Garden Shrubs

Peter Hunt

illustrated by Design Bureau

Hamlyn
London · New York · Sydney · Toronto

The months and seasons mentioned apply to temperate regions of the northern hemisphere; for readers in other regions a table of approximate equivalents has been included on page 156.

Published by The Hamlyn Publishing Group Limited
London · New York · Sydney · Toronto
Astronaut House, Feltham, Middlesex, England

Copyright © The Hamlyn Publishing Group Limited 1969
Reprinted 1972, 1974, 1976

ISBN 0 600 00089 3
Phototypeset by BAS Printers Limited, Wallop, Hampshire
Colour separations by Schwitter Limited, Zurich
Printed in Spain by Mateu Cromo, Madrid

CONTENTS

THE USE OF SHRUBS

Shrubs and small trees form the backbone, as it were, of a garden, as far as plant material is concerned and they have an important part to play in garden design. They are more permanent than other plants and, although a few lend themselves to being moved to fit in with an alteration of plan, most of them will remain where they are planted for many years.

Many shrubs are grown for the beauty of their flowers, others for their foliage, others for their colourful or interesting fruits. Some combine all attributes. There are shrubs ranging in height from a few inches to 15–20 feet and small trees may be expected to reach 20–25 feet in time. There are evergreen kinds and deciduous, or 'leaf-losing', kinds. Most of those available for our gardens will do well on any soil, although there are some that will not grow on alkaline soils – those containing chalk or lime.

Many of the most beautiful shrubs in flower, leaf or fruit are used as single specimens in a lawn where they can be seen in isolation and realize their full potential without competition from neighbours. They may be used, with other fine shrubs, in an area devoted solely to the cultivation of shrubs and small trees, usually known as a 'shrubbery'.

Outline of shrubs illustrated right
Key:
1. Prunus
2. Sorbus
3. Lonicera
4. Forsythia
5. Laurel
6. Weigela
7. Mahonia
8. Rhododendron
9. Ericas
10. Berberis
11. Ceratostigma
12. Senecio
13. Potentilla

Shrubs may also be used, with hardy herbaceous perennials, in a mixed border, to add height and to give an air of permanence. Many of them will provide with their flowers or foliage a certain interest during the winter months when the herbaceous perennials will, for the most part, have been cut down.

Some shrubs, and not only the less interesting kinds, may be used for hedging purposes, those which grow about 5 feet tall as boundary hedges, for example, with lower kinds as internal hedges. For this purpose it is not always necessary to use the same kind of shrub throughout the hedge, different kinds can often be used just as effectively. Taller kinds may be used to provide screens, to block out views of neighbouring houses or other features.

Some low-growing shrubs, many of them clump forming or spreading by layers or offsets, may be used as groundcover, to prevent the growth of weeds. Heathers and lings are good examples of these for, if closely planted, they will soon make dense ground-cover.

Shrubs, climbing by means of tendrils or with twining stems, are used to clothe walls or pergolas, and even to scramble over and hide ugly sheds and outbuildings. Others which are not true climbers may also be trained against walls.

Where a shrub border of reasonable size is being planned it is possible to plant specimens that will provide flowers throughout the entire year, without concentrating too much on spring and summer when the shrubs will be competing in colour with other garden plants. In general, where winter-flowering shrubs are being planted it is worth placing them so that they can be seen from the house and certainly be inspected closely from a pathway, for many of them have fragrant flowers.

Finally, resist the temptation to plant too closely. The small specimen received from the nursery may, in five years, be 10 feet high and as much wide. There is bound to be lots of bare ground in a shrub plantation in the early years, if shrubs are properly spaced, taking into account their ultimate spread, but this can be planted up with bulbs or temporary ground-cover plants.

Shrubs can be used in any part of the garden

Careful digging is essential
before any shrubs are planted.

PREPARATION OF THE SOIL

There is little point in buying a shrub, whatever the cost of it
might be, and then merely digging a hole that is large
enough to take the roots, replacing the soil around it and
firming it. The shrub will probably do reasonably well, but
will do far better if the ground is better prepared for it. It
ought to live for many years, considerably longer perhaps
than the planter, if it is properly dealt with from the very
beginning.

As the branch system extends, so will the root system, so
that, in order to allow free development, it is necessary to
dig the soil widely and reasonably deeply. Double-digging,
the cultivation of the soil to two spade-depths, is not often
done these days, but it does pay to cultivate deeply on
heavy soils and those which, after prolonged single-spit
digging, have developed a hard pan below the surface,

preventing free drainage and hindering the penetration of the roots. Clay soils are notoriously difficult in this respect for, although cultivation over a period of years may have made the top foot or so easier to work, below this there may be solid clay. Digging more deeply may be arduous, but is worth it in the long run.

Soils on the chalk formations vary widely. Some may have a deep chalky loam overlying the chalk, in others there may be a mere few inches of soil under which there is solid chalk. The former soils are easy to deal with, it is the thin types that present real problems. It is often necessary to compromise by breaking up the chalk below to a depth of a foot or so and as widely as possible, using, if necessary, a pick as well as a spade.

Sandy soils and those containing much peat present few problems as far as actual digging is concerned, but the former, in particular, tend to be so well drained that they retain little moisture in dry periods and plant foods tend to be washed down into them, out of the reach of roots. This is less likely to happen on the heavier soils. All soils benefit from having extra plant foods such as garden compost dug in while they are being prepared before shrubs are planted, but none so much as light, sandy soils. The object with these is to help them to retain moisture and to provide much-needed plant foods. Both can be obtained by digging in liberal quantities of humus-forming material. Moist peat helps to retain moisture, but contains little plant food and better materials are well-rotted garden compost, leafmould,

Plants should be chosen to suit particular situations.

made from fallen leaves rotted down in a heap. Other plant matter that can be used is spent hops, old mushroom compost available in certain areas, shoddy, again available in places, or seaweed that is obtainable in coastal areas. Even rotted bracken fronds can be used since bracken is a common weed of sandy places. Failing all else, or where there is not sufficient other material, it is possible to rot down bales of straw, to be bought reasonably cheaply from farmers who have surplus stocks. The bales are broken up, sulphate of ammonia is scattered among them and the straw is thoroughly watered. It should rot down quite quickly to a dark brown material that can then be dug into the soil.

Farmyard manure is, of course, the best material of all, but so little of it is available, especially in suburban areas, that its use in liberal quantities on light soils can hardly be considered. Where it is available it may be used, mixed with compost, or by itself as a mulch or dug in, but it should be well-rotted. If it is fresh, it should be well down in the soil and not placed immediately round roots that may be scorched by it. It is better to use fresh farmyard manure to help to rot down other plant materials, or to stack it for a period until it has rotted down better. It helps to rot down straw very quickly if the manure and straw are thoroughly mixed together.

If the shrubs are not planted immediately, the sacking should be kept moist. When finally planted they should be spaced the correct distance apart.

Larger shrubs need two people to plant them, one person to hold the shrub upright while the other returns the soil around it.

PLANTING

The planting season for leaf-shedding shrubs extends from October to March, depending on the weather, and even into April if March is exceptionally bad. Evergreens are best planted either in September, so that their roots can have a chance to become active before winter sets in, or in April or early May, when root growth should start immediately, preventing the loss of leaves. If May is a hot, dry month, newly-planted evergreens may need overhead spraying each day during May and June to prevent leaf-loss, an operation that is best carried out in the cool of the evening.

The improvement of the soil before planting has already been dealt with. The actual planting may be done at any time except when the ground is frozen, snow-covered or so rain-sodden that it is difficult to work. It is worth making preparations beforehand by keeping on one side, under cover, a supply of soil that is easily workable and can be put around the roots when planting. It can be kept, until

11

required, in a shed or out-house or covered with plastic sheeting. It is useful to add bonemeal at the rate of about $\frac{1}{4}$ lb to a barrow-load of the mixture. Even on lighter soils, or when planting is done in drier weather, bonemeal should be forked into the soil as it is an excellent, slow-acting plant food.

Small shrubs can be planted by one person but large plants may need two people, one to hold the shrub upright while the other returns the soil round the roots and firms it. Depth of planting is important and in general the soil mark on the stem acts as a guide to planting depth. Lavenders, ericas, callunas, *Hypericum calycinum, Fuchsia magellanica, Kerria japonica, Spiraea bumalda* and other plants that make spreading clumps, may be planted a little deeper to encourage clump formation. Large specimens, with a big root formation, should be shaken while planting to ensure that soil is properly worked in among the roots to leave no air gaps. Broken or damaged roots should be cut back before planting. The planting hole should be made sufficiently large to enable un-damaged roots to be spread

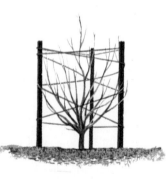

Shrubs must be staked firmly and prevented from rubbing their support, using sacking (*above*), cloth (*centre*) or twine (*below*).

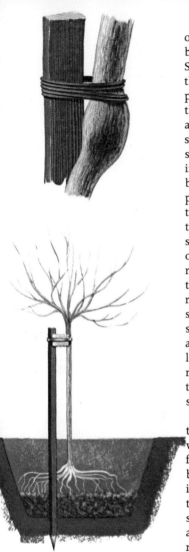

out properly without being bent back on each other. Spreading the roots out in this way will also help to provide firm anchorage for the plant, although trees and shrubs grown on a stem should be provided with a stout stake firmly driven into the centre of the hole before planting is started. To plant firmly is essential, though this does not mean trampling round the shrub so hard that roots are broken off. Some plants, notably rhododendrons, arrive from the nursery with their fibrous roots balled in sacking. In such instances the roots should not be spread out and all that is necessary is to loosen the sacking, plant the roots in a hole large enough to take the ball, and firm the soil round them.

If the root ball looks as though it will disintegrate when the sacking is removed from around it, the plant can be put into the ground, sacking and all, merely removing the string after planting. The sacking may be pulled away after planting, but if it does not pull away easily it can be left and will soon rot down. The roots will also grow up through the sacking as it rots.

The twine should not be too tight or deformities will result (*above*). The stake should fall below the crotch of the tree.

13

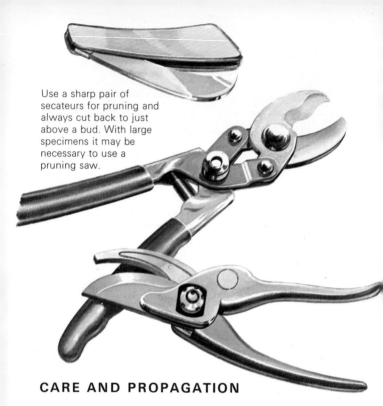

Use a sharp pair of secateurs for pruning and always cut back to just above a bud. With large specimens it may be necessary to use a pruning saw.

CARE AND PROPAGATION

Immediately after planting, damaged branches or shoots should be cut away making the cut immediately above a bud. Contrary to the beliefs held by many jobbing gardeners, many shrubs need little or no pruning at all. Certainly they do not need an annual hacking back in the winter or spring, an operation often carried out for the sake of 'tidiness' rather than to help the plant to produce more and better flowers or fruits, which should be the object of pruning. Where shrubs make reasonably symmetrical specimens in the normal course of events, there is no reason why the occasional 'wild' shoot should not be cut back, but this, like the removal of dead or dying shoots, is a mere tidying operation rather than real pruning.

Basically, shrubs may be divided into three groups: those that need no pruning; those that produce flowers in the spring on shoots made during the previous year; and those that flower in summer or autumn on shoots made in the current season. Those that flower on the previous season's growths should be pruned after the flowers have faded, cutting back those shoots that have borne flowers. Those that flower on the current season's wood are usually pruned the following spring, cutting back the old growths that flowered the previous year to within a few inches of the point where they spring from the main stem.

Many shrubs and trees, especially rhododendrons, azaleas, magnolias and camellias, benefit from an annual mulch in spring of such materials as moist peat, rotted compost or leafmould. The mulch should be spread over the soil round the shrub to a depth of several inches. It will gradually be absorbed into the soil by the action of worms or washed into the soil by rain. Any left on the surface in the autumn may be lightly forked into the top few inches of soil, taking care to avoid damage to roots near the surface.

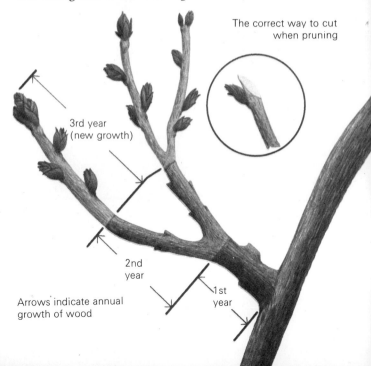

The correct way to cut when pruning

3rd year (new growth)

2nd year

1st year

Arrows indicate annual growth of wood

There are several ways of propagating shrubs, although not all of them can be relied upon to give good results. It is, for instance, possible to grow many shrubs from seed, though it can be a slow process. The seeds of tree paeonies, for example, may take a year or even two years to germinate. Germination of hard-coated seeds can be hastened by stratifying them. This consists of exposing them to the action of frost and weather to help to break down the hard outer coating. The method often adopted is to place, in the autumn, a layer of sand in a flower pot or seed pan, put in a layer of seeds, add another layer of sand, another layer of seeds, until the pot or other container is full and then leave this outdoors all winter in an exposed place. By the following spring the seed coats should have rotted or partially decomposed and it is then possible to sift out the seeds from the sand and sow them. This can be done in pots of seed compost in a cold frame or cold greenhouse, or outdoors, when germination should be quite rapid.

Propagation of many shrubs by cuttings is not

The seeds of many shrubs are berries and can be collected, dried, and planted.

Seeds stored in sand in a flower pot can be exposed to the weather to break down the hard outer coating.

Seed boxes should be carefully labelled.

16

Shoots should be selected with a heel, or cut below a bud.

If the cutting is placed in a pot surrounded with polythene and watered from below it should root satisfactorily.

difficult. Cuttings of half-ripe growths may be taken in summer, and rooted in a closed propagating case in the greenhouse, in a mixture of moist sand and peat or even in pure sand. If pure sand is used the cuttings must be potted into a soil mixture as soon as roots have formed. They are then grown in pots, until they can be planted out into a nursery bed the following spring and into their permanent place the following year.

Propagation by hard-wood or naked cuttings is successful with many shrubs. These are taken in October or November and are usually 6–12 inches long. As with most cuttings, the shoots are trimmed just below a joint or bud, the lower leaves, if any remain, are removed, and the cuttings are inserted 3–4 inches deep, either in pots of sandy compost placed in a well-ventilated cold frame, or out of doors, in a sheltered position. Out of doors it is usual to make a slit in the ground with a spade, scatter sharp sand in the bottom, insert the cuttings and then firm the soil around them. By the following spring they can be lifted carefully and planted out,

17

spaced 6–12 inches apart in a nursery bed. If evergreens are to be propagated in this way it is better to root them in a cold frame. Hormone rooting powders are available, but few gardeners require more than a small number of extra specimens and it is quite usual to expect a 50% 'strike' and not at all unusual to find that 90% of cuttings of certain shrubs have rooted.

Some shrubs are easily increased by layering their shoots. Some will even layer themselves as long shoots touch the ground and root from the point of contact. Shoots, preferably those that can easily be bent down to ground level, can be buried in the soil and, from the buds or nodes below soil level, roots should form. The rooted layer can eventually be cut off from the parent plant and start an existence of its own. With some shrubs all that is required is a long shoot

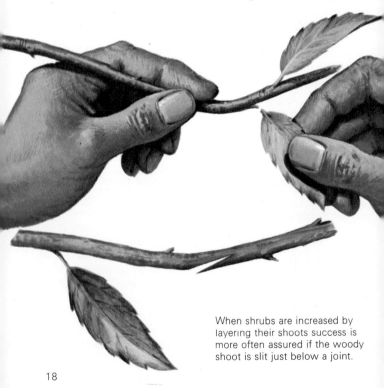

When shrubs are increased by layering their shoots success is more often assured if the woody shoot is slit just below a joint.

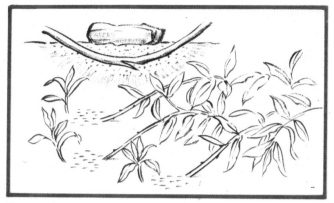

If a stone is placed over the point where the stem is buried in the ground it will conserve moisture below it.

bent down, buried in the soil and a stone or wire peg used to hold it in position. Success is more often assured, however, if the woody shoot is slit just below a joint, to form a 'tongue' at the point where it is buried in the soil. Alternatively, when the shoot is bent down it can be twisted and bent upwards at this point and then buried and held in place. On heavy soils it is advisable to provide a good rooting medium, such as a mixture of sand and peat, at the rooting place. A brick or stone, placed over the point where the stem is buried, is probably considerably better than a wire peg, because the soil beneath the brick will then remain moist, even in dry weather.

Division is a method of propagation often used where herbaceous perennials are concerned but is applicable to only a few shrubs, those that make masses of fibrous roots and clump-like growth, or make offsets, or sucker growth. It must be remembered that where varieties are grafted on to common stock, as in lilacs, the sucker growths will be those of the common stock, *Syringa vulgaris,* and not the desirable variety. Among the shrubs which may be propagated by division or by offsets are amelanchiers, *Fuchsia magellanica, Hypericum calycinum, Kerria japonica,* lavandulas, mahonias, rubus, certain spiraeas and syringas, remembering the proviso mentioned above.

BUYING SHRUBS

However early one orders shrubs, the arrival of the plants from the nursery is dictated by various factors not all under the control of the gardener. Accordingly, bundles of shrubs, well packed by the nursery, may arrive when it is quite impossible to plant them, perhaps because the ground is water-logged, frozen hard or covered with snow. The shrubs should be quite safe if the ties are loosened and they are left in their bundles, for two or three weeks, in a shed. But, as soon as the weather is suitable, even though it may not be convenient to carry out the actual planting, the shrubs should be removed from their bundles and heeled-in, until they can be planted out into their final places, normally not later than March.

Heeling-in consists merely of planting the shrubs temporarily. It is often recommended that a trench is dug and the roots of the plants set in this, laying them at an angle, and soil returned and firmed. It is much better, however, to choose a sheltered place, such as behind

Shrubs generally arrive from the nursery protected by sacking and straw. In bad weather they can safely be left in their bundles for about three weeks if the ties around them are loosened.

a hedge, and make a trench, planting the shrubs in this so that they are upright rather than slanting. This is because, in a bad winter, it may not be possible to move them to their permanent places until growth has well started and, when this happens, and the shrubs are laid at an angle, the new shoots will grow upright producing distorted growth.

On heavy clay soils it is a thankless task trying to heel-in shrubs and it is well worthwhile to keep a supply of friable soil mixture handy to place round the roots. Not only is this easier to handle, but it will also ensure that root development will begin without hindrance. All that remains to do then is to lift the shrubs carefully and plant them out in their permanent places after proper soil preparation.

The selection and arrangement of shrubs is very much a matter of personal choice but it is well to be guided by some general rules. In shrub borders, or other places where a number of shrubs and small trees are grown together, they should be planted in as naturalistic a manner as possible, avoiding rigidity. Rectangular shapes of beds and paths do not take full advantage of the natural symmetry of most

Heeling-in means planting temporarily. The plants are stood upright in a trench in a sheltered place.

shrubs. The natural sequence of height is trees, tall shrubs, shrubs of medium height, low growing types and finally ground-hugging kinds. Gradation of height will facilitate closer planting and give a concentration of flowers coupled with less maintenance work in weeding.

In recent years, flowering shrubs have taken an increasingly larger place in both large and small gardens. Personal likes and dislikes as regards plants vary widely but it is wise to have a plant that will grow vigorously under the conditions of the garden soil and climate. Unless the gardener is aiming at specialization in a particular group of plants, for competition purposes, for example, it is also advisable to choose shrubs that will not only blossom for a reasonable length of time but also make a decorative feature in the garden at all times of the year.

In the following pages, a variety of shrubs are discussed.

There are many shrubs that will be attractive for most of the year.

A. Syringa
B. Acer
C. Sorbus
D. Ilex

So many kinds of shrubs are now available that a selection for any type of garden should be possible. In many cases specific mention is made of varieties suitable for different types of soil, so that one can be certain of selecting the right plant for any particular area. When the specific names of hybrid races are mentioned they carry the usual multiplication sign, for example, *Berberis × rubrostilla*, but as far as possible botanical terms have been eliminated or explained immediately. If plants are being bought, it is well worthwhile obtaining them from a specialist nurseryman who stocks a wide range of plants. Many nurseries will also encourage visitors. If care is taken in the initial stages, an arrangement can be produced that will provide colour in the garden throughout the year. The choice of colour is again a personal matter and gardeners will have their own views on their favourite colour harmonies.

E. Lavandula
F. Crataegus
G. Vitis
H. Prunus

*Acer palmatum
heptalobum*

THE POPULAR SPECIES OF SHRUBS

Acer

Most of the acers or maples are big trees, *A. pseudoplatanus,* for instance, is the Sycamore. There are, however, many others, particularly Asiatic species and their varieties, that are no more than shrubs in this country, some of them slow-growing and eventually not too big for medium-sized gardens. Most of the leaves of these plants are maple-like, that is they have five or seven deep angular lobes. In some instances these are divided yet again into numerous other segments, sometimes so narrow that the leaves look more like the fronds of a fern than the leaves of a shrub.

The Japanese Maples, varieties of *A. palmatum,* are deservedly the most popular, because they are not too large and because their leaves turn such brilliant colours in the autumn. There are many from which to choose but, if there is room for one only, *A. palmatum heptalobum* 'Osakazuki' makes a strong claim as its autumn leaves turn the brightest of scarlets. For longer-term colour, *A. p. atropurpureum* is worth considering as its foliage is a good bronze-crimson throughout the summer and there are many others that grow slowly to 5–8 feet. The species itself is more vigorous and may reach 15–20 feet. There are a few varieties of *A. japonicum,* another Japanese Maple, of which *aureum* has yellow leaves while others provide good autumn colour.

Although these Japanese Maples will tolerate chalky soils, this is not really the correct medium. They prefer ordinary, well-drained loam, with fair quantities of moist peat dug in at planting time. Cutting winds can sear them so it is best to plant them where they get some protection from wind. Frost damaged and wind damaged shoots should be cut back in late spring but unless the size must be restricted no pruning is necessary.

Propagation of the choice garden forms is usually done by grafting on to seedlings of *A. palmatum,* preferably in a greenhouse during the spring. Seeds that are saved from good forms of these Japanese Maples will usually give quite good plants but it must not be expected that they will necessarily resemble the parent plants.

Amelanchier

There seems to be a certain amount of confusion over the correct name of the plant that is usually grown in our gardens under the name of *Amelanchier canadensis*. It may strictly be *A. laevis*. Correct name apart, it is a charming large shrub or small tree, its period of beauty extending throughout much of the spring, when the young leaves break from the buds and are pink in colour, to autumn when the foliage turns an attractive red before it falls.

The white flowers, which have five narrow petals, open in April and are so freely borne that the shrub becomes a mass of white. They are followed by fruits, that are red at first but which later ripen to a reddish-purple, providing the birds leave them on the twigs long enough.

A. ovalis, the Snowy Mespilus, and *A. oblongifolia*, the Swamp Sugar Pear, are two others, better perhaps for the smaller garden than *A. laevis,* as they seldom grow much more than a dozen feet tall, whereas *A. laevis* may, in time, grow to 20 feet. *A. ovalis* is distinguished by the woolly whiteness of its young twigs and leaves. *A. oblongifolia* tends to make sucker growths, though these are seldom a nuisance and, in fact, provide an easy way of propagating as it is only necessary to dig them up in the winter and transplant them. Otherwise, the flowers and fruits are very similar indeed and the leaves of both plants colour well during the autumn.

No pruning is necessary, nor do these useful and handsome shrubs make any particular soil demands. They will grow extremely well on chalk soils and in exposed positions in the garden.

Amelanchier laevis may in time grow to over twenty feet and is not very suitable for the small garden.

Berberis

There are probably around a hundred berberises readily obtainable from nurserymen in this country, so that the choice is apt to be somewhat bewildering. In the larger garden there may be room for twenty or thirty kinds but the smaller garden cannot normally accommodate more than a few.

Darwin's Barberry, *B. darwinii,* is still one of the best. It is an evergreen, growing to 6 feet with small, holly-like leaves and clusters of orange-red flowers in May, followed by blue fruits covered with a plum-like bloom.

B. thunbergii atropurpurea, a deciduous kind, grows to about 5 feet and is very colourful when in leaf, for the foliage is reddish-purple. The flowers are pale yellow. There is a dwarf form *nana* and both these are useful for making hedges, the latter for small interior hedges.

Two good hybrids are B. × *rubrostilla*, about 4 feet high, deciduous, with very large coral fruits, and *B. × stenophylla,* an evergreen, up to 10 feet tall, and sometimes more than this wide. It is very free-flowering, its golden flowers appearing in late April followed by blue fruits, and makes a fine informal hedge where there is room.

These barberries are easy to grow, with no special soil requirements. Little pruning is needed, though the growth of the deciduous kinds can be thinned periodically.

A bush of *Berberis darwinii*
(*bottom left*), the flowers (*right*),
and the fruit (*centre*).
Berberis thunbergii atropurpurea
(*bottom right*).

29

Buddleia

Buddleias, at least those commonly grown, which are varieties of *B. davidii* (*B. variabilis*), must be about the easiest of shrubs to grow. Perhaps because of this they are all too often neglected, and bushes 12–15 feet tall are seen producing flowers at the top and little or nothing lower down. This is one of those shrubs that flower on wood made the same year and if it is cut back in late winter it will send up new growths of varying lengths, each bearing their quota of heavily fragrant flower-spikes, covered with butterflies in late summer. There are numerous varieties in colours such as deep violet 'Black Night', lavender pink 'Charming', deep purple 'Dubonnet', lilac pink 'Pink Pearl', reddish-purple 'Royal Red' and white varieties such as 'White Bouquet' and 'White Cloud'.

B. globosa, known as the Orange Ball Tree, is a contrast, because its orange-yellow flowers, borne in May, are ball shaped and dangle from the branches. This grows to 12–15 feet and should be pruned after flowering, shortening the shoots that have borne flowers to about half their length.

There are many other buddleias, many of them too tender for most gardens. *B. × weyeriana* is a bit different and is a hybrid derived from the two previously described. This has ball-like flower-heads, mainly yellow and orange, but flushed or shaded with pink or mauve.

A bush of *Buddleia davidii*, Royal Red variety, (*left*) and flowers (*right*), with those of *Buddleia globosa*, the Orange Ball tree.

Calluna vulgaris, variety
H. E. Beale

Calluna

Calluna vulgaris, the single species in the genus, is the
common Heather or Ling, that makes so many of our hills
and moors colourful from late summer to autumn. In the wild
the plant has purplish-pink flowers, but it is so variable that
nurserymen specializing in heathers may list up to fifty
different kinds, varying in height from 3–4 inches to 2 feet
and showing great colour variation, both in flowers and
foliage. Some have double flowers and the best of these is

32

'H. E. Beale', flowering late, growing to about 2 feet, with tall spikes of rosy-pink flowers. If a dwarf double is required then it can be found in 'J. H. Hamilton', about 9 inches tall, with pink flowers.

The variety *searlei* has fine white flowers and there is a variety of this with golden leaves, called *searlei aurea*. *C. v. aurea* is another golden-leaved form, not so tall. In *C. v. argentea* the young growths are silvery. *C. v. nana* is one of the lowest growing, with purple flowers.

These callunas must have lime-free soil and they do best where the soil is dry and the position open and sunny. Plant them fairly closely together in drifts or clumps so that they grow together to make a continuous mat, to keep down weeds. A light clip over with shears after flowering will encourage new growth to form, and keep the plants neat and compact.

Calluna vulgaris aurea, a gold-leaved form

33

Camellia

The camellias are not difficult to grow provided they can be given the right conditions. They do not like chalky soils and although they will grow in exposed sites their buds are liable to be damaged by searing winds and spring frosts. Light woodland places are ideal or, in colder gardens, a place against a south, west or even north, but not east, wall. They make good tub plants, either for terraces or cold conservatories and this gives the gardener who has chalky soil a chance to enjoy these delightful plants.

Unless your garden is in one of the milder counties, stick to the varieties of *C. japonica* and the newer hybrids, the *williamsii* group, which are as hardy as any other shrub. The *japonica* forms vary in colour from white to rich crimson and there are kinds with single, semi-double and fully double flowers. The *williamsii* hybrids have excellent single or semi-double flowers. They appear to grow a little more quickly than the *japonica* forms, but both reach about 12–15 feet, the latter growing taller in ideal conditions. Both should begin to flower in late February or early March.

Dig in moist peat and leafmould before planting and mulch the shrubs each spring with the same materials.

Camellia × williamsii

Camellia japonica makes a delightful tub plant

The hybrid *Caryopteris* ×
clandonensis has small
bright blue flowers carried
in clusters.

Caryopteris

Shrubs which do not grow too tall, nor take up too much space, are decided assets for the small garden. Caryopteris, members of the Verbena family (*Verbenaceae*) come into this category and combine these assets with that of bearing blue flowers, uncommon in shrubs.

The most popular is *C. × clandonensis,* a hybrid that originated at Clandon, in Surrey, nearly 40 years ago. It can grow to about 5 feet tall, but it is easy to keep it to half this height or a little more, by cutting back each April the growths made the previous year, to within two buds of their base. New shoots quickly appear and in late summer will be bearing masses of small bright blue flowers which are carried in clusters springing from the axils of the leaves.

Even newer is 'Heavenly Blue', a hybrid from America, which makes a somewhat more upright bush, better, perhaps, for confined spaces, and with flowers of a slightly deeper blue.

Apart from these hybrids there is *C. mongholica,* a species introduced from China well over a century ago. It, too, has rich blue flowers, but is rather too tender for most gardens and, in any case, seems to be short-lived.

These caryopteris, sometimes called Blue Spiraeas or Bluebeard, because of the fringed flowers, do best in sheltered positions in full sun, though any reasonable garden soil, not too heavy, will suit them.

This shrub can grow to about 5 feet

Ceratostigma

Ceratostigma willmottianum, the species usually grown, is a hardy Plumbago. Its rich blue flowers, produced in clusters, much resemble those of the true Plumbago, that is often seen in conservatories and which has flowers that are a paler blue.

This shrub is perfectly hardy and can be grown in the open garden, where it makes a plant about 18 inches tall, its flowers beginning to appear soon after midsummer and continuing until September or October. The growths are usually cut by frost in the open garden, but no permanent damage results and it is only necessary to give the plant a trim over in April to remove the frost-killed shoots and new growth will soon start to appear. This in fact is the only form of pruning required.

Against a sunny, sheltered wall *C. willmottianum* may reach 3 feet in height and is less liable to frost damage. Another good place to grow it is in the herbaceous border, for its blue flowers associate well with the yellows and reds of the later summer border plants.

The foliage is a bonus for in the autumn it turns yellow and red, adding to the colourfulness of this useful shrub. It will grow in any kind of soil, including those containing much chalk. Plants may be lifted and divided for propagation purposes in much the same way as herbaceous perennials.

Ceratostigmas have rich clusters
of deep blue flowers. One of
the most popular species is
C. willmottianum (*above*).

The Judas Tree (*Cercis siliquastrum*) has purple-pink pea flowers (*below*).

Cercis

Cercis siliquastrum is the Judas Tree, sometimes seen as a tree 20–25 feet tall, sometimes as a shrub, reaching about 12–15 feet. It ought to be grown more often, as it is perfectly hardy and is a very fine sight when in full flower in May, just before the leaves are fully open. At that time each twig carries its quota of purple-pink pea flowers and these often appear in little clusters on the trunks of older-established plants. Purplish seed-pods, 3–4 inches long, follow the flowers.

Even out of flower the shrub is attractive for the greenish-grey leaves are round, almost heart-shaped. There is a white-flowered form, *alba*, where the leaves are paler in colour.

The Judas Tree does not require special soil and needs only a sunny situation to settle down, although it is best established from a pot as, like some other pea-flowered shrubs, it does not like root disturbance. Seeds germinate readily in pots of John Innes Seed Compost.

The related Western Redbud, *C. occidentalis,* is seen even less often because it is a tender shrub and prefers the milder conditions of western areas. It reaches about 15 feet and has bright green, kidney-shaped leaves and rose-coloured flowers. *C. canadensis,* the Red-Bud, is a hardier variety, but its rosy-pink flowers are smaller than those of the Judas Tree and the latter is to be preferred if there is room for only one to be grown.

41

Chaenomeles

Gardeners will always refer to this shrub as the 'Japonica', so deep-rooted is this old name. It is usually seen trained as a wall shrub, 8–10 feet tall, occasionally more, and it will cover a fairly wide area if it is properly looked after. If it is grown in this way, some pruning is absolutely essential to control the vigour of the plant development and to keep it from straggling. Basically the pruning consists of cutting away any forward-pointing branches as well as any very thin growths that are produced. Cutting back of new side-growths to 5 or 6 inches is also necessary, unless they are needed as extensions or to fill in a blank space on the wall. This is done during the summer and should be combined with tying in

Chaenomeles speciosa produces attractive flowers from January until June.

the new growths to nails set in the wall or on to any other support such as trellis-work or the side of an out-building or garden shed.

The 1½ inch wide flowers, produced on the leafless stems from January onwards, until May or June, are very attractive. Good colour forms are 'Apple Blossom', *nivalis,* white, *atrococcinea,* deep crimson, *cardinalis,* salmon-pink, and *rosea flore-plena*, which is a rose-pink, double variety. All these plants are varieties of *C. speciosa,* which is also known as *C. lagenaria* and *Cydonia japonica.* Apart from their use on walls the different varieties may be grown as open-ground shrubs, when less pruning is needed. They may also be used for hedging purposes but if this is the case they will need cutting back to keep them tidy and to prevent them from becoming too open. Whatever variety is chosen, none requires any special soil medium and will grow well on chalk. Oddly-shaped fruits, like those of the related quinces are very often produced and may be used for making such things as quince jelly.

Choisya

There is one species only of this plant, *C. ternata*, more familiar to gardeners as the Mexican Orange Blossom, because of the scented white flowers it produces in clusters in May and June, though the fragrance is definitely not that of orange-blossom.

It is an evergreen, with somewhat leathery leaves, made up of three leaflets. A well-grown plant will reach about 6 feet in height but rarely more even in the warmer parts of the country and scarcely less even in the colder districts. If it is allowed ample room it may be as wide as it is high, except in shady places when it is inclined to become straggly. For this reason it is better grown in the open, although some shelter is desirable from the cutting winds, which may damage the foliage in winter. In spring it may also be affected by late frosts.

This is a good plant for chalk, but will grow on any kind of soil, even the sandy, peaty soils on which rhododendrons thrive. Usually it makes a rounded bush, well-clothed to the ground, and no pruning is needed. Occasional 'wild' shoots may appear to spoil the symmetry and these may be cut away.

Choisya ternata is better known
as the Mexican Orange Blossom.

45

The hybrid *Cistus × purpureus,*
bush (*above*) and flowers (*below*).
(*Opposite*) The Silver Pink
variety is one of the hardiest hybrids.

Cistus

The cistus are the Rock Roses, plants from the Mediterranean region and, like so many others from that area, they prefer sunny places and dry, well-drained soils. They are beautiful shrubs, but even the hardiest of them are only on the border-line of hardiness, except in sheltered and warm gardens. In less well-favoured places some will survive for several years, but it is a wise precaution to take late summer cuttings and root them in bottom heat, overwintering them until they can be planted out in late spring.

One of the hardiest is the hybrid 'Silver Pink', a name which aptly describes the colour of its 3 inch wide flowers. This grows to 2 feet, or a little more. *C. × purpureus* is another hybrid, with beautiful purplish-crimson flowers, with a dark blotch at the base of each petal. This grows up to 6 feet high with a proportionate spread. The hardiest species is *C. laurifolius,* which again may reach to 6 feet, and has clusters of white flowers with yellow blotches at the bases of the petals.

In mild places it is worth trying other species and hybrids of these charming shrubs. Their individual flowers are usually over by noon on the day they open, but so many are borne in succession during June and July that the plants are never out of flower.

Clematis

This is another of those large genera that is bewildering in the variety it has to offer, for there are over 150 species and hybrids available of these pretty and indispensable climbers. Usually they are planted against walls, but there are so many other places where they can be accommodated that even in a small garden room might be found for several kinds. They are, for instance, excellent plants for pergolas or archways. The less vigorous kinds may be planted so that they scramble over low-growing and otherwise not particularly valuable shrubs, while the more vigorous kinds will climb up into taller trees.

Clematis montana (*left*) flowers in the spring and (*above*) the rich purple *C.* × *jackmanii* is a popular hybrid.

Cultivation is not difficult. Contrary to old gardeners' tales, lime or chalk in the soil is not essential and clematis do well on soils not containing chalk or lime, provided they are rich in plant foods. Clematis especially need more moisture-retentive soils, even heavy clay, provided it is well dug and broken up and plant foods are incorporated. What clematis do like is to have their roots cool and shaded, which means that they can be planted against shady walls, but, if so, they will send up their flowering shoots into the sunlight. So, it is better to plant them in sunny places and ensure the roots are cool. This can be arranged, if pieces of stone are placed over them, or if low-growing shrubs are planted in front of them. The soil should be enriched when digging and an annual mulch of rotted manure, leafmould, or compost given. They must be watered in dry weather, especially in spring and early summer.

Of the many kinds available, the old rich purple *C.* × *jackmanii* is still deservedly popular. 'Ville de Lyon' is a dark carmine-red flowering in late summer, and *C. montana rubens* is a pink form of the popular white *C. montana* flowering in spring. 'Comtesse de Bouchaud', pink, is one of the most free-flowering while 'Duchess of Edinburgh' is a double white but not a very vigorous kind. 'Lasursten' is one of the most popular of the large-flowered hybrids, with purple-blue flowers in summer.

Ville de Lyon is a late summer-flowering variety.

Clerodendrum trichotomum.
Leaves and flowers (*below*) and
outline of bush (*opposite*).

Clerodendrum

There is always a certain attraction about shrubs with blue berries and *Clerodendrum trichotomum* is one of the finest in this category, with turquoise-blue fruits, their colour enhanced by the crimson calyces in which they are held. The fruits turn black in time and drop off, but the calyces persist to give a certain amount of colour to this hardy shrub.

It grows to some 12 feet tall, perhaps even reaching 15 feet and so requires a fair amount of space. The leaves are large, about 9 inches long, oval in shape and have a somewhat unpleasant smell if they are handled. On the other hand the white flowers are sweetly scented. These appear from July onwards, in clusters, and are tubular in shape. The red calyces surrounding them add a good deal of colour.

This shrub will grow in most garden soils, but it does not like drought, so it pays to dig in a fair amount of leaf-mould, well-rotted garden compost, or moist peat, when the ground is prepared for planting. Although it is hardy, it does best in a sheltered situation where its young shoots are not liable to be damaged by cold winds.

Pruning, in the normal sense, is not required, but it is worth going over the shrub in late spring and cutting away dead wood or shoots affected by frost. Suckers appear round the base and may be dug up and used to form new plants.

Cornus

For some reason the dogwoods are not very common in gardens in this country, yet they are attractive shrubs, not difficult to grow. Some are grown for their flowers, others for their coloured bark, and some for a combination of their flowers and richly coloured autumn leaves. Seen most often is *Cornus mas*, the Cornelian Cherry, with its small yellow flowers in February and March that are sometimes followed by bright red berries.

There are more spectacular dogwoods, such as *C. kousa chinensis*, a shrub in which the individual flowers are tiny, but surrounded by large white bracts. In autumn the leaves turn a good crimson. Some peat or leafmould dug into the soil helps this shrub, which otherwise, like most of its relations, does not require special soil.

Among those grown for the beauty of their bark, especially in winter when they are leafless, are *C. alba sibirica*, with bright red shoots, *C. stolonifera*, dark dull red shoots, and its variety *flaviramea*, with yellow bark. *C. alba* also has some varieties with attractively variegated leaves. The kinds grown for their bark need cutting back hard each spring, practically to ground level and plenty of new shoots 4–5 feet long will appear afterwards to provide winter colour.

The flowers of *Cornus kousa chinensis (above)* are tiny, surrounded by large white bracts. *Cornus alba sibirica (below)* is often grown for the beauty of its bark.

Cotoneaster

Although the white flowers of cotoneasters are not individually spectacular they are usually borne freely in clusters. However, these plants are not grown for flowers as much as for the brilliance of their autumn fruits and the rich colours of their autumn leaves. There are many of these plants, most of them shrubs, ranging in height from a few inches to 20 feet, with one or two which may be classed as small trees, reaching 25 feet in time.

Some take up little space and are, therefore, perfectly suitable for small gardens. The most popular of these is the Fishbone Cotoneaster, *C. horizontalis,* its branches borne in herringbone formation. It is often planted by a wall, against which it will grow up to several feet, even on a north aspect, spreading itself almost flat against the bricks. In the open, over a rock or tree stump, or planted by the side of an inspection cover, it will spread fairly horizontally. The flowers are not particularly beautiful, although they cover the shoots and are attractive to insects, but the berries are bright red and the small leaves turn red and orange before falling.

C. dielsianus grows to about 6 feet and has arching branches, bright scarlet berries and brightly coloured autumn leaves. *C. dammeri* is even better for planting beside an inspection cover for its long growths are quite prostrate, its leaves are evergreen and the freely-borne fruits are bright red. For sheer spectacle there is little to surpass in autumn 'Cornubia', an evergreen hybrid, growing to 15–20 feet, its branches laden down with its scarlet fruits. This shrub is among the largest of the cultivated cotoneasters. *C. salicifolius,* is a 12–15 feet tall, evergreen species that also fruits heavily. The variety *floccosus* has narrower leaves and big crops of small fruits while the *fructuluteo* variety is distinct in having yellow fruits. *C. simonsii,* semi-evergreen, is a species that is often used for hedging or screening purposes. It grows to about 15 feet tall eventually and is of rather stiff, upright habit usually bearing plenty of scarlet fruits.

Cotoneaster horizontalis is suitable for small gardens. The hybrid Cornubia has branches laden with scarlet fruit in autumn.

These cotoneasters are easy to grow in any kind of soil, in sun or a semi-shade. They are perfectly hardy, even in windswept coastal conditions. None need pruning, other than removing dead wood. They may seed themselves in favourable situations, but are hardly likely to become a nuisance.

The blossoms of the Double Crimson Thorn, *Crataegus oxyacantha coccinea plena*.

Crataegus

This genus contains the well-known hawthorns, quicks or Mays, useful for informal hedges and a magnificent sight when they foam with white flowers in May, but not really ornamental shrubs in the normal way. However, there is a very fine form of one of the hawthorns, *C. oxyacantha*, known botanically as *coccinea plena*, but possibly better recognized by gardeners as the Double Crimson Thorn. This makes a neat, round-headed tree, about 15 feet in height, useful as a lawn specimen or for a position perhaps by the garden gate. Two, one on each side of the gate, with their heads allowed to grow together, would be even better, especially when they produce their long-lasting crimson flowers in May and June. No pruning is needed except to remove dead wood or straying growths that would otherwise spoil the symmetrical shape. The plant is native to the British Isles and will grow in almost any situation.

There are plenty of other crataegus, some, such as *C. monogyna aurea,* a variant of the common May, with yellow fruits. Others, such as *C. arnoldiana,* have very large fruits, as big as cherries, while those of *C. arkansana,* are even bigger. *C. arnoldiana,* incidentally, is fearsomely armed, its thorns sometimes 3 inches long.

One of the daintiest of this genus is *C. tanacetifolia,* the Tansy-leaved Thorn, with attractive deeply-lobed grey-green leaves and large flowers, up to an inch across. The yellow fruits have the same diameter, hanging like small apples. This eventually makes a taller tree than most of these crataegus, reaching about 30 feet in height.

The round trees are suitable for lawns.

Cytisus battandieri (below) needs wall protection in most gardens.

Cytisus

Not all gardens are blessed with good soil and, while it is possible to improve the soil, this is often a lengthy process. Meanwhile, it is worth planting those shrubs that not only put up with poor conditions, but actually thrive on them. Among these are the cytisus, which, like the genistas and *Spartium junceum* described elsewhere, are called brooms. They are very much shrubs for dry, stony, well-drained soils.

There are many cytisus, in a wide range of colours, and among the finest are those in which the pea-shaped flowers are of two colours, the standard, back petal, of one colour, the wing petals another. In some the petals are streaked with other colours. Habits vary greatly and some kinds such as *C. decumbens,* with bright yellow flowers, are prostrate in growth, while others, such as the white-flowered *C. albus* and 'Johnson's Crimson', with clear crimson blooms, may reach 6 or 7 feet. The Moroccan Broom, *C. battandieri,* grows even taller, reaching 15–20 feet, but it needs wall protection in most gardens. However, it is one of the finest, with silvery leaves and upright spikes of yellow flowers in July.

Most brooms tend to become straggly unless they are pruned after they have flowered. Light pruning of the stems that have carried blooms is all that is needed.

Cytisus scoparius

Daphne

The daphne most usually seen is our native *D. mezereum*, the Mezereon, now rare as a native plant, but easily obtainable from nurseries. It is an old 'cottage garden' plant, grown for the sake of its sweetly-scented purplish-red flowers, that smother the twigs in February and March and often into April. Round red fruits follow in autumn and these provide a ready means of increase. It grows about 4 feet tall, tolerating most soils, except very dry ones, and it does well on the chalk and in partially shaded situations. There is a fine white-flowered variety *alba,* a pink form *rosea,* and a form, *grandiflora*, producing larger flowers a good deal earlier.

Not all daphnes are so easy to grow. *Daphne × burkwoodii,* a semi-evergreen hybrid, about 3 feet tall, with very fragrant pale pink flowers in May and June, is not at all difficult. It is also worth trying the variegated leaf form, *D. odora aureo-marginata.* This is harder than the species and is an evergreen, slow-growing to perhaps 3 feet, although much depends on soil and situation. Like other exotic daphnes, it prefers a well-drained, though moisture-retaining loam. Peat and leafmould dug in before planting may do something towards ensuring success with this aristocratic plant, although shelter from frosts and cutting winds is probably more important.

None of the daphnes described here requires pruning, unless it is to remove frost-killed wood.

Daphne × burkwoodii, a semi-evergreen hybrid.

Sweetly-scented
Daphne mezereum
(*above*) with
outline of the shrub.

Deutzia

The deutzias flower in June, at about the same time as the philadelphus and, although their flowers lack the sweet fragrance of those of the best of the mock oranges, they are worth planting for their beauty. They are easy to grow and are not too big for small gardens as the tallest reaches only about 10 feet and most of them have a maximum height of 6 feet. Some varieties can be bought that are not much more than 4 feet tall.

One of the best is *D. scabra candidissima*, about 10 feet tall, with pure white double flowers. 'Pride of Rochester' (*D. scabra plena*) is another good double-flowered kind, the petals rosy-purple on the outside and white within. 'Perle

Deutzia Perle Rose
is suitable for
restricted spaces.

Rose' is only 6 feet tall and, therefore, suitable for more restricted spaces and has flowers that are a soft rose-pink. *D. gracilis*, 3–4 feet, with graceful arching stems, has white flowers and is the kind forced into flower for sale in florists' shops. *D. × elegantissima,* which grows to 5–6 feet, is exceptional in having fragrant flowers, clear rosy-pink in colour.

Some pruning is needed with these shrubs. They produce most of their flowers on shoots made during the previous year, so that immediately after flowering a proportion of the older branches should be cut away. It is inadvisable to cut away too many for from them may spring new shoots to flower the following season.

Deutzia scabra plena is a double flowered kind that is easily cultivated.

Erica carnea (left) and
Erica vagans (right)

Erica

The callunas described earlier are usually referred to as lings
or heathers but their close relations, the ericas, which have
given their name to the whole family (*Ericaceae*) are also
known as heathers, or heaths. Whereas there is but one
species of calluna there are over 500 erica species, although
most of these are of little importance to the shrub gardener
as they are tender, greenhouse plants from South Africa.

There is a wide range of hardy ericas, however, mostly
from Europe, including the British Isles and, by choosing the
right kinds, it is possible to have them in flower throughout
the twelve months of the year. Like the lings, they make
fine ground cover if planted fairly closely together so that
they eventually merge. Heights range from a few inches to a
maximum of about 2 feet with the exception of the 'tree
heaths'. There is a good colour variation and some differences
in foliage colour.

Callunas may be grown only on lime-free soil, but there
are one or two ericas that will grow perfectly well on chalky,

or limey soils, which is a great help to the thousands of gardeners who have to put up with these soils. The same kinds will also grow on any other soil, so it is worth describing them first. The principal species is *E. carnea*, about a foot tall, with rosy-purple flowers from December to April. There are numerous varieties of this, some, such as 'Eileen Porter', flowering from October onwards and bearing carmine flowers, others, such as *vivellii*, are dwarfer. Colours include rosy-red, shades of pink, dark red, carmine and white.

The hybrid *E.* × *darleyensis* is also lime-tolerant. It grows to 18 inches tall and has rose-coloured flowers from November onwards until March or April. It has one or two varieties, including the white-flowered 'Silberschmelz'. One parent is *E. carnea,* the other *E. mediterranea* which is a good deal taller, at least 4 feet and in favoured places nearer 8 feet. It has rosy-red flowers from March or April, into June, so extending the season for these lime-tolerant heaths.

There is a wide range of others for lime-free soils, including several 'tree heaths' and the Cornish Heath *E. vagans* which will reach 2 feet. As far as the lower-growing kinds are concerned pruning is best carried out after flowering. It consists in trimming the plants lightly after the flowers have faded. Less vigorous kinds need no pruning. All need a sunny site on well-drained soil and should be planted firmly.

Erica mediterranea will grow to four feet and has red flowers from March until June.

Escallonia

The finest escallonias are seen by the sea, where *E. macrantha* is often used as a hedging plant. Its rosy-crimson flowers, which have a honey fragrance, set among the dark green leaves are a familiar sight in the late spring and summer of most coastal areas. It is most particularly found in the south and west of England.

The escallonias are, with few exceptions, evergreen shrubs, although they tend to be semi-evergreen in colder areas, where they are best given the shelter of a wall. They all do well near the sea, although some of them are hardy enough to be grown in inland gardens. Among the hardiest are *E.* × *langleyensis*, a hybrid with rosy carmine flowers, that grows to about 5–6 feet, or up to 10 feet near the coast. *E.* × *edinensis*, another not quite so tall hybrid, has rosy-pink flowers, while 'Slieve Donard', apple-blossom pink in colour, is one of a number of hybrids developed at a well-known nursery in Northern Ireland, in various shades of pink.

In general, escallonias do not require special soil, though they do best in rich loam. They make good hedges and in coastal areas grow densely enough to form excellent windbreaks. Their growths tend to be somewhat arching and, if neglected, straggly, but this can be controlled by hard pruning, which entails cutting off flowered shoots once the flowers are over. Half-ripe cuttings, taken in August, will root readily in bottom heat.

Escallonia × *langleyensis* is one of the hardiest escallonias and will grow to ten feet under good conditions.

Eucryphia

There are not many of these beautiful shrubs and two only have any claim to hardiness. One of these is the species *E. glutinosa*, which makes a deciduous shrub about 12–15 feet tall, or is occasionally seen as a small tree. It will not do well on lime or chalky soils, but will flourish in the southern counties, at least, on any reasonably rich loamy soil, if given a sheltered position. It bears from July onwards, beautiful fragrant white flowers, 2 inches or more across, with a central boss of stamens. In the autumn the leaves turn to rich colours before falling.

The other hardy kind is the evergreen hybrid, *E. × nymansay*, a cross between *E. glutinosa* and a less hardy species, *E. cordifolia*. *E. × nymansay* is a vigorous shrub which may reach 25 feet or more, but takes up less room than one might think as it is seldom more than 10 feet wide and would therefore not be out of place in a medium-sized garden. It produces its handsome flowers, which are like large white single roses with a central mass of yellow stamens, during August and September. Unlike its parents, *E. × nymansay* will tolerate lime or chalk in the soil, but it is not a shrub for thin soils overlying chalk. It will tolerate a deep chalky loam, but it does appreciate some shelter, particularly in its young state.

Eucryphias need no pruning unless it is to remove dead or frost-damaged wood, an operation best carried out in April or May.

Flowers of the hybrid *Eucryphia ×
nymansay (above)* and the
shrub form (*left*).

Forsythia

The spring garden would be incomplete without the golden-yellow flowers of the forsythias. These are among the hardiest and easiest of shrubs to grow, and for that reason are sometimes neglected, when a little attention would produce even better results. In general hard pruning is not necessary. Particularly in open situations in colder gardens, however, the tips of the shoots made the previous year, on which most of the flowers are borne, sometimes die back and to prevent these from looking bare it is a good plan to cut them back. Apart from this these shrubs need little pruning other than the occasional cutting out of the oldest wood.

Those grown in the open are usually forms or varieties of the hybrid, *F. × intermedia,* of which the best variety is perhaps the modern 'Lynwood', with large, golden-yellow flowers that are freely borne. 'Beatrix Farrand' has flowers nearly as large and makes an upright bush. *F. spectabilis*, the kind usually seen, also blooms freely, although its flowers are not so large. An interesting kind is 'Arnold Dwarf' which makes a low spreading bush, 6 feet or so across, but only 2 feet or so high.

Forsythia suspensa is another fine species, but although it can be grown in the open, the best position is against a south or west wall, trained as a wall shrub, where it will grow 10 feet tall or more, producing lemon-yellow flowers along its arching branches.

These shrubs will grow in any ordinary garden soil.

Forsythia suspensa (opposite) and the hybrid *Forsythia × intermedia (above)* which has large, freely borne, golden-yellow flowers.

Fuchsia magellanica (below) and its varieties are hardy enough to survive outdoors in most places and it is not uncommon to see it grown as a hedge.

Fuchsia

Most of the fuchsias are not hardy enough to qualify for inclusion in a book devoted to describing shrubs that are hardy in these islands. However, *F. magellanica* and its varieties and one or two others, are certainly hardy enough to survive outdoors in most places, even though in less favoured gardens they may be cut to the ground by frost each year. *F. magellanica* will grow where frosts are less severe and has red and purple flowers that are very freely borne. It may reach 10 feet and it is not uncommon to see it grown as a delightful flowering hedge in the West. Cut by frost it seldom fails to recover, sending up new stems from the base, but will then only grow to about 5 feet in height.

The variety usually grown is *riccartonii,* with crimson and purple flowers. There is a white flowered variety *alba,* one rather more slender in growth, *gracilis,* sometimes classed as a species, and also one (*versicolor*) in which the leaves are variegated with crimson, pink and cream. This does not grow so tall. 'Mrs. Popple' is another hardy fuchsia, with larger flowers, scarlet and deep purple in colour, while 'Madame Cornelissen' has attractive crimson and white flowers.

These hardy fuchsias will grow in any ordinary soil and sunny position. Except in very exposed gardens, where a covering of bracken will help, there is no need to give them extra protection; if they are damaged by frost it is a simple matter to cut the stems down to ground level in spring.

Garrya

The only species that is commonly grown is *Garrya elliptica,* which is sometimes, for reasons that are obvious when the plant is in flower, known as the Silk Tassel Bush. It comes from North America and is quite hardy in most parts of the country, although in the North and East it does better if given the protection of a wall. It grows rapidly and in a few years will reach 12–15 feet in height and a well-grown plant may be 6–8 feet wide.

It is not the flowers themselves that make the plant so attractive, but the long, silvery-green catkins in which they

Garrya elliptica will cover a wall even in a shady position.

The flowers give it the name of Silk Tassel Bush.

are borne. These, on male plants, may reach a foot long and they make the shrub a most handsome specimen when it is in full flower. The catkins start to appear in November and are very much in evidence until late in February.

This is an easily grown shrub flourishing well on poor soils as well as on chalk or in sea-side gardens. It does not object to a shady position, thus making it suitable for a north or east wall, and does not need pruning. Perhaps the only point which can be made against it is that it is not easy to transplant, and is best planted out, as a young specimen, from a pot. If you grow one plant only get the male, for the catkins of the female plant are much shorter.

Genista

The genistas are among those plants popularly referred to as brooms, the others are the cytisus and *Spartium junceum,* the Spanish broom. Whereas the pea-shaped flowers of cytisus may be of various colours, those of genistas, with very few exceptions, are yellow or golden-yellow. There are other slight botanical differences, although the two genera are closely related.

One of the most spectacular when it is in full flower in July is the Mount Etna broom, *G. aethnensis,* which may grow to 12 feet or more tall, with long drooping shoots, clothed with small golden-yellow flowers.

By contrast, *G. lydia* seldom exceeds 2 feet in height, although its growths are equally drooping in habit and hidden beneath golden-yellow flowers in May and June.

The Spanish Gorse, *G. hispanica,* is another dwarf kind, about 2 feet tall, sometimes less and sometimes a little more. It is very spiny and equally floriferous, with golden-yellow flowers appearing at about the same time or a little later than those of *G. lydia.*

Genista lydia

The attractive flowers
(*above*) and bush (*opposite*)
of *Genista aethnensis*.

There are other, mostly dwarf, varieties, although one good exception is *G. cinerea*, some 8 feet tall, with greyish leaves and fragrant yellow flowers in June and July.

These genistas do well in poor dry soil but must have full sun. Prune them after flowering, cutting away those stems that have carried blooms, but avoiding cutting into the older wood. Always plant them out from pots as they resent root disturbance.

Hamamelis mollis
with the outline of its
shrub form.

Hamamelis

The Hamamelis are the Wych Hazels or Witch Hazels as they are perhaps better known and are very valuable because they flower in winter, on the leafless branches. These shrubs grow slowly, but will eventually reach a height of 10 feet or more, with a proportionate spread and so require a fair amount of room. However, in order that the flowers and their fragrance can be appreciated, it is well worth planting them fairly near a pathway.

H. mollis is probably the best of the genus and it produces flowers from late December until late February or early March. These are golden-yellow blossoms, with strap-shaped petals that are about $\frac{1}{2}$ inch in length. The leaves are large and turn bright orange in autumn before falling. There is a variety, *pallida*, with paler flowers.

H. japonica in contrast has less fragrant flowers and the narrow petals are wavy with the flowers surrounded by red bracts. It flowers at about the same time as *H. mollis* and has one or two varieties, including *arborea*, which is considerably taller, and *zuccariniana* with flowers of lemon-yellow. There is a variety 'Carmine Red', so called because of the colour of its flowers and another variety 'Hiltingbury' from the hybrid *H.* × *intermedia*, which has coppery-red flowers. 'Copper Beauty', sometimes known as 'Jelena', has flowers of coppery-orange.

These wych hazels do well in any ordinary garden soil, are perfectly hardy and need no pruning other than the normal trimming necessary to keep the shrub in shape.

Hebe

These are the Shrubby Veronicas, still sometimes listed in catalogues under Veronica, though the name Hebe has now become more familiar to gardeners. Certainly it serves to distinguish these evergreen shrubs from their hardy herbaceous relatives.

There are many varieties, most of them from New Zealand, but not all are hardy and it is unfortunate that the tender ones have the brightest coloured flowers. However, the hardier kinds are beautiful, free-flowering shrubs and well worth their place. One of the finest that is known is 'Midsummer Beauty' that reaches about 4 feet tall. 'Autumn Glory', which actually comes into flower in summer and goes on until October, makes a widespread bush, about $1\frac{1}{2}$ feet high, with rich violet-blue flowers carried in short spikes. *H. brachysiphon* (*H. traversii*) is the commonest kind, often used for hedging purposes in coastal areas, but a fine specimen by itself when given room to develop. It reaches 5–6 feet and has multitudes of white flowers in short spikes. 'White Gem' is an improved dwarf form.

H. elliptica, also useful for hedging, is reasonably hardy. This makes a symmetrical, dome-shaped shrub and has mauve or sometimes very pale, almost white flowers. Its form *variegata* is more handsome as the leaves have broad creamy-white edges. Another fine variegated hebe is *H.* × *andersonii variegata*, eventually 4–5 feet tall, but often seen at about a foot, used for foliage effect in summer bedding in public parks, especially in coastal towns.

These hebes make few demands on the soil, growing well in quite poor kinds and those containing much chalk. They stand up well to salt-laden winds.

Hebe elliptica is a good hedging shrub.

The variety Midsummer Beauty bears hundreds of long spikes of lavender flowers throughout the summer and early autumn.

The colourful Sun Roses grow well on dry sunny banks or rockeries.

Helianthemum

The Sun Roses are charming little plants, that are very useful for many places in the garden, but practically indispensable for helping to clothe dry, sunny banks or, because they grow a mere 9 inches or so tall, for planting in sunny pockets on the rock garden.

H. nummularium (*H. chamaecistus*) is a native plant that has inch-wide yellow flowers. The many hybrids and varieties are very popular indeed, especially as they are easy to grow and have a wide colour range. Named kinds include 'Ben Afflick' which has orange and buff flowers,

'Firedragon' with crimson, 'Marigold', double yellow and 'Rose of Leeswood' with double flowers of a soft pink. There is a white variety called 'The Bride' and, in contrast, 'Henfield Brilliant' is brick red. There are many others, of which some have grey or silvery-grey leaves.

Left to themselves these plants are inclined to become straggly, but this can generally be overcome by hard pruning after flowering is over, usually in late July. This is not necessary merely for the sake of tidiness, but will encourage new flowering growth to appear. Sometimes this summer pruning may even cause the plants to produce more flowers in the autumn.

These shrubs do well in poor, but well-drained soils and their only real requirement is a sunny place, where they will produce their flowers freely without much attention. They dislike cold, wet soils.

A variety of *Helianthemum nummularium* has inch-wide pink flowers.

Hibiscus

Hibiscus syriacus and its numerous varieties, sometimes known as Tree Hollyhocks, are invaluable shrubs for they flower late, when a good many shrubs are already over. They begin to flower in July and it is sometimes October before the last flowers appear. The flowers are trumpet-shaped, much like those of the popular hollyhocks to which they are related, and there is now a fair colour range. These plants grow slowly to about 6–8 feet, making upright, rather than spreading bushes. They will grow in any reasonable garden soil but must have a sunny position. Dead wood should be removed when the plants are well in leaf which may not be until May.

Apart from the late-summer flowering, two of these shrubs at least are useful in that they have blue flowers. These are 'Blue Bird' and 'Coeleste'. *H. syriacus coeruleus plenus* has double purplish-blue flowers, *roseus plenus* has double lilac-red flowers and *violaceus plenus* double reddish-purple. 'Hamabo', a popular kind, has pale pink blooms with a crimson blotch at the petal bases and often with pink-tipped petals. 'Duc de Brabant' is a double red and *monstrosus plenus* a double white, purplish at the centre.

Hibiscus syriacus Coeleste
has blue flowers in late summer.

The Woodbridge variety is rose-pink
with maroon blotches.

Hydrangea petiolaris

Hydrangea

Most people think of hydrangeas as the shrubs with large mop-heads of flowers, in blue or pink, often seen at their best in the gardens of seaside towns in late summer. These, the 'hortensia' varieties of *H. macrophylla,* are deservedly popular, as they flower well, look spectacular when in bloom and are not difficult to grow, succeeding in sun or semi-shade. On chalk or lime the flowers are pink or red and the colours are so pleasant that it is hardly worth going to the considerable trouble of trying to make them blue by adding 'blueing' powder or aluminium sulphate to the soil in considerable quantities at frequent intervals. On acid soils the flowers are blue while on neutral soils they may be either or both on the same shrub and, in fact, this may happen on fairly deep soils overlying chalk. There are a number of named varieties, in shades of pink and red, not all of them guaranteed to blue. There are also one or two white-flowered varieties.

A variation is the 'Lace-cap' hydrangea, with flat heads of flowers, large sterile florets surrounding small fertile florets. 'Blue Wave' is a fine variety and 'Lanarth White' always attracts attention.

These varieties of *H. macrophylla* are not the only hydrangeas. Among the other hardier kinds are *H. paniculata grandiflora,* with cone-shaped spikes of white flowers and

H. arborescens grandiflora, which has large heads of white flowers. *H. quercifolia,* the Oak-leaved Hydrangea, is not quite so hardy but has attractive leaves that turn bright colours in autumn.

Different in habit from all these, is *H. petiolaris,* the Climbing Hydrangea, a self-clinging climber, a most unusual plant for a wall of any aspect, or for growing up a tree.

Hydrangeas must have a moisture retaining soil otherwise the shrubs will flag noticeably in dry periods and look very sorry for themselves. Even then it may be necessary to give them a really thorough watering in periods of drought.

Pruning, where necessary, is done in April and consists of cutting away weak growths and frost-damaged wood.

Hydrangea macrophylla (left) and a Lace-cap variety (*right*).

The Hidcote hybrid of Hypericum (*left*) and *Hypericum calycinum* (*below*).

Hypericum

Hypericum calycinum, usually referred to as Rose of Sharon, and often looked upon as almost a weed, is a useful plant for clothing dry banks, for those places under trees and shrubs where little else will grow, or for the tops of double walls. Its bright yellow flowers, with a big brush of stamens in the centre, are a familiar sight in many gardens and in railway cuttings in the chalk of the southern counties.

There are better, much more aristocratic kinds than this, however, fully worthy of a place of honour in the garden. The hybrid 'Hidcote', for instance, bears large, saucer-shaped flowers freely from July to autumn and grows to 5–6 feet tall. 'Rowallane Hybrid' is somewhat better as it easily reaches 6 feet in the milder counties and has flowers that may be 3 inches across. Unfortunately it is not hardy enough for the open garden except in warmer places and elsewhere it needs the shelter of a wall or a protected site.

Other good kinds include 'Elstead Variety', about 4 feet tall, *patulum henryi,* 3–4 feet, with good autumn leaf colour, and *patulum grandiflorum,* about 3 feet tall. In addition there are several dwarfer forms suitable for the rock garden, ranging from the 6 inches of *H. polyphyllum* to the 18 inches of *H. kalmianum.*

All these shrubs are sun-lovers and they do well in hot, dry situations, particularly on the chalk. *H. calycinum,* an evergreen, should be trimmed over with shears. 'Hidcote' and 'Rowallane Hybrid' may be hard pruned in spring but others need little attention except for the removal of dead wood.

This is a useful plant for dry banks

Jasminum nudiflorum will provide colour every winter without fail.

Jasminum

Winter flowers are always welcome, particularly if they are produced unfailingly, whatever the weather. The Winter Jasmine, *Jasminum nudiflorum* can always be guaranteed to open its bright yellow flowers on the leafless stems, even in hard frost or when deep snow covers the ground, unless pruning has been neglected. The flowers are produced on young growths made the previous year so that after flowering is over some thinning out of older shoots is needed, otherwise in a very few years, the bush will make a mass of tangled growths and flowering will be diminished. Specimens are normally grown against walls or fences, of any aspect, or may be trained over pergolas or arches. They may reach 12–15 feet in height.

The Summer Jessamine *J. officinale* is also a plant for a wall, though it should be a sunny one. Its white, sweetly fragrant flowers appear from June onwards into early autumn. It produces long twining growths and, properly trained, can cover a house side. Regular pruning is unnecessary, but it does pay to carry out some thinning out of shoots every two or three years, otherwise the growth is so vigorous that it will make a tangled mass several feet thick.

A hybrid between the Summer Jasmine and *J. beesianum* is *J. stephanense,* which is almost as vigorous and bears sweet-scented pale pink flowers in June and July. Like its parent it needs a sunny wall. Otherwise, like the others described here, it will grow in any normal garden soil.

Flowers of *Jasminum officinale* the fragrant summer species (*below*) and in shrub form (*left*).

Kalmia

Allied to the rhododendrons and belonging to the same family as the heathers (*Ericaceae*), the Kalmias need a lime-free, preferably peaty soil. In its native America *K. latifolia*, the most commonly grown species is known as the Mountain Laurel and its bright pink flowers make the mountains of the Eastern States very colourful in May and June. There it grows to 25–30 feet, although in Britain it seldom exceeds about 8–10 feet, but is well worth growing where the soil is

suitable. No pruning is needed, but, as with rhododendrons, it is worth removing dead flowers.

K. angustifolia, the Sheep Laurel, is a good deal less tall, reaching at the most 3 feet and usually less. It has narrow leaves and rosy-red flowers. An even more dwarf form is *K. polifolia,* about a foot or so in height, flowering earlier than the others, its purplish flowers opening in April.

All these kalmias prefer semi-shade and moist, though not perpetually boggy, soil. Peat and leafmould dug in at planting time and also used subsequently as a surface mulch, will do much to create the right conditions.

Kalmia latifolia has evergreen leaves like those of rhododendrons and the flowers are borne in clusters at the end of the stems. These are attractive in bud, looking like pink boxes, opening to bell-shaped blossoms.

Kerria

There is one species only of Kerria, *K. japonica*, although there are several varieties of it. One does not often see *K. japonica* itself, as most people prefer to grow the larger double-flowered form, *pleniflora* (or *flore-plena*) which makes a considerably larger plant. Yet the ordinary kind has its merits. It grows about 5–6 feet tall when planted against a wall or fence of any aspect, not quite so tall when grown in the open. It makes a clump of green stems, somewhat arching in habit, on which, mainly in April and May but also at other times of the year, appear numerous orange-yellow flowers, not unlike small single roses or large buttercups.

There is also a dwarf form, *picta* (or *variegata*), which has leaves edged with silvery-white.

Any kind of soil seems suitable for this shrub provided it is not too poor and dry. If it is to be planted in the open, a reasonably sheltered position should be chosen and it does not matter if this is in semi-shade. Pruning is not generally required. However, as plants make fairly extensive thickets it is worth thinning out the stems occasionally to let in light and air.

Kerria japonica pleniflora is the variety generally cultivated and often trained against a wall (*left*). It has large two-inch double flowers and grows to about eight feet with stiff upright stems.

The hybrid *Laburnum* × *vossii* is more upright and tree-like in growth.

Laburnum

The laburnums are strictly small trees, but they never grow very tall and although they may be grown as standards on a single stem, often fork low down, giving the appearance of a tall shrub. They grow quite quickly, but rarely to more than 20 feet in height and it is more usual to see them at about 15 feet. The common laburnum (*L. anagyroides*) is pleasant enough in late May and June with its trails of golden flowers, and it does well near the sea and in exposed, windy gardens. It is not, however, as good as the hybrid, *L.* × *vossii*, which has longer trails of flowers, some 15–18 inches in length, borne a little later. This kind also has the advantage of

producing fewer of the poisonous black seeds that make some gardeners with small children reluctant to plant the beautiful laburnums.

Another kind which flowers later than the ordinary laburnum is its variety *autumnale* and with this, too, the flower trails are longer.

Laburnums grow in any kind of soil, including those containing much chalk. They do not require pruning, but, where there are small children about it is advisable to go over the trees after flowering and cut off the dead flower trails to prevent the seed from setting.

Lavandula

One of the most pleasant ways of growing that old garden favourite, the lavender, is to use it as a hedge, either as a low boundary hedge or an internal hedge to divide one part of the garden from another. Lavenders, with their ever-grey leaves, associate well with other silvery or grey-leaved plants in the shrub or herbaceous border. A few separate plants in a broad paved area, planted in the space gained by removing a flagstone, looks very effective.

L. spica is the Old English Lavender and there are several forms of it, of which 'Grappenhall Variety' at about 3 feet, sometimes reaching 4 feet, is the tallest and 'Beechwood Blue' at less than 1 foot is about the shortest. This kind has flowers of a good blue and there are others such as *rosea* with pink flowers and 'Twickel Purple' with deep purple blooms, as well as several other dwarfs at about 15 inches. These dwarfs are particularly useful in very small gardens where the bigger kinds would look out of place.

Any well-drained soil and sunny position suits the lavenders and it is all the better if the soil is really well-drained and on the dry side in summer. Apart from the pruning the plants get when the stems are cut for drying or decoration it is as well to trim them over in April, avoiding cutting into the old wood.

The many varieties of *Lavandula spica* look very attractive as internal hedges flanking a pathway. They should be planted at least 1½ feet from the edge to allow for development without impeding progress along the path.

Lonicera

The loniceras are the Honeysuckles and the native *L. periclymenum* is also known as the Woodbine. This has a couple of varieties, more often planted in gardens than the wild kind and both deserving a place because they follow each other in flower, giving a continuous display between them from May to October. The Early Dutch Honeysuckle, *L. periclymenum belgica,* with reddish-purple flowers, starts the season in late spring, and the Late Dutch, *L. p. serotina,* with somewhat richer coloured flowers, carries it into the autumn.

There are numerous others, however, some more vigorous, some lacking the delicious fragrance one associates with

Lonicera periclymenum is native to Britain and selected varieties are easy to cultivate, especially over garden arches (*right*).

these plants, but with larger flowers. One of the finest is the hybrid, *L. × americana*, which is extremely free-flowering with large flowers opening white but ageing to deep yellow, in big clusters in June or July. They lack fragrance but the plant is worth growing for the speed with which it covers a pergola, fence or other support.

The native Woodbine flourishes on heavy clay soils and all loniceras do well in shade, although they will not object to sunnier situations. The twiners need some support for their growths and often look well if they are allowed to scramble through other shrubs or into trees. They need pruning only if they become too vigorous, when it is sufficient to shorten the strongest shoots in autumn.

Lupinus

The lupins that are most well known are the hardy herbaceous perennials, especially the Russell lupins in a wide colour range. But there is a fine shrub, popularly known as the Tree Lupin, which has very similar flowers, although the spikes are shorter at about 9 inches long. This is *Lupinus arboreus,* an excellent shrub for dry soils, for hot sunny banks and for poor, stony soils that sometimes present problems. In fact it does better on these soils than on richer, moisture-retaining kinds, which is understandable, as it originated in California.

Its maximum height is about 6 feet, but in most places it rarely seems to exceed 4–5 feet. So rapidly does it grow, however, that it can attain its eventual height in no more than two or three years. Its sweetly fragrant flowers are produced throughout most of June and July. Normally they are a fairly bright yellow, but there are various named colour forms available including the deep yellow 'Golden Spire' and 'Yellow Boy', 'Mauve Queen', rosy-mauve, and the pure white 'Snow Queen'. Plants are easily raised from seed and other colour forms may appear among the seedlings.

There is no need to prune this shrub, though it is worth deadheading it to conserve its strength. It does not like being transplanted so that it is best to plant out from pots.

Lupinus arboreus is an excellent shrub for dry soils.

The Tree Lupins make shrubby plants that develop sweetly fragrant flowers in June.

Magnolia

The magnolias are among the most beautiful of all shrubs, though they are not planted as widely as they might be because they have a reputation for being 'difficult' and because, generally, they are slow growing. Several, however, are reasonably easy to grow provided they are given the right soil and, if carefully planted, some flower very early in life. Certainly not the least beautiful is *M. stellata*, which produces starry flowers with drooping white petals. Plants a mere 18 inches tall will start to flower the year following planting.

Magnolia stellata produces starry white flowers in March and April.

M. soulangeana is no more difficult to grow and also flowers early in life. It has a number of varieties but *lennei* is the best. In June this produces flowers that look much like large tulips, purplish-rose on the outside, white inside.

By contrast, *M. grandiflora*, a wall evergreen, may take many years to flower, unless 'Exmouth Variety' or 'Goliath', two kinds that flower much younger, are planted. This, one of the most magnificent of all magnolias, flowers in late summer producing enormous fragrant creamy flowers, 9–10 inches across. It may grow to 30 feet, with a proportionate spread.

These magnolias do not mind chalky soils, provided they

are not thin and deep, well-cultivated alkaline soil is probably preferable to a hot, dry sandy acid soil. Before planting the opportunity should be taken to incorporate moist peat and leafmould in lavish quantities and it is worth lightening heavier clay soils with sharp sand in addition. An annual mulch in spring with moist peat and leafmould, or rotted garden compost is always beneficial to magnolias. They require no pruning, apart from the removal of any dead wood, but they must have plenty of water during droughts, particularly when young. When planting great care should be taken not to damage the roots.

Magnolia soulangeana (above) with outline of the shrub form (*left*) is one of the commonly grown deciduous species.

Mahonia aquifolium is an
excellent shrub for shady
conditions but will grow in more
open situations (*right*).

Mahonia

Related to the berberis and sometimes included under berberis in catalogues, these evergreen shrubs differ mainly in having large leathery leaves divided into a number of leaflets. The kind mainly grown is *M. aquifolium,* an excellent shrub for under the shade of trees though it will grow in more open situations, in time reaching some 3–6 feet tall, with a spread of 3–5 feet. The large leaves have up to seven pairs of spiny toothed leaflets. As winter approaches these turn purplish or are often flushed or edged with red. These colours persist until the spring. In late winter the shrub flowers, producing lemon-yellow deliciously fragrant blooms, in long clusters, springing from a central point. The flowers are followed by berries, green at first, changing to dark purple with a plum-like bloom, almost as handsome as the flowers. The shrub spreads by underground suckers, but seldom at a rate to make it a nuisance and this habit makes it useful for ground cover under trees. It also makes it easy to propagate by digging up pieces of sucker growth.

M. japonica is a taller plant, with even more fragrant flowers, with a distinct lily-of-the-valley scent. These are produced in late winter in longer clusters or sprays.

These mahonias are not demanding in their soil requirements. The leafy soil beneath trees suits them admirably though they will flourish in any kind of garden soil including chalky ones.

The hybrid *Malus ×
purpurea* in flower

Malus

These are the crab-apples and, like several other plants
mentioned in this book, they are small trees rather than
shrubs. They are grown for their flowers as much as for their
richly coloured fruits and some provide an added bonus
when their leaves turn bright colours in autumn, before
falling. Some, indeed, have purplish coppery leaves throughout. One with this characteristic is *M. × eleyi,* which grows
to about 20 feet tall, with rosy-crimson flowers in late
April and early May, followed by masses of small purplish
crabs. *M. × purpurea* is another fine hybrid that has purplish
leaves and reddish crimson flowers, produced rather earlier
than those of *M. × eleyi.*

Malus × purpurea

John Downie (*right*) is planted chiefly for its large fruit.

'John Downie' is the kind planted more than any other, for the sake of its large scarlet and yellow fruits that follow the white flowers. 'Dartmouth Crab', another white-flowered kind, crops heavily, its fruits crimson with a bluish plum-bloom. The yellow-fruited kinds such as 'Golden Hornet' are unusually handsome, though their fruits are smaller. There are also several kinds with double flowers, including 'Katherine', pink at first, ageing to white, with red fruits.

These Crabs will grow in all kinds of soil, particularly those containing lime, preferably in open, sunny positions. Pruning is unnecessary except for shape or to restrict over-lush growth.

Olearia

The olearias are the Daisy Bushes, natives of Australia and New Zealand, evergreen shrubs, many of them tender, though suitable for coastal gardens in the milder counties. Though not fully hardy, *O. haastii* is hardy enough to be grown successfully in quite cold northern gardens, where one can see old specimens, 4–5 feet tall, bearing numerous clusters of small white daisy flowers in late summer. It makes an unusual and informal evergreen hedge.

In warmer gardens near the coast, even in the south-east, provided it is planted there in a sheltered place, the hybrid *O. × scilloniensis* will put up a good show. Its flowers are much larger and a well-grown bush, 3–5 feet tall, is a handsome sight when it flowers in May and early June. Even when out of flower it is attractive for its leaves are a good grey-green. In somewhat milder but exposed seaside areas, it is possible to grow *O. gunniana*, the Tasmanian Daisy Bush, which again flowers in May and June, white in the species, but also available with flowers that are rosy-pink, blue or lavender in colour.

These Daisy Bushes will grow in any normal garden soil and do not object to slight shade. A trim with shears after they have flowered will improve their appearance. If they become leggy and gaunt they may be pruned quite hard.

Olearia gunniana

Olearia × *scilloniensis* is a hybrid that has larger than average flowers in May and June.

Paeonia

The shrubby paeonies, varieties of *P. suffruticosa*, known as Moutan paeonies, are among the most showy of garden plants for a few weeks in April and May. Their large semi-double or fully double flowers in shades of crimson, pink, carmine, purple and white, often splashed with another colour, are among the glories of the garden at that time. They grow to 4–6 feet tall and a well-grown plant may be 3–4 feet wide. They are not difficult plants to grow but, although hardy, they may be damaged by frosts and for that reason are best planted in sheltered situations, particularly where the morning sun cannot reach them, because rapid evaporation of dew or frost will damage the delicate blooms. They will grow in any reasonably rich and well-dug soil.

The single, deep crimson flowers of *P. delavayi* which is a 5 feet tall Chinese species will always attract attention. A very good effect can also be obtained with the large bright yellow single blooms of *P. lutea* of which the best form is *ludlowii*. This variety should reach 6 feet with ease. *P. lutea* has been crossed with *P. suffruticosa* to produce the *lemoinei* hybrids, such as 'Alice Harding', a double canary yellow, and 'Souvenir de Maxine Cornu', which has very large bright yellow flowers and petals edged with red.

These tree paeonies need no pruning but dead wood should be cut away in the spring.

The colourful flowers of the paeonies always attract attention during the flowering period of May and June.

The Mock Orange variety,
Sybille, has richly scented
flowers and reaches 5 feet
in height.

114

Philadelphus

These are the well-loved Mock Oranges, known to most gardeners for the scent of their early summer flowers, although not all of them have the piercingly sweet 'orange-blossom' fragrance of the old-fashioned, commonly grown *P. coronarius* with its creamy-white flowers. This may grow to 10 feet tall, producing annually a mass of young shoots, either springing from the base or from the older wood, and it is on this young growth that the Mock Oranges produce most of their flowers, which gives the clue to pruning. This consists in thinning out some of the oldest stems each year, after the flowers have faded, thus giving the younger growth a better chance to ripen. These young growths are always paler in colour so that it is an easy matter to differentiate when pruning.

There is a particularly beautiful variety of *P. coronarius*, known as *aureus*, with golden-yellow leaves which, after midsummer, turn greenish-yellow. In spring it is an outstanding sight.

The Mock Oranges are easy plants to grow but prefer a sunny position. The old vernacular name 'Syringa' still persists, although the true syringas are the lilacs.

Philadelphus coronarius is the old-fashioned, commonly grown, form.

Pieris

Double value shrubs are usually worth growing and anyone with a lime-free soil, of the type on which rhododendrons thrive, should grow pieris. If there is room for one only it should be *P. forrestii* (*P. formosa forrestii*) in one of its finest forms, such as 'Exbury Form' or 'Wakehurst Variety'. The great glory of this evergreen shrub is in the spring or early summer, when the young growths are developing. These bear a resemblance to shuttlecocks on the ends of the branches, are brilliant red and remain so for some weeks before turning a light green, which turns darker as the summer advances. Sprays of white, fragrant flowers similar to lily-of-the-valley appear in April and May when the red young growths are at their best.

Pieris forrestii, sometimes known as *Pieris formosa forrestii*

The shrub will reach 10 feet in milder places, with a proportionate spread. In less protected places a height of about 6 feet is more usual. In general, pruning is unnecessary, except to remove dead or dying wood.

Where space allows, other species of pieris may be grown. *P. floribunda*, for instance, does not take up much room, as it usually grows only to about 4 feet and is, in any case, a slow-grower. *P. japonica*, which ultimately grows to about 10 feet, has larger flowers that are produced in March and April, a little earlier than other species. Another of these plants, is *P. taiwanensis*, which reaches the same height and flowers freely during April and May. None, however, has quite the attraction of the best forms of *P. forrestii*.

This shrub will reach 10 feet in mild situations.

Potentilla

These are the Shrubby Cinquefoils, mostly varieties of *P. fruticosa*, a deciduous shrub about 4 feet tall, although its named forms range in height from 1 foot upwards to over 4 feet. They flower over a very long period, usually from June to September, or even later into the autumn and are invaluable from this point of view alone. In the species itself the flowers are yellow, but there are many subtle shades of this colour and in the varieties it is possible to find pale primrose as in, 'Katherine Dykes', one of the best of all, reaching 4 feet, canary yellow, as in 'Elizabeth', 2½ feet tall, and golden-yellow, in such varieties as *farreri*.

Potentilla fruticosa is invaluable because it flowers from June until late autumn.

This variety grows to 2 feet and comes into flower earlier than the others. A coppery yellow, or orange, can be obtained with the 'Tangerine' variety and a creamy-yellow with *vilmoriniana*. This is an excellent variety because its silvery, almost white leaves add to its attraction. Apart from these there are white-flowered kinds, of which the 1 foot tall *mandschurica,* with grey leaves, is one of the best.

Although the potentillas do best in sunny, open positions, they will tolerate a little shade and the quality of soil appears to be immaterial. They do not require pruning. Those of more upright growth may be used to make pleasant internal hedges, flowering as they do over such a long period.

Prunus

This is a big genus containing the almonds, apricots, cherries, peaches, plums, sloes and related fruits, as well as a wide range of ornamentals, principally the Japanese flowering cherries. It also includes various hedging plants such as laurels and myrobalan plums, some of which, like *P.* × *cistena,* are becoming increasingly popular for making coloured-leaf hedges.

As there are some two hundred or more prunus in cultivation the choice can be somewhat bewildering. For sheer colour in spring there is nothing to beat the hybrid Japanese cherries, although they need choosing with care as some grow too large for small gardens. For really confined spaces there is 'Amanogawa', in growth like a Lombardy Poplar, with fragrant, semi-double pink flowers. Small, too, is 'Kiku Shidare Zakura', also known as 'Cheal's Weeping Cherry', with arching shoots bearing fully double, deep pink flowers. Larger, with wide-spread branches, is 'Kanzan', with deep pink, double flowers, very freely borne. There are many

(*From left to right*) Cherry Laurel, Flowering Almond, Japanese Cherry and Purple Cherry.

others, in pinks pale and deep, and some good white-flowered kinds.

P. subhirtella autumnalis, a small tree, is popular because it produces its white, single or semi-double flowers from November onwards, particularly when the weather is mild.

More shrubby in growth is *P. triloba multiplex,* a dwarf almond, which grows to about 6 feet tall, or more against a wall, and has delightful rosy-pink, 'bachelor's button' flowers in March and April.

P. cerasifera atropurpurea (*pissardii*) is the Purple-leaved Plum, a decorative small tree, also used for hedging. *P. c. nigra* has darker, almost black leaves and pink flowers.

An attractive bush is made by the dwarf almond, *P. amygdalus tenella* 'Fire Hill', which grows to 4 feet with a similar spread and in April bears many rosy-crimson flowers.

All the prunus do well on chalk. Little pruning is required for trees and shrubs in the open but those against walls require pruning and training to keep their shape.

Pyracantha coccinea lalandii is a delightful wall-trained shrub with orange-red fruit.

Pyracantha

Seen more often as wall-trained shrubs rather than in the open, pyracanthas or Firethorns are notable for their freely produced colourful berries that follow the pretty clusters of white flowers, much like those of our native hawthorn. Against walls these plants will grow to 10–20 feet but in the open, where they may be used as hedges or as specimen plants, they are a good deal less tall. They will grow in sun or shade, do well on north walls, and do not have any special soil requirements, growing well on those containing much chalk.

Berry colours range from bright crimson, through orange to yellow. One of the best of the crimson-fruited kinds is the tall-growing *P. atalantoides* (*P. gibbsii*), which also has a fine yellow-berried form *aurea*. In *P. coccinea* the fruits are orange-red and it is the variety of this known as *lalandii,* with larger berries of a similar colour, that is the most popular pyracantha. However, orange is not everyone's colour and those who prefer something quieter may like to plant *P. crenulata flava,* which has bright yellow fruits.

Against walls these shrubs need pruning occasionally as they grow vigorously and long growths can become a nuisance. In the open little attention is necessary. Pruning is best undertaken wearing gloves as the aptly-named fire-thorns are indeed thorny.

Rhododendron

This is a large and bewildering genus, particularly as it includes the azaleas. It contains a vast range of plants, both deciduous and evergreen, in a wonderful colour range, varying in height from less than 1 foot to the 20–30 feet of some tree-like species grown in the milder counties. Most kinds are hardy outdoors anywhere in the British Isles, some can only be grown properly in warmer places while some need the protection of a cool greenhouse.

Although the normal flowering period is April and May there are some which come into flower earlier than this, while others delay their flowering until June or July, so that the rhododendron season is not as short as may be supposed.

The Princess Morika variety of the Rhododendrons (*left*) and *R. azalea mollis* (*right*).

R. yakusimanum (left) and *R. augustinii*

However diverse these shrubs may be, they have, with one or two minor exceptions, one thing in common and that is their dislike of lime or chalk in the soil or even in the water that may be used to water them. Acid woodland soils, those containing much leafmould or peat, in lime-free districts suit them best.

It is possible to mention here a few kinds only from the very many available. The Hardy Hybrids are among the best for the normal garden. They include such kinds as the old favourites 'Pink Pearl', the rosy-carmine 'Cynthia', 'Handsworth Scarlet', 'Gomer Waterer', blush-pink, and many others, some with handsome darker blotches on their petals.

Among the species *R. augustinii* with blue flowers is outstanding and *R. repens* is a fine prostrate kind for woodland ground cover, with scarlet flowers. *R. impeditum,* mauve, *R. calostrum,* pink to mauve, and *R. hanceanum nanum,* yellow, are all dome-shaped plants good as rock garden shrubs.

The Kurume hybrids are among the best of the evergreen azaleas, with many good colours. The *mollis* hybrids, 4–5 feet tall, with large flowers are excellent deciduous azaleas.

Rhus

The rhus most commonly seen in gardens is *R. typhina*, the well-known Stag's Horn Sumach. It will grow anywhere, but has a bad habit of sending up suckers yards away, so be warned. For this reason it is not a good specimen for a lawn, although it is often seen in this situation. It usually grows 12–15 feet tall, so needs a fair amount of space.

By far the best of the rhus is *R. cotinus*, correctly known nowadays as *Cotinus coggygria,* but described here as it is still found under Rhus in many catalogues. This is the Smoke Tree, Wig Tree or Venetian Sumach, although the latter name is hardly ever heard. Smoke Tree and Wig Tree are much more appropriate names as when it is in flower the flower-stems, many of them flowerless, are so slender that it looks as though the shrub is wearing a huge pale pink wig. In autumn these fine stems turn grey and one can see why the name Smoke Tree has been given to this shrub.

This is another plant for a poor soil, otherwise it may not flower freely, but will produce too much foliage. On the other hand the variety known as *atropurpurea foliis purpureis* 'Notcutt's Variety' might be given better treatment, as the main attraction lies in the deep maroon leaves.

These are good plants for the busy or lazy gardener as no pruning is needed except to remove dead wood or any branches that spoil the shape.

The crimson spikes of *Rhus typhina* are a common sight in late summer and the leaves turn scarlet before they fall.

Ribes sanguineum, known as the Flowering Currant, is one of the easiest shrubs to grow in any soil in a sunny position.

Ribes

Most gardeners know the Flowering Currant, *Ribes sanguineum,* one of the easiest of plants to grow in any soil and sunny situation, although it is not the most aristocratic of shrubs. The species itself has rosy-pink flowers in March and April but the pink is not a very good colour. There are several good red-flowered cultivars, however, such as 'King Edward VII' which is deep crimson, and 'Pulborough

Scarlet', as well as an unusual one, *brocklebankii,* with golden leaves and pink flowers. All these reach from 6–10 feet in height and benefit from hard pruning after the flowers are over. The shoots that have flowered may then be cut out or cut back as required.

There are other ornamental currants worthy of a more prominent position. The Buffalo Currant or Golden Currant *R. aureum* (*R. odoratum*) has short trails of sweetly-scented yellow flowers in spring. It grows to about 6–8 feet tall and its leaves turn a good yellow in autumn. *R.* × *gordonianum,* a hybrid between the two species described above, has bronze-red and yellow flowers and red autumn leaves. The Fuchsia-flowered Gooseberry, *R. speciosum,* is an evergreen and belongs to the gooseberry side of the genus. It makes a good wall shrub, with drooping red fuchsia-like flowers.

This shrub should be planted from October to March. *R. speciosum* will sometimes suffer from frost damage but the other species are quite hardy. All the varieties of this shrub can be increased by taking cuttings of the firm young stems. These should be between 6–8 inches in length, and can be inserted in ordinary soil outdoors during October. Most cuttings treated in this way should root satisfactorily by the following spring.

R. aureum has sweetly-scented yellow flowers.

Rosa

Roses, in all their varied forms and colours, are among the aristocrats of flowering shrubs. Few shrubs come into flower in June and continue flowering until October or later, as the modern hybrid tea and floribunda roses do.

There are roses for practically all purposes and no other shrub is so diverse in its flower colour. In the hybrid teas and floribundas, pinks, reds and yellows predominate, with a few good white varieties and, in recent years, a good many on the orange or vermilion side of red have been introduced, with a few others verging on lilac. In the older roses it is possible to find purples, maroons, magentas, and mauves as well as the deepest crimsons and delicate pinks. There are the striped roses such as 'Rosa Mundi' and partly-coloured varieties such as 'York and Lancaster', grown for over four centuries, with its petals sometimes pink and sometimes almost white, usually with both kinds on the same flower.

Among these 'old' roses, are the most heavily fragrant kinds, their scent quite unlike the light fragrance of most of the modern roses. Many have a short flowering period, around midsummer, but others have recurrent or 'perpetual' flowers. In contrast *R. rubrifolia* is grown for its purple leaves.

In this short space it is impossible to mention further names, particularly as new varieties of hybrid teas, floribundas and even shrub roses, appear annually. There are many suppliers of fine hybrid teas and floribundas in the country and it would be invidious to recommend particular nurseries. There are, however, few nurseries that have a really wide range of 'old' roses, Bourbons, hybrid musks, hybrid perpetuals, China roses, and species roses. The widest selection is held by Sunningdale Nurseries, Windlesham, Surrey, an establishment that is well worth a visit around midsummer or during late June, when most of these roses are in bloom.

The Rose Garden – still as popular as ever it was.

Roses will do well on clay soils provided they are properly cultivated, just as they will flourish on most soils except the very thin ones overlying chalk, which provide the most difficult conditions for most shrubs. Mulching in spring is necessary to keep them growing vigorously.

Hybrid teas and floribundas are usually pruned in late March. For ordinary garden display hard pruning is not necessary and reducing stems by about a third or a half their length, cutting back to above an outward-pointing bud, is usually sufficient, cutting out thin growths at the same time and endeavouring to keep the centre of the bush open.

Rambler roses are pruned immediately after they have flowered, cutting away the old flowered shoots. Climbing hybrid teas are pruned by thinning out some of the old flowered shoots once the blooms are over; the plants are gone over again in April to cut off dead growth and thin, weakly shoots and tipping back the ends of unripened shoots.

Little pruning is required for the 'old' roses. Some of the oldest stems can be cut away each year after flowering and the longest growths are shortened by one third in February or March.

The species roses also need little pruning, though when bushes become overgrown it is necessary to cut out the oldest shoots and thin growth, to encourage the production of new, strong shoots on which the best flowers are produced.

Flowers and fruit of *Rosa moyesii*

A. Mrs Pierre S. Dupont
B. Ellen Poulsen
C. *R. mundi*
D. Hips of a species rose
E. Masquerade
F. Constance Spry

Rubus

The Brambles are grown for their flowers, their fruits, or their white stems. Some are valuable for shady places or rough banks. Of the twenty or more kinds in cultivation, pride of place as far as flowers go must be given to the hybrid, 'Tridel', because of its shining, paper-white flowers, with a central mass of yellow stamens, looking not unlike single roses. These are freely borne in April and May, on arching shoots which may reach 9–10 feet in length.

Of the white-stemmed kinds, *R. cockburnianus* and *R. thibetanus* are about the best. They are seen at their best in winter when the leaves are off and the ghostly-white stems can be appreciated.

Rubus thibetanus has white stems and is at its best in winter.

An unusual kind is *R. ulmifolius bellidiflorus,* which makes a wide spreading clump in a wild garden or may be trained back against a wall, or over a pergola or fence. It has double pink flowers in July and August.

All these shrubs can be grown in any kind of soil and may either be cut hard back to keep them within bounds, or be left to grow at will, merely cutting out the oldest wood each spring. The white-stemmed kinds look more attractive if they are pruned hard each spring so as to encourage the formation of new stems.

The best ornamental Rubus
is Tridel, a hybrid
from *R. delicosus* and
R. trilobus.

135

Senecio

There are not many daisy-flowered shrubs available for the garden and this genus includes 1,300 species, very few of garden value. The senecio usually grown in gardens, referred to as either *S. greyi* or *S. laxifolius,* is probably neither of these species, but a hybrid. It attracts attention not only because of its bright yellow daisies, but also because of the silvery grey appearance of its young leaves, which makes them look as though they are covered with felt. In older leaves the greyness is confined to the edges. Underneath the leaves are white.

Fine specimens of this plant, up to 3–4 feet tall, are to be seen in gardens near the sea round most of the coast, for this shrub will tolerate well the wind and salt sea spray. However, it grows well inland, provided it can be given a fairly sheltered position in full sunlight. It is also a useful plant for the chalk garden. Gardeners who plant mainly for

Senecio laxifolius is one of the few daisy-flowered shrubs available.

the foliage effect often remove the flower-heads before they open to preserve the grey-white appearance of the plant, but most people generally prefer to let the handsome yellow daisies develop fully. Little pruning is needed, although after severe winters there may be a fair amount of dead growth to be cut away.

There are many other senecios available, although they are not often seen. *S. compactus* is very much like the plant that has been described above, except that it does not exceed 3 feet in height and is usually considerably less, and both its leaves and flowers are smaller. *S. elaeagnifolius* grows to about 4 feet in height and is much denser and more stiff in habit. Both this and the taller *S. hectori,* which has white centres and white petals to the flowers, are really only suitable for seaside planting in milder areas such as the south-west and the west of Britain.

Sorbus aucuparia is valued for its orange-red fruits, copiously produced in autumn.

Sorbus

The Mountain Ash or Rowan (*Sorbus aucuparia*), a native plant, will, in time, reach 20–30 feet, making a round-headed tree, so its position should be chosen with some care. The leaves, divided into many narrow leaflets, are graceful, and the small white flowers are produced in clusters in May.

Although this is among the best of small trees, it does have the disadvantage that the fruits seldom stay long enough for them to be fully appreciated for they are eagerly devoured by birds. Fortunately there is a yellow-fruited form, *xanthocarpa,* which is less attractive to birds. There are other forms, too, including *asplenifolia,* with deeply-cut, fern-like leaves, and *fastigiata,* more upright in growth and thus more suitable for restricted spaces.

There are many other sorbuses and among these *S. discolor* is worth growing for its bright red, long-lasting autumn foliage. *S. hupehensis,* somewhat taller, attracts attention because of its white or pale pink fruits. *S. essertauiana,* 20–25 feet, carries great clusters of rather small scarlet fruits which hang on the leafless trees well into winter.

Sorbus hupehensis

(*Above*) Fruit and flowers
of *Sorbus aucuparia*

Spartium

The only species here is *S. junceum,* the Spanish Broom, familiar to many gardeners. It is an attractive shrub but peculiar because it is almost leafless, with green, rush-like stems. The species name *junceum* acknowledges the similarity to the rushes, called *Juncus.* The real attraction lies in the large yellow pea flowers that are borne all summer. These are worth cutting to bring indoors for the sake of the scent of lilies that they exhale.

S. junceum thrives best in poor, dry, stony soils and is one answer to what to plant in such places. It does very well on chalk and is a good plant for seaside gardens as it stands up well to searing winds and salt spray.

It is not very elegant as far as habit is concerned, especially if pruning is neglected, for then it will grow nearly 10 feet tall, but look leggy and straggly. Hard pruning in March will help and the more straggly shoots can be cut hard back and the other shoots reduced in length. Even so, after a few years, plants will inevitably become leggy. To prevent this spoiling the effect it pays to plant a lower-growing shrub or a clump of herbaceous perennials in front of the Spanish Broom.

Planting out, as this shrub does not like root disturbance, should be done from pot plants. Transplanting from the open ground should only be done if absolutely essential as it usually kills the plant.

Spartium junceum will not make an elegant shrub if allowed to grow freely. It should be hard pruned in March.

Spiraea

This is another biggish group of shrubs, with about fifty kinds available, though for the normal shrub garden the selection can be limited to a few. Even these are varied in height, habit and flower colour.

The most familiar kind is the hybrid *S. × arguta*, known to many gardeners as the Bridal Wreath, a shrub eventually about 6 feet tall, with slender arching stems, wreathed in April and May with multitudes of tiny white flowers. To ensure that the shrub has ample opportunity to produce the long new shoots on which the flowers appear, it is necessary to prune after flowering at about the end of May, cutting back hard the old stems that have flowered.

The equally popular *S. × bumalda* 'Anthony Waterer' must be treated even more drastically for in April it should be cut practically down to the ground. It will then produce masses of stems, about 2 feet tall, which, in late summer will bear flattish heads of crimson flowers. If these are cut off after they have faded, more may be produced well into September. Those who like variegated foliage should note that very often the leaves of this shrub are variegated with pink and creamy-white.

S. thunbergii starts the season by flowering in late March

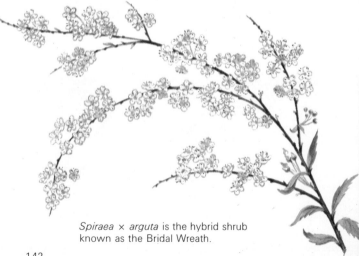

Spiraea × arguta is the hybrid shrub known as the Bridal Wreath.

or early April. In habit and in flower it is not unlike *S.* ×
arguta, but it is not so tall, reaching 4 feet. It should be
pruned in the same way.

S. × *vanhouttei,* again similar in habit and flower to
S. × *arguta,* flowers in June, but is taller, growing to about
7–8 feet.

All these spiraeas, flowering as they do on new growth,
benefit from reasonably generous treatment and annual
pruning. They have no particular soil requirements but
do better if the soil is well dug and enriched with compost at
planting time and if it is given an annual mulch of compost,
rotted manure or hop manure.

The hybrid *S.* × *bumalda*
has crimson flowers and
variegated foliage.

Syringa yunnanensis

Syringa

The syringas are the lilacs, not the philadelphus, as explained elsewhere. They have long been popular for their fragrant flowers, appearing from about the middle of May to early June, but although this is a short flowering period few gardeners would wish to omit lilacs from their gardens.

The ordinary lilac, *S. vulgaris,* with its mauve flowers, is a good shrub, but there are finer kinds, developed from it over the past sixty years or so. Because lilacs are easy to grow they are apt to be neglected and allowed to look after themselves, so that all too often they do not give of their best. The trouble is, perhaps, that they will literally grow almost anywhere, in sunny places, no matter what type of soil they have to put up with. They will do much better, however, if they are mulched annually with well-rotted compost or a general fertilizer, although this should not be dug in but spread around, to be absorbed gradually into the soil. The shrubs will flower better if time can be found to cut off dead flower-heads and to remove sucker growths.

Among the most magnificent kinds are the double-flowered varieties such as 'Katherine Havemeyer', deep lavender-purple, 'Madame A. Buchner', pinkish-mauve, 'Mrs Edward Harding', rosy-carmine, and 'Souvenir de Alice Harding', white. All these have large fragrant flowers in large trusses.

Good single-flowered varieties include 'Clarke's Giant', 'Marchal Foch', and 'Primrose'.

The double forms of the ordinary lilac, *Syringa vulgaris,* produce magnificent displays.

Viburnum

There are about seventy-five viburnums in cultivation but most of these are little known. Some of the more popular kinds are evergreen, others deciduous, some are grown for their flowers, some for their fruit. A few add brilliant autumn leaf colour to their other attributes.

The winter-flowering kinds are good value as they bloom at a time when flower-interest is at a premium. The old *V. tinus*, commonly known as Laurustinus, is widely planted, usually as a specimen, although it makes a good evergreen hedge. Its heads of white flowers begin to appear in Novem-

Viburnum davidii

ber and it is early spring before flowering ceases. *V.* × *burkwoodii*, an evergreen hybrid, with fragrant white flowers that open from early in the New Year to early spring, is outstanding. It is followed into flower by *V. carlesii,* a deciduous species with clusters of fragrant white flowers. One of the most striking of the spring-flowering kinds is *V. rhitidophyllum*, an evergreen, 10 feet or more tall, with large leaves, white below, and large clusters of white flowers.

This, however, is not as fine as *V. tomentosum* in its forms 'Lanarth' or *mariesii*. This is a leaf-losing shrub, eventually about 6 feet tall, its branches held out horizontally. Along these in May and June appear flat heads of white flowers not unlike those of some hydrangeas in that the inner, fertile ones are surrounded by larger sterile flowers. The leaves of this viburnum are briefly magnificent in autumn when they turn crimson.

The leaves of our native Guelder Rose, *V. opulus,* also colour well in autumn and add to the value of the shrub for its white flowers in May and June and its clusters of red fruits in autumn. Old specimens may reach 15 feet.

Worth growing for its fruit alone is the dwarf evergreen species, *V. davidii,* about 2 feet tall, with bright blue berries on female plants. Both male and female types must be planted to ensure fruiting.

All these are easy shrubs to grow, and do well on chalky soils. Normal ground preparation is sufficient and no pruning is needed unless it is to remove dead wood. All are hardy. *V. davidii* is a good kind to grow in groups.

V. opulus sterile and
V. fragrans (*right*)

Species of *Parthenocissus* are excellent for covering house walls.

Vitis

These are the Vines and vine relatives, the Virginia Creepers and similar plants that, for the sake of convenience, the closely related genera *Ampelopsis* and *Parthenocissus* are included under this heading, particularly as from the gardener's point of view there is little to differentiate them. Those grown in British gardens are all deciduous climbers, some of them self-clinging by means of small 'sucker-pads', others needing support. Most of them are notable for their brilliant autumn foliage tints, a few produce bunches of grape-like fruits following their greenish, insignificant flowers. They are usually seen clothing walls, and many of them are excellent on north or east walls, but they are also good plants for fences, pergolas, archways, tree stumps or for growing into trees. Like wisterias, they may be used to smother outhouses, sheds, garages and the like, without doing structural damage to the buildings.

None of these useful climbers is fussy about soil, but, like any climber planted near a wall, it is worth enriching the soil before planting, since these sites are usually poor and dry

Vitis coignetiae covers the arch.
(*Above*) a leaf of *Parthenocissus quinquefolia*.

and overhanging eaves may keep them dry, even in wet weather. Compost, moist peat or leafmould dug into the soil in generous quantities, with the site widely and deeply dug, should ensure that the plants get a good start and will continue to make rapid growth. No pruning is needed.

The most striking plant for shady walls is *Parthenocissus* (*Vitis*) *henryana*, a tendril climber, with delightful purple and white variegated leaves that turn red in autumn. The true Virginia Creeper is *Parthenocissus* (*Vitis*) *quinquefolia*, with bright scarlet and orange leaves in autumn. The popular large-leaved 'Virginia Creeper' is *P. tricuspidata*, the leaves of which turn the most fiery colours in October. Of the true Ampelopsis, *A. brevipeduculata* is the best because not only do its hop-like leaves colour well but it also has bunches of china-blue grapes in autumn.

Another striking plant is *Vitis coignetiae*, with leaves up to 1 foot across, turning to all imaginable shades of crimson and orange in autumn. This is better for a pergola, or for covering an outhouse, rather than for a wall.

149

The garden varieties (*above*)
are derived from *W. florida*.

Weigela

The weigelas, still sometimes catalogued as diervillas, are among those shrubs that give their best if they are properly pruned, the old, flowered shoots cut back hard to encourage the production of new flowering growth. However, they are easy shrubs to grow and even if pruning is neglected they still put up a reasonably good show.

They will grow well in any normal garden soil, including those that contain much chalk or lime. They will survive in exposed, wind-swept positions, but, to look their best they should be given ample space, for, although they do not grow more than 5–6 feet tall, their arching growths cover an area of about 6 feet in diameter.

Weigela florida, the commonest kind, has rosy-pink flowers in May and early June, sometimes followed by a later flush, but there are better and brighter hybrids. Among these 'Newport Red', the crimson 'Eva Rathke', the white 'Mont Blanc' and the large-flowered pink 'Conquete' are among the best.

Weigela florida variegata adds leaf variegation to its attraction and is among the best of variegated leaf shrubs, slower-growing than the type, but a constant pleasure from spring to autumn, with its leaves broadly edged with white. The purple-leaved form, *foliis purpureis*, has its own attraction. Both varieties have pink flowers.

Weigela florida variegata

Wisteria

Wisterias are very vigorous climbing shrubs, most useful for covering walls, pergolas, fences and the like, and even capable of smothering garages and other out-buildings beneath their growths, or growing up into trees. However, by careful attention to pruning, they can be kept within reasonable bounds and it is, in fact, possible to train them as standard trees, their long growths weeping down to the ground. Pruning is done in autumn or winter, when the plants are gone over to see which shoots are to be retained to extend the growth. The remainder are then cut back to within about 3 inches of the point at which they spring from the older shoots. Longer shoots retained for extension purposes may be tipped and, to restrict growth further, all shoots may be lightly pruned in August. But, where plants are grown over trees no pruning is needed.

W. sinensis is the species usually grown. It has a white variety, *alba,* and one with double flowers, *plena.*

Wisterias are not particularly fussy about the soil in which they are grown, but the planting site should be well prepared, deeply and widely dug, with ample quantities of well-rotted compost or leafmould incorporated.

Wisteria sinensis has foot long
trails of fragrant mauve flowers.

SPECIAL PURPOSE SHRUBS

* The inclusion of a particular shrub in this list does not mean that it will not grow in more open, sunny positions. In any case, few shrubs will grow in deep shade.

FOR SHADE*

Berberis darwinii
Berberis × stenophylla
Camellias
Choisya ternata
Cornus kousa
Cotoneaster simonsii
Daphne mezereum
Forsythia spectabilis
Hydrangea macrophylla
Hydrangea paniculata
Hypericum calycinum
Kerria japonica
Olearia haastii
Prunus laurocerasus
Prunus lusitanicus
Pyracanthas
Rhododendron (Azalea)
    Kurume Hybrids
    Mollis Hybrids
Ribes sanguineum
Viburnum tinus

FOR CHALKY SOILS

Berberis
Buddleias
Caryopteris
Cercis
Chaenomeles
Choisya ternata
Cistus
Clematis
Clerodendrum
Cornus
Cotoneasters
Crataegus
Cytisus
Daphne mezereum
Deutzias

Erica carnea
Forsythias
Fuchsias
Garrya elliptica
Genistas
Hebe
Helianthemums
Hibiscus
Hypericums
Laburnum
Lavandulas
Loniceras
Malus
Philadelphus
Potentillas
Prunus
Rhus
Ribes
Rosa
Senecio
Sorbus
Spartium
Spiraea
Syringa
Vibusnum
Weigela

FOR DRY SOILS AND SUNNY SITES

Acer
Berberis
Calluna
Caryopteris
Chaenomeles
Cistus
Cotoneasters
Cytisus
Ericas
Genistas

Hebes
Helianthemums
Hypericums
Lavandulas
Olearias
Potentillas
Rhus
Senecio,
Spartium
Spiraea

FOR TOWN GARDENS

Amelanchiers
Berberis
Caryopteris
Chaenomeles
Cornus
Cotoneasters
Cytisus
Deutzias
Forsythias
Hibiscus
Hypericums
Jasminums
Kerrias
Laburnums
Malus
Olearias
Philadelphus
Prunus
Pyracanthas
Rhododendrons
Rhus
Ribes
Senecio
Sorbus
Spiraea
Syringa
Viburnum
Weigela

MONTHS AND SEASONS

The months and seasons
mentioned in this book apply
to temperate regions of the
northern hemisphere (Europe,
Canada and the northern
United States). For readers
living in other regions, the
following table gives
approximate equivalents.

*Subtropical regions of the
northern hemisphere
(Mediterranean sea, southern
United States)*
Plants will tend to shoot and
flower a month or so earlier
in these regions.

*Tropical regions
(around the equator)*
No seasons exist in the tropical
regions. There are no set times
for planting, and the suitability
of growing an individual plant
will depend on local climatic
conditions.

*Subtropical regions of the
southern hemisphere
(Australasia, South America,
southern Africa)*
The seasons are reversed in
these regions. Spring is
approximately from September
to November, summer from
December to February, autumn
from March to May, and winter
from June to August.

INDEX

Page numbers in bold type refer to illustrations.

SOME OTHER TITLES IN THIS SERIES

■ **Arts**
Antique Furniture/Architecture/Art Nouveau for Collectors/Clocks and Watches/Glass for Collectors/Jewellery/Musical Instruments/Porcelain/Pottery/Silver for Collectors/Victoriana

■ **Domestic Animals and Pets**
Budgerigars/Cats/Dog Care/Dogs/Horses and Ponies/Pet Birds/Pets for Children/Tropical Freshwater Aquaria/Tropical Marine Aquaria

■ **Domestic Science**
Flower Arranging

■ **Gardening**
Chrysanthemums/Garden Flowers/Garden Shrubs/House Plants/Plants for Small Gardens/Roses

■ **General Information**
Aircraft/Arms and Armour/Coins and Medals/Espionage/Flags/Fortune Telling/Freshwater Fishing/Guns/Military Uniforms/Motor Boats and Boating/National Costumes of the world/Orders and Decorations/Rockets and Missiles/Sailing/Sailing Ships and Sailing Craft/Sea Fishing/Trains/Veteran and Vintage Cars/Warships

■ **History and Mythology**
Age of Shakespeare/Archaeology/Discovery of: Africa/The American West/Australia/Japan/North America/South America/Great Land Battles/Great Naval Battles/Myths and Legends of: Africa/Ancient Egypt/Ancient Greece/Ancient Rome/India/The South Seas/Witchcraft and Black Magic

■ **Natural History**
The Animal Kingdom/Animals of Australia and New Zealand/Animals of Southern Asia/Bird Behaviour/Birds of Prey/Butterflies/Evolution of Life/Fishes of the world/Fossil Man/A Guide to the Seashore/Life in the Sea/Mammals of the world/Monkeys and Apes/Natural History Collecting/The Plant Kingdom/Prehistoric Animals/Seabirds/Seashells/Snakes of the world/Trees of the world/Tropical Birds/Wild Cats

■ **Popular Science**
Astronomy/Atomic Energy/Chemistry/Computers at Work/The Earth/Electricity/Electronics/Exploring the Planets/Heredity/The Human Body/Mathematics/Microscopes and Microscopic Life/Physics/Psychology/Undersea Exploration/The Weather Guide

CONTENTS

Printed by Butler Tanner and Dennis   Maps by The XYZ Digital Map Company

WHO'S WHO IN SCOTLAND'S GARDENS

SCOTTISH CHARITY NO SC011337

Mario Testino ©

As the President of Scotland's Gardens, I am delighted that, even in one of the wettest years in living memory, so many owners have managed to open their beautiful gardens to visitors from all over the world. It is a tribute to the dedication of the garden owners and to the hardiness of their visitors.

Over the past year, Scotland's Gardens has expanded its scope. Most notably, the Fife Diamond Garden Festival celebrating Her Majesty The Queen's Diamond Jubilee was a new, and very successful, venture.

It is wonderful that so many charities, both local and nationwide, benefit each year from the efforts of all the garden owners and volunteers who work so hard to ensure the success of Scotland's Gardens' programme. I wish them all every possible good fortune, and better weather, in 2013!

Camilla

CHAIRMAN'S MESSAGE

My term in office has only just begun and has coincided with one of the wettest and most miserable summers I can remember. In taking over from Tricia Kennedy I have a hard act to follow. Tricia immersed herself in Scotland's Gardens and was active in meeting garden openers, visiting District and Area organisers and talking to garden visitors. In her time in office Scotland's Gardens raised record sums of money for our own beneficiaries and for those chosen by our garden openers. She also introduced a gentle programme to ensure that Scotland's Gardens remains vital and energetic. I would like to continue to develop the reforms now in train. We rely entirely on the goodwill of our garden openers, our volunteers and our paying visitors so it is very important that we grow and develop Scotland's Gardens with their support. Over the next year I am intending to visit as many garden openers, volunteers and districts as I possibly can, to ensure that we remain topical and relevant.

As a garden opener, a member of our East Lothian District team and responsible for persuading our local village to open its gardens every other year, I am only too well aware of all the effort that goes into a successful open day. To all those of you who work so hard to make your gardens look so glorious despite sometimes dreadful weather, to those of you who energetically volunteer to facilitate the opening of gardens and to those of you who visit our gardens so faithfully and enthusiastically, a very big thank you.

I am writing this note in my office at home, in late September. The rain is once more lashing against the window and any hope of an Indian summer is fast evaporating. Perhaps by the time that the spring and summer of 2013 is upon us we shall have drained the sky of rain and shifted the Jetstream to its more normal path. Whatever the weather may bring I wish you a contented and happy 2013 growing and giving season.

Mark Hedderwick
Chairman

SPONSORS

We would like to acknowledge and thank the following organisations that will be sponsoring Scotland's Gardens in 2013. Their support is invaluable and enables us to maximise the funds we give to our beneficiary charities.

Investec Wealth & Investment

Corney & Barrow

D C Thomson & Co

Lycett, Browne Swinburn Douglas Ltd

Rettie & Co

Savills (L&P) Ltd

The Edinburgh International Conference Centre

Escrivo Internet Consulting

In addition we would like to say how grateful we are to the many private donors who have given us their support.

 As principal sponsor
we congratulate
Scotland's Gardens
on its success

Jonathan Wragg
Chief Executive
Investec Wealth & Investment

| Individuals | International | Financial Advisers | Charities | Court of Protection |

Offices at: Bath Belfast Birmingham Bournemouth Cheltenham Edinburgh Exeter Glasgow Guildford Leeds Liverpool London
Manchester Reigate Sheffield

Wealth & **Investment.**
Well-tended expertise

Visit us soon at our Edinburgh or Glasgow offices

Just like Scotland's Gardens, we are a national network with a local feel, and our offices in Glasgow and Edinburgh are well placed to tend to your investments, pensions or other financial matters.

Our specialist teams manage over £19.6 billion* on behalf of our clients, seeking the best and most tax-efficient returns on their capital. To see how we could best be of service to you please visit our website.

Please bear in mind that the value of investments and the income derived from them can go down as well as up and that you may not get back the amount that you have put in.

For more information on how we have supported Scotland's Gardens please visit **investecwin.co.uk/sponsorships**

Edinburgh **0131 226 5000**
Glasgow **0141 333 9323**

WHAT HAPPENS TO THE MONEY RAISED?

All garden owners who participate in the Scotland's Gardens programme are able to nominate a charity of their choice to receive 40% of the funds raised at their openings. 209 different worthy charities will be supported in this manner in 2013 and these vary from small local ones to several large well known organisations. Examples include:

- Alzheimer Scotland
- Atlantic Salmon Trust
- AICR
- Camphill Blair Drummond
- Cancer Research UK
- Children 1st
- Children's Hospice Association Scotland
- Christchurch Duns
- Colmonell Primary School
- Highland Hospice

- Kilmelford Village Charities
- Kilpatrick Durham Church
- Macmillan Cancer Support
- Marie Curie
- Parkinson's UK
- Riding for the Disabled
- RNLI
- Scottish Motor Neurone Disease Association
- The Order of St John
- Trellis

60%, net of expenses, of the funds raised at each garden is given to Scotland's Gardens beneficiaries:

- Maggie's Cancer Caring Centres
- The Queen's Nursing Institute Scotland
- The Gardens Fund of the National Trust for Scotland
- Perennial

Information on these organisations is provided on the following pages.

Several garden owners who open their garden on a regular basis and generously support Scotland's Gardens give a donation and the net sum is split between Scotland's Gardens beneficiaries.

In this book details of the charities nominated by the Garden Owners are provided and those gardens giving a donation are also indicated.

BENEFICIARY MESSAGES

maggie's

It is with great pleasure that I offer my thanks again to Paddy Scott and Scotland's Gardens for their support of Maggie's Centres. It has not been the best of summers, with the records showing it was the wettest since records began, but despite this there was still a fantastic turnout for all the gardens opened by members of Scotland's Gardens.

The support we receive from Scotland's Gardens is invaluable as it allows us to plan for the year ahead with confidence. The income that was generated helped us to facilitate an amazing 1,500 visits to our centres by people with cancer and their friends and family across Scotland. I would like to take this opportunity to thank you all for your efforts for not only Maggie's but the many other charities who benefit from your kindness in opening your gardens for others to enjoy.

Best wishes,

Laura Lee
Chief Executive
Maggie's Centres

Please call 0300 123 1801 or visit
www.maggiescentres.org for more information.

Maggie's newest centre at Gartnavel General Hospital, Glasgow.

THE QUEEN'S NURSING INSTITUTE SCOTLAND
Patron: Her Majesty The Queen
31 Castle Terrace, Edinburgh EH1 2EL
Tel: 0131 229 2333 Fax: 0131 228 9066
Registered Scottish Charity No: SC005751

The Queen's Nursing Institute Scotland (QNIS) is a registered independent charity and its main aim is to promote excellence in community nursing in Scotland. QNIS has a long relationship with Scotland's Gardens and is enormously grateful for the financial support it receives, enabling nurse led projects to be undertaken throughout Scotland. The Projects Co-ordinator provides practical support for nurses to develop project proposals and ultimately to disseminate learning and good practice from projects.

QNIS works closely with the National Health Service and the professional bodies involved in the support, training and further education of Community Nurses. The NHS has ever increasing demands and regardless of how worthy the cause cannot meet every demand.

QNIS is governed by Council. The day to day business is managed by the Nurse Director with the help of a small dedicated administrative team. As a non political organisation, QNIS is uniquely placed to listen to and support nurses working at grass roots level. The work of QNIS can be summarised as follows:-

- Raises awareness to influence policy and decision making at local and national level
- Supports the professional development of nurses by providing a QNIS Fellowship programme, education grants and research fellowships
- Organises conferences and workshops on current community nursing issues throughout Scotland
- Addresses the welfare needs of retired Queen's Nurses (pensions, special grants, holidays, Newsletters and Annual Gatherings)
- Funds innovative Community Nurse led projects to improve patient care.

Over the last ten years, QNIS has funded 26 Projects, 17 Partnerships in Practice Awards and 2 Partnerships in Research Awards. This funding has provided important opportunities for nurses to develop professionally and personally within the current climate of austerity.

Pilot of a Health Promoting Residential Unit
Looked-after children consistently have poorer health than other children. A QNIS Fellow led a two year project that aimed to make one residential unit in Renfrewshire a healthier place for the children who live there. The QNIS funding was used to offer healthier food choices and increase opportunities for exercise for the young people and also provide training for the staff. As a result, staff morale increased, young people have become more active and are keen to take part in more of the outdoor activities such as cycling, camping and canoeing. The young peoples' self-esteem and confidence also improved. This is an example where a small amount of money and a large commitment from a community nurse has made a difference to the lives of a vulnerable group of young people.

Congratulations go to the Heart 2 Heart Cardiac Rehab Group. This Clackmannanshire exercise class, for people who have had a heart attack, received a small amount of funding from QNIS two years ago. This inspirational group is now being funded by Chest, Heart and Stroke and has won a prestigious prize in the Octagon Challenge. Well done!

A VERY BIG THANK YOU – to Scotland's Gardens, the organisers, garden owners and the visiting public. QNIS is extremely grateful for your support in enabling enthusiastic nurses to lead innovative projects and share new knowledge to improve patient care.

the National Trust for Scotland

a place for everyone

On behalf of the National Trust for Scotland's Gardens Community I would like to thank all of Scotland's Gardens owners for their ongoing support to the National Trust for Scotland in general and its gardens portfolio in particular. We really appreciate the financial (and other) support which you provide and which enables so much of the work that goes on in our gardens. Our gardens continue to flourish and grow, prove popular with our visitors, providing perfect places to escape for the pressures of daily life. We are grateful to those people who support our work and the work of Scottish Gardens by continuing to visit and enjoy the places in our care.

During 2012 twenty five Trust gardens opened in support of Scotland's Gardens. There were some very interesting and successful events – like Geilston Garden's Japanese-themed cookery demonstration, as well as guided walks, tours, demonstrations and workshops where our expert gardeners shared their knowledge and experience with over 4000 visitors.

In 2013 twenty four of our gardens will support Scotland's Gardens opening on 35 different occasions throughout the year at which we plan to host daffodil teas at Brodie; and Evening Encounter at Broughton House; Pruning- and wildlife gardening workshops at Crathes and Greenbank, respectively; Romancing the Rose at Drum Castle and a guided tour of the garden at Fyvie followed by dinner in the Castle. We are also pleased to announce that Haddo House Garden will be opening on behalf of Scotland's Gardens for the first time since 2010.

Through the School of Heritage Gardening, in part supported by Scotland's Gardens, the Trust continues to play an important part in growing future gardeners. There is a high quality framework to support gardener training in our gardens across the country, with student placements at Threave Garden, Kellie Castle, Inverewe

and Geilston House Garden, Branklyn, Drum Castle & Crathes Castle Gardens (pictured).

Thanks to your generous financial donation, visitors can enjoy our gardens every year, at all times of year, and see the results of the hard work and expertise of our dedicated gardens staff and your vital and generous support, creating such beautiful places for so many to enjoy.

Kate Mavor
Chief Executive

PERENNIAL
GARDENERS' ROYAL BENEVOLENT SOCIETY
Helping Horticulturists In Need Since 1839

PERENNIAL – LOOKING AFTER THOSE WHO LOOK AFTER OUR GREEN SPACES.

We all enjoy wonderful gardens and appreciate the hard work which goes into making them look so beautiful, however often the role the gardener, landscaper, tree surgeon , garden designer and plant grower plays in developing and maintaining our green spaces is overlooked. Low pay, illness and injury are just some of the problems these horticulturalists encounter.

That's why Perennial's work is so important – and why we're committed to offering practical, hands-on help whenever it's needed. This begins with a personal visit from one of our caseworkers who will investigate all the difficulties a client is facing. Our support could be in the form of a grant to helping with benefit forms and appeals, advising on home and residential care and liaising with social services. Over the past year we have seen a huge upsurge in clients who are benefiting from our comprehensive debt advice service.

Perennial receives no statutory funding, so the donation we receive through Scotland's Gardens is an important source of income for Perennial. We would like to thank Scotland's Gardens, the garden owners and visitors for their kind support. Please find out more about Perennials' work and the variety of ways you could get involved, for example by joining our team of volunteers, our friends scheme or by making a one off or regular donation. Simply visit www.perennial.org.uk or call 0845 230 1839.

Focusing on the things that matter to you

Turcan Connell offers a comprehensive service to private individuals and their families; charities; and the owners and managers of land. Our focus has always been on providing trusted counsel over the long term. Our combination of legal and financial expertise allows us to provide focused and tailored advice on the issues that really matter.

- Asset Protection
- Charity Law
- Turcan Connell Charity Office
- Dispute Resolution
- Employment Law
- Family Business Advice
- Family Law

- Financial Planning
- Investment Management
- Land & Property
- Pensions
- Tax Services
- Trust and Succession
- Turcan Connell Family Office

TURCAN CONNE
LEGAL • WEALTH MANAGEMENT •

Edinburgh   Glasgow   London   Gue

Princes Exchange, 1 Earl Grey Street, Edinburgh EH3 9EE Tel: 0131 22

Sutherland House, 149 St Vincent Street, Glasgow G2 5NW Tel: 0141 44

Follow us on Twitter @TurcanC
enquiries@turcanconnell.com   www.turcanconne

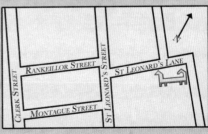

the National Trust
for Scotland
a place for everyone

GIVE A GIFT OF MEMBERSHIP

THE PRESENT THAT LASTS A WHOLE YEAR

Join online at www.nts.org.uk or call
0844 493 2100 quoting *Scotland's Gardens*

Gardening therapy: helping our brave veterans

Research shows that around **20%** of veterans are likely to develop mental health symptoms stemming from their time in the Armed Forces.

Symptoms include flashbacks, nightmares and anxiety. In the garden, therapy helps to reduce isolation, improve motor skills, memory, and concentration, and reduce anxiety. Working with plants promotes a sense of purpose and hope for the future.

Our projects (three in Scotland and one London) are all based in walled gardens, a unique feature that is instrumental in our success with veterans who often suffer from hyper-vigilance. You know the joy of gardens – help spread that joy.

£20 will pay for a gardening therapy session for a veteran.

£250 will pay for a course of 12 sessions.

Find out more about our work at **www.gardeningleave.org** or by calling 01292 521444. Donations can be sent to Room 1, Gardening Leave, SAC Auchincruive, Ayrshire, KA6 5HW

GARDENING LEAVE

Celebrate
Life with
RBGE

Celebrate Life

A Commemorative Programme from the Royal Botanic Garden Edinburgh

The Hope Tree | Tree Adoption | Bench Adoption
Online Commemorative Book | Leave a Legacy

Celebrate Life is a wonderful programme which
allows supporters and friends of the Garden
to commemorate the life of a loved one,
celebrate an event or purchase a
unique gift for someone special
in the beautiful surroundings
of the Royal Botanic
Garden Edinburgh.

For more details please visit **celebratelife.rbge.org.**
or call the Development Office on **0131 248 2855**

NCHMARLO

Retirement living around 'a garden paradise' on Royal Deeside

The opening of the Inchmarlo Continuing Care Retirement Community in 1986 pioneered a new way of living in Scotland for those over 55 years old. We are proud that 250 people call Inchmarlo "home"

We offer services that will enable you to live independently in your own home and if, or when, health patterns change we provide additional services, which can be tailored to enable you to continue living n your own home longer than might be the case elsewhere. By postponing a permanent move into a Care Home, significant savings can be made of £35,000 per year.

- 24-hour security warden • care support
- help call system • home delivery of meals
- customer liaison officer
- priority entry to Inchmarlo Care Home
- respite care • social committee and events programme • private function room

1 and 2 bedroom apartments and 2 – 4 bedroom houses are available for resale throughout the year from £95,000 to £350,000.

HUMPHREY Therapy Assistant (canine)
Read my Blog
http://inchmarlo.wordpress.com

Telephone Sales Office: 01330 826242 or visit www.inchmarlo-retirement.co.uk

"THE CHELSEA BELLADONNA"

In summer 2012 Scotland's Gardens collaborated with Square Peg Productions in facilitating the production of a remarkable promenade performance which involved audience participation in five of the gardens taking part in our programme. Although the bad weather affected the audience numbers there were several performances that were well attended.

"The Chelsea Belladonna" tells the story of the life of Elizabeth Blackwell, the Aberdeen born botanical illustrator. Born at the dawn of the 18th century Elizabeth eloped with Alexander her reckless young husband and cousin to London. Very soon Alexander found himself in the debtor's prison and Elizabeth resolved to raise the funds needed to free her husband and herself. After much scheming and in a felicitous arrangement with Sir Hans Sloane of the Chelsea Physic Garden, she embarked upon the creation and illustration of "A Curious Herbal". Upon publication the Herbal released Alexander and became a veritable apothecaries' bible in Britain and abroad, rooting Elizabeth's name firmly and for ever in British Botanical history.

The promenade was acted superbly by Irene Allan and Kenny Blyth and received rave reviews from the press and from the audiences.

We hope to work with Square Peg Productions in the future and bring such remarkable and clever performances to gardens in Scotland once again.

Chelsea Belladonna - Blair Castle

Chelsea Belladonna - Lands of Loyal Hotel

NEW GARDENS FOR 2013

Aberdeenshire

Birken Cottage
Middle Cairncake

Angus

The Walled Garden at Logie

Argyll

Barochreal
Kames Bay
Maolachy's Garden
Melfort House Kitchen Garden

Ayrshire

10 Grange Terrace
Cairn Hall House
Kilmaurs Village Gardens

Berwickshire

Preston Gardens

Caithness, Sutherland, Orkney & Shetland

Caergarth
Keldaberg

Dunbartonshire

Shandon Gardens

East Lothian

Belhaven Hill School and Belhaven House

Edinburgh & West Lothian

The Glasshouses at the Royal Botanic Garden Edinburgh

Ettrick & Lauderdale

2 Whytbank Row
Ravensheugh House

Barholm Castle, Kirkcudbrightshire

Fife

Kemback House
Fife Garden Trail

Kincardine & Deeside

Mallamauch
Woodend House

Kirkcudbrightshire

Barholm Castle
Seabank
Steadstone

Lanarkshire

Allium Croft
Thankerton / Covington Village Gardens

Midlothian

Harvieston Walled Garden

Perth & Kinross

Bonhard Garden

Ross, Cromarty, Skye & Inverness

Aultgowrie Mill
Oldtown of Leys Garden

Roxburghshire

Lanton Tower

Stirlingshire

Drymen Gardens
Row House
Stirling Gardens
The Walled Garden

Birken Cottage, Aberdeenshire

SNOWDROP OPENINGS

Snowdrops remain as popular as ever and several properties will be opening in February and March to enable visitors to enjoy the stunning displays of these flowers. Once again VisitScotland will be supporting the openings with their heavily marketed Snowdrop Festival which has become an important part of their successful Winter White campaign.

The following properties will be opening and most will be participating in the Snowdrop Festival:

Angus

Dunninald
Pitmuies Gardens

East Lothian

Shepherd House

Fife

Cambo House

Kincardine & Deeside

Ecclesgreig Castle

Kirkcudbrightshire

Danevale

Lanarkshire

Cleghorn

Midlothian

Kevock Garden

Peeblesshire

Dawyck Botanic Garden
Kailzie
Traquair

SCOTTISH SNOWDROP FESTIVAL

Scotland's Gardens season starts with the popular Snowdrop Openings.

We are very keen to add more Snowdrop Gardens in 2014 so please let us know if you would like to share your snowdrops with us next year.

Perth & Kinross

Blair Castle Gardens
Cluny House
Fingask Castle
Kilgraston

Renfrewshire

Ardgowan

Ross, Cromarty, Skye & Inverness

Abriachan Garden Nursery

Stirlingshire

Gargunnock House
Kilbryde Castle
The Linns
West Plean House

Wigtownshire

Castle Kennedy & Gardens
Dunskey Garden and Maze
Kirkdale

Danevale © Mary McIlvenna

FIFE GARDEN TRAIL

South Flisk

Scotland's Gardens is introducing a new experience into their 2013 programme – **The Fife Garden Trail**.

In May and June nine gardens will open their gates on a number of days, some into the long summer evenings. Ticket holders will be able to visit all the gardens in three days early in June (4th-6th and/or 11th -13th) or if a more leisurely tour is wanted over the two month period on the days the gardens will be open.

The gardens participating in the Trail represent a mixture of designs. Some exploit natural characteristics with border shape and planting fitting, enhancing or exaggerating the landscape. Some gardens are symmetrical and formal while others are flowing and irregular. Some have designs that link house and garden, others have been designed to link the house with the surrounding landscape so as to create a cohesive whole. All gardens aim to achieve a lively effect and a long season of interest with planting schemes of unusual plants, different colour combinations and a variation in texture and foliage.

A ticket for The Garden Trail makes a perfect gift - and do treat yourself as well!

Logie House

Earlshall

Willowhill

Greenhead Farmhouse, Greenhead of Arnot

Admission: £15.00 for all gardens.
Accompanied children free.
Entry to all gardens by pre-sold ticket only.

Tickets: A limited number of tickets are available
and may be purchased by credit card at www.
scotlandsgardens.org or by cheque payable to
Scotland's Gardens from S. Lorimore, Willowhill,
Forgan, Newport on Tay, Fife DD6 8RA.

Information Leaflet: Tickets will be despatched with an
information leaflet providing details of all the gardens,
including directions, when and where teas and plant
stalls will be available etc.

Beneficiary Charities: 60% (net) of the proceeds from
The Fife Trail will go to Scotland's Gardens' beneficiary
charities with the remaining 40% going to The
Association for International Cancer Research (AICR),
a St Andrews based charity that supports fundamental
cancer research worldwide.

Gilston House

Rosewells

Barham

The Tower, Wormit

CHAMPION TREES

What is a Champion Tree?

A champion tree is the best of its kind in its area. Conventionally the accolade goes to the tallest, and the one with the fattest trunk. Often the tallest tree is not the fattest and so there may be two champions for each species. Over 600 trees in Scotland are the champions for Britain and Ireland, with several considered to be unbeaten in Europe. Inevitably many champions are rare species found only in the botanic gardens such as Edinburgh, Logan, Benmore and Dawyck. But champions can be found in urban areas and public parks, and many are in domestic gardens. Currently almost 2,000 trees are recorded as being champions of Scotland and 6,000 trees are Scottish county champions, from 169 in Fife to 764 in Perth and Kinross. (2011)

One of Britain's widest trees - Cluny Garden

Yew - Lindores

Who Records these Trees?

The Tree Register of the British Isles –TROBI – is a registered charity collating and updating a database of exceptionally large, historic, rare and remarkable trees throughout Britain and Ireland. This unique register comprises of a computer database with details of more than 190,000 trees. It includes historical records going back more than 200 years, and provides information on the size and growth of trees which is not available from any other source. Thus it has the definitive record of Britain and Ireland's champion trees.

Monkey Puzzle Avenue - Castle Kennedy

Champion Trees in Scottish Gardens

The importance, appreciation and enjoyment of any tree can be greatly enhanced by knowing it is of particular significance as an exceptional specimen, or of great heritage value. Garden owners often have trees which are far more unusual than they realise - maybe they are the oldest, the biggest or rarest of their species in Scotland.

Volunteer recorders often find new champion trees when gardens are open to the public and the list is always growing as trees are discovered! Several of the gardens in which there are champion trees, or trees of special interest, are indicated within this guidebook. Look out for some of Scotland's finest trees when you next plan a visit to an open garden.

The owners of these gardens will have some information about the trees and on some open days there may be a local TROBI recorder on hand to talk to the public about them. For more information about champion trees visit www.treeregister.org.

Laburnum - Megginch

Rhodo - Castle Kennedy

Abies alba - Ardkinglas

CAROLSIDE

Carolside was a dream for me. It was the garden which lured me without my ever knowing.

As a child I had always gardened. My memories are of waiting eagerly each year for certain plants to flower, planting all sorts of things from a very young age, my maternal grandmother who adored roses and of staying with a friend, aged perhaps nine or ten, and drinking the dew from the roses in the early morning. These must have been the memories which led me to see Carolside as a blank canvas. It had a romantic setting and a beautiful valley. The vision of the trees, changing colour with the seasons and the mists that get caught on the valley floor, captivated me.

Carolside has had a long history of good gardeners long before I ever came there. It had a well-known rose garden as long ago as the First World War and after the Second World War, Lady Mary Gilmour, a remarkable plantswoman, revived the garden. She too had a great love of roses.

My first project was to plant hedges to give privacy to the garden, to put back pergolas and arbours where I thought necessary and to completely reorganise and make much deeper, the main herbaceous border in the oval walled garden which involved planting the back of the border with very tall perennials such as *Cephalaria*, *Cicerbita* and *Thalictrum flavum* in order to create a wonderful walk from which one would be unable to see into the vegetable, fruit and cutting flower borders beyond. I wanted to create a sense of mystery.

I do think that it is so necessary to create a sense of mystery in one's design and not be able to see everything at once. There is nothing new in this concept but it was something that I instinctively discovered and without consciously realising I began to create rooms, one after the other, each with a different atmosphere.

The main herbaceous border is very much a July border, flowering in all its glory, starting with pale pastel shades leading up to a crescendo of stronger pinks and magentas with roses such as 'Lady of Megginch'. There

Blush Rambler and Filipendula Venusta

re no reds or strong yellows. I prefer pale pinks against
deep black purples eg Lupin... Masterpiece, the apricot
colour of the lovely rose 'Abraham Derby', underplanted with pale sky blue 'Baby Blue Eyes' (annual)
or the pretty viola 'Broughton Blue' and using lots of
white and soft primrose shades found in *Anthemis* 'E.C.
Buxton', which cast a soft light in the border. I also
love to use pale lilac colours eg. *Campanula persicifolia*
'Cornish Mist'. This colour can light the garden so well
in the early evening. Honeysuckles clamber up walls and
through roses to give scent which can be particularly
wonderful on warm days after the rain. The front of
this long border is edged in *Nepeta* 'Six Hills Giant'
alternating with *Alchemilla mollis* which creates a frilly
edge to the border and leads the eye. Many heritage
pinks, of which I am fond, grow between, particularly
'Mrs. Sinkins' and the 'Earl of Essex'.

The pretty, oval shape of the walled garden lends itself
to roses and they are everywhere, growing through
the apple trees on the wall, over arches even in the
herbaceous border where they can add their different
shades of pink after the peonies have bloomed and
before the phlox appears. The parterre at the end of
garden is mono-planted in 'Eglantine', a strong rose
which will flower until the first frosts and opposite are
delphinium beds, planted in Blackmore and Langdon's
wonderful varieties.

Rosa Mundi

Through the door from the main walled garden is a small
herb garden, edged in box. Here grow roses, all of which
have a history of being used in former times, grow eg
Rosa Gallica 'Officinalis' and 'Blush Damask'. The Secret
Garden into which one walks next has a central arbour
covered in the pretty Victorian looking rose 'Debutante'
and the Clematis 'Prince Charles' which flowers most of
the summer. In this garden I use 'Manningtons Mauve
Rambler', another Victorian looking rose in mauve grey
colour which looks very good with the grey *Artemisia*.
Philadelphus in different varieties is used for scent.

Debutante

The collection of roses that Carolside now holds was
never meant to be a collection but through the love
of them I now have a considerable number of gallicas,
damasks, albas, mosses and bourbons. As time has
gone on I look for the rarer varieties, eg. 'Chateau de
Namur', an incredibly beautiful gallica or the powdery
mauve of 'Orpheline de Juillet', each one different and
unforgettable.

The remainder of the garden is a meandering path
leading towards the garden room, always under trees
and therefore planted with shade loving plants. *Cornus
aurea* under planted with hostas, tree peony *P. lutea*,
Rheum palmatum with its huge leaves, *Ligularia* and all
interplanted with Martagon lilies, foxgloves and tulips
in the Spring such as 'White Triumphator'. In another
bed, *Philadelphus* 'Innocence' with it's pretty variegated

leaves flowers remarkably well in the shade and lights up under the trees. I have also used *Philadelphus coronarius* 'Aureus' and the beautiful *alba* rose 'Celestial' with its grey, green leaves and soft pink flowers. Alba roses do very well in the shade and in contrast, damasks must be grown in the sun.

Around the garden room is *Magnolia wilsonii* which needs the protection of the wall and *Abutilon, Wisteria* on the wall and pots of lilies, roses and hostas round the door. From this door one looks over to the rose gates in the

beech hedge which lead to the serenity and peace of the river walk, much needed after the intensity of the flower garden and to remind us that the wildness of nature is every bit as beautiful as the design of the garden.

Rose Foyle

Blush Rambler

Eglantine, Ethel on the arbour, Blackmore & Langdon delphiniums

Ombrée Parfaite

Alain Blanchard

SINCE 1931

SCOTLAND'S
GARDENS
GROWING AND GIVING

Autumn Seminar

**TUES 1
OCTOBER
10:30am - 4:00pm**

SPEAKERS:
- Elizabeth Banks, Chairman, RHS
- Richard Baines, Curator,
  Logan Botanical Gardens
- Chris Marchant, Orchard Dene
  Nurseries

VENUE:
The Albert Halls, Dumbarton Road,
Stirling FK8 2QL

Morning Coffee, Sandwich Lunch, Wine & Stalls
Tickets £45.00, children free.

For tickets please contact :
Lady Edmonstone, Duntreath Castle, Blanefield, Glasgow G63 9AF
Tel: 01360 770215
Email: juliet@edmonstone.com

Visit four iconic Gardens in Scotland

Dawyck

Benmore

Edinburgh

Logan

Experience
400 years of plant hunting
when you visit the four Gardens of th
Royal Botanic Garden Edinburgh

*Year of Natural
Scotland 2013*

Royal
Botanic Garden
Edinburgh

One of the world's finest Gardens
Inverleith Row | Edinburgh EH3 5LR

Open daily (except 25 Dec & 1 Jan)

Royal Botanic Garden Edinburgh at **Dawyck**

Dawyck Botanic Garden
Stobo, Scottish Borders EH45 9JU

Open daily 1 Feb To 30 Nov

Royal Botanic Garden Edinburgh at **Benmore**

Benmore Botanic Garden
Nr Dunoon, Argyll PA23 8QU

Open daily 1 Mar to 31 Oct

Royal Botanic Garden Edinburgh at **Logan**

Logan Botanic Garden
Nr Stranraer, Dumfries & Galloway D

Open daily 15 Mar to 31 Oct

www.rbge.org.

SINCE 1931
SCOTLAND'S
GARDENS
GROWING AND GIVING

Two wonderful Private Garden Tours for 2013

Kallizie   Photo: Ray Cox

Private Gardens of Argyll
17 May 2013
Four days' half board from £425.00pp

The gentle climate of Argyll allows gardeners here in the ancient Kingdom of Dalriada to grow rare and unusual plants, while the acid soil is perfect for azaleas, rhododendrons and magnolias.

What's included

Visits to the gardens of Ross Priory, Parkhead, An Cala, Ardmaddy Castle, Drim na Vullin, Lip na Cloiche nursery, Ardtornish, Ard-Daraich and Conaglen. Based at the Royal Hotel, Oban.

Gardens of the Scottish Borders
19 July 2013
Three days' half board from £295.00pp

Broadly following the course of the River Tweed, which runs like a silver thread through this tour, we visit a carefully selected series of wonderful private gardens from our base in Melrose.

What's included

Visits to the the gardens of Kailzie, Carolside, Anton's Hill, Bughtrig, Lennel Bank, Floors Castle, Corbet Tower, West Leas and Monteviot. Based at the George and Abbotsford Hotel, Melrose.

For full details on both tours contact:

01334 657155

brightwater
holidays

Brightwater Holidays Ltd
Eden Park House,
Cupar, Fife KY15 4HS
info@brightwaterholidays.com
www.brightwaterholidays.com

Parkhead

Blair Castle and Gardens

Blair Castle's Hercules Garden, recently restored to its original Georgian design, is a peaceful walled garden of fruit trees and vegetables, featuring a large landscaped pond, Chinese bridge and a trail of contemporary and 18th century sculptures. The glory of this garden in summer are the herbaceous borders which run along the 275m south facing wall. The castle grounds also feature a 2 acre woodland grove with some of Britain's finest and tallest trees.

Atholl Estates
Blair Castle
& Gardens

Tel: 01796 481207 or visit www.blair-castle.co.uk
Blair Castle, Blair Atholl, Pitlochry Perthshire PH18 5TL

SCONE PALACE

THE CROWNING PLACE OF SCOTTISH KINGS

See the crowning place of Scottish Kings and the site of the Stone of Scone.

Roam around the extensive grounds containing the Murray Star Maze, Pinetum, Plant Hunters Pavilion, Cyril the Squirrel's Wildlife Trail, children's play area and glorious gardens.

Browse around our food and gift shops, enjoy refreshments in our coffee shop.

Only 45 minutes from Edinburgh Airport, 2 miles north of Perth on the A93. Open 1 April - 31 October, 7days from 9.30am.

t: 01738 552300
e: visits@scone-palace.co.uk
www.sconepalace.co.uk

GARDENS OPEN ON A SPECIFIC DATE

January

Saturday 26 January
Kincardine & Deeside   Crathes Castle, Banchory

February

To be advised
Kirkcudbrightshire   Danevale Park, Crossmichael

Sunday 10 February
Wigtownshire   Kirkdale, Carsluith, Newton Stewart

Saturday 16 February
Wigtownshire   Dunskey Gardens and Maze, Portpatrick

Sunday 17 February
Renfrewshire   Ardgowan, Inverkip
Wigtownshire   Dunskey Gardens and Maze, Portpatrick

Saturday 23 February
Angus   Dunninald, Montrose
East Lothian   Shepherd House, Inveresk
Peeblesshire   Traquair, Traquair House, Innerleithen
Wigtownshire   Dunskey Gardens and Maze, Portpatrick

Sunday 24 February
Angus   Dunninald, Montrose
East Lothian   Shepherd House, Inveresk
Kincardine & Deeside   Ecclesgreig Castle, St Cyrus
Lanarkshire   Cleghorn , Stable House, Cleghorn Farm, Lanark
Peeblesshire   Traquair House, Innerleithen
Perth & Kinross   Kilgraston, Bridge of Earn
Stirlingshire   West Plean House, Denny Road, By Stirling
Wigtownshire   Dunskey Gardens and Maze, Portpatrick

March

Sunday 3 March
Midlothian   Kevock Garden, 16 Kevock Road, Lasswade
Peeblesshire   Kailzie Gardens, Peebles
Stirlingshire   Kilbryde Castle, Dunblane

Saturday 9 March
Glasgow & District   Greenbank Garden, Flenders Road, Clarkston

Sunday 10 March

Stirlingshire   The Linns, Sheriffmuir, Dunblane

Sunday 24 March

Dumfriesshire   Dalswinton House, Dalswinton

April

Sunday 7 April

Ayrshire   Caprington Castle, Kilmarnock

East Lothian   Winton House, Pencaitland

Edinburgh & West Lothian   61 Fountainhall Road, Edinburgh

Edinburgh & West Lothian   Dean Gardens , Edinburgh

Saturday 13 April

Edinburgh & West Lothian   10 Pilton Drive North, Edinburgh

Moray & Nairn   Brodie Castle, Brodie

Sunday 14 April

Aberdeenshire   Westhall Castle, Oyne, Inverurie

Dunbartonshire   Kilarden, Rosneath

Edinburgh & West Lothian   61 Fountainhall Road, Edinburgh

Moray & Nairn   Brodie Castle, Brodie

Perth & Kinross   Megginch Castle, Errol

Monday 15 April

Ross, Cromarty, Skye & Inverness   Brackla Wood, Culbokie

Tuesday 16 April

Ross, Cromarty, Skye & Inverness   Brackla Wood, Culbokie

Wednesday 17 April

Ross, Cromarty, Skye & Inverness   Brackla Wood, Culbokie

Thursday 18 April

Ross, Cromarty, Skye & Inverness   Brackla Wood, Culbokie

Ross, Cromarty, Skye & Inverness   Dundonnell House, Dundonnell, Little Loch Broom

Friday 19 April

Ross, Cromarty, Skye & Inverness   Brackla Wood, Culbokie

Saturday 20 April

Argyll   Stratholm, Clachan

Renfrewshire   SG Plant Sale at Kilmacolm, Lochwinnoch Road

Sunday 21 April

Argyll   Benmore Botanic Garden, Benmore, Dunoon

Argyll   Crarae Garden, Inveraray

Argyll   Stratholm, Clachan

Stirlingshire   The Pass House, Kilmahog, Callander

May

Saturday 4 May

Argyll	Kames Bay, Kilmelford
Argyll	Maolachy's Garden, Lochavich, by Taynuilt
East Lothian	Shepherd House, Inveresk
Lochaber & Badenoch	Canna House Walled Garden, Isle of Canna

Sunday 5 May

Angus	Brechin Castle, Brechin
Argyll	Kames Bay, Kilmelford
Argyll	Maolachy's Garden, Lochavich, by Taynuilt
Dumfriesshire	Portrack House, Holywood
East Lothian	Inwood, Carberry, Musselburgh
East Lothian	Shepherd House, Inveresk
Fife	Falkland Palace and Garden, Falkland
Isle of Arran	Brodick Castle & Country Park, Brodick
Perth & Kinross	Branklyn, Perth
Perth & Kinross	Glendoick, by Perth
Wigtownshire	Logan House Gardens, Port Logan

Saturday 11 May

Argyll	Knock Cottage, Lochgair

Sunday 12 May

Angus	Dalfruin, Kirriemuir
Argyll	Arduaine, Oban
Argyll	Knock Cottage, Lochgair
Berwickshire	Charterhall, Duns
Dumfriesshire	Drumpark, Irongray
East Lothian	Tyninghame House, Dunbar
Edinburgh & West Lothian	61 Fountainhall Road, Edinburgh
Fife	Culross Palace, Culross
Fife	Tayfield, Forgan, Newport-on-Tay
Fife	Willowhill, Forgan, Newport-on-Tay
Kirkcudbrightshire	Threave Garden, Castle Douglas
Perth & Kinross	Bonhard Garden, Perth
Perth & Kinross	Glendoick, by Perth
Stirlingshire	Kilbryde Castle, Dunblane
Wigtownshire	Claymoddie Garden, Whithorn, Newton Stewart

Saturday 18 May

Argyll	Colintraive Gardens
Argyll	Drim na Vullin, Blarbuie Road, Lochgilphead
Argyll	Knock Cottage, Lochgair
Edinburgh & West Lothian	Rocheid Garden, 20 Inverleith Terrace, Edinburgh
Glasgow & District	5 Ellergreen Road, Bearsden
Perth & Kinross	Rossie House, Forgandenny

Sunday 19 May

Angus	Dunninald, Montrose
Argyll	Colintraive Gardens
Argyll	Drim na Vullin, Blarbuie Road, Lochgilphead
Argyll	Knock Cottage, Lochgair
Ayrshire	Kirkhill Castle, Colmonell
Dumfriesshire	Dalswinton House, Dalswinton
Dunbartonshire	Ross Priory, Gartocharn
Edinburgh & West Lothian	61 Fountainhall Road, Edinburgh
Edinburgh & West Lothian	Moray Place & Bank Gardens, Edinburgh
Glasgow & District	Kilsyth Gardens, Allanfauld Road, Kilsyth
Isle of Arran	Strabane, Brodick
Lanarkshire	Nemphlar Village Garden Trail, Lanark
Stirlingshire	Drymen Gardens

Wednesday 22 May

Ross, Cromarty, Skye & Inverness	Inverewe, Poolewe

Saturday 25 May

Fife	Tayport Gardens
Midlothian	SG & Midlothian Council Plant Sale, Vogrie

Sunday 26 May

Angus	Gallery, Montrose
Dumfriesshire	Dabton, Thornhill
Dumfriesshire	Westerhall, Bentpath, Langholm
East Lothian	Belhaven Hill School and Belhaven House, Dunbar
Fife	Lindores House, by Newburgh
Fife	Tayport Gardens
Isle of Arran	Strabane, Brodick
Kincardine & Deeside	Woodend House, Banchory
Kirkcudbrightshire	Corsock House, Corsock, Castle Douglas
Perth & Kinross	Croftcat Lodge, Grandtully
Perth & Kinross	Fingask Castle, Rait
Renfrewshire	Carruth, Bridge of Weir
Ross, Cromarty, Skye & Inverness	Aultgowrie Mill, Aultgowrie, Urray, Muir of Ord
Stirlingshire	Gargunnock House, Gargunnock
Wigtownshire	Logan Botanic Garden, Port Logan

Wednesday 29 May

Aberdeenshire	Cruickshank Botanic Gardens, Aberdeen
Ross, Cromarty, Skye & Inverness	House of Gruinard, Laide, by Achnasheen

Thursday 30 May

Aberdeenshire	Leith Hall, Huntly
Ross, Cromarty, Skye & Inverness	Dundonnell House, Little Loch Broom

June

Saturday 1 June

Caithness, Sutherland, Orkney & Shetland	Amat, Ardgay

Sunday 2 June

Aberdeenshire	Kildrummy Castle Gardens, Alford
Aberdeenshire	Tillypronie, Tarland
Angus	Cortachy Castle, Cortachy, By Kirriemuir
Ayrshire	10 Grange Terrace, Kilmarnock
Caithness, Sutherland, Orkney & Shetland	Amat, Ardgay
Dumfriesshire	Cowhill Tower, Holywood
Dunbartonshire	Geilston Garden, Main Road, Cardross
East Lothian	Broadwoodside, Gifford
Edinburgh & West Lothian	The Glass Houses at The Royal Botanic Gardens
Fife	Earlshall Castle, Leuchars
Lochaber & Badenoch	Aberarder, Kinlochlaggan
Lochaber & Badenoch	Ardverikie, Kinlochlaggan
Ross, Cromarty, Skye & Inverness	Novar, Evanton
Wigtownshire	Woodfall Gardens, Glasserton

Wednesday 5 June

Ross, Cromarty, Skye & Inverness	Brackla Wood, Culbokie, Dingwall
Ross, Cromarty, Skye & Inverness	Inverewe, Poolewe

Saturday 8 June

Ayrshire	Holmes Farm, Drybridge, By Irvine
Glasgow & District	Kirklee Circus Pleasure Garden and Beyond
Kincardine & Deeside	Inchmarlo House Garden, Inchmarlo

Sunday 9 June

Aberdeenshire	Birken Cottage, Burnhervie, Inverurie
Ayrshire	Holmes Farm, Drybridge, By Irvine
Berwickshire	Lennel Bank, Coldstream
Dumfriesshire	Glenae, Amisfield
Ettrick & Lauderdale	2 Whytbank Row, Clovenfords, Galashiels
Fife	Freuchie Plant Sale and the Garden at Karbet
Kincardine & Deeside	Kincardine, Kincardine O'Neil
Perth & Kinross	Explorers Garden, Pitlochry
Ross, Cromarty, Skye & Inverness	Field House, Belladrum, Beauly
Stirlingshire	Kilbryde Castle, Dunblane
Wigtownshire	Glenwhan Gardens, Dunragit, By Stranraer

Tuesday 11 June

Caithness, Sutherland, Orkney & Shetland	Keldaberg, Cunningsburgh

Thursday 13 June

Kirkcudbrightshire	Broughton House Garden, 12 High Street, Kirkcudbright
Perth & Kinross	Bradystone House, Murthly

Saturday 15 June

Caithness, Sutherland, Orkney & Shetland	Keldaberg, Cunningsburgh
East Lothian	Shepherd House, Inveresk
Edinburgh & West Lothian	Dr Neil's Garden, Duddingston Village
Edinburgh & West Lothian	Rocheid Garden, 20 Inverleith Terrace, Edinburgh
Midlothian	Kevock Garden, 16 Kevock Road, Lasswade

Sunday 16 June

Angus	Letham Village
Dumfriesshire	Newtonairds Lodge, Newtonairds
Dunbartonshire	Kirkton Cottage, Cardross, Dumbarton
East Lothian	Athelstaneford Village
East Lothian	Shepherd House, Inveresk
Edinburgh & West Lothian	Dr Neil's Garden, Duddingston Village
Fife	Old Inzievar House, Dunfermline
Kincardine & Deeside	Ecclesgreig Castle, St Cyrus
Lanarkshire	Allium Croft, 21 Main Street, Braehead
Midlothian	Kevock Garden, 16 Kevock Road, Lasswade
Stirlingshire	Stirling Gardens
Wigtownshire	Castle Kennedy & Gardens, Stranraer

Tuesday 18 June

Caithness, Sutherland, Orkney & Shetland	Keldaberg, Cunningsburgh

Thursday 20 June

Perth & Kinross	Bradystone House, Murthly

Saturday 22 June

Argyll	Dal an Eas and Dalnaneun, Kilmore
Caithness, Sutherland, Orkney & Shetland	Keldaberg, Cunningsburgh
Edinburgh & West Lothian	101 Greenbank Crescent, Edinburgh
Kincardine & Deeside	Crathes Castle, Banchory

Sunday 23 June

Angus	Edzell Village & Castle
Argyll	Dal an Eas and Dalnaneun, Kilmore
Dunbartonshire	8 Laggary Park, Rhu
East Lothian	Gifford Bank, Gifford
Edinburgh & West Lothian	101 Greenbank Crescent, Edinburgh
Edinburgh & West Lothian	61 Fountainhall Road, Edinburgh
Ettrick & Lauderdale	Fairnilee House, Near Clovenfords
Ettrick & Lauderdale	Harmony Garden, St. Mary's Road, Melrose
Ettrick & Lauderdale	Priorwood Gardens, Abbey Road, Melrose
Fife	Craigfoodie, Dairsie
Kincardine & Deeside	Finzean House, Finzean, Banchory
Kirkcudbrightshire	The Waterhouse Gardens at Stockarton, Kirkcudbright
Lanarkshire	Dippoolbank Cottage, Carnwath
Renfrewshire	Sma' Shot Cottages , 2 Sma' Shot Lane, Paisley

Tuesday 25 June
Caithness, Sutherland, Orkney & Shetland   Keldaberg, Cunningsburgh

Thursday 27 June
Aberdeenshire   Leith Hall, Huntly
Perth & Kinross   Bradystone House, Murthly

Saturday 29 June
Caithness, Sutherland, Orkney & Shetland   Keldaberg, Cunningsburgh
Ettrick & Lauderdale   Gattonside Village Gardens
Moray & Nairn   Cuddy's Well, Clephanton, Inverness
Perth & Kinross   The Bield at Blackruthven, Tibbermore   .

Sunday 30 June
Aberdeenshire   Mansefield, Alford
Angus   Newtonmill House, By Brechin
East Lothian   Tyninghame House, Dunbar
Ettrick & Lauderdale   Lowood House , Melrose
Fife   Pittenweem: Gardens in the Burgh
Fife   Strathmiglo Village Gardens
Isle of Arran   Dougarie
Kirkcudbrightshire   Cally Gardens, Gatehouse of Fleet
Lanarkshire   Thankerton/Covington Village Gardens
Moray & Nairn   Cuddy's Well, Clephanton, Inverness
Renfrewshire   Duchal, Kilmacolm
Ross, Cromarty, Skye & Inverness   House of Aigas and Field Centre, by Beauly
Stirlingshire   Blair Drummond Gardens

July

Wednesday 3 July
Caithness, Sutherland, Orkney & Shetland   The Castle & Gardens of Mey, Mey
Stirlingshire   Row House, Dunblane

Thursday 4 July
Kincardine & Deeside   Drum Castle, Drumoak, by Banchory
Perth & Kinross   Bradystone House, Murthly

Saturday 6 July
Aberdeenshire   Hillockhead, Glendeskry, Strathdon
Aberdeenshire   Middle Cairncake, Cuminestown, Turriff
Fife   Kemback House, Kemback, Cupar
Wigtownshire   Woodfall Gardens, Glasserton

Sunday 7 July
Aberdeenshire   23 Don Street, Old Aberdeen
Aberdeenshire   Bruckhills Croft, Rothienorman, Inverurie
Aberdeenshire   Middle Cairncake, Cuminestown, Turriff
Angus   Montrose and Hillside Gardens, Montrose
Ayrshire   Gardens of Largs, Greenock Road

Berwickshire	Netherbyres, Eyemouth
Caithness, Sutherland, Orkney & Shetland	Bighouse Lodge, By Melvich
Dunbartonshire	Shandon Gardens
East Lothian	Bowerhouse with Bowerhouse Walled Garden, Dunbar
Isle of Arran	Brodick Castle & Country Park, Brodick
Kincardine & Deeside	Findrack, Torphins
Lochaber & Badenoch	Craigmore Mill , Dorback Road, Nethybridge

Wednesday 10 July

Ross, Cromarty, Skye & Inverness	House of Gruinard, Laide, by Achnasheen
Stirlingshire	Row House, Dunblane

Thursday 11 July

Kincardine & Deeside	Drum Castle, Drumoak, by Banchory
Perth & Kinross	Bradystone House, Murthly

Saturday 13 July

Angus	Gallery, Montrose
Argyll	Seafield, 173 Marine Parade, Hunter's Quay, Dunoon
Ettrick & Lauderdale	Carolside , Earlston
Kincardine & Deeside	Drumlithie Village
Ross, Cromarty, Skye & Inverness	Hugh Miller's Birthplace Cottage & Museum, Cromarty

Sunday 14 July

Argyll	Seafield, 173 Marine Parade, Hunter's Quay, Dunoon
Ayrshire	Cairnhall House, Mauchline Road, Ochiltree
Berwickshire	Preston Gardens, Duns
Ettrick & Lauderdale	Ravensheugh House, Selkirk
Fife	Wormistoune House, Crail
Kincardine & Deeside	Douneside House, Tarland
Kirkcudbrightshire	Crofts, Kirkpatrick Durham, Castle Douglas
Moray & Nairn	Bents Green, 10 Pilmuir Road West, Forres
Roxburghshire	Yetholm Village Gardens, Town Yetholm

Tuesday 16 July

Ayrshire	Culzean, Maybole

Wednesday 17 July

Caithness, Sutherland, Orkney & Shetland	The Castle & Gardens of Mey, Mey
Stirlingshire	Row House, Dunblane

Thursday 18 July

Kincardine & Deeside	Drum Castle, Drumoak, by Banchory

Saturday 20 July

Aberdeenshire	Middle Cairncake, Cuminestown, Turriff
Fife	Crail: Small Gardens in the Burgh

Sunday 21 July

Aberdeenshire	Leith Hall, Huntly
Aberdeenshire	Middle Cairncake, Cuminestown, Turriff
Argyll	Crarae Garden, Inveraray
Ayrshire	Skeldon, Dalrymple
Berwickshire	Anton's Hill and Walled Garden, Leitholm, Coldstream
Dunbartonshire	Rhu Gardens
Edinburgh & West Lothian	15 Morningside Park, Edinburgh
Fife	Crail: Small Gardens in the Burgh
Kincardine & Deeside	Mill of Benholm Project, Benholm by Johnshaven
Kirkcudbrightshire	Glensone Walled Garden, Southwick
Lanarkshire	Dippoolbank Cottage, Carnwath
Peeblesshire	8 Halmyre Mains, West Linton
Perth & Kinross	Auchleeks House, Calvine
Perth & Kinross	Boreland, Killin
Stirlingshire	The Walled Garden, Righead Farm, Kincardine

Tuesday 23 July

Stirlingshire	Gean House , Tullibody Road, Alloa

Wednesday 24 July

Stirlingshire	Row House, Dunblane

Thursday 25 July

Kincardine & Deeside	Drum Castle, Drumoak, by Banchory

Friday 26 July

Aberdeenshire	Fyvie Castle, Fyvie, Turriff

Saturday 27 July

Argyll	Barochreal, Kilninver, Oban
Argyll	Melfort House Kitchen Garden, Kilmelford
Caithness, Sutherland, Orkney & Shetland	House of Tongue, Tongue

Sunday 28 July

Aberdeenshire	Birken Cottage, Burnhervie, Inverurie
Aberdeenshire	Castle Fraser, Sauchen, Inverurie
Aberdeenshire	Glenkindie House, Glenkindie, Alford
Angus	The Walled Garden at Logie, Logie House, Kirriemuir
Argyll	Ardchattan Priory, North Connel
Argyll	Barochreal, Kilninver, Oban
Argyll	Melfort House Kitchen Garden, Kilmelford, By Oban
Ayrshire	Carnell, By Hurlford
Caithness, Sutherland, Orkney & Shetland	Lea Gardens, Tresta, Shetland
Edinburgh & West Lothian	Hunter's Tryst, 95 Oxgangs Road, Edinburgh
Fife	Balcaskie, Pittenweem
Fife	Kellie Castle, Pittenweem
Kincardine & Deeside	Mallamauch, Banchory
Kirkcudbrightshire	Southwick House, Southwick

Peeblesshire   Portmore, Eddleston
Perth & Kinross   Croftcat Lodge, Grandtully
Ross, Cromarty, Skye & Inverness   House of Aigas and Field Centre, by Beauly
Stirlingshire   The Tors, 2 Slamannan Road, Falkirk

Monday 29 July
Kirkcudbrightshire   Southwick House, Southwick

Tuesday 30 July
Caithness, Sutherland, Orkney & Shetland   Keldaberg, Cunningsburgh
Kirkcudbrightshire   Southwick House, Southwick

Wednesday 31 July
Kirkcudbrightshire   Southwick House, Southwick
Stirlingshire   Row House, Dunblane

August

Thursday 1 August
Kirkcudbrightshire   Southwick House, Southwick

Friday 2 August
Kirkcudbrightshire   Southwick House, Southwick

Saturday 3 August
Aberdeenshire   Pitscurry Project, Whiteford, Pitcaple
Caithness, Sutherland, Orkney & Shetland   Keldaberg, Cunningsburgh
Wigtownshire   Woodfall Gardens, Glasserton

Sunday 4 August
Aberdeenshire   Pitscurry Project, Whiteford, Pitcaple
Caithness, Sutherland, Orkney & Shetland   Langwell, Berriedale
Dumfriesshire   Newtonairds Lodge, Newtonairds
Edinburgh & West Lothian   15 Morningside Park, Edinburgh
Ettrick & Lauderdale   2 Whytbank Row, Clovenfords
Fife   Earlshall Castle, Leuchars
Kincardine & Deeside   Glenbervie House, Drumlithie
Kirkcudbrightshire   Seabank, Merse Road, Rockcliffe
Kirkcudbrightshire   Threave Garden, Castle Douglas
Midlothian   Silverburn Village, Nr. Penicuik
Moray & Nairn   Castleview, Auchindoun, Dufftown
Perth & Kinross   Drummond Castle Gardens, Crieff
Perth & Kinross   Mount Tabor House, Perth
Ross, Cromarty, Skye & Inverness   Aultgowrie Mill, Aultgowrie

Wednesday 5 August
Aberdeenshire   Pitscurry Project, Whiteford, Pitcaple

Tuesday 6 August
Aberdeenshire   Pitscurry Project, Whiteford, Pitcaple
Caithness, Sutherland, Orkney & Shetland   Keldaberg, Cunningsburgh

Wednesday 7 August

| Aberdeenshire | Haddo House, Methlick, Ellon |
| Aberdeenshire | Pitscurry Project, Whiteford, Pitcaple |

Thursday 8 August

| Aberdeenshire | Pitscurry Project, Whiteford, Pitcaple |

Friday 9 August

| Aberdeenshire | Pitscurry Project, Whiteford, Pitcaple |

Saturday 10 August

Aberdeenshire	Pitscurry Project, Whiteford, Pitcaple
Ayrshire	Avonhill Cottage, Drumclog, Strathaven
Caithness, Sutherland, Orkney & Shetland	Keldaberg, Cunningsburgh
Edinburgh & West Lothian	45 Northfield Crescent, Longridge, Bathgate

Sunday 11 August

Aberdeenshire	Pitscurry Project, Whiteford, Pitcaple
Caithness, Sutherland, Orkney & Shetland	Langwell, Berriedale
Edinburgh & West Lothian	45 Northfield Crescent, Longridge, Bathgate
Kirkcudbrightshire	Barholm Castle, Gatehouse of Fleet
Lanarkshire	Wellbutts, Elsrickle, by Biggar
Peeblesshire	West Linton Village Gardens
Stirlingshire	Thorntree, Arnprior

Wednesday 14 August

| Lochaber & Badenoch | Canna House Walled Garden, Isle of Canna |

Thursday 15 August

| Ross, Cromarty, Skye & Inverness | Dundonnell House, Little Loch Broom, Wester Ross |

Saturday 17 August

| Caithness, Sutherland, Orkney & Shetland | The Castle & Gardens of Mey, Mey |

Sunday 18 August

Aberdeenshire	Haddo House, Methlick, Ellon
Aberdeenshire	Pitmedden Garden, Ellon
Ayrshire	Kilmaurs Village Gardens
Kirkcudbrightshire	Cally Gardens, Gatehouse of Fleet
Lanarkshire	Culter Allers, Coulter, Biggar
Lanarkshire	New Lanark Roof Garden, New Lanark Mills, Lanark
Midlothian	Harvieston Walled Garden, Harvieston Cottage, Gorebridge
Roxburghshire	West Leas, Bonchester Bridge

Saturday 24 August

| Fife | Gilston House, By Largoward, Leven |

Sunday 25 August

Aberdeenshire	Tillypronie, Tarland
Caithness, Sutherland, Orkney & Shetland	Springpark House, Laurie Terrace, Thurso
East Lothian	Amisfield Walled Garden, Haddington

| Fife | Tayfield, Forgan, Newport-on-Tay |
| Fife | Willowhill, Forgan, Newport-on-Tay |

Thursday 29 August

| Aberdeenshire | Leith Hall, Huntly |

September

Sunday 1 September

| Dunbartonshire | SG Hill House Plant Sale, Helensburgh |

Saturday 7 September

| Edinburgh & West Lothian | Rocheid Garden, 20 Inverleith Terrace, Edinburgh |
| Wigtownshire | Woodfall Gardens, Glasserton |

Sunday 8 September

| Edinburgh & West Lothian | 61 Fountainhall Road, Edinburgh |

Saturday 14 September

| Edinburgh & West Lothian | The Archivists' Garden, 2 Princes Street, Edinburgh |
| Renfrewshire | SG Plant Sale at St Fillan's Episcopal Church, Kilmacolm |

Sunday 15 September

| Edinburgh & West Lothian | 61 Fountainhall Road, Edinburgh |
| Edinburgh & West Lothian | The Archivists' Garden, 2 Princes Street, Edinburgh |

Thursday 19 September

| Ross, Cromarty, Skye & Inverness | Dundonnell House, Little Loch Broom, Wester Ross |

Sunday 22 September

| Kincardine & Deeside | Drum Castle, Drumoak, by Banchory |

Sunday 29 September

| Aberdeenshire | Kildrummy Castle Gardens, Alford |

October

Tuesday 1 October

| Stirlingshire | Scotland's Gardens Autumn Seminar, Stirling |

Saturday 5 October

| Wigtownshire | Woodfall Gardens, Glasserton |

Sunday 6 October

| Fife | Hill of Tarvit Plant Sale and Autumn Fair, Cupar |
| Peeblesshire | Dawyck Botanic Garden, Stobo |

Sunday 20 October

| Kincardine & Deeside | Inchmarlo House Garden, Inchmarlo |

GARDENS OPEN BY ARRANGEMENT

Aberdeenshire

Grandhome, Danestone, Aberdeen	On request
Greenridge, Craigton Road, Cults	On request
Hatton Castle, Turriff	On request
Laundry Cottage, Culdrain, Gartly, Huntly	On request
Tillypronie, Tarland	On request

Angus

Cortachy Castle, by Kirriemuir	On request
Dunninald, Montrose	On request
Kirkside of Lochty, Menmuir, by Brechin	On request

Argyll

Knock Cottage, Lochgair	15 April to 15 June

Ayrshire

Carnell, By Hurlford	1 May to 30 September

Berwickshire

Anton's Hill and Walled Garden, Leitholm	1 May to 30 September
Lennel Bank, Coldstream	On request
Netherbyres, Eyemouth	1 May to 31 August

Caithness, Sutherland, Orkney & Shetland

Caergarth, Scatness, Virkie, Shetland	1 June to 30 September
Cruisdale, Sandness, Shetland	1 May to 31 August
Gerdi, Hillswick, Shetland	1 July to 31 August
Highlands, East Voe, Scalloway, Shetland	On request
Langwell, Berriedale	On request
Nonavaar, Levenwick, Shetland	On request
Norby, Burnside, Sandness, Shetland	On request

Dumfriesshire

Grovehill House , Burnhead, Thornhill	1 April to 30 September

Dunbartonshire

Parkhead, Rosneath	1 April to 30 September

East Lothian

Bowerhouse, Dunbar	15 April to 30 September
Humbie Dean, Humbie	1 April to 31 July
Stobshiel House , Humbie	On request

Edinburgh & West Lothian

45 Northfield Crescent, Longridge, Bathgate	On request
61 Fountainhall Road, Edinburgh	On request
Hunter's Tryst, 95 Oxgangs Road, Edinburgh	On request
Newliston, Kirkliston	On request
Rocheid Garden, 20 Inverleith Terrace, Edinburgh	On request

Ettrick & Lauderdale

Fairnilee House, Near Clovenfords	1 May to 31 August

Fife

Barham, Bow of Fife	1 April to 30 September
Earlshall Castle, Leuchars	On request
Glassmount House, by Kirkcaldy	1 April to 30 September
Teasses Gardens, Nr. Ceres	On request
Willowhill, Forgan, Newport-on-Tay	1 June to 30 August
Wormistoune House, Crail	On request

Glasgow & District

Kilsyth Gardens, Allanfauld Road, Kilsyth	1 April to 30 September

Kirkcudbrightshire

Corsock House, Corsock, Castle Douglas	1 April to 30 June
Cosy Cottage, Borgue	On request
Danevale Park, Crossmichael	Until 1 June
Margrie Cottage, Borgue	On request
Steadstone, Colvend Road, Dalbeattie	On request
Stockarton, Kirkcudbright	1 April to 31 August

Lanarkshire

Baitlaws, Lamington, Biggar	1 June to 31 August
Biggar Park, Biggar	1 May to 31 July
Carmichael Mill, Hyndford Bridge	On request
The Scots Mining Company House	On request

Lochaber & Badenoch

Ard-Daraich, Ardgour, by Fort William	On request

Midlothian

The Old Sun Inn, Newbattle, Dalkeith	1 June to 31 July

Moray & Nairn

Bents Green, 10 Pilmuir Road West, Forres	1 July to 1 September

Peeblesshire

Portmore, Eddleston	On request

Perth & Kinross

Bradystone House, Murthly	On request
Croftcat Lodge, Grandtully, Perthshire	On request
Easter Meikle Fardle, Meikleour	On request
Glendoick, by Perth	On request
Parkhead House, Burghmuir Road, Perth	1 June to 31 August

Ross, Cromarty, Skye & Inverness

Brackla Wood, Culbokie, Dingwall	20 April and 21 April & 8 September - 14 September
Coiltie Garden, Divach, Drumnadrochit	On request
Dundonnell House, Little Loch Broom	On request
Dunvegan Castle and Gardens, Isle of Skye	3 January to 31 March & 16 October to 31 December
House of Aigas and Field Centre, by Beauly	On request
Leathad Ard, Upper Carloway, Isle of Lewis	1 April to 30 September
The Lookout, Kilmuir, North Kessock	1 April to 31 October

Roxburghshire

Lanton Tower, Jedburgh	On request
West Leas, Bonchester Bridge	On request

Stirlingshire

Arndean, by Dollar	15 May to 15 June
Camallt, Fintry	1 April to 15 May
Duntreath Castle, Blanefield	On request
Gargunnock House, Gargunnock	15 September to 31 October
Kilbryde Castle, Dunblane	On request
Milseybank, Bridge of Allan	On request
Rowberrow, 18 Castle Road, Dollar	On request
The Tors, 2 Slamannan Road, Falkirk	On request
Thorntree, Arnprior	On request

Wigtownshire

Castle Kennedy & Gardens, Stranraer	1 November to 31 December
Claymoddie Garden, Whithorn, Newton Stewart	On request
Craichlaw, Kirkcowan, Newton Stewart	On request
Dunskey Gardens and Maze, Portpatrick, Stranraer	On request
Woodfall Gardens, Glasserton	On request

CANCELLATIONS

On the rare occassions that garden openings are cancelled, details will be posted on the Cancellation page of our website www.scotlandsgardens.org

GARDENS OPEN ON A REGULAR BASIS

Angus

Dunninald, Montrose	29 June to 28 July, except Mondays
Pitmuies Gardens, House of Pitmuies, Guthrie	2 February to 18 March
	& 1 April to 31 October

Argyll

An Cala, Ellenabeich, Isle of Seil	1 April to 31 October
Ardchattan Priory, North Connel	25 March to 31 October
Ardkinglas Woodland Garden, Cairndow	Daily
Ardmaddy Castle, By Oban	Daily
Barguillean's "Angus Garden", Taynuilt	Daily
Benmore Botanic Garden, Benmore, Dunoon	1 March to 31 October
Crinan Hotel Garden, Crinan	1 May to 31 August
Druimneil House, Port Appin	29 March to 31 October
Fairwinds, Hunter's Quay, Dunoon	All summer
Inveraray Castle Gardens, Inveraray	29 March to 31 October
Kinlochlaich House Gardens, Appin	Daily
Oakbank, Ardrishaig	1 May to 31 August

Berwickshire

Bughtrig, Near Leitholm, Coldstream	1 June to 1 September

Caithness, Sutherland, Orkney & Shetland

15 Linkshouse , Mid Yell, Shetland	11 July to 8 August, Thursdays
Caergarth, Scatness, Virkie, Shetland	15 June to 29 July, Saturdays, Sundays and Mondays
	and not open 6, 7, 8 July
Holmlea, Mid Yell, Shetland	7 July to 18 August
Lea Gardens, Tresta, Shetland	1 April to 31 October
Nonavaar, Levenwick, Shetland	2 June to 28 August, Wednesdays and Sundays
The Castle & Gardens of Mey, Mey	1 May to 24 July
	& 8 August to 30 September

Dunbartonshire

Glenarn, Glenarn Road, Rhu, Helensburgh	23 March to 21 September

East Lothian

Inwood, Carberry, Musselburgh	2 May to 12 September, Tues, Thurs and Sats

Shepherd House, Inveresk	12 February to 28 February, Tuesdays and Thursdays & 16 April to 4 July, Tuesdays and Thursdays

Edinburgh & West Lothian

Newliston, Kirkliston	1 May to 2 June, except Mondays and Tuesdays

Ettrick & Lauderdale

Carolside , Earlston	23 June to 4 August, Wednesdays, Fridays and Sundays

Fife

Cambo House, Kingsbarns	Daily
The Fife Garden Trail	1 May to 30 June
The Tower, 1 Northview Terrace, Wormit	18 April to 12 September, Thursdays
Willowhill, Forgan, Newport-on-Tay	26 June to 28 August, Wednesdays

Lanarkshire

New Lanark Roof Garden, Lanark	Daily

Lochaber & Badenoch

Ardtornish, By Lochaline, Morvern	Daily

Moray & Nairn

Boath House, Auldearn, Nairn	1 June to 30 September

Peeblesshire

Dawyck Botanic Garden, Stobo	1 February to 30 November
Kailzie Gardens, Peebles	Daily
Traquair House, Innerleithen	29 March to 30 November, open weekends only in Nov.

Perth & Kinross

Ardvorlich, Lochearnhead	1 May to 31 May
Blair Castle Gardens, Blair Atholl	12 January to 25 October
Bolfracks, Aberfeldy	1 April to 31 October
Braco Castle, Braco	1 March to 31 October
Cluny House, Aberfeldy	Daily
Dowhill, Cleish	2 May to 27 June, Tuesdays and Thursdays
Drummond Castle Gardens, Crieff	1 May to 31 October
Easter Meikle Fardle, Meikleour	12 April to 31 August, Fridays
Fingask Castle, Rait	10 February to 10 March, Sundays
Glenbeich, Lochearnhead	22 July to 4 August
Glendoick, by Perth	1 April to 31 May

Ross, Cromarty, Skye & Inverness

Abriachan Garden Nursery, Loch Ness Side	1 February to 30 November
Applecross Walled Garden, Strathcarron	15 March to 31 October

Attadale, Strathcarron	28 March to 31 October, except Sundays
Balmeanach House, Struan, Isle of Skye	6 May to 30 October, Mondays and Wednesdays
Clan Donald Skye, Armadale, Isle of Skye	Daily
Dunvegan Castle and Gardens, Isle of Skye	1 April to 15 October
Leathad Ard, Upper Carloway, Isle of Lewis	1 June to 31 August, except Fridays and Sundays also closed Wednesday 7 August
Leckmelm Shrubbery & Arboretum, Ullapool	1 April to 31 October
Oldtown of Leys Garden, Inverness	Daily
The Lookout, Kilmuir, North Kessock	2 April to 26 September

Roxburghshire

Floors Castle, Kelso	1 May to 31 October
Monteviot, Jedburgh	1 April to 31 October

Stirlingshire

Gargunnock House, Gargunnock	2 February to 17 March, daily & 14 April to 16 June, Saturdays and Sundays
The Walled Garden, Righead Farm, Kincardine	23 January to 29 December, except Mons and Tues

Wigtownshire

Ardwell House Gardens, Ardwell, Stranraer	1 April to 30 September
Castle Kennedy & Gardens, Stranraer	4 February to 30 October
Claymoddie Garden, Whithorn, Newton Stewart	31 March to 29 September, Fris, Sats and Suns
Dunskey Gardens and Maze, Portpatrick, Stranraer	29 March to 31 October
Glenwhan Gardens, Dunragit, by Stranraer	1 April to 31 October
Logan Botanic Garden, Port Logan, by Stranraer	1 March to 31 October

PLANT SALES

Renfrewshire

| Plant Sale at Kilmacolm | Saturday 20 April | 10:00am - 12:00pm |

Perth & Kinross

| Rossie House, Forgandenny | Saturday 18 May | 11:00am - 5:00pm |

Midlothian

| Plant Sale at Vogrie Country Park | Saturday 25 May | 10:00am - 4:00pm |

Fife

| Freuchie Plant Sale and the Garden at Karbet | Sunday 9 June | 12:00pm - 4:00pm |

Dunbartonshire

| 8 Laggary Park, Rhu, Helensburgh | Sunday 23 June | 2:00pm - 5:00pm |
| Hill House Plant Sale, Helensburgh | Sunday 1 September | 11:00am - 4:00pm |

Renfrewshire

| Plant Sale at St Fillan's Episcopal Church, Kilmacolm | Saturday 14 September | 10:00am - 12:00pm |

Fife

| Hill of Tarvit Plant Sale and Autumn Fair, Cupar | Sunday 6 October | 10:30am - 4:00pm |

Cheshire's gardens
Different every day

There are over **25 beautiful Gardens of Distinctio**
in Cheshire and each promises a unique adventure

From stately homes and secret gardens, the
quintessentially English to exotic oriental planting –
Cheshire is Home to England's Finest Gardens.

Discover more at visitcheshire.com/garden

Cheshire's Gardens
of Distinction
Home of England's Finest Gardens

The David Welch Winter Gardens

at Duthie Park, Polmuir Road, Aberdeen are one of Europe's largest indoor gardens. It boasts a beautiful floral paradise all year round, with many rare and exotic plants on show from all around the world.

Open daily from 9:30am Tel: 01224 583 155

Email: wintergardens@aberdeencity.gov.uk
Web-site:www.aberdeencity.gov.uk

Free Admission

Escape to Auchlochan Village to see our beautifully landscaped grounds, mature woodlands, spectacular gardens and expansive lochs.

Auchlochan Garden

Escape to Auchlochan Garden Village to see our beautifully landscaped grounds, mature woodlands, spectacular gardens and lochs.

The gardens at Auchlochan are its undoubted glory, offering a wide range of attractions to visitors, walkers and residents alike.

Laid out over a 50 acre estate, the gardens feature not only the lochs that gave the village its name, but stunning herbaceous borders, terrace gardens, rhododendron beds and heather gardens. Along the River Nethan valley, the gardens merge with mature woodland which feature our prominent Sequoiadendron giganteum - giant Redwoods - which are native to California.

At Auchlochan's heart is the delightful 1.5 acre walled garden. Built around 1900, the garden was originally designed as a source of fruit and vegetables for the estate. Under the care of the current gardening team it has been transformed into a show garden.

The Auchlochan grounds attract many visitors - come and see why - and enjoy a relaxing cup of tea or coffee or even lunch in our bistro, at the same time.

nd Grounds

Auchlochan
Garden Village

01555 893592
www.auchlochan.com

Auchlochan Garden Village, New Trows Road,
Lesmahagow, South Lanarkshire ML11 0GS

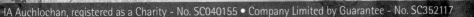

WOODBURY ESTATE

WHOLESALE FOREST TREE AND POTTED STOCK NURSERY

Kiln House, Newton of Glenisla, Blairgowrie, PH11 8PE

Tel/Fax 01575 582288 email: chris@woodburyestate.co.uk

Nursery visits by appointment only. Hours Mon-Sat 8 till 5pm. Ring for your copy of our full catalogue.

Nursery owned and managed by John and Chris Watkinson. John has over 35 years experience in the nursery trade. Our nursery is in the heart of the beautiful Angus Glens and well worth a visit.

Bare root. Nov to April. (Min.order 100) Forestry broadleaves & conifers, hedging, shrubs, willows and game cover. We supply farmers and estates for hedge and woodland planting schemes thoughout Scotland.

Potted stock. All year round. Huge range of potted native and ornamental trees & shrubs from 3L to 20L pot size, 30cm to 3m height. We pot between 10 and 100 of a species and can supply larger numbers than most garden centres. We stock ornamental Rowan, Birches, Crab apples, Acers, Flowering Cherries and many other beautiful and unusual trees, shrubs & fruit trees.

MAP OF DISTRICTS

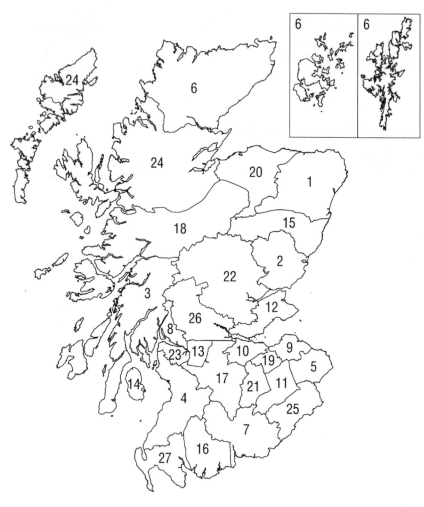

1. Aberdeenshire
2. Angus
3. Argyllshire
4. Ayrshire
5. Berwickshire
6. Caithness, Sutherland, Orkney and Shetland
7. Dumfriesshire
8. Dunbartonshire
9. East Lothian
10. Edinburgh and West Lothian
11. Ettrick and Lauderdale
12. Fife
13. Glasgow and District
14. Isle of Arran
15. Kincardine and Deeside
16. Kircudbrightshire
17. Lanarkshire
18. Lochaber and Badenoch
19. Midlothian
20. Moray and Nairn
21. Peeblesshire
22. Perth and Kinross
23. Renfrewshire
24. Ross, Cromarty, Skye and Inverness
25. Roxburghshire
26. Stirlingshire
27. Wigtownshire

GENERAL INFORMATION

MAPS
A map of each district is provided at the start of each section. These show the location of gardens as per the postal codes provided. Directions can be found in the garden descriptions.

HOUSES
Houses are not open unless specifically stated; where the house or part of the house is open, an additional charge is usually made.

TOILETS
Private gardens do not normally have outside toilets. For security reasons owners have been advised not to admit visitors into their houses.

PHOTOGRAPHY
No photographs taken in a garden may be used for sale or reproduction without the prior permission of the garden owner.

CHILDREN
Children are always welcome but must be accompanied by an adult. Children's activities are often available at openings.

CANCELLATIONS
All cancellations will be posted on our website www.scotlandsgardens.org

KEY TO SYMBOLS

	New in 2013		Homemade teas		Accommodation
	Teas		Dogs on a lead allowed		Plant stall
	Cream teas		Wheelchair access		Scottish Snowdrop Festival

ABERDEENSHIRE

District Organiser

Mrs V Walters	Tillychetly, Alford AB33 8HQ

Area Organisers

Mrs H Gibson	6 The Chanonry, Old Aberdeen AB24 1RP
Mrs C Hamilton	Ardneidly, Monymusk, Inverurie AB51 7HX
Mrs F G Lawson	Asloun, Alford AB33 8NR
Mrs A Robertson	Drumblade House, Huntly AB54 6ER
Mrs F M K Tuck	Stable Cottage, Allargue, Gorgarff AB36 8YP

Treasurer

Lesley Mitchell	13 Highgate Gardens, Ferryhill, Aberdeen AB11 7TZ

Gardens open on a specific date

Westhall Castle, Oyne, Inverurie	Sunday 14 April	1:00pm	-	4:00pm
Cruickshank Botanic Gardens, Aberdeen	Wednesday 29 May	6:30pm	-	8:30pm
Leith Hall, Huntly	Thursday 30 May	7:00pm		
Kildrummy Castle Gardens, Alford	Sunday 2 June	10:00am	-	5:00pm
Tillypronie, Tarland	Sunday 2 June	2:00pm	-	5:00pm
Birken Cottage, Burnhervie	Sunday 9 June	2:00pm	-	6:00pm
Leith Hall, Huntly	Thursday 27 June	7:00pm		
Mansefield, Alford	Sunday 30 June	2:00pm	-	5:00pm
Hillockhead, Glendeskry	Saturday 6 July	2:00pm	-	5:00pm
Middle Cairncake, Cuminestown	Saturday 6 July	2:00pm	-	5:00pm
23 Don Street, Old Aberdeen	Sunday 7 July	1:30pm	-	6:00pm
Bruckhills Croft, Rothienorman	Sunday 7 July	12:00pm	-	5:00pm
Middle Cairncake, Cuminestown	Sunday 7 July	2:00pm	-	5:00pm
Middle Cairncake, Cuminestown	Saturday 20 July	2:00pm	-	5:00pm
Leith Hall, Huntly	Sunday 21 July	12:00pm	-	4:30pm
Middle Cairncake, Cuminestown	Sunday 21 July	2:00pm	-	5:00pm
Fyvie Castle, Fyvie, Turriff	Friday 26 July	7:00pm	-	10:00pm
Birken Cottage, Burnhervie	Sunday 28 July	2:00pm	-	6:00pm
Castle Fraser, Sauchen	Sunday 28 July	12:00pm	-	4:30pm
Glenkindie House, Glenkindie	Sunday 28 July	1:00pm	-	5:00pm
Pitscurry Project, Whiteford, Pitcaple	Saturday 3 August	10:00am	-	3:00pm
Pitscurry Project, Whiteford, Pitcaple	Sunday 4 August	10:00am	-	3:00pm

ABERDEENSHIRE

Scotland's Gardens 2013 Guidebook is sponsored by **INVESTEC WEALTH & INVESTMENT**

Pitscurry Project, Whiteford, Pitcaple	Monday 5 August	10:00am - 3:00pm
Pitscurry Project, Whiteford, Pitcaple	Tuesday 6 August	10:00am - 3:00pm
Haddo House, Methlick	Wednesday 7 August	9:00am - 5:00pm
Pitscurry Project, Whiteford, Pitcaple	Wednesday 7 August	10:00am - 3:00pm
Pitscurry Project, Whiteford, Pitcaple	Thursday 8 August	10:00am - 3:00pm
Pitscurry Project, Whiteford, Pitcaple	Sunday 9 August	10:00am - 3:00pm
Pitscurry Project, Whiteford, Pitcaple	Sunday 10 August	10:00am - 3:00pm
Pitscurry Project, Whiteford, Pitcaple	Sunday 11 August	10:00am - 3:00pm
Haddo House, Methlick	Sunday 18 August	9:00am - 5:00pm
Pitmedden Garden, Ellon	Sunday 18 August	10:00am - 5:30pm
Tillypronie, Tarland	Sunday 25 August	2:00pm - 5:00pm
Leith Hall, Huntly	Thursday 29 August	7:00pm
Kildrummy Castle Gardens, Alford	Sunday 29 September	10:00am - 5:00pm

Gardens open by arrangement

Grandhome, Danestone	On request	01224 722202
Greenridge, Cults	On request	01224 860200
Hatton Castle, Turriff	On request	01888 562279
Laundry Cottage, Culdrain	On request	01466 720768
Tillypronie, Tarland	On request	01339 881529
		M: 07796 946309

Key to symbols

	New in 2013		Homemade teas		Accommodation
	Teas		Dogs on a lead allowed		Plant stall
	Cream teas		Wheelchair access		Scottish Snowdrop Festival

Garden locations

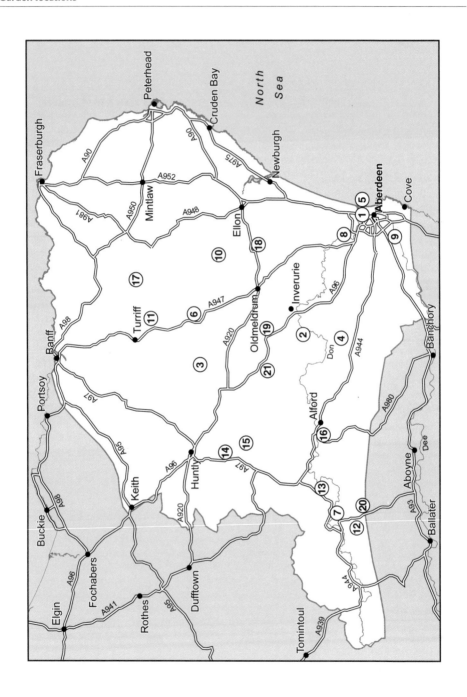

23 DON STREET
Old Aberdeen AB24 1UH
Miss M and Mr G Mackechnie

Atmospheric walled garden in historic Old Aberdeen. Wide range of rare and unusual plants and old-fashioned scented roses.

Directions: Park at St Machar Cathedral, short walk down Chanonry to Don Street, turn right. City plan ref: P7.

Disabled Access:
Full

Opening Times:
Sunday 7 July
1:30pm - 6:00pm

Admission:
£4.00, concessions £3.50

Charities:
Cat Protection receives 40%, the net remaining to SG Beneficiaries.

BIRKEN COTTAGE
Burnhervie, Inverurie AB51 5JR
Clare and Ian Alexander T: 01467 623013

This steeply sloping garden of just under 1 acre is packed with plants. It rises from a wet streamside gully and woodland, past sunny terraces and a small parterre, to dry flowery banks.

Directions: Burnhervie is about 3 miles west of Inverurie. Leave Inverurie by the B9170 (Blackhall Road) or B993 (St James' Place).

Disabled Access:
None

Opening Times:
Sunday 9 June
2:00pm - 6:00pm
Sunday 28 July
2:00pm - 6:00pm

Admission:
£4.00

Charities:
The Friends of the Cruickshank Botanic Garden receives 40%, the net remaining to SG Beneficiaries.

BRUCKHILLS CROFT
Rothienorman, Inverurie AB51 8YB
Paul and Helen Rushton T: 01651 821596
E: helenrushton1@aol.com

A slate built croft-house surrounded by an informal country cottage garden with numerous flower borders, an orchard and a productive fruit and vegetable patch with poly tunnel. Flowers range from the tiny Primula scotica to the giant Himalayan Lily. Below the main garden is a wildflower meadow and pond which attracts a great deal of wildlife. You can relax on the decking overlooking the fledgling River Ythan, or, new for 2013, try out the labyrinth.

Other Details: The plant stall will include for sale a large selection of herbaceous perennials from the garden.

Directions: From Rothienorman take the B9001 north, just after Badenscoth Nursing Home (approx 2.5 miles) turn left, after 1 mile you will be directed into a field behind the Croft.

Disabled Access:
Partial

Opening Times:
Sunday 7 July
12:00pm - 5:00pm

Admission:
£4.00, concessions £3.00, children free.

Charities:
Advocacy Service Aberdeen receives 20%, Befriend A Child receives 20%, the net remaining to SG Beneficiaries.

CASTLE FRASER
Sauchen, Inverurie AB51 7LD
The National Trust for Scotland T: 0844 493 2164
E: castlefraser@nts.org.uk www.nts.org.uk

Castle Fraser's designed landscape and parkland is the work of Thomas White in 1794. Castle Fraser, one of the most spectacular of the Castles of Mar, has a traditional walled garden of trees, shrubs and herbaceous plantings, a medicinal and culinary border and organically grown fruit and vegetables. You can stroll through the woodland garden with its azaleas and rhododendrons or take the young at heart to the Woodland Secrets adventure playground and trails.

Other Details: Self catering accommodation. Buy a raffle ticket for a chance to win the Castle Fraser gardeners for half a day. Bring the family for live music, a puppet show and games.

Directions: Near Kemnay, off A944.

Disabled Access:
Full

Opening Times:
Sunday 28 July
12:00pm - 4:30pm

Admission:
£4.00 including NTS members, children under 16 free. N.B. Prices correct at time of going to print

Charities:
Donation to SG Beneficiaries.

CRUICKSHANK BOTANIC GARDENS
23 St. Machar Drive, Aberdeen AB24 3UU
Cruickshank Botanic Garden Trust/Aberdeen University
www.abdn.ac.uk/botanic-garden/

An evening tour with the Curator, Mark Paterson and Head Gardener, Richard Walker. The garden comprises: a sunken garden with alpine lawn, a rock garden built in the 1960s complete with waterfalls and pond system, a long unbroken herbaceous border, a formal rose garden with drystone walling, and an arboretum. It has a large collection of flowering bulbs and rhododendrons, and many unusual shrubs and trees including two mature Camperdown Elms. It is sometimes known as The Secret Garden of Old Aberdeen.

Other Details: National Plant Collection ®: Baptisia, Zanthoxylum, Nomocharis.

Directions: Come down St Machar Drive over the mini-roundabout, just before the first set of traffic lights turn left into the Cruickshank Garden car park. The pedestrian Garden entrance is off the Chanonry.

Disabled Access:
Partial

Opening Times:
Wednesday 29 May
6:30pm - 8:30pm

Admission:
£5.00 per person, includes tea/coffee and biscuits

Charities:
Cruickshank Botanic Garden receives 40%, the net remaining to SG Beneficiaries.

FYVIE CASTLE
Fyvie, Turriff AB53 8JS
The National Trust for Scotland T: 01651 891363 or 01651 891266
E: gthomson@nts.org.uk www.nts.org.uk

An 18th century walled garden developed as a garden of Scottish fruits and vegetables. There is also the American garden, Rhymer's Haugh woodland garden, loch and parkland to visit. An evening guided walk round the gardens with the Head Gardener (meeting in the Walled Garden). Learn about the collection of Scottish fruits and their cultivation, and exciting projects for the future. The evening will end with a three course dinner with produce from the kitchen garden and a glass of wine in the Victorian Tea Room.

Other Details: Dinner booking essential and must be booked by Wednesday 24 July. Self catering accommodation available. Fruit from the Fyvie garden may be available for sale.

Directions: Off A947 8miles SE of Turriff and 25miles NW of Aberdeen.

Disabled Access:
Full

Opening Times:
Friday 26 July
7:00pm - 10:00pm

Admission:
£26.00 includes guided walk, a 3 course dinner made with Fyvie produce and a glass of wine.

Charities:
Donation to SG Beneficiaries.

GLENKINDIE HOUSE
Glenkindie, Alford AB33 8SU
Mr & Mrs JP White

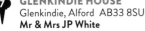

Large country garden containing herbaceous borders, rose beds, hedges and topiary surrounded by mature conifers and hardwoods.

Directions: On the A97 Alford/Strathdon road, 12 miles west of Alford.

Disabled Access:
Full

Opening Times:
Sunday 28 July
1:00pm - 5:00pm

Admission:
£4.00, concessions £3.00.

Charities:
Willow Foundation receives 40%, the net remaining to SG Beneficiaries.

GRANDHOME
Danestone, Aberdeen AB22 8AR
Mr & Mrs D R Paton T: 01224 722202
E: davidpaton@btconnect.com

18th century walled garden, incorporating rose garden (replanted 2010); policies with daffodils, tulips, rhododendrons, azaleas, mature trees and shrubs. At its best in April - October.

Directions: From north end of North Anderson Drive, continue on A90 over Persley Bridge, turning left at Tesco roundabout. 1¾ miles on left, through the pillars on a left hand bend.

Disabled Access:
Partial

Opening Times:
By arrangement on request

Admission:
£4.00, concessions £2.00

Charities:
Children 1st receives 40%, the net remaining to SG Beneficiaries.

GREENRIDGE
Craigton Road, Cults AB15 9PS
BP Exploration T: 01224 860200 or Fax 01224 860210
E: greenrid@bp.com

Large secluded garden surrounding 1840 Archibald Simpson house. For many years winner of Britain in Bloom 'Best Hidden Garden'. The garden includes mature specimen trees and shrubs, sloping walled rose garden and terraces and a kitchen garden.

Directions: Will be advised when booking.

Disabled Access:
Partial

Opening Times:
By arrangement on request

Admission:
£3.50

Charities:
Cancer Research Scotland receives 40%, the net remaining to SG Beneficiaries.

HADDO HOUSE
Methlick, Ellon AB41 7EQ
The National Trust for Scotland T: 0844 493 2179
E: haddo@nts.org.uk www.nts.org.uk

The Haddo Terrace Garden's geometric flower beds and fountain are being transformed through a lavish restoration. Meet the gardeners and learn about this exciting project. Visitors will also enjoy the secluded glades and knolls. A magnificent avenue of lime trees leads to adjacent Haddo country park with its lakes, monuments, walks and wildlife.

Other Details: Guided garden walks at 2:00pm, meet in courtyard. Light refreshments available in the courtyard.

Directions: Off B999 near Tarves, at 'Raxton' crossroads, 19m north of Aberdeen, 4m north of Pitmedden and 10m NW of Ellon. Cycle: 1m from NCN 1 Bus: Stagecoach Bluebird from Aberdeen bus station 01224 212666, c. 4mile walk.

Disabled Access:
Partial

Opening Times:
Wednesday 7 August
9:00am - 5:00pm
Sunday 18 August
9:00am - 5:00pm

Admission:
Guided tour £4.00 including NTS members. N.B. Prices correct at time of print

Charities:
Donation to SG Beneficiaries

HATTON CASTLE
Turriff AB53 8ED
Mr and Mrs James Duff T: 01888 562279
E: jjdgardens@btinternet.com

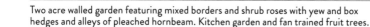

Two acre walled garden featuring mixed borders and shrub roses with yew and box hedges and alleys of pleached hornbeam. Kitchen garden and fan trained fruit trees. Lake and woodland walks.

Other Details: Teas and lunch parties available by arrangement.

Directions: On A947, 2 miles south of Turriff.

Disabled Access:
Full

Opening Times:
By arrangement on request

Admission:
£4.50, children free

Charities:
Juvenile Diabetes Research Foundation receives 40%, the net remaining to SG Beneficiaries.

HILLOCKHEAD
Glendeskry, Strathdon AB36 8XL
Stephen Campbell and Sue Macintosh

This garden is set against the stunning backdrop of Morven, at an altitude of 1300 feet, where wilderness meets cultivation. Wildflower areas, herbaceous borders, and organic fruit and vegetables are punctuated by numerous sit-ooteries, quiet corners and meandering dry stone dykes. There is an infinity pool for frogs, and probably the world's smallest grouse moor! Weather permitting this year there will be an extensive display of Alliums.

Directions: From Deeside, take A97 north for 9 miles, turn sharp left at crossroads. After ½ mile take first left at Ardgeith Fishings, go two miles, Hillockhead on right. Grass verge parking.

Disabled Access:
Partial

Opening Times:
Saturday 6 July
2:00pm - 5:00pm

Admission:
£3.00, concessions £2.50

Charities:
The Silver Circle receives 40%, the net remaining to SG Beneficiaries.

KILDRUMMY CASTLE GARDENS
Alford AB33 8RA
Kildrummy Garden Trust T: 01975 571203
www.kildrummy-castle-gardens.co.uk

April shows the gold of the lysichitons in the water garden and the small bulbs naturalised beside the copy of the 14th century Brig o' Balgownie. Rhododendrons and azaleas from April (frost permitting). September/October brings colchicums and brilliant colour with acers, fothergillas and viburnums.

Other Details: Children's play area.

Directions: On A97, 10 miles from Alford, 17 miles from Huntly. Car park free inside hotel main entrance. Coaches park up at hotel delivery entrance.

Disabled Access:
Partial

Opening Times:
Sunday 2 June
10:00am - 5:00pm
Sunday 29 September
10:00am - 5:00pm

Admission:
£4.50, concessions £4.00, children free

Charities:
Aberdeen Branch Multiple Sclerosis Society receives 40%, the net remaining to SG Beneficiaries.

LAUNDRY COTTAGE
Culdrain, Gartly, Huntly AB54 4PY
Simon and Judith McPhun T: 01466 720768
E: simon.mcphun@btinternet.com

An informal, cottage-style garden of about 1½ acres. Upper garden around the house of mixed borders, vegetables and fruit. Steep grass banks to the south and east are planted with native and non-native flowers, specimen trees and shrubs. Narrow grass paths, not suitable for wheelchairs, lead down to the River Bogie.

Directions: 4 miles south of Huntly on A97.

Disabled Access:
Partial

Opening Times:
By arrangement on request

Admission:
£3.00, children free

Charities:
Amnesty International receives 40%, the net remaining to SG Beneficiaries.

LEITH HALL
Huntly AB54 4NQ
The National Trust for Scotland T: 01464 831148
E: clow@nts.org.uk www.nts.org.uk

An open day and a series of evening guided tours with the head gardener. The west garden was made by Mr and The Hon Mrs Charles Leith-Hay around the beginning of the 20th century. In summer the magnificent zigzag herbaceous and serpentine catmint borders provide a dazzling display. A lot of project work is ongoing in the garden including a rose catenary along with large borders being redeveloped in a Gertrude Jekyll style and a Laburnum archway with spring interest borders.

Directions: On B9002 1 mile west of Kennethmont.

Disabled Access:
Partial

Opening Times:
Thursdays 30 May, 27 June & 29 August at 7:00pm
Sunday 21 July 1
2:00pm - 4:30pm

Admission:
£5.00 including NTS Members. N.B. Prices correct at time of going to print. Booking essential for all dates apart from 21 July.

Charities:
Donation to SG Beneficiaries.

MANSEFIELD
Alford AB33 8NL
Diane and Derek Neilson T: 019755 63086
E: info@mansefieldgarden.co.uk www.mansefieldgarden.co.uk

A 3 acre country garden which has been extensively replanted and developed over the past 10 years. Features include woodland gardens, a burnside walk as well as a more formal walled garden where homemade teas are served.

Directions: On A980 Alford/Lumphanan road, adjacent to Alford West Church.

Disabled Access:
Partial

Opening Times:
Sunday 30 June
2:00pm - 5:00pm

Admission:
£4.00, concessions £3.00, children under 12 free.

Charities:
Alford Car Transport Service receives 40%, the net remaining to SG Beneficiaries.

MIDDLE CAIRNCAKE
Cuminestown, Turriff AB53 5YS
Mr and Mrs N Orpwood

The garden has been planned and planted by the owners over the last six years. Features include a kitchen garden with soft fruit and vegetables, a greenhouse, herbaceous beds, heathers and a walled rose garden. New for 2013 is a polytunnel and a pond. It is a windy site with light, sandy soil. The walls have been built with stone dug from the garden.

Directions: Middle Cairncake is on the A9170 between New Deer and Cuminestown. It is clearly signposted.

Disabled Access:
Partial

Opening Times:
Saturday & Sunday 6/7 July
2:00pm - 5:00pm
Saturday & Sunday 20/21 July 2:00pm - 5:00pm

Admission:
£3.00

Charities:
RNLI receives 40%, the net remaining to SG Beneficiaries.

PITMEDDEN GARDEN
Ellon AB41 7PD
The National Trust for Scotland T: 0844 493 2177
E: sburgess@nts.org.uk www.nts.org.uk

Garden created by Sir Alexander Seton in 1675. Elaborate floral designs in parterres of box edging, inspired by the garden at the Palace of Holyroodhouse, have been recreated by the Trust. Fountains and sundials make fine centrepieces to the garden, filled in summer with forty thousand annual flowers. Also herb garden, herbaceous borders, trained fruit, museum of farming life, visitor centre, nature hut, woodland walk and wildlife garden. Meet and chat with our expert garden staff.

Other Details: Self catering accommodation available. Light refreshments available for purchase in the tearoom.

Directions: On A920, 1 mile west of Pitmedden village and 14 miles north of Aberdeen.

Disabled Access:
Partial

Opening Times:
Sunday 18 August
10:00am - 5:30pm

Admission:
£6.00, concessions £5.00, families £15.00. N.B. Prices correct at time of going to print.

Charities:
Donation to SG Beneficiaries.

PITSCURRY PROJECT
Whiteford, Pitcaple, Inverurie AB51 5DY
Aberdeenshire Council T: 01467 681773

Aberdeenshire Council, together with PEP Ltd and local industry have created a 6 acre garden providing work experience for adults with learning disabilities. The gardens are fully accessible and are divided into several themed areas: sensory, heritage, wildlife and production. There are also displays of sculpture, art and crafts, hand crafted garden furniture and recycling activities.

Other Details: Disabled access toilets and changing facilities available.

Directions: The site is located next to Pitcaple Quarry which is sign-posted from most local junctions. Be wary of using the postcode in a satnav as it covers a number of properties.

Disabled Access:
Full

Opening Times:
Saturday 3 August to Sunday 11 August 10:00am - 3:00pm

Admission:
£4.00

Charities:
Pitcaple Environmental Project receives 40%, the net remaining to SG Beneficiaries.

TILLYPRONIE
Tarland AB34 4XX
The Hon Philip Astor T: 01339 881529, M: 07796 946309

Late Victorian house for which Queen Victoria laid a foundation stone. Herbaceous borders, terraced garden, heather beds, water garden and new rockery. New Golden Jubilee garden still being laid out. Shrubs and ornamental trees, including pinetum with rare specimens. There is a fruit garden and greenhouses as well as superb views from the garden.
In June there is a wonderful show of azaleas and spring heathers.

Other Details: Plant stall June opening only. Homemade teas June opening, cream teas August opening.

Directions: Off A97 between Ballater and Strathdon.

Disabled Access:
Partial

Opening Times:
Sunday 2 June
2:00pm - 5:00pm
Sunday 25 August
2:00pm - 5:00pm
Also by arrangement on request

Admission:
£5.00, children £2.00.

Charities:
All proceeds to SG Beneficiaries.

WESTHALL CASTLE
Oyne, Inverurie AB52 6RW
**Mr Gavin Farquhar and Mrs Pam Burney
E: enquiries@ecclesgreig.com**

Set in an ancient landscape in the foothills of the impressive foreboding hill of Bennachie. A circular walk through glorious daffodils with outstanding views. Interesting garden in early stages of restoration, with large groupings of rhododendrons and specimen trees. Westhall Castle is a 16thC. tower house, incorporating a 13thC building of the bishops of Aberdeen. There were additions in the 17th, 18th & 19thC. The castle is semi derelict, but stabilized from total dereliction. A fascinating house encompassing 600 years of alteration and additions.

Directions: Marked from the A96 at Old Rayne and from Oyne village.

Disabled Access:
Partial

Opening Times:
Sunday 14 April
1:00pm - 4:00pm

Admission:
£4.00, children under 12 free.

Charities:
Bennachie Guides receives 40%, the net remaining to SG Beneficiaries.

ANGUS

Scotland's Gardens 2013 Guidebook is sponsored by INVESTEC WEALTH & INVESTMENT

District Organiser

| Mrs Terrill Dobson | Logie House, Kirriemuir DD8 5PN |

Area Organisers

Mrs Helen Brunton	Cuthlie Farm, Arbroath DD11 2NT
Mrs Katie Dessain	Lawton House, Inverkeilor, by Arbroath DD11 4RU
Mrs Susan Macgregor	Lundie Castle, Edzell DD9 7QW
Mrs Rosanne Porter	West Scryne, By Carnoustie DD7 6LL
Mrs Sue Smith	Balintore House, Balintore, by Kirriemuir DD8 5JS
Mrs Gladys Stewart	Ugie-Bank, Ramsay Street, Edzell DD9 7TT
Mrs Annabel Stormonth Darling	Lednathie, Glen Prosen, Kirriemuir DD8 4RR
Mrs Tracey Williams	Alma Lodge, 51 Duncan Road, Letham DD8 2PN

Treasurer

| Mrs Mary Stansfeld | Dunninald, By Montrose DD10 9TD |

Gardens open on a specific date

Dunninald, Montrose	Saturday 23 February	12:00pm - 5:00pm
Dunninald, Montrose	Sunday 24 February	12:00pm - 5:00pm
Brechin Castle, Brechin	Sunday 5 May	2:00pm - 5:00pm
Dalfruin, Kirriemuir	Sunday 12 May	2:00pm - 5:00pm
Dunninald, Montrose	Sunday 19 May	2:00pm - 5:00pm
Gallery, Montrose	Sunday 26 May	2:00pm - 5:00pm
Cortachy Castle, by Kirriemuir	Sunday 2 June	2:00pm - 6:00pm
Letham Village	Sunday 16 June	12:00pm - 6:00pm
Edzell Village & Castle	Sunday 23 June	1:00pm - 5:00pm
Newtonmill House, by Brechin	Sunday 30 June	2:00pm - 5:00pm
Montrose and Hillside Gardens	Sunday 7 July	1:00pm - 6:00pm
Gallery, Montrose	Saturday 13 July	2:00pm - 5:00pm
The Walled Garden at Logie, Logie House, Kirriemuir	Sunday 28 July	2:00pm - 5:00pm

Gardens open regularly

Dunninald, Montrose	29 Jun - 28 Jul, except Mons	12:00pm - 5:00pm
Pitmuies Gardens, Guthrie	2 February - 17 March	10:00am - 5:00pm
	& 1 April - 31 October	10:00am - 5:00pm

ANGUS

Gardens open by arrangement

Cortachy Castle, by Kirriemuir	On request	01575 570108
Dunninald, Montrose	On request	01674 672031
Kirkside of Lochty, Menmuir, by Brechin	On request	01356 660431

Cortachy Castle

Key to symbols

New in 2013	Homemade teas	Accommodation
Teas	Dogs on a lead allowed	Plant stall
Cream teas	Wheelchair access	Scottish Snowdrop Festival

Garden locations

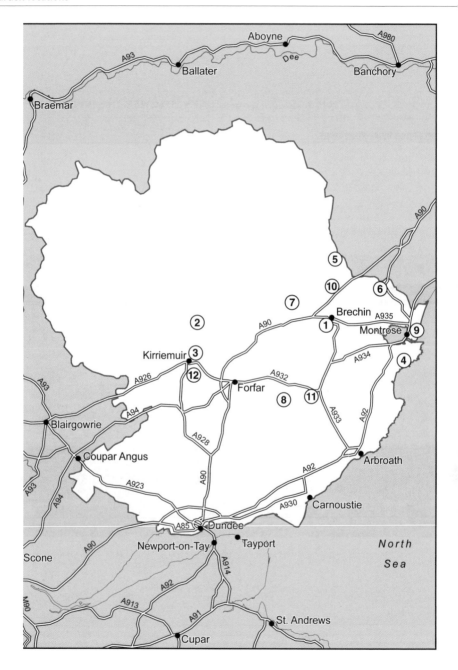

BRECHIN CASTLE
Brechin DD9 6SG
The Earl and Countess of Dalhousie T: 01356 624566
E: mandyferries@dalhousieestates.co.uk www.dalhousieestates.co.uk

The uniquely curving walls of the garden at Brechin Castle are just the first of many delightful surprises in store. The luxurious blend of ancient and modern plantings is the second. Find charm and splendour in the wide gravelled walks, secluded small paths and corners. May sees the rhododendrons and azaleas hit the peak of their flowering to wonderful effect; and with complementary under-planting and a framework of great and beautiful trees to set the collection in the landscape. This is a lovely garden at any time of year and a knock-out in the spring.

Other Details: Tombola and childrens activities. Dogs on leads please.

Directions: A90 southernmost exit to Brechin, 1 mile past Brechin Castle Centre, castle gates on right.

Disabled Access:
Partial

Opening Times:
Sunday 5 May
2:00pm - 5:00pm

Admission:
£4.00, OAPs £3.00,
accompanied children free.

Charities:
Dalhousie Day Care receives 20%, Unicorn Preservation Society receives 20%, the net remaining to SG Beneficiaries.

CORTACHY CASTLE
Cortachy, By Kirriemuir DD8 4LX
The Earl and Countess of Airlie T: 01575 570108
E: office@airlieestates.com www.airlieestates.com

16th century castellated house. Additions in 1872 by David Bryce. Spring garden and wild pond garden with a mass of azaleas, primroses and rhododendrons. Garden of fine American species trees and river walk along South Esk.

Other Details: Pipe band. Ice creams.

Directions: B955 Kirriemuir 5 miles.

Disabled Access:
None

Opening Times:
Sunday 2 June
2:00pm - 6:00pm
Also by arrangement on request

Admission:
£5.00, accompanied children free.

Charities:
Arbroath Lifeboats RNLI receives 40%, the net remaining to SG Beneficiaries.

DALFRUIN
Kirktonhill Road, Kirriemuir DD8 4HU
Mr & Mrs James A Welsh

A well-stocked connoisseur's garden of about one-third of an acre situated at end of a short cul-de-sac. There are many less common plants like varieties of trilliums, meconopsis (blue poppies), tree peonies (descendants of ones collected by George Sherriff and grown at Ascreavie), dactylorhiza and codonopsis. There is a scree and collection of ferns. Vigorous climbing roses, Kiftsgate and Paul's Himalayan Musk, grow over pergolas. Interconnected ponds encourage wildlife.

Other Details: Good plant stall which may include trilliums, meconopsis and tree peonies. Teas served at St Mary's Episcopal Church.

Directions: From centre of Kirriemuir turn left up Roods. Kirktonhill Rd is on left near top of hill. Please park on Roods or at St Mary's Episcopal Church. Disabled parking only in Kirktonhill Road.

Disabled Access:
Full

Opening Times:
Sunday 12 May
2:00pm - 5:00pm

Admission:
£3.00, accompanied children free.

Charities:
St Mary's Episcopal Church receives 40%, the net remaining to SG Beneficiaries.

DUNNINALD
Montrose DD10 9TD
The Stansfeld Family T: 01674 672031
E: visitorinformation@dunninald.com   www.dunninald.com

Dunninald is a family home built in 1824, set in policies developed during the seventeenth and eighteenth centuries. It offers many attractive features to the visitor including a beech avenue planted around 1670. Snowdrops in spring and bluebells in May carpet the woods and wild garden. At its best in July, the highlight of Dunninald is the walled garden planted with traditional mixed borders, vegetables, soft fruits, fruit trees and a greenhouse.

Other Details: Castle open 29 June - 28 July 1:00pm-5:00pm (closed Mondays).

Directions: 2 miles south of Montrose, signposted off A92 Arbroath/Montrose road (Turning marked Usan).

Disabled Access:
Partial

Opening Times:
Sat & Sun 23/24 Feb.
12:00pm - 5:00pm for
Snowdrop Festival
Sunday 19 May 2:00pm -
5:00pm for Bluebell Sunday
29 June to 28 July except
Mondays 12:00pm - 5:00pm
By arrangement on request

Admission:
£4.00, accomp. children free.

Charities:
All proceeds to SG
Beneficiaries.

EDZELL VILLAGE & CASTLE
EdzellDD9 7TT
The Gardeners of Edzell & Historic Scotland

Walk round several fabulous and different gardens in Edzell village including those of Edzell Castle.

Other Details: Tickets are on sale in the village and a map will be issued with the tickets.

Directions: On B966.

Disabled Access:
Full

Opening Times:
Sunday 23 June
1:00pm - 5:00pm

Admission:
£4.00, accompanied children free.

Charities:
Stracathro Cancer Care
Fund UK receives 40%,
the net remaining to SG
Beneficiaries.

GALLERY
Montrose DD10 9LA
Mr John Simson
E: galleryhf@googlemail.com

Redesign and replanting of this historic garden have preserved and extended its traditional framework of holly, privet and box. A grassed central alley, embellished with circles, links themed gardens, incl. a fine collection of old roses, yellow and blue floral borders of the entrance garden and the fountain and pond in the formal white garden. A walk through the woodland garden, home to rare breed sheep, with its extensive border of mixed heathers, leads to the river North Esk. From there rough paths lead both ways along the bank.

Directions: From A90 south of Northwater Bridge take exit to Hillside and next left to Gallery & Marykirk. From A937 west of rail underpass follow signs to Gallery & Northwater Bridge.

Disabled Access:
Partial

Opening Times:
Sunday 26 May
2:00pm - 5:00pm
Saturday 13 July
2:00pm - 5:00pm

Admission:
£4.00, accompanied children free.

Charities:
Practical Action receives
40%, the net remaining to
SG Beneficiaries.

KIRKSIDE OF LOCHTY
Menmuir, by Brechin DD9 6RY
James & Irene Mackie T: 01356 660431

The garden contains a large collection of plants, several rare and unusual, also many different varieties of ferns. It is approached by a strip of woodland and expands into various compartments in an overall area of two acres, part of which is cultivated as a flowering meadow.

Other Details: No dogs allowed.

Directions: Leave the A90 two miles south of Brechin and take the road to Menmuir. After a further two miles pass a wood on the left and a long beech hedge in front of the house.

Disabled Access:
None

Opening Times:
By arrangement on request

Admission:
£3.50, accompanied children free.

Charities:
All proceeds to SG Beneficiaries.

LETHAM VILLAGE
Letham DD8 2PD
Letham Gardening Club

Be inspired by the diverse range of gardens from cottage style to shady gardens to small gardens and those newly developed by keen gardeners.

Other Details: Tickets and maps available in village with teas and plant stall at the Scout Hall, Auldbar Road (opposite the village hall).

Directions: From north take A90 exiting for Forfar town centre, then take A932 towards Arbroath and pickup signs to Letham. From south via Dundee take B978 Kellas/Wellbank Road, pick up signs.

Disabled Access:
Partial

Opening Times:
Sunday 16 June
12:00pm - 6:00pm

Admission:
£4.00, accompanied children free.

Charities:
1st Letham & Dunnichen Scouting Group receives 40%, the net remaining to SG Beneficiaries.

MONTROSE AND HILLSIDE GARDENS
Montrose DD10 8SB
Montrose & Hillside Gardeners

An eclectic mix of fascinating and sometimes hidden gardens in Montrose and neighbouring Hillside. These range from older established gardens to newly designed and planted. In 2012 Straton House won a national award. Parking around the town.

Other Details: No dogs allowed. Refreshments available at various gardens. Tickets and maps available at The Croft, Main Street, Hillside, DD10 9HZ; Dorward House, 24 Dorward Road, Montrose, DD10 8SB; and, Straton House, 10 Castle Place, Montrose, DD10 8AL.

Directions: Approach Montrose on A92 or A90 via Brechin.

Disabled Access:
Partial

Opening Times:
Sunday 7 July
1:00pm - 6:00pm

Admission:
£4.00, accompanied children free.

Charities:
Dorward House receives 40%, the net remaining to SG Beneficiaries.

NEWTONMILL HOUSE
By Brechin DD9 7PZ
Mr & Mrs S Rickman

Newtonmill House looks over and into the semi-formal walled garden. The entrance to the garden is through a wrought iron gate that reflects the mill wheel from which Newtonmill derives its name. The central pathway is flagged by herbaceous borders, sheltered by a fine prunus pissardi hedge. The garden is divided into four squares of vegetables, fruit, spring garden and croquet lawn with summer house. The construction of an autumn garden in this area will involve work in progress. Through the rose arch at the south end of the garden are peony and shrub rose beds, a small pond area and doocot. Adjacent to the house is a rose-garlanded terrace and raised beds.

Directions: From A90, exit B966 Brechin/Edzell towards Edzell.

Disabled Access:
Full

Opening Times:
Sunday 30 June
2:00pm - 5:00pm

Admission:
£4.00, accompanied children free.

Charities:
RNLI (Montrose) receives 40%, the net remaining to SG Beneficiaries.

PITMUIES GARDENS
House of Pitmuies, Guthrie, By Forfar DD8 2SN
Mrs Farquhar Ogilvie

Two semi-formal wall gardens adjoin 18th century house and shelter long borders of herbaceous perennials, superb delphiniums, old fashioned roses and pavings with violas and dianthus. Spacious lawns, river and lochside walks beneath fine trees. A wide variety of shrubs with good autumn colours. Interesting picturesque turreted doocot and 'Gothick' wash-house. Myriad spring bulbs include carpets of crocus following the massed snowdrops.

Directions: A932. Friockheim 1½ miles.

Disabled Access:
Partial

Opening Times:
2 February to 17 March
10:00am - 5:00pm for the Snowdrop Festival
1 April to 31 October
10:00am - 5:00pm

Admission:
£3.50, accompanied children free

Charities:
Donation to SG Beneficiaries.

THE WALLED GARDEN AT LOGIE
Logie House, Logie, Kirriemuir DD8 5PN
Gavin & Terrill Dobson
www.angusherbalists.co.uk

This Herbalists's garden is set amid an 18th century walled garden and large Victorian greenhouse within Logie's organic farm. Featuring more than 150 herbs, the physick garden is divided into 8 rectangles including medicinal herbs for different body systems. All the herbs are labelled with a brief description of actions to help novices learn more about this ancient art. The garden also features a Herbaceous border and productive Fruit & Vegetable garden.

Directions: From the A926 leaving Kirriemuir, fork left at Beechwood Place onto the single track road (or if approaching Kirrie take sharp left after "Welcome to Kirriemuir sign". Take the first left and follow signs to The Walled Garden.

Disabled Access:
Partial

Opening Times:
Sunday 28 July
2:00pm - 5:00pm

Admission:
£3.00, accompanied children free.

Charities:
Trellis (supporting health through horticulture) receives 40%, the net remaining to SG Beneficiaries.

ARGYLL

District Organiser

Minette Struthers	Ardmaddy Castle, Balvicar, By Oban PA34 4QY

Area Organisers

Mrs G Cadzow	Duachy, Kilninver, Oban PA34 4RH
Mrs E B Ingleby	Braighbhaille, Crarae, Inveraray PA32 8YA
Mary Lindsay	Dal an Eas, Kilmore, Oban PA34 4XU
Mrs P McArthur	Bute Cottage, Newton, Strachlachan PA27 8DB

Treasurer

Minette Struthers	Ardmaddy Castle, Balvicar, By Oban PA34 4QY

Gardens open on a specific date

Stratholm, Clachan	Saturday 20 April	10:00am	-	5:00pm
Benmore Botanic Garden, Benmore	Sunday 21 April	10:00am	-	6:00pm
Crarae Garden, Inveraray	Sunday 21 April	10:00am	-	5:00pm
Stratholm, Clachan	Sunday 21 April	10:00am	-	5:00pm
Kames Bay, Kilmelford	Saturday 4 May	12:00pm	-	5:00pm
Maolachy's Garden, Lochavich	Saturday 4 May	12:00pm	-	5:00pm
Kames Bay, Kilmelford	Sunday 5 May	12:00pm	-	5:00pm
Maolachy's Garden, Lochavich	Sunday 5 May	12:00pm	-	5:00pm
Knock Cottage, Lochgair	Saturday 11 May	1:00pm	-	5:30pm
Arduaine, Oban	Sunday 12 May	9:30am	-	6:00pm
Knock Cottage, Lochgair	Sunday 12 May	1:00pm	-	5:30pm
Colintraive Gardens	Saturday 18 May	1:00pm	-	5:00pm
Drim na Vullin, Lochgilphead	Saturday 18 May	2:00pm	-	5:00pm
Knock Cottage, Lochgair	Saturday 18 May	1:00pm	-	5:30pm
Colintraive Gardens, Colintraive	Sunday 19 May	1:00pm	-	5:00pm
Drim na Vullin, Lochgilphead	Sunday 19 May	2:00pm	-	5:00pm
Knock Cottage, Lochgair	Sunday 19 May	1:00pm	-	5:30pm
Dal an Eas and Dalnaneun, Kilmore	Saturday 22 June	1:30pm	-	6:00pm
Dal an Eas and Dalnaneun, Kilmore	Sunday 23 June	1:30pm	-	6:00pm
Seafield, Hunter's Quay, Dunoon	Saturday 13 July	2:00pm	-	5:00pm
Seafield, Hunter's Quay, Dunoon	Sunday 14 July	2:00pm	-	5:00pm
Crarae Garden, Inveraray	Sunday 21 July	10:00am	-	5:00pm

ARGYLL

Scotland's Gardens 2013 Guidebook is sponsored by **INVESTEC WEALTH & INVESTMENT**

Barochreal, Kilninver, Oban	Saturday 27 July	12:00pm	- 5:00pm
Maolachy's Garden, Lochavich	Saturday 27 July	2:00pm	- 5:00pm
Melfort House Kitchen Garden, Kilmelford, by Oban	Saturday 27 July	2:00pm	- 5:00pm
Ardchattan Priory, North Connel	Sunday 28 July	12:00pm	- 4:00pm
Barochreal, Kilninver, Oban	Sunday 28 July	12:00pm	- 5:00pm
Maolachy's Garden, Lochavich	Sunday 28 July	2:00pm	- 5:00pm
Melfort House Kitchen Garden, Kilmelford, by Oban	Sunday 28 July	2:00pm	- 5:00pm

Gardens open regularly

An Cala, Ellenabeich, Isle of Seil	1 April - 31 October	10:00am	- 6:00pm
Ardchattan Priory, North Connel	25 March - 31 October	9:30am	- 5:30pm
Ardkinglas Woodland Garden, Cairndow	Daily	Dawn	- Dusk
Ardmaddy Castle, by Oban	Daily	9:00am	- Dusk
Barguillean's "Angus Garden", Taynuilt	Daily	9:00am	- Dusk
Benmore Botanic Garden, Benmore, Dunoon	1 March - 31 October	10:00am	- 6:00pm
Crinan Hotel Garden, Crinan	1 May - 31 August	Dawn	- Dusk
Druimneil House, Port Appin	29 March - 31 October	Dawn	- Dusk
Fairwinds, Hunter's Quay, Dunoon	All summer	9:00am	- 6:00pm
Inveraray Castle Gardens, Inveraray	29 March - 31 October	10:00am	- 5:45pm
Kinlochlaich House Gardens, Appin	Daily	9:30am	- 5:00pm
Oakbank, Ardrishaig	1 May - 31 August	10:30am	- 5:30pm

Gardens open by arrangement

Knock Cottage, Lochgair	15 April - 15 June	01546 886331

Key to symbols

	New in 2013		Homemade teas		Accommodation
	Teas		Dogs on a lead allowed		Plant stall
	Cream teas		Wheelchair access		Scottish Snowdrop Festival

Garden locations

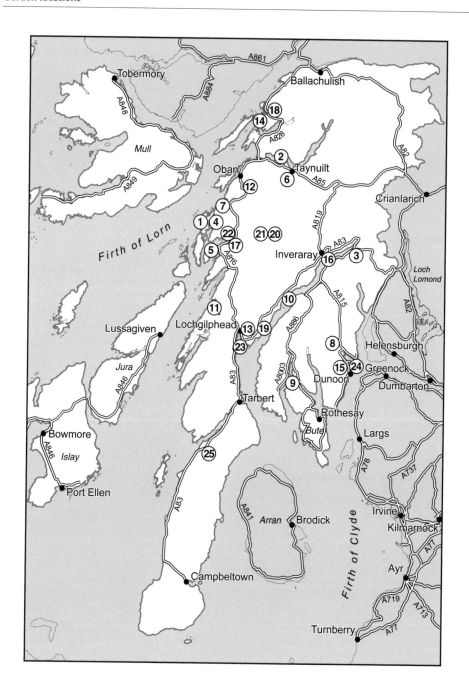

AN CALA
Ellenabeich, Isle of Seil PA34 4RF
Mrs Thomas Downie T: 01852 300237
www.gardens-of-argyll.co.uk

A wonderful example of a 1930s designed garden, An Cala sits snugly in its horseshoe shelter of surrounding cliffs. A spectacular and very pretty garden with streams, waterfall, ponds, many herbaceous plants as well as azaleas, rhododendrons and cherry trees in spring. Archive material of Mawson's design found recently.

Directions: Proceed south from Oban on Campbeltown road for 8 miles, turn right at Easdale sign, a further 8 miles on B844; garden between school and village.

Disabled Access:
Partial

Opening Times:
1 April to 31 October
10:00am - 6:00pm

Admission:
£3.50

Charities:
Cancer Research UK receives 40%, the net remaining to SG Beneficiaries.

ARDCHATTAN PRIORY
North Connel PA37 1RQ
Mrs Sarah Troughton T: 01796 481355
E: sh.troughton@virgin.net www.gardens-of-argyll.co.uk

Beautifully situated on the north side of Loch Etive. In front of the house there is a rockery, extensive herbaceous and rose borders, with excellent views over the loch. West of the house there are shrub borders and a wild garden, numerous roses and over 30 different varieties of sorbus providing excellent autumn colour. The Priory, founded in 1230, is now a private house. The ruins of the chapel and graveyard, with fine early stones, are in the care of Historic Scotland and open with the garden.

Other Details: Garden fete, homemade teas, catering, plant and other stalls on 28th July only.

Directions: Oban 10 miles. From north, left off A828 at Barcaldine onto B845 for 6 miles. From East/Oban on A85, cross Connel Bridge and turn first right, proceed east on Bonawe Road. Well signed.

Disabled Access:
Partial

Opening Times:
Sunday 28 July
12:00pm - 4:00pm
25 March to 31 October
9:30am - 5:30pm

Admission:
£3.50

Charities:
Donation to SG Beneficiaries

ARDKINGLAS WOODLAND GARDEN
Cairndow PA26 8BH
Ardkinglas Estate T: 01499 600261
www.ardkinglas.com

In a peaceful setting overlooking Loch Fyne the garden contains one of the finest collections of rhododendrons and conifers in Britain. This includes the tallest tree in Britain, a 'Grand Fir' measured at over 64 metres. as well as many other champion trees. Gazebo with unique "Scriptorium" based around a collection of literary quotes. Woodland lochan, ancient mill ruins and many woodland walks. Visit Scotland 3* garden.

Other Details: Champion Trees: 'Grand Fir' tallest tree in Britain and other champion trees.   Nearby Tree Shop offers take-away food.

Directions: Entrance through Cairndow village off A83 Loch Lomond/Inveraray road.

Disabled Access:
Partial

Opening Times:
Daily Dawn - Dusk

Admission:
£4.50, concessions £3.50, children under 16 free, season ticket available for £16.00

Charities:
Donation to SG Beneficiaries

ARDMADDY CASTLE
By Oban PA34 4QY
Mr & Mrs Charles Struthers T: 01852 300353
E: ardmaddycastle@btinternet.com www.gardens-of-argyll.co.uk

Ardmaddy Castle gardens, in a most spectacular setting, are shielded to the north by mature woodlands, carpeted with bluebells and daffodils and protected from the Atlantic winds by the elevated Castle. The Walled Garden is full of magnificent rhododendrons, some huge, an increasing collection of rare and unusual shrubs and plants, the 'Clock Garden' with its cutting flowers, fruit and vegetables grown with labour saving formality, all within dwarf box hedging. Beyond, a woodland walk, with its amazing hydrangea climbing to 60 feet, leads to the water gardens - in early summer a riot of candelabra primulas, irises, rodgersias and other damp loving plants and grasses. Lovely autumn colour. A garden for all seasons.

Disabled Access:
Full

Opening Times:
Daily 9:00am - Dusk

Admission:
£4.00, children free.

Charities:
Donation to SG Beneficiaries

Other Details: Stall for veg. and summer fruits in season. Toilet suitable for disabled. Six self catering cottages, details can be found at www.ardmaddy.com.

Directions: Take A816 south of Oban for 8 miles. Turn right B844 to Seil Island/ Easdale. 4 miles on, take Ardmaddy road for further 2 miles.

ARDUAINE
Oban PA34 4XQ
The National Trust for Scotland T: 0844 493 2216
E: mwilkins@nts.org.uk www.nts.org.uk

Outstanding twenty acre coastal garden created over a 100 years ago on the south facing slope of a promontory separating Asknish Bay from Loch Melfort. This remarkable hidden paradise, protected by tall shelterbelts and influenced favourably by the North Atlantic Drift, grows a wide variety of plants from all over the globe. Internationally known for the rhododendron species collection, the garden also features magnolias, camellias, azaleas and other wonderful trees and shrubs, many being tender and rarely seen. A broad selection of perennials, bulbs, ferns and water plants ensure year-long interest.

Disabled Access:
Partial

Opening Times:
Sunday 12 May
9:30am - 6:00pm

Admission:
£6.00 including NTS members N.B. These prices are correct at the time of going to print.

Charities:
Donation to SG Beneficiaries

Other Details: Garden staff walks at 11:00am and 2:30pm. Teas in local hotel.

Directions: Off A816 Oban-Lochgilphead, sharing an entrance with the Loch Melfort Hotel.

BARGUILLEAN'S "ANGUS GARDEN"
Taynuilt PA35 1HY
The Josephine Marshall Trust T: 01866 822333
E: info@barguillean.co.uk www.barguillean.co.uk

Nine acre woodland garden around an eleven acre loch set in the Glen Lonan hills. Spring flowering shrubs and bulbs, extensive collection of rhododendron hybrids, deciduous azaleas, conifers and unusual trees. The garden contains a large collection of North American rhododendron hybrids from famous contemporary plant breeders. Some paths can be steep. Three marked walks from thirty minutes to one and a half hours.

Disabled Access:
None

Opening Times:
1 January to 31 December
9:00am - Dusk

Admission:
£3.00, under 14 free.

Charities:
Donation to SG Beneficiaries

Other Details: Self catering accommodation in traditional farmhouse. Coach Tours by arrangement - contact Sean Honeyman T: 01866 822335.

Directions: 3 miles south off A85 Glasgow/Oban road at Taynuilt; road marked Glen Lonan; 3 miles up single track road; turn right at sign.

BAROCHREAL (JOINT OPENING WITH MAOLACHY'S GARDEN & MELFORT HOUSE)
Kilninver, Oban, Argyll PA34 4UT
Nigel & Antoinette Mitchell T: 01852 316 151
E: toni@themitchells.co.uk www.Barochreal.co.uk

A young garden evolving since 2006. After much fencing, stone clearing and rewalling, digging and ditching, each year another area has been completed to give a bank of rhodies and azaleas, a rose garden, water feature with rockery, a small pond, raised vegetable beds and a wild garden with beehives, waterfall and burn. The two hard winters of 2010/11 and 2011/12 destroyed many plants in their infancy which are being replaced and constantly added to.

Other Details: Homemade teas served at Melfort House.

Directions: On the A816 Oban to Lochgilphead road just to the south of the village of Kilninver on the left hand side of the road.

Disabled Access:
Partial

Opening Times:
Saturday 27 July
2:00pm - 5:00pm
Sunday 28 July
2:00pm - 5:00pm

Admission:
£3.00

Charities:
Argyll Animal Aid receives 40%, the net remaining to SG Beneficiaries.

BENMORE BOTANIC GARDEN
Benmore, Dunoon PA23 8QU
Regional Garden of the Royal Botanic Garden Edinburgh T: 01369 706261
E: benmore@rbge.org.uk www.rbge.org.uk

World famous for magnificent conifers and its extensive range of flowering trees and shrubs, including over 250 species of rhododendron. From a spectacular avenue of Giant Redwoods numerous marked walks lead, via a formal garden and pond, through hillside woodlands to a dramatic viewpoint overlooking the Eachaig valley and the Holy Loch. The newly restored Benmore Fernery is open from 11:00am, closing an hour before the Garden closes. Guided tours Tue, Wed, Thu & Sun at 2:00pm.

Directions: 7 miles north of Dunoon or 22 miles south from Glen Kinglass below Rest and Be Thankful pass. On A815.

Disabled Access:
Partial

Opening Times:
Sunday 21 April
10:00am - 6:00pm
1 March to 31 October
10:00am - 6:00pm

Admission:
£5.50, concessions £4.50, children £1.00, family ticket (2 adults and up to 4 children) £11.00.

Charities:
Donation to SG Beneficiaries

COLINTRAIVE GARDENS
Colintraive PA22 3AR
The Gardeners of Colintraive

Two delightful and varied spring gardens in this very beautiful corner of Argyll - within easy reach of each other on the old B866 shore road looking out over Loch Riddon and the Kyles of Bute. The gardens are Altavoil (Mrs Caroline Sinclair) and Caol Ruadh (Mr and Mrs C Scotland). Caol Ruadh has the additional attraction of a unique outdoor sculpture park featuring works from a variety of Scottish artists.

Other Details: Tickets can be obtained at both gardens. Teas in community hall beside community gardens.

Directions: A815 and A866 (Dunoon 20 miles via B836, Strachur 22 miles).

Disabled Access:
None

Opening Times:
Saturday 18 May
1:00pm - 5:00pm
Sunday 19 May
1:00pm - 5:00pm

Admission:
£4.00 (includes both gardens), children free.

Charities:
All proceeds to SG Beneficiaries

CRARAE GARDEN
Inveraray PA32 8YA
The National Trust for Scotland T: 0844 4932210
E: nprice@nts.org.uk   www.nts.org.uk

A spectacular 50 acre garden in a dramatic setting. Crarae has a wonderful collection of woody plants centred on the Crarae Burn, which is spanned by several bridges and tumbles through a rocky gorge in a series of cascades. A wide variety of shrubs and trees chosen for spring flowering and autumn colour grow in the shelter of towering conifers. The lush naturalistic planting and rushing water gives the garden the feel of a valley in the Himalayas.

Other Details: National Plant Collection ®: Nothofagus (Southern Beech). This colliection is the most northerly of its type in the UK. Sturdy footwear is recommended.

Directions: On A83 10 miles south of Inveraray.

Disabled Access:
Partial

Opening Times:
Sunday 21 April
10:00am - 5:00pm
Sunday 21 July
10:00am - 5:00pm

Admission:
£6.00 including NTS members. Price includes behind the scenes guided walks. N.B. Prices correct at time of going to print.

Charities:
Donation to SG Beneficiaries

CRINAN HOTEL GARDEN
Crinan PA31 8SR
Mr & Mrs N Ryan T: 01546 830261
E: nryan@crinanhotel.com   www.crinanhotel.com

Small rock garden with azaleas and rhododendrons created into a steep hillside over a century ago with steps leading to a sheltered, secluded garden with sloping lawns, herbaceous beds and spectacular views of the canal and Crinan Loch.

Other Details: Raffle of painting by Frances Macdonald (Ryan), tickets at coffee shop, art gallery and hotel. Homemade teas available in the coffee shop.

Directions: Lochgilphead A83, then A816 to Oban, then A841 Cairnbaan to Crinan.

Disabled Access:
None

Opening Times:
1 May to 31 August
Dawn - Dusk

Admission:
By donation

Charities:
Feedback Madagascar receives 40%, the net remaining to SG Beneficiaries.

DAL AN EAS AND DALNANEUN
Kilmore, Oban PA34 4XU
Mary Lindsay and Ms C Boswell T: 01631 770 246 or 209
E: dalaneas@live.com

Recently created informal country garden with the aim of increasing the biodiversity of native plants and insects while adding interest and colour with introduced trees, shrubs and naturalised perennials. It has a structured garden with pond, a burn with pool, wildflower meadow with 5 different species of native orchid and a vegetable plot. Grass paths lead to waterfalls, views and ancient archaeological sites. The enclosed garden of Dalnaneun is accessed through the Dal an Eas garden and comprises lawns, flowerbeds, vegetables and herbs. A burn runs through the garden and local stone has been imaginatively used for various features.

Other Details: Sturdy footwear is recommended.

Directions: Take A816 to Kilmore turn (3½ miles S of Oban) on the road marked Barran and Musdale. Keep left at junction. Follow the Connel road. Dal an Eas is on the left over the cattle grid.

Disabled Access:
Partial

Opening Times:
Saturday 22 June
1:30pm - 6:00pm
Sunday 23 June
1:30pm - 6:00pm

Admission:
£4.00

Charities:
Mary's Meals receives 40%, the net remaining to SG Beneficiaries.

DRIM NA VULLIN

Blarbuie Road, Lochgilphead PA31 8LE
Mr & Mrs Robin Campbell Byatt T: 01546 602615
E: byatt.drim@virgin.net

Drim na Vullin, originally a mill, and its woodland garden have been owned by the same family since 1829. Most of the development of the garden was landscaped and planted in the 1950s by Sybil Campbell OBE, Britain's first female professional magistrate, assisted by Percy Cane the garden designer. It lies along a cleft formed by the Cuilarstitch Burn with a spectacular waterfall at the top. Mature species and hybrid rhododendrons, magnolias, azaleas and other shrubs are under a canopy of mostly native trees. The present owners' planting brings the developed area to about 5 acres.

Directions: A83 to Lochgilphead. At the top of main street in front of parish church, turn right up Manse Brae. The garden is ⅓ mile up hill on left. Beyond the houses on left a high fence leads to Drim na Vullin's entrance. Please park on road.

Disabled Access:
None

Opening Times:
Saturday 18 May
2:00pm - 5:00pm
Sunday 19 May
2:00pm - 5:00pm

Admission:
£3.00

Charities:
Christchurch Episcopal Church, Lochgilphead receives 40%, the net remaining to SG Beneficiaries.

DRUIMNEIL HOUSE

Port Appin PA38 4DQ
Mrs J Glaisher (Gardener: Mr Andrew Ritchie) T: 01631 730228

Large garden overlooking Loch Linnhe with many fine varieties of mature trees and rhododendrons and other woodland shrubs. Nearer the house, an impressive bank of deciduous azaleas is underplanted with a block of camassia and a range of other bulbs. A small Victorian walled garden is currently being restored.

Other Details: Teas normally available. Lunch by prior arrangement.

Directions: Turn in for Appin off A828 (Connel/Fort William Road). 2 miles, sharp left at Airds Hotel, second house on right.

Disabled Access:
None

Opening Times:
29 March to 31 October
Dawn - Dusk

Admission:
By donation

Charities:
Donation to SG Beneficiaries

FAIRWINDS

14 George Street, Hunter's Quay, Dunoon PA23 8JU
Mrs Carol Stewart T: 01369 702666
E: carol.argyll@talk21.com

This mature garden was created in the fifties from a small orchard. The present owner is constantly trying to add colour and interest for all seasons. Spring brings a flourish of spring flowers, rhododendrons and azaleas. Trees of all kinds display their constantly changing shades throughout the year and in autumn the acers and copper beech are at their very best. Around every corner there is yet another plant of interest, a goldfish pond or a swing.

Other Details: Please call if coming from a distance. Tea on request.

Directions: On A815. Enter Dunoon on loch side road, right up Cammesreinach Brae just before the Royal Marine Hotel opp W Ferries terminal. The Brae becomes George Street, Fairwinds is on left.

Disabled Access:
Partial

Opening Times:
All summer
9:00am - 6:00pm

Admission:
£2.50, children free.

Charities:
The Cowal Hospice receives 40%, the net remaining to SG Beneficiaries.

INVERARAY CASTLE GARDENS
Inveraray PA32 8XF
The Duke and Duchess of Argyll T: 01499 302203
E: enquiries@inveraray-castle.com   www.inveraray-castle.com

Rhododendrons and azaleas abound and flower from April to June. Very fine specimens of Cedrus deodars, Sequoiadendron wellingtonia, Cryptomeria japonica, Taxus baccata and others thrive in the damp climate. The 'Flag-Borders' on each side of the main drive and with paths in the shape of Scotland's National flag, the St. Andrew's Cross, are outstanding in spring with Prunus "Ukon" and "Subhirtella" and are underplanted with rhododendrons, Eucryphias, shrubs and herbaceous plants giving interest all year.

Other Details: Tearoom open for teas, coffees, homebaking and light lunches. Only guide dogs allowed.

Directions: Inveraray is 60 miles north of Glasgow on the banks of Loch Fyne on the A83 with a regular bus service from Glasgow and 15 miles from Dalmally on A819.

Disabled Access:
Partial

Opening Times:
29 March to 31 October
10:00am - 5:45pm

Admission:
£4.00

Charities:
Donation to SG Beneficiaries

KAMES BAY (JOINT OPENING WITH MAOLACHY'S GARDEN)
Kilmelford PA34 4XA
Stuart Cannon T: 01852 200 205
E: stuartcannon@kames.co.uk

The garden and house were first established from a wild hillside in 1982. The garden and woodland were extended in 2001. It is principally a spring garden with ornamental trees, rhododendrons and azaleas, some of the rhodies from Arduaine and Ardanasaig gardens, as well as other friend's gardens.   A pond was created while landscaping the hill to provide a flatter area for a shed and green house. There are some pleasant walks in the woodland with wild primroses, violets, and other wild flowers, with various seats to rest and enjoy the special views over Loch Melfort and the Islands to the west.

Other Details: Some grass paths - suitable walking shoes are recommended as access is up a steep private drive.

Directions: On A816 Oban to Lochgilphead road opposite Kames Bay and the fish farm. 2½ miles south of Kilmelford and 2½ miles north of Arduaine.

Disabled Access:
None

Opening Times:
Saturday 4 May
12:00pm - 5:00pm
Sunday 5 May
12:00pm - 5:00pm

Admission:
£4.00

Charities:
Kilmelford Village
Charities receives 40%,
the net remaining to SG
Beneficiaries.

KINLOCHLAICH HOUSE GARDENS
Appin PA38 4BD
Mr & Mrs D E Hutchison and Miss F M M Hutchison T: 07881 525754
E: gardens@kinlochlaich-house.co.uk   www.kinlochlaichgardencentre.co.uk

Walled garden incorporating the Western Highlands' largest Nursery Garden Centre. Amazing variety of plants growing and for sale. Extensive grounds with woodland walk, spring garden, vegetable gardens, fruit polyhouse and formal garden. Extensive display of rhododendrons, azaleas, trees, shrubs and herbaceous, including many unusuals - Embothrium, Davidia, Magnolia, Eucryphia and Tropaeolum.

Other Details: Plant stall at Western Highlands' largest Nursery Garden Centre. Self-catering accommodation. We do not sell teas but are happy to make you one if possible.

Directions: On the A828 in Appin. Oban 18 miles south, Fort William 27 miles north. The entrance is next to the Police Station.

Disabled Access:
Partial

Opening Times:
Daily 9:30am - 5:00pm

Admission:
£2.50, accompanied children
free

Charities:
Appin Village Hall receives
40%, the net remaining to
SG Beneficiaries.

KNOCK COTTAGE
Lochgair PA31 8RZ
Mr David Sillar T: 01546 886331
E: birkhill@btinternet.com

A 5 acre woodland and water garden centred round a small loch and lily pond. Started in the 1960s most of the garden dates from the creation of the lochan in 1989 and the plantings of the 1990s. Development entered a new phase following the severe storms of 2011/12. Some 80 different rhododendron species and hybrids along with camelias, azaleas and other shrubs are scattered throughout the garden in a natural setting, sheltered by conifers, eucalyptus, birch, rowan, alder and beech.

Other Details: Very limited parking. Waterproof footwear recommended.

Directions: On the A83, ½ mile south of Lochgair Hotel on west side of the road between two sharp bends.

Disabled Access:
Partial

Opening Times:
Saturday & Sunday 11/12 May
1:00pm - 5:30pm
Saturday 18/19 May
1:00pm - 5:30pm
Also by arrangement 15 April
to 15 June

Admission:
£3.50

Charities:
Marie Curie Cancer
Care receives 40%, the
net remaining to SG
Beneficiaries.

MAOLACHY'S GARDEN (JOINT OPENING WITH BAROCHREAL AND MELFORT HOUSE)
Lochavich, by Taynuilt PA35 1HJ
Georgina Dalton T: 01866 844212

Three acres of Woodland Garden with a tumbling burn - created in a small glen over thirty years.
At an altitude of 450 feet and two weeks behind the coast we have a shorter growing season. By not struggling to grow tender or late species we can enjoy those that are happy to grow well here and give us all much pleasure.
Snowdrops, followed by early rhodies, masses of daffodils in many varieties, bluebells, wild flowers and azaleas, primulas and irises. Herbaceous blooms flower on into summer's greenery. Later flowering shrubs and autumn colours and berries make something to see and enjoy all year. A productive vegetable patch and tunnel feeds the gardener and family!

Other Details: The main path is gravelled, but some others are narrow, steep and not for the faint hearted! Sensible shoes are recommended. Homemade teas served at Melfort House.

Directions: A816 south of Oban at Kilmelford - it is exactly 4 miles to the Maolachy drive. Turn uphill between the shop and church, signposted Lochavich 6 - a steep and twisty road with a hairpin bend shortly after leaving the village. Check where the passing places are! Cross 3 county cattle grids; after the third, ignore the forestry tracks, to left and right. Continue downhill towards loch Avich, and Maolochy is up on the left - the first house after Kilmelford. Ignore satnav.

Disabled Access:
None

Opening Times:
Saturday 27 July
2:00pm - 5:00pm
Sunday 28 July
2:00pm - 5:00pm

Admission:
£3.50

Charities:
Erskine Hospital receives
40%, the net remaining to
SG Beneficiaries.

MAOLACHY'S GARDEN (JOINT OPENING WITH KAMES BAY)
Lochavich, by Taynuilt PA35 1HJ
Georgina Dalton T: 01866 844212

For garden details and directions see entry for Maolachy's Garden (joint opening with Barochreal and Melfort House).

Disabled Access:
None

Opening Times:
Saturday 4 May
12:00pm - 5:00pm
Sunday 5 May
12:00pm - 5:00pm

Admission:
£3.50

Charities:
Kilmelford Village
Charities receives 40%,
the net remaining to SG
Beneficiaries.

MELFORT HOUSE KITCHEN GARDEN (JOINT OPENING WITH BAROCHREAL AND MAOLACHY'S GARDEN)
Kilmelford, By Oban, Argyll PA34 4XD
Yvonne Anderson E: yvonne@melforthouse.co.uk www.melforthouse.co.uk

Melfort house is a family home and country house dinner, bed and breakfast on the shores of Loch Melfort, set in a mature two acre garden with specimen trees, a water feature and a variety of rhododendron and azaleas. In the quest for the most exquisite tastes and flavours for our table we were inspired to "'grow our own". Two years ago the kitchen garden was born. Now over 40 types of vegetables are grown from seed, including rarer heritage seed varieties, in a 54 feet. long polytunnel. Whatever the weather, the polytunnel has become a place to relax and enjoy the colour, texture and aromas of the whole growing experience from seed to plate.

Directions: Leave A816 Oban to Lochgilphead road in the village of Kilmelford. Turn west following sign for "Melfort 1¼" for just over 1 mile. Immediately after the stone bridge turn right through stone pillars and then bear left into our drive.

Disabled Access:
Full

Opening Times:
Saturday 27 July
2:00pm - 5:00pm
Sunday 28 July
2:00pm - 5:00pm

Admission:
£3.00

Charities:
Local Kilmelford charities
receives 40%, the
net remaining to SG
Beneficiaries.

OAKBANK
Ardrishaig PA30 8EP
Helga Macfarlane T: 01546 603405
E: helgamacfarlane@onetel.com www.gardenatoakbank.blogspot.com

This unusual and delightful garden was formed by clearing some three acres of hillside and creating a series of paths that wind amongst a varied collection of trees, shrubs, bulbs and wild flowers. There are several small ponds, many wonderful wood carvings, an active visiting population of red squirrels and a viewpoint overlooking Loch Fyne to the Isle of Arran. The garden also has huge appeal for children with lots to explore, including a secret garden.

Directions: On the Tarbert side of Ardrishaig. Entry to the garden is at the junction of Tarbert and Oakfield Roads and immediately opposite the more southerly Scottish Water lay-by.

Disabled Access:
None

Opening Times:
1 May to 31 August
10:30am - 5:30pm

Admission:
£3.00, children free.

Charities:
Diabetes UK receives 40%,
the net remaining to SG
Beneficiaries.

SEAFIELD

173 Marine Parade, Hunter's Quay, Dunoon PA23 8HJ
Scoular Anderson
E: scoulara9@aol.com

Stunning seaside garden on a hillside with clever plantings, divided into separate smaller gardens including gravel garden, damp pond garden, heather garden, shady garden, herbaceous beds, shrubs, ferns and grasses.

Directions: Situated on the Cowal Peninsula at Hunter's Quay on A815 a few hundred yards south (Dunoon side) of the Western Ferries' terminal. Parking on promenade.

Disabled Access:
None

Opening Times:
Saturday 13 July
2:00pm - 5:00pm
Sunday 14 July
2:00pm - 5:00pm

Admission:
£4.00, children free

Charities:
Children's Hospice
Association Scotland receiv
40%, the net remaining to
SG Beneficiaries.

STRATHOLM

Clachan PA29 6XL
Don and Paddy Alderson T: 01880 740654
E: dons.barite@btopenworld.com

This sheltered two acre garden on a south-facing hillside has pleasant views across the fields and woodland of the opposite side of the valley. There are many and varied mature camellias, azaleas, rhododendrons and other shrubs planted by the first owner, Jeanie McCallum. Over five years the present owners have added pergolas with roses, clematis, honeysuckle etc, herbaceous beds, a gravel area with hostas and ferns, pools and watercourse, a greenhouse, fruit trees, soft fruits, vegetable beds. There is a burnside pathway plus extra pathways and steps accessing all parts of the garden.

Other Details: There is a delightful summerhouse at highest point where you can have tea.

Directions: On A83, on the right, before Clachan Filling Station, if approaching from Tarbert. Turn immediately after first 40mph sign.

Disabled Access:
Partial

Opening Times:
Saturday 20 April
10:00am - 5:00pm
Sunday 21 April
10:00am - 5:00pm

Admission:
£3.00, accompanied childre
under 16 free.

Charities:
Clachan Village Hall receive
40%, the net remaining to S
Beneficiaries.

Druimneil

AYRSHIRE

Scotland's Gardens 2013 Guidebook is sponsored by INVESTEC WEALTH & INVESTMENT

District Organisers

Mrs Glen Collins	Grougarbank House, Kilmarnock KA3 6HP
Mrs R F Cuninghame	Caprington Castle, Kilmarnock KA2 9AA

Area Organisers

Mrs Hywel Davies	Peatland, Gatehead, Kilmarnock KA2 9AN
Mrs Michael Findlay	Carnell, By Hurlford, Kilmarnock KA1 5JS
Mrs John MacKay	Pierhill, Annbank KA6 5AW
Mrs A J Sandiford	Harrowhill Cottage, Kilmarnock KA3 6HX
Mrs Heidi Stone	3 Noddsdale Cottage, Brisbane Glen Rd, Largs KA30 8SL

Treasurer

Brigadier A J Sandiford	Harrowhill Cottage, Kilmarnock KA3 6HX

Gardens open on a specific date

Caprington Castle, Kilmarnock	Sunday 7 April	1:30pm	-	5:00pm
Kirkhill Castle, Colmonell	Sunday 19 May	2:00pm	-	5:00pm
10 Grange Terrace, Kilmarnock	Sunday 2 June	2:00pm	-	5:00pm
Holmes Farm, Drybridge	Saturday 8 June	1:00pm	-	5:00pm
Holmes Farm, Drybridge	Sunday 9 June	1:00pm	-	5:00pm
Gardens of Largs, Largs	Sunday 7 July	2:00pm	-	5:00pm
Cairnhall House, Ochiltree	Sunday 14 July	2:00pm	-	5:00pm
Culzean, Maybole	Tuesday 16 July	9:30am	-	5:00pm
Skeldon, Dalrymple	Sunday 21 July	2:00pm	-	5:00pm
Carnell, By Hurlford	Sunday 28 July	2:00pm	-	5:00pm
Avonhill Cottage, Drumclog	Saturday 10 August	2:00pm	-	5:00pm
Kilmaurs Village Gardens, Kilmaurs	Sunday 18 August	1:30pm	-	4:30pm

Gardens open by arrangement

Carnell, By Hurlford	1 May - 30 September	01563 884236

Key to symbols

🍸	New in 2013	🇭🇵	Homemade teas	B&B	Accommodation
🍵	Teas	🐕	Dogs on a lead allowed	🌷	Plant stall
☕	Cream teas	♿	Wheelchair access	🌿	Scottish Snowdrop Festival

Garden locations

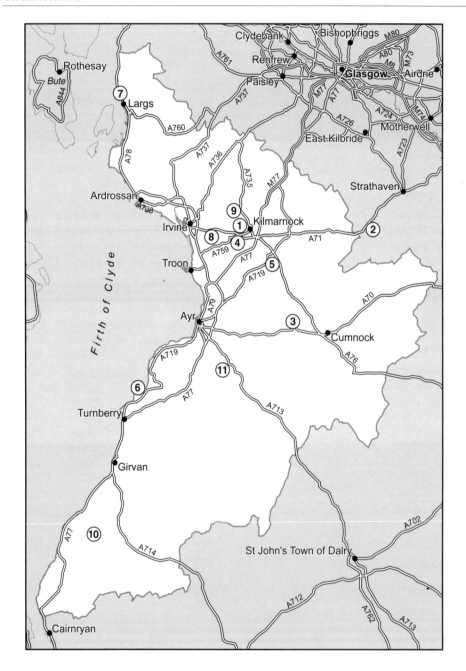

10 GRANGE TERRACE
Kilmarnock KA1 2JR
Mr & Mrs Iain Linton

This south facing established garden has a diversity of well chosen shrubs and herbaceous borders. A vegetable plot with soft fruit and top fruit trees complete a delightful triangular garden.

Directions: From A77 Bellfield interchange take the A71 dual carriageway marked Irvine to first roundabout and take Crosshouse exit. Over a small roundabout directing to Hospital (B7081) and at T junction turn right to Kilmarnock Town Centre past Annanhill Park/Golf Course through set of lights to turn right off Irvine Road before filling station into Grange Terrace. Route signposted in yellow "Garden Open"

Disabled Access:
Partial

Opening Times:
Sunday 2 June
2:00pm - 5:00pm

Admission:
£3.50, children free

Charities:
Annanhill Walled Garden receives 40%, the net remaining to SG Beneficiaries.

AVONHILL COTTAGE
Drumclog, Strathaven ML10 6QG
Mr & Mrs E Chang

A garden of approximate 3.5 acres created from a field in an exposed site over the past 20 years. The planting is varied and includes woodland shelter belts, herbaceous plants, shrubs, grasses and a bank of rhododendrons overlooking the river. There are also three ponds, fruit and vegetable beds and free range chickens.

Other Details: Bric a brac and home produce stall for Stella's Voice.

Directions: 5 miles west from Strathaven or 15 miles east from Kilmarnock on A71. Turn into B745 to Muirkirk at Drumclog Memorial Kirk. Avonhill is on right over hump back bridge.

Disabled Access:
Partial

Opening Times:
Saturday 10 August
2:00pm - 5:00pm

Admission:
£2.50, children free.

Charities:
Stella's Voice receives 40%, the net remaining to SG Beneficiaries.

CAIRNHALL HOUSE
Mauchline Road, Ochiltree KA18 2QA
Ian and Sarah Hay

A nature lover's garden created over seven years from a thistle-filled field into an organic 2 acre garden of extensive flower beds, large pond and vegetable plot, a clematis meadow (new for 2013) and laburnum tunnel all designed to appeal to insects, butterflies, birds and people.

Other Details: Whilst possible to drop off infirm at house, wheelchair users would find the gravel difficult.

Directions: From A70 into Ochiltree where road forks to Cumnock, turn left up Mauchline Road. Drive is 150yds on left. Please note parking is limited. Cemetery car park nearby option. See drop off info above.

Disabled Access:
Partial

Opening Times:
Sunday 14 July
2:00pm - 5:00pm

Admission:
£4.00, children free.

Charities:
Sight Savers receives 20%, Waste Water receives 20%, the net remaining to SG Beneficiaries.

CAPRINGTON CASTLE
Kilmarnock, Ayrshire KA2 9AA
Mrs Robert Cuninghame and Mr William Cuninghame T: 01563 526157
E: caprington@googlemail.com

Open this year for daffodils and spring flowers - swathes of daffodils along with primroses and wood anemones in attractive grounds. Large walled garden with fruit trees, soft fruit, vegetables and borders mainly undergoing renovation.

Other Details: Demonstration of daffodils: growing and classification. Please bring cut samples, preferably named. Show table with prizes for group of 5 large trumpet, 5 smaller cup, 5 Cyclamineus or Jonquilla Narcissus and 5 of own favourites (can be mixed). Children's classes - posy or garden on plate. Strong waterproof footwear recommended.

Directions: Route from M77 take A71 to Irvine and exit first roundabout to Gatehead, Dundonald, Troon. Gatehead over railway line, river bridge and take 1st left at Old Rome Farmhouse. Twin Lodges about ½ mile on. Yellow signposted from Ayr -Kilmarnock road after Bogend Toll.

Disabled Access:
Partial

Opening Times:
Sunday 7 April
1:30pm - 5:00pm

Admission:
£4.00, children free.

Charities:
The Order of St John Scotland receives 40%, the net remaining to SG Beneficiaries.

CARNELL
By Hurlford KA1 5JS
Mr & Mrs John Findlay and Mr & Mrs Michael Findlay T: 01563 884236
E: carnellestates@aol.com   www.carnellestates.com

The 16th century Peel Tower looks down over a 10 acre garden which has featured in the "Beechgrove Garden", "Country Life", "The Good Gardens Guide" as well as Suki Urquhart's book "The Scottish Gardener". Carnell has a traditional walled garden with a 100 yard long herbaceous border, as well as a rock and water garden, gazebo with Burmese statues, lawns and many other features of interest. Herbaceous, rose and phlox borders are in full bloom during July.

Other Details: Ice-cream, craft stalls and silver band on the lawn.

Directions: From A77 (Glasgow/Kilmarnock) take A76 (Mauchline/Dumfries) then right on to the A719 to Ayr for 1½ miles.

Disabled Access:
Partial

Opening Times:
Sunday 28 July
2:00pm - 5:00pm
Also by arrangement on request

Admission:
£4.00, children under 12 free.

Charities:
Craigie Church receives 20%, Craigie Village Hall receives 10%, SSPCA receives 10%, the net remaining to SG Beneficiaries.

CULZEAN
Maybole KA19 8LE
The National Trust for Scotland T: 0844 493 2148
E: culzean@nts.org.uk   www.nts.org.uk

A major Scottish attraction and a perfect day out for all the family. Robert Adam's romantic 18th-century masterpiece is perched on a cliff high above the Firth of Clyde. The Fountain Garden lies in front of the castle with terraces and herbaceous borders reflecting its Georgian elegance. The extensive country park offers beaches and rock pools, parklands, gardens, woodland walks and adventure playground. It contains fascinating restored buildings contemporary with the castle.

Other Details: Castle and estate open, see NTS website for details. Homemade wine from Culzean. The tour starts at 2:00pm.

Directions: On A719 12 miles S of Ayr, 4m W of Maybole. Bus: Stagecoach, Ayr/Girvan via Maidens (No 60) to entrance. 1 mile walk downhill from stop to Castle/Visitor Centre.

Disabled Access:
Partial

Opening Times:
Tuesday 16 July
9:30am - 5:00pm

Admission:
£2.00 including NTS members, for a guided walk with the Head Gardener.

Charities:
Donation to SG Beneficiaries.

GARDENS OF LARGS
96 Willowbank Hotel, Greenock Road KA30 8PG
The Gardens of Largs T: 01475 673155
E: heidistone@btinternet.com

The gardens of Largs are opening with a selection of very different gardens.

Other Details: Home made cream teas will be served in a wild life garden situated in the beautiful glen countryside, where there will also be a plant stall.

Directions: A78 south from Greenock and north from Irvine. Admission tickets and maps available from the Willowbank Hotel.

Disabled Access:
Partial

Opening Times:
Sunday 7 July
2:00pm - 5:00pm

Admission:
£4.00, children free.

Charities:
Alzheimer's Scotland receives 20%, MacMillan receives 20%, the net remaining to SG Beneficiaries.

HOLMES FARM
Drybridge, By Irvine KA11 5BS
Mr Brian A Young T: 01294 311210
E: yungi@fsmail.net

A plantsman's garden created by a confirmed plantaholic. Meandering paths guide the eye through plantings predominantly herbaceous, with small trees and shrubs. Some plant collections are housed permanently in polytunnels. The garden opening will hopefully be timed for peak bloom of some of the 300 iris in the garden. Some areas of the garden are currently undergoing a partial replant and redesign.

Other Details: Arts and crafts gallery, various stalls.

Directions: Holmes is the only farm between Drybridge and Dreghorn on B730.

Disabled Access:
None

Opening Times:
Saturday 8 June
1:00pm - 5:00pm
Sunday 9 June
1:00pm - 5:00pm

Admission:
£4.00, children free.

Charities:
Plant Heritage receives 40%, the net remaining to SG Beneficiaries.

KILMAURS VILLAGE GARDENS
Kilmaurs KA3 2QS
The Gardeners of Kilmaurs

A selection of gardens, promising a great variety of planting and styles including sculpture in this historic and picturesque village with a designated conservation centre.

Other Details: Tickets and maps from 1.30pm at Community Centre East Park Drive. Teas 1:45 - 4:00pm (Hall closes 4:30pm). Guide dogs only.

Directions: From M77 north take B751 turnoff at Fenwick for Kilmaurs. From A77 from east and south A71 Irvine and turn off to Crosshouse, Knockentiber on B751. Yellow signposted from A735 and B751.

Disabled Access:
Partial

Opening Times:
Sunday 18 August
1:30pm - 4:30pm

Admission:
£4.00, children free.

Charities:
Riding for the Disabled (Winton Group) receives 20%, The Prostate Cancer Charity receives 10%, Alzheimer Scotland receives 10%, the net remaining to SG Beneficiaries.

KIRKHILL CASTLE
Colmonell KA26 0SB
Mr & Mrs Paul Gibbons

8½ acre garden with rhododendrons, magnolias and camellias. Azalea walk, rose garden, and woodland walkways, with newly restored Vine House and Peach House.

Other Details: Piper on the lawn. No dogs please.

Directions: Kirkhill Castle is in Colmonell Village next to the village hall.

Disabled Access:
Partial

Opening Times:
Sunday 19 May
2:00pm - 5:00pm

Admission:
£3.50, children free.

Charities:
Colmonell Primary School receives 40%, the net remaining to SG Beneficiaries.

SKELDON
Dalrymple KA6 6AT
Mr S E Brodie QC

One and a half acres of formal garden with herbaceous borders and arched pathways. Large Victorian glasshouse with a substantial collection of plants. Four acres of woodland garden within a unique setting on the banks of the River Doon.

Other Details: Silver Band on Lawn.

Directions: From Dalrymple take B7034 Dalrymple/Hollybush road and follow yellow signs.

Disabled Access:
Partial

Opening Times:
Sunday 21 July
2:00pm - 5:00pm

Admission:
£4.00, children free.

Charities:
Help For Heroes receives 40%, the net remaining to SG Beneficiaries.

Holmes Farm

BERWICKSHIRE

Scotland's Gardens 2013 Guidebook is sponsored by **INVESTEC WEALTH & INVESTMENT**

District Organiser

| Mrs F Wills | Anton's Hill, Coldstream TD12 4JD |

Treasurer

| Mr F Wills | Anton's Hill, Coldstream TD12 4JD |

Gardens open on a specific date

Charterhall, Duns	Sunday 12 May	1:30pm	- 5:00pm
Lennel Bank, Coldstream	Sunday 9 June	10:30am	- 5:00pm
Netherbyres, Eyemouth	Sunday 7 July	2:00pm	- 5:30pm
Preston Gardens, Duns	Sunday 14 July	2:00pm	- 5:30pm
Anton's Hill and Walled Garden, Leitholm	Sunday 21 July	2:00pm	- 5:30pm

Gardens open regularly

Bughtrig, Near Leitholm, Coldstream	1 June - 1 September	11:00am	- 5:00pm

Gardens open by arrangement

Anton's Hill and Walled Garden, Leitholm	1 May - 30 September	01890 840203/468
Lennel Bank, Coldstream	1 January - 31 December	01890 882297
Netherbyres, Eyemouth	1 May - 31 August	01890 750337

Key to symbols

	New in 2013		Homemade teas		Accommodation
	Teas		Dogs on a lead allowed		Plant stall
	Cream teas		Wheelchair access		Scottish Snowdrop Festival

Garden locations

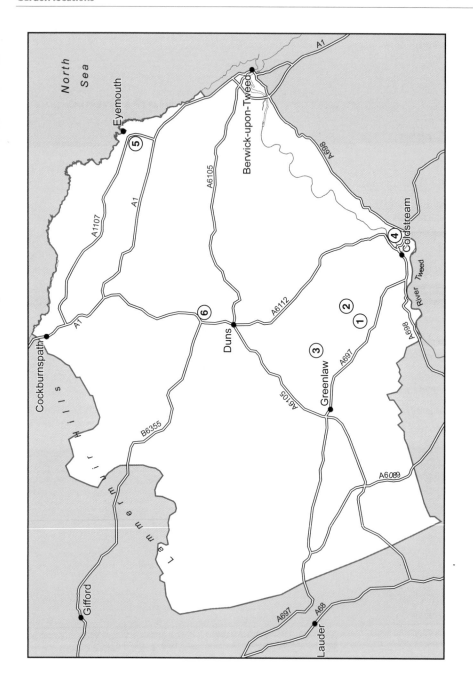

1 ANTON'S HILL AND WALLED GARDEN
Leitholm, Coldstream TD12 4JD
Mr & Mrs F Wills, Alec West & Pat Watson T: 01890 840203/468
E: cillawills@antonshill.co.uk

Well treed mature garden which has been improved and added to since 1999. There are woodland walks including a stumpery and a large well planted pond, shrubberies and herbaceous borders. Topiary elephant family of yew and a new woodland pond. A restored organic walled garden and greenhouse with an apple and pear orchard containing a growing collection of over 230 varieties.

Other Details: Dogs are not allowed in the walled garden.

Directions: Signed off B6461 west of Leitholm.

Disabled Access:
Full

Opening Times:
Sunday 21 July
2:00pm - 5:30pm
Also by arrangement 1 May to
30 September

Admission:
£4.00, children free.

Charities:
"Oakfield Ltd" Home for
people with special needs,
Northants. receives 40%,
the net remaining to SG
Beneficiaries.

2 BUGHTRIG
Near Leitholm, Coldstream TD12 4JP
Major General C and The Hon Mrs Ramsay T: 01890 840678
E: ramsay@bughtrig.co.uk

A traditional hedged Scottish family garden with an interesting combination of herbaceous plants, shrubs, annuals and fruit. It is surrounded by fine specimen trees which provide remarkable shelter.

Other Details: Small picnic area.

Directions: ¼ mile east of Leitholm on B6461

Disabled Access:
Partial

Opening Times:
1 June to 1 September
11:00am - 5:00pm

Admission:
£3.00, children under 18
£1.00.

Charities:
Donation to SG Beneficiaries.

3 CHARTERHALL
Duns TD11 3RE
Major and Mrs A Trotter

A well-established woodland garden, surrounding a lovely family home with an outstanding view. Wide range of rhododendrons and azaleas planted by family for the past 100 years. Flower garden with fine collection of roses, bulbs and perennial plants, with a heated greenhouse and vegetable garden.

Other Details: Delicious homemade teas.

Directions: On B6460, 6 miles south west of Duns and 3 miles east of Greenlaw.

Disabled Access:
Full

Opening Times:
Sunday 12 May
1:30pm - 5:00pm

Admission:
£4.00, children £1.00.

Charities:
St John's South East Scotland
receives 20%, Christ
Church, Duns receives 20%,
the net remaining to SG
Beneficiaries.

LENNEL BANK
Coldstream TD12 4EX
Mrs Honor Brown T: 01890 882297

Lennel Bank is a terraced garden overlooking the River Tweed, consisting of wide borders packed with shrubs and perennial planting, some unusual. The water garden, built in 2008, is surrounded by a rockery and utilises the slope ending in a pond. There is a small kitchen garden with raised beds in unusual shapes. Different growing conditions throughout the garden from dry, wet, shady and sun lend themselves to a variety of plants, which hopefully enhance the garden's interest.

Directions: On A6112 Coldstream to Duns road. 1 mile from Coldstream.

Disabled Access:
None

Opening Times:
Sunday 9 June
10:30am - 5:00pm
Also by arrangement on request

Admission:
£4.00, children free.

Charities:
British Heart Foundation receives 40%, the net remaining to SG Beneficiaries.

NETHERBYRES
Eyemouth TD14 5SE
Col S J Furness and Leonard Cheshire Disability T: 018907 50337

A unique 18th century elliptical walled garden. Annuals, roses, herbaceous borders, fruit and vegetables in summer.

Directions: ½ mile south of Eyemouth on A1107 to Berwick.

Disabled Access:
Full

Opening Times:
Sunday 7 July
2:00pm - 5:30pm
Also by arrangement
1 May to 31 August

Admission:
£4.00, concessions £3.00, children under 12 free.

Charities:
Friends of Netherbyres receives 40%, the net remaining to SG Beneficiaries.

PRESTON GARDENS
Duns TD11 3TQ
Mr & Mrs R Eggo and Mr W Laidlaw

Angus Cottage TD11 3TQ: A charming garden with interesting shrubs and long curving herbaceous border, full of perennials, climbing roses and clematis. Gravel garden with small pond.
Cumledge Mill House TD11 3TD: The garden is surrounded by an attractive new wall, a good backdrop for the herbaceous borders, mature trees and spacious lawns. The garden enclosed part of a former blanket factory, which was run by the owner's family 1850's - 1970's.

Other Details: Teas served in Preston Village Hall.

Directions: Preston Village is 2 miles north of Duns on the Duns - Grantshouse Road. Cumledge Mill House is located between the village and the river Whiteadder, ref. blocks of white mill cottages.

Disabled Access:
Full

Opening Times:
Sunday 14 July
2:00pm - 5:30pm

Admission:
£4.00 for entry to both gardens

Charities:
Macmillan Cancer Support receives 40%, the net remaining to SG Beneficiaries.

CAITHNESS, SUTHERLAND, ORKNEY & SHETLAND

Scotland's Gardens 2013 Guidebook is sponsored by **INVESTEC WEALTH & INVESTMENT**

District Organiser

Mrs Judith Middlemas	22 Miller Place, Scrabster, Thurso KW14 7UH

Area Organisers

Mrs Kathy Greaves	Caregarth, Scatness, Birkie ZE3 9JW
Mrs Mary Leask	VisitShetland, Market Cross, Lerwick ZE1 0LU
Mr Steve Mathieson	VisitShetland, Market Cross, Lerwick ZE1 0LU
Mrs Jonny Shaw	Amat, Ardgay, Sutherland IV24 3BS

Treasurer

Mr Chris Hobson	Braeside, Dunnet, Caithness KW14 8YD

Gardens open on a specific date

Amat, Ardgay	Saturday 1 June	2:00pm	- 5:00pm
Amat, Ardgay	Sunday 2 June	2:00pm	- 5:00pm
The Castle & Gardens of Mey, Mey	Wednesday 3 July	10:00am	- 5:00pm
Bighouse Lodge, by Melvich	Sunday 7 July	2:30pm	- 5:30pm
The Castle & Gardens of Mey, Mey	Wednesday 17 July	10:00am	- 5:00pm
House of Tongue, Tongue, Lairg	Saturday 27 July	2:00pm	- 6:00pm
Langwell, Berriedale	Sunday 4 August	2:00pm	- 5:00pm
Langwell, Berriedale	Sunday 11 August	2:00pm	- 5:00pm
The Castle & Gardens of Mey, Mey	Saturday 17 August	10:00am	- 5:00pm
Springpark House, Laurie Terrace, Thurso	Sunday 25 August	11:00am	- 5:00pm

Gardens open regularly

The Castle & Gardens of Mey, Mey	1 May - 24 July	10:00am	- 5:00pm
	& 8 August - 30 September	10:00am	- 5:00pm

Gardens open by arrangement

Langwell, Berriedale	On request	01593 751278/751237

Key to symbols

	New in 2013		Homemade teas		Accommodation
	Teas		Dogs on a lead allowed		Plant stall
	Cream teas		Wheelchair access		Scottish Snowdrop Festival

Garden locations

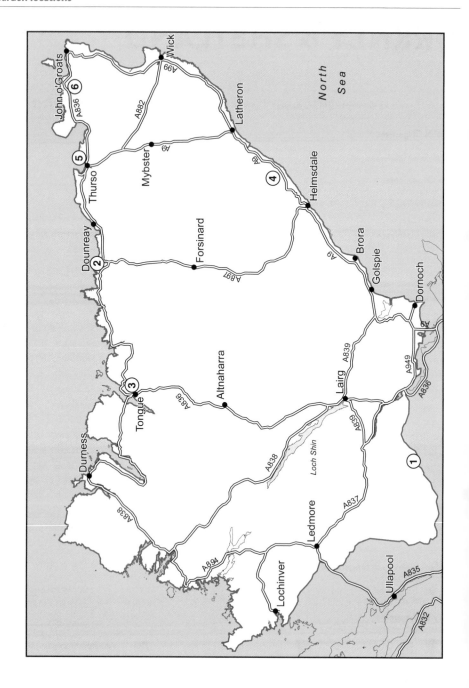

AMAT
Ardgay IV24 3BS
Jonny & Sara Shaw
E: saraamat@btinternet.com

Riverside garden set in Amat forest. Herbaceous borders and rockery set in large lawn looking onto salmon pool. Old and new rhododendrons with woodland and river walk.

Other Details: Teas £2.50.

Directions: Take road from Ardgay to Croick 9 miles. Turn left at red phone box. 500 yards on left

Disabled Access:
Partial

Opening Times:
Saturday 1 June
2:00pm - 5:00pm
Sunday 2 June
2:00pm - 5:00pm

Admission:
£4.00

Charities:
Croick Church receives 20%, Wireless for the Blind receives 20%, the net remaining to SG Beneficiaries.

BIGHOUSE LODGE
By Melvich KW14 7YJ
Bighouse Estate
E: info@bighouseestate.com   www.bighouseestate.com

Bighouse Lodge is situated on the north coast of Sutherland at the mouth of the River Halladale. The 2 acre walled garden, originally laid out in 1715, consists of a central axis leading to a charming bothy with lawn, herbaceous borders, a sunken garden and four separate conceptual gardens behind the hedgerows. Each garden contains a sculpture to reflect the aspects of the Bighouse Estate namely the River, the Forest, the Strath and the Hill. The garden has recently been restored and is now a most interesting place to visit.

Other Details: Teas £3.00.

Directions: Off A836 ½ mile East of Melvich.

Disabled Access:
Partial

Opening Times:
Sunday 7 July
2:30pm - 5:30pm

Admission:
£4.00 Children under 12 £1.00

Charities:
RNLI receives 40%, the net remaining to SG Beneficiaries.

HOUSE OF TONGUE
Tongue, Lairg IV27 4XH
The Countess of Sutherland
E: ginrik@btopenworld.com

17th century house on Kyle of Tongue. Walled garden with herbaceous borders, lawns, old fashioned roses, vegetables, soft fruit and small orchard.

Other Details: Teas £3.50.

Directions: Half a mile from Tongue village. House just off main road approaching causeway. Well signposted.

Disabled Access:
Partial

Opening Times:
Saturday 27 July
2:00pm - 6:00pm

Admission:
£4.00, OAPs £3.00, children under 12 50p

Charities:
Children 1st receives 40%, the net remaining to SG Beneficiaries.

LANGWELL
Berriedale KW7 6HD
Welbeck Estates T: 01593 751278/751237
E: macanson@hotmail.com

A beautiful and spectacular old walled garden with outstanding borders situated in the secluded Langwell Strath. Charming wooded access drive with a chance to see deer.

Other Details: Teas will be under cover.

Directions: A9 Berriedale 2 miles.

Disabled Access:
Partial

Opening Times:
Sunday 4 August
2:00pm - 5:00pm
Sunday 11 August
2:00pm - 5:00pm
Also by arrangement on request

Admission:
£4.00, OAPs £3.00, children under 12 free

Charities:
RNLI receives 40%, the net remaining to SG Beneficiaries.

SPRINGPARK HOUSE
Laurie Terrace, Thurso KW14 8NR
Mr Ronald and Mrs Kirsty Gunn T: 01847 894797

Several individually styled gardens within one walled garden. Collection of old farming implements and household memorabilia on show. Vegetable garden with large polytunnel. The garden is on one level with good wheelchair access and plenty of parking space.

Other Details: Teas £2.00

Directions: In Thurso off the Castletown road at Mount Pleasant Road, continue up the hill until you see Laurie Terrace (last road on the right), house is at the end. Park in garden or road.

Disabled Access:
Full

Opening Times:
Sunday 25 August
11:00am - 5:00pm

Admission:
£3.50

Charities:
Cancer Research UK receives 40%, the net remaining to SG Beneficiaries.

ORDER FORM ON PAGE 270

Copies of this guidebook can be purchased on our website or using the order form in this book.

WWW.SCOTLANDSGARDENS.ORG

THE CASTLE & GARDENS OF MEY
Mey KW14 8XH
The Queen Elizabeth Castle of Mey Trust T: 01847 851473
E: enquiries@castleofmey.org.uk www.castleofmey.org.uk

Originally a Z plan castle bought by the Queen Mother in 1952 and then restored and improved. The walled garden and the East Garden were also created by the Queen Mother. An animal centre has been established over the last 3 years and is proving very popular with all ages.

Other Details: Tearoom, shop and animal centre. Castle opens 10:20am, last entries 4.00pm. Please check Castle website as dates subject to change.

Directions: On A836 between Thurso and John O'Groats.

Disabled Access:
Partial

Opening Times:
Wednesday3 July
10:00am - 5:00pm
Wednesday 17 July
10:00am - 5:00pm
Saturday 17 August
10:00am - 5:00pm
1 May to 24 July
10:00am - 5:00pm
8 August to 30 September
10:00am - 5:00pm

Admission:
£10.50, concessions. £9.50, children £6.00, family £28.00
Garden and animal centre only: £6.00 family £18.00

Charities:
Alzheimers Scotland receives 40%, the net remaining to SG Beneficiaries.

House of Tongue

Gardens open on a specific date

Keldaberg, Cunningsburgh	Tuesday 11 June	2:00pm	- 4:00pm
Keldaberg, Cunningsburgh	Saturday 15 June	2:00pm	- 4:00pm
Keldaberg, Cunningsburgh	Tuesday 18 June	2:00pm	- 4:00pm
Keldaberg, Cunningsburgh	Saturday 22 June	2:00pm	- 4:00pm
Keldaberg, Cunningsburgh	Tuesday 25 June	2:00pm	- 4:00pm
Lea Gardens, Tresta	Sunday 28 July	2:00pm	- 5:00pm
Keldaberg, Cunningsburgh	Saturday 29 June	2:00pm	- 4:00pm
Keldaberg, Cunningsburgh	Tuesday 30 July	2:00pm	- 4:00pm
Keldaberg, Cunningsburgh	Saturday 3 August	2:00pm	- 4:00pm
Keldaberg, Cunningsburgh	Tuesday 6 August	2:00pm	- 4:00pm
Keldaberg, Cunningsburgh	Saturday 10 August	2:00pm	- 4:00pm

Gardens open regularly

15 Linkshouse , Mid Yell	11 July - 8 August, Thurs	10:00am	- 7:00pm
Caergarth, Scatness, Virkie	15 June - 29 July Sats, Suns & Mons and not open 6, 7, 8 July	11:00am	- 5:00pm
Holmlea, Mid Yell	7 July - 18 August	10:00am	- 7:00pm
Lea Gardens, Tresta	1 April - 31 October	2:00pm	- 5:00pm
Nonavaar, Levenwick	2 June - 28 August Weds and Suns	2:00pm	- 4:00pm

Gardens open by arrangement

Caergarth, Scatness, Virkie	1 June - 30 September	01950 460576
Cruisdale, Sandness	1 May - 31 August	01595 870739
Gerdi, Hillswick	1 July - 31 August	01806 503776
Highlands, East Voe	On request	01595 880526
Nonavaar, Levenwick	On request	01950 422447
Norby, Burnside, Sandness	On request	01595 870246

Key to symbols

	New in 2013		Homemade teas		Accommodation
	Teas		Dogs on a lead allowed		Plant stall
	Cream teas		Wheelchair access		Scottish Snowdrop Festival

Garden locations

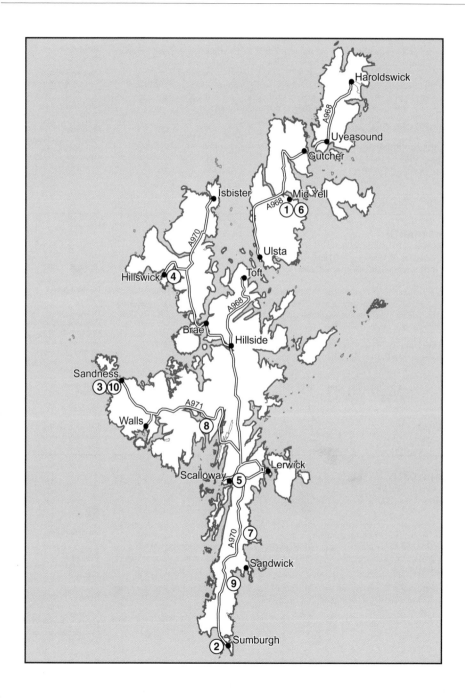

15 LINKSHOUSE
Mid Yell ZE2 9BP
Mr Charlie Inkster T: 01957 702049
E: cjinkster@btinternet.com

A small cottage garden with a greenhouse full of plants and colour, a pond complete with fountain and water lilies, and a small aviary with canaries and finches. The garden is well established with trees, bushes and a good variety of plants giving plenty of colour. Fuschias are a favourite providing a good selection of different varieties both in the garden and in the greenhouse. Also in the greenhouse are many varieties of streptocarpus adding to the colourful display.

Other Details: Small aviary.

Directions: In Yell head north on the A968, turn right to Mid Yell. Drive down through Mid Yell and turn towards Linkshouse Pier. The garden is at the far end of the row of white cottages.

Disabled Access:
None

Opening Times:
11 July to 8 August, Thursdays
10:00am - 7:00pm

Admission:
£3.00

Charities:
Yell for Cancer Support receives 40%, the net remaining to SG Beneficiaries.

CAERGARTH
Scatness, Virkie ZE3 9JW
Mr and Mrs M Greaves T: 01950 460576
E: Kathy.caergarth@btinternet.com

New garden site of ½ acre with 360 degree views of Sumburgh Head, Fair Isle, Fitful Head and Virkie landscapes. Despite being new we have already established in the garden a polytunnel, vegetable garden and greenhouse all full of plants with shrubs, a rose garden, wildlife pond and meadow.

Other Details: The garden is situated close to Viking archaelogical digs, sandy beaches and a Pictish Blockhouse.

Directions: Head south on the A970 towards Sumburgh Airport. Once over the runway take the road signposted Scatness, with bus shelter on the corner. Caergarth is 100 yards on the left.

Disabled Access:
Partial

Opening Times:
15 June to 29 July
11:00am - 5:00pm
Sats, Suns & Mons
except 6, 7 & 8 July.
Also by arrangement 1 June to 30 September

Admission:
£3.00

Charities:
MacMillan Nurses Shetland receives 40%, the net remaining to SG Beneficiaries.

CRUISDALE
Sandness ZE2 9PL
Alfred Kern T: 01595 870739

The garden is in a natural state with many willows, several ponds and a variety of colourful hardy plants that grow well in the Shetland climate. It is a work in progress, started about seven years ago and growing bigger over the years with more work planned.

Directions: In Sandness, on the west side of Shetland. Opposite the school, on the right hand side with a wind generator in the field.

Disabled Access:
None

Opening Times:
By arrangement 1 May to 31 August

Admission:
£3.00

Charities:
WRVS receives 40%, the net remaining to SG Beneficiaries.

GERDI
Hillswick ZE2 9RW
Alison Charleson T: 01806 503776

A small, new garden, surrounded by moorland full of wild flowers. The beds surrounding the house contain a mixture of herbaceous plants and grasses with trees and shrubs to give shelter and colour throughout the summer. Meandering stone paths allow the plants to be enjoyed close up.

Directions: Follow the A970 north from Lerwick to Hillswick, continuing on past the public hall and Stucca. Gerdi is a pale blue wooden chalet on the left just before the Hillswick Hotel.

Disabled Access:
None

Opening Times:
By arrangement 1 July to 31 August

Admission:
£3.00

Charities:
All proceeds to SG Beneficiaries.

HIGHLANDS
East Voe, Scalloway ZE1 0UR
Sarah Kay T: 01595 880526
E: info@easterhoull.co.uk

The garden is in two parts. The upper garden includes a rockery built with large rocks and a wide selection of plants. The lower garden is on a steep slope with a spectacular sea view over village of Scalloway. Path to lead visitors around. Wide selection of plants, pond and vegetable patch.

Directions: Follow A970 main road towards village of Scalloway. Take a sharp turn on the left, signposted for Easterhoull Chalets and follow road, stop at greenhouse!

Disabled Access:
None

Opening Times:
By arrangement on request

Admission:
£3.50

Charities:
All proceeds to SG Beneficiaries.

HOLMLEA
Mid Yell ZE2 9BT
John and Sandra Robertson T: 01957 702062

The garden has a greenhouse, conservatory and drystane dyke, with a mixture of flowers, shrubs and vegetables. Enjoy wandering around admiring the variety of different shrubs and herbaceous plants interspersed with colourful annuals, then see the plot of mixed vegetables before moving on into the greenhouse where tomatoes, cucumber and peppers grow.

Other Details: Waterwheel.

Directions: Once on the island of Yell head for Mid Yell, going down to Linkshouse Pier. From there go up past the shop about 150yds. Holmlea is right on the corner with garage and basement.

Disabled Access:
Partial

Opening Times:
7 July to 18 August Sundays 10:00am - 7:00pm

Admission:
£3.00

Charities:
RNLI receives 40%, the net remaining to SG Beneficiaries.

KELDABERG
Cunningsburgh ZE2 9HG
Mrs L Johnston T: 01950 477331
E: linda.keldaberg@btinternet.com

A 'secret garden' divided into 4 areas. A beach garden of grasses, flowers and driftwood. The main area is a sloping perennial border, leading down to a greenhouse, vegetable plot, up to a decked area with containers and exotic plants including agaves, pineapple lilies, cannas and gunneras. The new part has trees, raised vegetable beds, a rockery, retaining walls and an arbour to rest in. There is a pond complete with goldfish, golden orf and koi plus aquatic plants, and a water lily.

Directions: On the A970 south of Lerwick is Cunningsburgh, take the Gord junction on the left after passing the village hall. Continue along the road to the 1st house past the Kenwood sign.

Disabled Access:
Partial

Opening Times:
11 June to 29 June
Tuesdays and Saturdays
2:00pm - 4:00pm
30 July to 10 August
Tuesdays and Saturdays
2:00pm - 4:00pm

Admission:
£3.00

Charities:
Chest Heart & Stroke Scotland receives 40%, the net remaining to SG Beneficiaries.

LEA GARDENS
Tresta ZE2 9LT
Rosa Steppanova T: 01595 810454

Lea Gardens, started in the early 1980s, now covers almost 2 acres. The plant collection, the largest north of Inverewe Gardens, consists of 1,500 different species and cultivars from all over the world, including phyto-geographic elements of collections of plants from New Zealand, South Africa and South America. Planted to provide all-year-round interest it has been divided into a variety of habitats: woodland and shade, borders, wetland, raised beds, and acid and lime lovers. A winner of the 2011 Shetland Environmental Award.

Directions: From Lerwick take A970 north, turn left at Tingwall onto A971 past Weisdale along Weisdale Voe and up Weisdale hill. Coming down, Lea Gardens is on your right surrounded by trees.

Disabled Access:
Partial

Opening Times:
Sunday 28 July
2:00pm - 5:00pm
for Scotland's Gardens
1 April to 31 October
2:00pm - 5:00pm

Admission:
£3.00

Charities:
All proceeds to SG Beneficiaries for 28 July and donation to SG Beneficiaries for other dates.

NONAVAAR
Levenwick ZE2 9HX
James B Thomason T: 01950 422447

This is a delightful country garden, sloping within drystone walls, overlooking magnificent coastal views. It contains ponds, terraces, areas of lawn, trees, bushes, varied perennials, annuals, vegetable garden and greenhouse.

Other Details: Arts and Crafts Studio.

Directions: Head south from Lerwick. Turn left at Levenwick sign soon after Bigton turnoff. Follow road to third house on left after Midway stores. Park where there is a 'Garden Open' sign.

Disabled Access:
None

Opening Times:
2 June to 28 August
Wednesdays and Sundays
2:00pm - 4:00pm
Also by arrangement on request

Admission:
£3.00

Charities:
Cancer Research receives 40%, the net remaining to SG Beneficiaries.

NORBY
Burnside, Sandness ZE2 9PL
Mrs Gundel Grolimund T: 01595 870246
E: gislinde@tiscali.co.uk

A small but perfectly formed garden and a prime example of what can be achieved in a very exposed situation. Blue painted wooden pallets provide internal wind breaks and form a background for shrubs, climbers and herbaceous plants, while willows provide a perfect wildlife habitat. There are treasured plants such as chionocloa rubra, pieris, Chinese tree peonies, and a selection of old-fashioned shrub roses. Narrow raised beds contain salads and herbs decorated by beach finds.

Other Details: Historic old house.

Directions: At Sandness, take road to Norby, turn right at Methodist Church, 'Burnside' at end.

Disabled Access:
None

Opening Times:
By arrangement on request
Due to remote location phone or email before visit.

Admission:
£3.00

Charities:
Survival International receives 40%, the net remaining to SG Beneficiaries.

DUMFRIESSHIRE

Scotland's Gardens 2013 Guidebook is sponsored by **INVESTEC WEALTH & INVESTMENT**

District Organiser

Mrs Sarah Landale   Dalswinton House, Dalswinton, Auldgirth DG2 0XZ

Area Organiser

Mrs Fiona Bell-Irving   Bankside, Kettleholm, Lockerbie DG11 1BY

Treasurers

Mr Harold Jack   The Clachan, Newtonairds DG2 0JL

Gardens open on a specific date

Dalswinton House, Dalswinton	Sunday 24 March	11:00am	- 4:00pm
Portrack House, Holywood	Sunday 5 May	12:00pm	- 5:00pm
Drumpark, Irongray	Sunday 12 May	2:00pm	- 5:00pm
Dalswinton House, Dalswinton	Sunday 19 May	2:00pm	- 5:00pm
Dabton, Thornhill	Sunday 26 May	2:00pm	- 5:00pm
Westerhall, Bentpath, Langholm	Sunday 26 May	2:00pm	- 5:00pm
Cowhill Tower, Holywood	Sunday 2 June	2:00pm	- 5:00pm
Glenae, Amisfield	Sunday 9 June	2:00pm	- 5:00pm
Newtonairds Lodge, Newtonairds	Sunday 16 June	5:00pm	- 9:00pm
Newtonairds Lodge, Newtonairds	Sunday 4 August	1:00pm	- 5:00pm

Gardens open by arrangement

Grovehill House , Burnhead, Thornhill	1 April - 30 September	01848 331637

Key to symbols

	New in 2013		Homemade teas		Accommodation
	Teas		Dogs on a lead allowed		Plant stall
	Cream teas		Wheelchair access		Scottish Snowdrop Festival

Garden locations

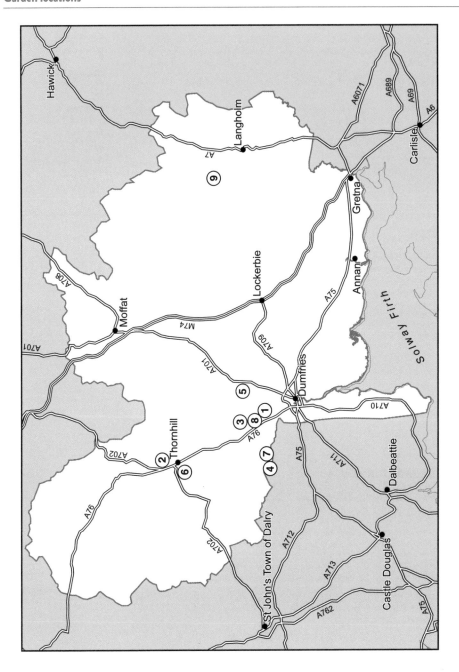

COWHILL TOWER
Holywood DG2 0RL
Mr & Mrs P Weatherall T: 01387 720304

Interesting walled garden. Topiary animals, birds and figures. Woodland walk.
Splendid views from lawn down the Nith valley. Variety of statues from the Far East.

Directions: Holywood 1½ miles off A76, 5 miles north of Dumfries.

Disabled Access:
Partial

Opening Times:
Sunday 2 June
2:00pm - 5:00pm

Admission:
£4.00, children £0.50p

Charities:
Maggie's Cancer Caring
Centres receives 40%,
the net remaining to SG
Beneficiaries.

DABTON
Thornhill DG3 5AR
The Duke and Duchess of Buccleuch T: 01848 330467
E: phunter@buccleuch.com

19th century house built of pink stone. Extensive walled garden. 95 yards long
herbaceous border, roses, island beds and shrubs, ponds with azaleas and primulas,
woodland walk, vegetable garden and greenhouses.

Directions: Entrance off A76 between Thornhill and Carronbridge.

Disabled Access:
Partial

Opening Times:
Sunday 26 May
2:00pm - 5:00pm

Admission:
£4.00, children free

Charities:
The supported charity is still
to be decided and will receive
40%, the net remaining to
SG Beneficiaries.

DALSWINTON HOUSE
Dalswinton DG2 0XZ
Mr & Mrs Peter Landale T: 01387 740220

Late 18th century house sits on top of a hill surrounded by herbaceous beds and
well established shrubs, including rhododendrons and azaleas overlooking the loch.
Attractive walks through woods and around the loch. It was here that the first
steamboat in Britain made its maiden voyage in 1788 and there is a life-size model
beside the water to commemorate this. A recently established plant centre is now in
the old walled garden.

Other Details: Soup available at the daffodil opening in March.
Homemade teas in May.

Directions: Seven miles North of Dumfries off A76.

Disabled Access:
Partial

Opening Times:
Sunday 24 March 11:00am
4:00pm for daffodils
Sunday 19 May
2:00pm - 5:00pm

Admission:
24 Mar: £3.00, children f
19 May: £4.00, children f

Charities:
Marie Curie receives 40%
March opening, Kirkmaho
Parish Church receives
40% June opening, the ne
remaining to SG Beneficia

DRUMPARK
Irongray DG2 9TX
Mr and Mrs Iain Mitchell T: 01387 820323

Well contoured woodland garden and extensive policies with mature azaleas, rhododendrons and rare shrubs among impressive specimen trees. Water garden with primulas and meconopsis. Victorian walled garden with fruit trees and garden produce. Herbaceous border. All set in a natural bowl providing attractive vistas.

Directions: From Dumfries by-pass, head north on A76 for ½ mile, turn left at signpost to "Lochside Industrial Estates" and immediately right onto Irongray Road; continue for 5 miles; gates in sandstone wall on left (½ mile after Routin' Brig).

Disabled Access:
Partial

Opening Times:
Sunday 12 May
2:00pm - 5:00pm

Admission:
£4.00, children free

Charities:
Loch Arthur Community (Camphill Trust) receives 40%, the net remaining to SG Beneficiaries.

GLENAE
Amisfield DG1 3NZ
Mr and Mrs Sebastian Morley T: 01387 710236

A beautiful walled garden, well stocked with interesting plants, four small lawns surrounded by colourful herbaceous borders, a woodland garden and a restored Victorian glass-house.

Other Details: Bouncy castle.

Directions: 1½ miles north of Amisfield on A701. Turn left to Duncow and Auldgirth and 1 mile on right.

Disabled Access:
Partial

Opening Times:
Sunday 9 June
2:00pm - 5:00pm

Admission:
£4.00, children £0.50p

Charities:
Yorkhill Children's Foundation receives 40%, the net remaining to SG Beneficiaries.

GROVEHILL HOUSE
Burnhead, Thornhill DG3 4AD
Mr and Mrs Allen & Penelope Paterson T: 01848 331637

Two-acre plantsman's garden designed for year-round interest. The steep site has been terraced to offer sheltered borders and garden 'rooms'. Small productive walled garden. There are fine views down the Nith Valley and to the surrounding hills.

Directions: In Burnhead on the A702. Approx 1 mile, coming from Thornhill. House on left on steep corner with sandstone lodge and red phone box opposite.

Disabled Access:
None

Opening Times:
By arrangement Monday 1 April to Monday 30 September

Admission:
£3.00

Charities:
Loch Arthur Community (Camphill Trust) receives 40%, the net remaining to SG Beneficiaries.

NEWTONAIRDS LODGE
Newtonairds DG2 0JL
Mr & Mrs J Coutts
www.newtonairds-hostasandgarden.co.uk

An interesting 1.2 acre Plantsman's garden punctuated with topiary, trees and shrubs, surrounding a 19th century listed baronial lodge. The National Collection is integrated with a further 150 other Hosta varieties on a natural terraced wooded bank.

Other Details: National Plant Collection ®: Hosta Plantagirea Hybrids and CVS
16 June: Wine and nibbles available.
4 August: Scottish Piper during the afternoon.

Directions: From Dumfries take A76 north. At Holywood take B729 (Dunscore). After 1 mile turn left (Morrinton). After 3 miles red sandstone lodge is on right behind black iron railings.

Disabled Access:
Partial

Opening Times:
Sunday 16 June
5:00pm - 9:00pm
Sunday 4 August
1:00pm - 5:00pm

Admission:
£4.00 for both openings.

Charities:
Peter Pan Moat Brae Trust receives 40% June opening, SWSRnR receives 40% August opening, the net remaining to SG Beneficiaries.

PORTRACK HOUSE
Holywood DG2 0RW
Charles Jencks
www.charlesjencks.com

Original 18th century manor house with Victorian addition; octagonal folly-library. Twisted undulating landforms and terraces designed by Charles Jencks as "The Garden of Cosmic Speculation"; lakes designed by Maggie Keswick; rhododendrons, large new greenhouse in a geometric kitchen garden of the Six Senses; Glengower Hill plantation and view; woodland walks with Nonsense Building (architect: James Stirling); Universe cascade and rail garden of the Scottish Worthies; interesting sculpture including that of DNA and newly completed Comet Bridge.

Other Details: Please note: this year the garden is undergoing some necessary repair and renovation work around the mounds and ponds but everything will be open to see as usual.
Local Pipe Band.

Directions: Holywood 1½ miles off A76, five miles north of Dumfries.

Disabled Access:
Partial

Opening Times:
Sunday 5 May
12:00pm - 5:00pm

Admission:
£6.00

Charities:
Maggie's Cancer Caring Centres receives 40%, the net remaining to SG Beneficiaries.

WESTERHALL
Bentpath, Langholm DG13 0NQ
Mrs Peter Buckley

An extensive collection of azaleas, rhododendrons, rare shrubs and mature trees set in a landscape of follies, sculpture and stunning vistas. The redesigned walled garden contains a glasshouse with some exotic plants which have been collected from around the world.

Directions: From Langholm: Take B709 towards Eskdalemuir. After approx. 5miles in village of Bentpath, turn right by white house. Go down through village, over small/narrow bridge and turn right by church. Carry on this road for approx. 1 mile. Parking at farm, signed.

Disabled Access:
Partial

Opening Times:
Sunday 26 May
2:00pm - 5:00pm

Admission:
£4.00, children free

Charities:
Westerkirk Parish Trust receives 40%, the net remaining to SG Beneficiaries.

DUNBARTONSHIRE

Scotland's Gardens 2013 Guidebook is sponsored by INVESTEC WEALTH & INVESTMENT

District Organiser

Mrs K Murray	7 The Birches, Shandon, Helensburgh G84 8HN

Area Organisers

Mrs M Greenwell	Avalon, Shore Road, Mambeg Garelochhead G84 0EN
Mrs R Lang	Ardchapel, Shandon, Helensburgh G84 8NP
Mrs R Macaulay	Denehard, Garelochhead G84 0EL
Mrs S Miller	8 Laggary Park, Rhu G84 8LY
Mrs M Rogers	Station House, Station Road, Tarbet G83 7DA
Mrs J Theaker	19 Blackhill Drive, Helensburgh G84 9AF
Mrs H Wands	Lindowan, Rhu G84 8NH

Treasurer

Mrs S Miller	8 Laggary Park, Rhu G84 8LY

Gardens open on a specific date

Kilarden, Rosneath	Sunday 14 April	2:00pm	-	5:00pm
Ross Priory, Gartocharn	Sunday 19 May	2:00pm	-	5:00pm
Geilston Garden, Cardross	Sunday 2 June	1:00pm	-	5:00pm
Kirkton Cottage, Cardross	Sunday 16 June	2:00pm	-	5:00pm
Shandon Gardens, Shandon	Sunday 7 July	2:00pm	-	5:00pm
Rhu Gardens, Rhu	Sunday 21 July	2:00pm	-	5:00pm
SG Hill House Plant Sale, Helensburgh	Sunday 1 September	11:00am	-	4:00pm

Gardens open regularly

Glenarn, Rhu	23 March - 21 September	Dawn	-	Dusk

Gardens open by arrangement

Parkhead, Rosneath	1 April - 30 September	01436 831448

DUNBARTONSHIRE

Scotland's Gardens 2013 Guidebook is sponsored by **INVESTEC WEALTH & INVESTMENT**

Plant sales

8 Laggary Park, Rhu	Sunday 23 June	2:00pm	- 5:00pm
SG Hill House Plant Sale, Helensburgh	Sunday 1 September	11:00am	- 4:00pm

Glenearn © Ray Cox

Key to symbols

New in 2013	Homemade teas	Accommodation
Teas	Dogs on a lead allowed	Plant stall
Cream teas	Wheelchair access	Scottish Snowdrop Festival

Garden locations

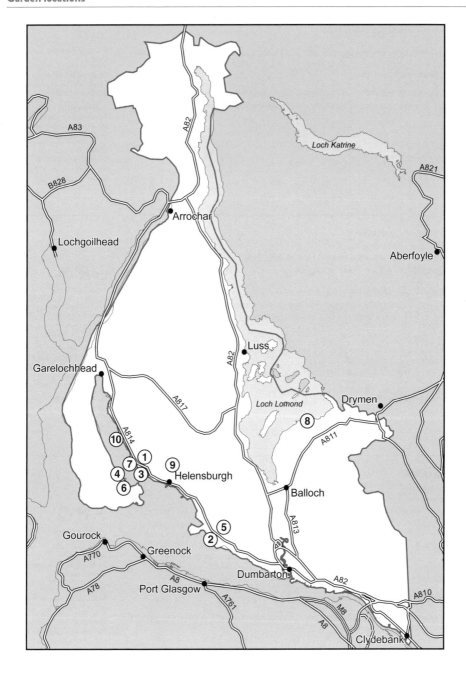

8 LAGGARY PARK
Rhu, Helensburgh G84 8LY
Susan and Jim Miller T: 01436 821314
E: susan.miller17@btinternet.com

Large plant sale comprising perennials and shrubs propagated from the collection growing in the garden, including hardy geraniums, penstemons, meconopsis, delphiniums and violas.

Directions: Take A814 shore road from Helensburgh to Rhu Marina. Turn right into Pier Road and take second turn right (signposted) into Laggary Park and bear right.

Disabled Access:
Partial

Opening Times:
Plant Sale Sunday 23 June
2:00pm - 5:00pm

Admission:
Free but donation requested from those wishing to go round the garden

Charities:
SSPCA receives 40%, the net remaining to SG Beneficiaries.

GEILSTON GARDEN
Main Road, Cardross G82 5HD
The National Trust for Scotland T: 0844 4932219
E: jgough@nts.org.uk www.nts.org.uk

Geilston Garden has many attractive features including the walled garden with the herbaceous border providing summer colour, the tranquil woodland walks along the Geilston Burn and a large working kitchen garden.

Other Details: There will be a plant sale offering a range of herbaceous perennials, and geraniums, a live band playing classical music, teas and home baking plus a strawberries and cream stall!
Don't miss the toy duck race for children starting at 2.30pm in the Geilston Burn!

Directions: On the A814, 1 mile from Cardross.

Disabled Access:
Partial

Opening Times:
Sunday 2 June
1:00pm - 5:00pm

Admission:
£4.00, children under 12 free
N.B. Prices correct at time of going to print

Charities:
Donation to SG Beneficiaries

GLENARN
Glenarn Road, Rhu, Helensburgh G84 8LL
Michael and Sue Thornley T: 01436 820493
E: masthome@dsl.pipex.com www.gardens-of-argyll.co.uk

Glenarn survives as a complete example of a 10 acre garden which spans from 1850 to the present day. There are winding paths through glens under a canopy of oak and lime, sunlit open spaces, a vegetable garden with beehives, and a rock garden with views over the Gareloch. It is famous for its collection of rare and tender rhododendrons but horticulturally there is much more besides.

Other Details: Catering for groups by prior arrangement.

Directions: On A814, two miles north of Helensburgh. Cars to be left at gate unless passengers are infirm.

Disabled Access:
Partial

Opening Times:
23 March to 21 September
Dawn - Dusk

Admission:
£4.00, accompanied children under 16 free.

Charities:
Donation to SG Beneficiaries

4

KILARDEN
Rosneath G84 0PU
Mr and Mrs J E Rowe

Sheltered hilly 10 acre woodland with notable collection of species and hybrid rhododendrons gathered over a period of 50 years by the late Neil and Joyce Rutherford as seen on "Beechgrove Garden".

Other Details: St Modan's church open. Organ music. Homemade tea in church hall. Paths may be muddy.

Directions: ¼ mile from Rosneath off B833.

Disabled Access:
Partial

Opening Times:
Sunday 14 April
2:00pm - 5:00pm

Admission:
£2.50, children free

Charities:
Friends of St Modan's receives 40%, the net remaining to SG Beneficiaries.

5

KIRKTON COTTAGE
Cardross, Dumbarton G82 5EZ
Mr and Mrs T Duggan

A garden of just under one acre on a south facing slope with a burn running through, which provides a variety of growing conditions. Mixed borders, fruit, vegetables, herbs and bog garden.

Other Details: Homemade teas at Kirkton House.

Directions: ½ mile up Darleith Road at west end of Cardross off A814.

Disabled Access:
None

Opening Times:
Sunday 16 June
2:00pm - 5:00pm

Admission:
£3.00, children free

Charities:
Macmillan Nurses receives 20%, Alzheimer's Scotland, Dementia Nurse Appeal receives 20%, the net remaining to SG Beneficiaries.

6

PARKHEAD
Rosneath, Helensburgh G84 0QR
Ian & Susan McKellar T: 01436 831448
E: imckellaris@gmail.com

Early 18th century building attached to an older walled garden which was a field by the 1960s. Since then the current owners have restored the burnt out property and laid out the architectural Italianate garden, featuring Box, Yew, Beech, Hornbeam, Holly and Prunus in hedges parterre and topiary. Pots and bedding plants set off the clipped evergreens. A lily pond, foot maze and sundial garden occupy three circular Yew "rooms". There is a hen run and walled enclosure for vegetables and soft fruit.

Directions: One mile beyond Rosneath on B833 fork left at sign for caravan park for ¼ mile then track on right (sign on tree). Exercise caution. Helensburgh/Coulport Service bus 316 hourly.

Disabled Access:
Partial

Opening Times:
By arrangement 1 April to 30 September

Admission:
£4.00, children free, group charge by arrangement

Charities:
Friends of St. Modan's receives 40%, the net remaining to SG Beneficiaries.

RHU GARDENS
Rhu G84 8NF
Mr and Mrs Jim Miller/Mr and Mrs Peter Proctor

Glebeside House, Spy's Lane G84 8RA (Mr and Mrs Peter Proctor). Traditional Scottish house built in 1834 with ⅓ acre of ground. Natural rockery, laburnum arch and 4 or 5 'rooms', mixed herbaceous islands and borders, shrubs, lawn and greenhouse.
8 Laggary Park, G84 8LY (Mr and Mrs Jim Miller) ½ acre garden with flowering shrubs and specimen trees. New clematis arbour, pergola, fernery and woodland. Mixed borders with hardy geraniums, hydrangeas and penstemons.

Directions: Take A814 shore road from Helensburgh to Rhu Marina. Turn right into Pier Road. Spy's Lane is uphill on left and Laggary Park on right. Park on Pier Road.

Disabled Access:
Partial

Opening Times:
Sunday 21 July
2:00pm - 5:00pm

Admission:
£4.00 (includes both gardens), accompanied children under 12 free

Charities:
Riding for the Disabled receives 20%, SSPCA receives 20%, the net remaining to SG Beneficiaries.

ROSS PRIORY
Gartocharn G83 8NL
University of Strathclyde

1812 Gothic addition by James Gillespie Graham to house of 1693 overlooking Loch Lomond. Rhododendrons, azaleas, selected shrubs and trees. Walled garden with glasshouses, pergola, ornamental plantings. Family burial ground. Nature and garden trails.

Other Details: House not open to view. Putting green. Teas are served in the house.

Directions: Gartocharn 1½ miles off A811. Bus: Balloch to Gartocharn leaves Balloch at 1:00pm and 3:00pm.

Disabled Access:
Full

Opening Times:
Sunday 19 May
2:00pm - 5:00pm

Admission:
£4.00, children free

Charities:
CHAS receives 40%, the net remaining to SG Beneficiaries.

SG HILL HOUSE PLANT SALE
Helensburgh G84 9AJ
The National Trust for Scotland/SG T: 01436 673900
E: gsmith@nts.org.uk www.nts.org.uk

The Plant Sale is held in the garden of The Hill House which has fine views over the Clyde estuary and is considered Charles Rennie Mackintosh's domestic masterpiece. The sale includes nursery grown perennials and locally grown trees, shrubs, herbaceous, alpine and house plants. The gardens continue to be restored to the patron's planting scheme with many features that reflect Mackintosh's design.

Other Details: Tea served in house from 11.00am.

Directions: Follow signs to The Hill House.

Disabled Access:
Full

Opening Times:
Plant sale 1 September
11:00am - 4:00pm
Garden also open

Admission:
No admission charge but donations to Scotland's Gardens welcome

Charities:
All proceeds to SG Beneficiaries

SHANDON GARDENS
Shandon G84 8HN
Mr and Mrs Ian Chatten & Mr and Mrs Robin Murray

West Garemount: Open to the public for the first time this steeply terraced garden with burn running through has many unusual trees and shrubs. Gravel garden and rose arbour. Patios on different levels with fine views over the Gareloch. Very steep steps.
7 The Birches: Recently completed Crevice Garden adds new interest to the structure and planting. Rockery, raised beds, gravel garden, ferns, grasses, roses and good mixed borders.

Other Details: Cake and candy stall.

Directions: Three and three quarter miles north of Helensburgh on A814. Take Ardchapel exit and park on service road below houses.

Disabled Access:
None

Opening Times:
Sunday 7 July
2:00pm - 5:00pm

Admission:
£3.00, children under 12 free

Charities:
SSPCA receives 40%,
the net remaining to SG
Beneficiaries.

Parkhead

PLANT SALE DONATIONS WANTED

DONATIONS OF PLANTS ARE ALWAYS EXTREMELY WELCOME.

EAST LOTHIAN

Scotland's Gardens 2013 Guidebook is sponsored by **INVESTEC WEALTH & INVESTMENT**

District Organiser

Mr W Alder	Granary House, Kippielaw, Haddington EH41 4PY

Area Organisers

Mr P Atkins	Mizzentop, Westerdunes Park, North Berwick EH39 5HJ
Mrs J Flockhart	Belton Hill Road, Gullane EH31 2BE
Mrs C Gwyn	The Walled Garden, Tyninghame, Dunbar EH42 1XY
Mr M Hedderwick	Gifford Bank, Gifford EH41 4JE
Mrs J Lindsay	Kirkland, Whittingehame EH41 4QA
Mrs N Parker	Steading Cottage, Stevenson, Haddington EH41 4PU

Treasurer

Mr S M Edington	Meadowside Cottage, Strathearn Road, North Berwick EH39 5BZ

Gardens open on a specific date

Shepherd House, Inveresk	Saturday 23 February	11:00pm	-	4:00pm
Shepherd House, Inveresk	Sunday 24 February	11:00am	-	4:00pm
Winton House, Pencaitland	Sunday 7 April	12:00pm	-	4:30pm
Shepherd House, Inveresk	Saturday 4 May	11:00am	-	4:00pm
Inwood, Carberry	Sunday 5 May	2:00pm	-	5:00pm
Shepherd House, Inveresk	Sunday 5 May	11:00am	-	4:00pm
Tyninghame House, Dunbar	Sunday 12 May	1:00pm	-	5:00pm
Belhaven Hill School and Belhaven House, Dunbar	Sunday 26 May	2:00pm	-	5:00pm
Broadwoodside, Gifford	Sunday 2 June	2:00pm	-	6:00pm
Shepherd House, Inveresk	Saturday 15 June	11:00am	-	5:00pm
Athelstaneford Village,	Sunday 16 June	2:00pm	-	5:00pm
Shepherd House, Inveresk	Sunday 16 June	11:00am	-	5:00pm
Gifford Bank, Gifford	Sunday 23 June	1:00pm	-	5:00pm
Tyninghame House, Dunbar	Sunday 30 June	1:00pm	-	5:00pm
Bowerhouse with Bowerhouse Walled Garden, Dunbar	Sunday 7 July	2:00pm	-	5:00pm
Amisfield Walled Garden, Haddington	Sunday 25 August	2:00pm	-	5:00pm

EAST LOTHIAN

Scotland's Gardens 2013 Guidebook is sponsored by **INVESTEC WEALTH & INVESTMENT**

Gardens open regularly

Inwood, Carberry	2 May - 12 September Tues, Thurs & Sats	2:00pm - 5:00pm
Shepherd House, Inveresk	12 February - 28 February Tues & Thurs	2:00pm - 4:00pm
	16 April - 4 July Tues & Thurs	2:00pm - 4:00pm

Gardens open by arrangement

Bowerhouse, Dunbar	15 April - 30 September	rebecca@tyndall.co.uk
Humbie Dean, Humbie	1 April - 31 July	07768 996382
Stobshiel House, Humbie	On request.	01875 833646

Shepherd House

Key to symbols

New in 2013		Homemade teas			Accommodation
Teas		Dogs on a lead allowed			Plant stall
Cream teas		Wheelchair access			Scottish Snowdrop Festival

Garden locations

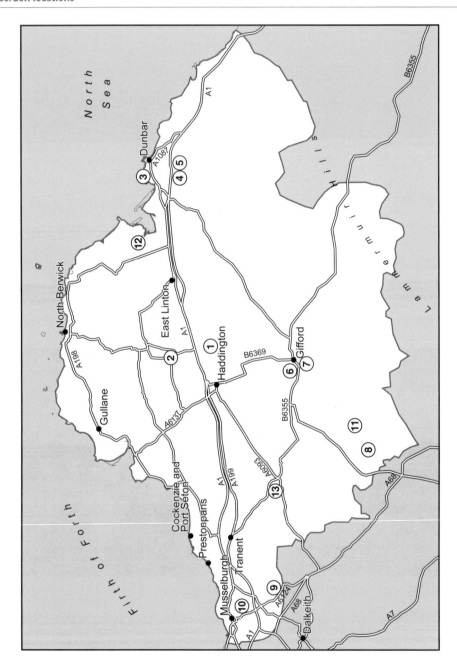

AMISFIELD WALLED GARDEN
Haddington EH41 4PU
Amisfield Preservation Trust (Leased from East Lothian Council)
www.amisfield.org.uk

18th century walled garden, abandoned for many years. The garden, which has an area of approximately 8 acres, is completely enclosed by 16ft high walls of dressed stone. Each corner features a stone pavilion, all of whose domed roofs have been lost. Over the last 5 years, herbaceous borders, vegetable plots and fruit trees have been planted and new paths laid. A hornbeam walk was planted in 2010 and is maturing well. Apple trees were planted on the diagonal pathways and small orchards have been introduced within the last two years, and willow beds planted in the Winter Garden. A wild flower meadow has been introduced as a further step in our bio-diversity plan. Archaeologists are starting to uncover the former 'pinery vinery' glasshouse.

Directions: Follow the A199 from Haddington; turn south about 1 mile east of Haddington at the Stevenson/Hailes Castle junction. Garden is on right just after the bridge over the River Tyne.

Disabled Access:
Full

Opening Times:
Sunday 25 August
2:00pm - 5:00pm

Admission:
£4.00

Charities:
Amisfield Preservation Trust receives 40%, the net remaining to SG Beneficiaries.

ATHELSTANEFORD VILLAGE
EH39 5BE
Gardeners of Athelstaneford

A variety of interesting village gardens of historical interest all within walking distance.

Directions: On B1343.

Disabled Access:
Partial

Opening Times:
Sunday 16 June
2:00pm - 5:00pm

Admission:
£4.50, children free

Charities:
The Village Hall, Church and School share 40%, the net remaining to SG Beneficiaries.

BELHAVEN HILL SCHOOL AND BELHAVEN HOUSE
Belhaven Road, Dunbar, East Lothian EH42 1NN
Mr Innes MacAskill and Mr and Mrs Jon Bruneau

Originally called Winterfield House the School has retained the formal garden in front of the walled garden which is accessed through an ornate gate and archway and is laid to lawn with box-edged borders, some containing wild flowers. A gate from the playing field leads to Belhaven House which has 4 acres of formal Georgian gardens, walled vegetable and fruit garden and woodland. Owned for a while by Sir George Taylor a former director of Kew gardens and famous botanist.

Other Details: Champion Trees: Arbutus unedo, Dividia involucrata, Eucryphia nymansensis etc.   Car parking at the school. Teas, cakes and sandwiches served in front hall of school by main entrance. Toilet facilities in main school building.

Directions: Approaching Dunbar from A1 on A1087 Belhaven House is opposite Brewery Lane on the junction with Duke Street and the school entrance is a further 300 yards past a high stone wall.

Disabled Access:
Partial

Opening Times:
Sunday 26 May
2:00pm - 5:00pm

Admission:
£4.00, children under 12 free

Charities:
East Lothian Special Needs Play Schemes receives 40%, the net remaining to SG Beneficiaries.

BOWERHOUSE
Dunbar EH42 1RE
Mark and Rebecca Tyndall
E: rebecca@tyndall.co.uk

The formal gardens with courtyards and water features enhance the 1835 David Bryce Mansion House set in 17 acres of parkland, orchard and woodland walks.

Directions: 1 mile south of Dunbar off the westbound carriage of the A1.

Disabled Access:
Full

Opening Times:
By arrangement
15 April to 30 September

Admission:
£4.00

Charities:
Leuchie House receives 40%, the net remaining to SG Beneficiaries.

BOWERHOUSE WITH BOWERHOUSE WALLED GARDEN
Dunbar EH42 1RE
Mark & Rebecca Tyndall and Ian & Moira Marrian

Two contrasting but complementary gardens set in 26 acres of parkland, orchard and woodland walks, close to Dunbar and Spott but completely self-contained. The formal gardens with courtyards and water features enhance the 1835 David Bryce Mansion House while the 18th century walled garden is a riot of flowers, shrubs, fruit and vegetables.

Directions: 1 Mile South of Dunbar off the westbound carriageway of the A1.

Disabled Access:
Full

Opening Times:
Sunday 7 July
2:00pm - 5:00pm

Admission:
£4.00 for both gardens.
Children under 12 free

Charities:
Save the Children Fund receives 40%, the net remaining to SG Beneficiaries.

BROADWOODSIDE
Gifford EH41 4JQ
Anna and Robert Dalrymple
www.broadwoodside.co.uk

Selected by "The Independent" as one of Britain's "50 Best Homes and Gardens", the garden at Broadwoodside is planted in and around a farm steading that was rescued from dereliction in 2000. Two sheltered courtyards are encircled by the old buildings. Around the outside of the steading the garden extends into the surrounding farmland and woods on an ambitious scale.
"Fast becoming one of the most influential new gardens in Scotland" Caroline Donald, The Sunday Times, 2012.

Directions: On B6355 going out of Gifford towards Pentcaitland, at the Golf Course junction.

Disabled Access:
Partial

Opening Times:
Sunday 2 June
2:00pm - 6:00pm

Admission:
£5.00

Charities:
Cancer Research Scotland receives 40%, the net remaining to SG Beneficiaries.

GIFFORD BANK
Gifford EH41 4JE
Mr and Mrs M Hedderwick

A constantly evolving garden of three acres surrounding the Georgian house with seperate garden rooms for roses, an Italianate rill, a pond and bog beds. The walled garden has extensive herbaceous beds with vegetable plots and fruit trees. Some of the garden is deliberately left wild to encourage birds and insects. The woodland walk around the perimeter of the garden has undergone quite a refit and work is ongoing to gently continue its development.

Other Details: Champion Trees: Monterey Cypress.

Directions: Gifford Bank is the last house on the right on the B6355 going out of Gifford towards the Golf Course.

Disabled Access:
Partial

Opening Times:
Sunday 23 June
1:00pm - 5:00pm

Admission:
£5.00

Charities:
Cancer Research
Campaign receives 40%,
the net remaining to SG
Beneficiaries.

HUMBIE DEAN
Humbie EH36 5PW
Frank Kirwan T: 07768 996382
E: frank.kirwan@which.net

A two acre woodland garden at 600 feet with the core created in the 1960s, under renovation and major extension since 2008. It is bounded by burns and woodland and on different levels. Renovation entails tree clearance; creation of light; access to the woodland; replanting; construction of paths, steps, a bridge, and a woodland walk. New planting includes an Oudolf-style autumn border; extensive candelabra primula and bulb planting; and extension of the mature azalea and rhododendron planting.

Directions: Enter Humbie from A68, pass school and village hall on left then turn right into lane (Shell sign in hedge). Take second left. Humbie Dean is first house on left between two small bridges.

Disabled Access:
None

Opening Times:
By arrangement
1 April to 31 July

Admission:
£4.00

Charities:
Oxfam receives 40%,
the net remaining to SG
Beneficiaries.

INWOOD
Carberry, Musselburgh EH21 8PZ
Mr and Mrs I Morrison T: 0131 665 4550
E: lindsay@inwoodgarden.com www.inwoodgarden.com

Created from scratch, Inwood Garden sits snugly around the house, with a fine Cornus contraversa 'Variagata' at the centre and a sheltering backdrop of mature woodland. This 0.4 ha (1 acre) enthusiast's garden is packed with interesting plants in generously proportioned island beds. It's worth a visit at any time during the season with massed tulips and rhododendrons in spring, rambling roses and clematis in high summer and hydrangeas and late flowering perennials in early autumn. Greenhouses with begonias and streptocarpus collections and a pond invite further exploration. An "RHS Recommended Garden".

Directions: From the A1 take A6094 exit signed Wallyford and Dalkeith. At roundabout turn left on A6124. Continue up hill for 1½ miles. Turn left at Inwood sign on left.

Disabled Access:
Partial

Opening Times:
Sunday 5 May
2:00pm - 5:00pm
2 May to 12 September
2:00pm - 5:00pm Tuesdays,
Thursdays & Saturdays
Groups welcome

Admission:
£4.00, children under 12 free

Charities:
All proceeds to SG
Beneficiaries

SHEPHERD HOUSE
Inveresk, Musselburgh EH21 7TH
Sir Charles and Lady Fraser T: 0131 665 2570
E: annfraser@talktalk.net   www.shepherdhousegarden.co.uk

Shepherd House and its one-acre garden form a walled triangle in the middle of the 18th century village of Inveresk. The main garden is to the rear of the house where the formality of the front garden is continued with a herb parterre and two symmetrical potagers. A formal rill runs the length of the garden, beneath a series of rose and clematis arches and connects the two ponds. The snowdrops are mainly grown in beds and borders. However there is a growing collection of "specialist snowdrops" around 50 different cultivars at present some of which will be displayed in our "Snowdrop Theatre".

Other Details: No teas will be served on any of the open days.

Directions: Near Musselburgh. From A1 take A6094 exit signed Wallyford and Dalkeith and follow signs to Inveresk.

Disabled Access:
Full

Opening Times:
Saturday 23 February
11:00pm - 4:00pm
Sunday 24 February
11:00am - 4:00pm
For the snowdrop festival.
Saturday 4 May
11:00am - 4:00pm
Sunday 5 May
11:00am - 4:00pm
Saturday 15 June
11:00am - 5:00pm
Sunday 16 June
11:00am - 5:00pm
12 February to 28 February
Tuesdays and Thursdays
2:00pm - 4:00pm
16 April to 4 July
2:00pm - 4:00pm
Tuesdays and Thursdays

Admission:
£4.00, children free

Charities:
Mary's Meals receives 40%,
the net remaining to SG
Beneficiaries.

STOBSHIEL HOUSE
Humbie EH36 5PD
Mr Maxwell and Lady Sarah Ward T: 01875 833646
E: stobshiel@gmail.com

A large garden to see for all seasons. Walled garden adjacent to the house, box-edged borders filled with bulbs, roses and lavender beds. Rustic summerhouse. Castellated yew hedge. Glasshouse. Shrubbery with rhododendrons, azaleas and bulbs. Water and woodland garden with meconopsis and primulas. Formal lily pond. Woodland walks.

Other Details: Groups welcome.

Directions: B6368 Haddington/Humbie road; sign to Stobshiel 1 mile.

Disabled Access:
None

Opening Times:
By arrangement on request

Admission:
£4.00, children under 12 free

Charities:
Camphill Blair Drummond
receives 40%, the
net remaining to SG
Beneficiaries.

TYNINGHAME HOUSE
Dunbar EH42 1XW
Tyninghame Gardens Ltd

Splendid 17th century pink sandstone Scottish baronial house, remodelled in 1829 by William Burn, rises out of a sea of plants. Herbaceous border, formal rose garden, Lady Haddington's secret garden with old fashioned roses, formal walled garden with sculpture and yew hedges. The "wilderness" spring garden with magnificent rhododendrons, azaleas, flowering trees and bulbs. Grounds include one mile beech avenue to sea, "apple walk", Romanesque ruin of St Baldred's Church, views across Tyne estuary and Lammermuir Hills. Tyninghame is one of only seven estates in Scotland to have been awarded 'Outstanding' for every category in the Inventory of Gardens and Designed Landscapes of Scotland.

Other Details: Champion Trees: Two British and seven Scottish.

Directions: Gates on A198 at Tyninghame Village.

Disabled Access:
Full

Opening Times:
Sunday 12 May
1:00pm - 5:00pm
Sunday 30 June
1:00pm - 5:00pm

Admission:
£5.00, children free

Charities:
Cyrenians receives 40% 12 May opening, Dunbar RNLI receives 40% 30 June opening, the net remaining to SG Beneficiaries.

WINTON HOUSE
Pencaitland EH34 5AT
Sir Francis Ogilvy Winton Trust T: 01875 340222
www.wintonhouse.co.uk

The gardens continue to develop and improve, in addition to the natural areas around Sir David's Loch and the Dell, extensive mixed borders are taking shape for the terrace borders and walled garden. In spring a glorious covering of daffodils make way for cherry and apple blossoms. Enjoy an informative tour of this historic house and walk off delicious lunches and homebaking around the estate.

Directions: Entrance off B6355 Tranent/Pencaitland Road.

Disabled Access:
Full

Opening Times:
Sunday 7 April
12:00pm - 4:30pm

Admission:
Estate £4.00, guided house tours £5.00/£3.00, children under 10 free

Charities:
Maggie's Centre receives 40%, the net remaining to SG Beneficiaries.

Tynninghame House

EDINBURGH & WEST LOTHIAN

Scotland's Gardens 2013 Guidebook is sponsored by **INVESTEC WEALTH & INVESTMENT**

District Organiser

Mrs Victoria Reid Thomas   Riccarton Mains Farmhouse, Currie EH14 4AR

Treasurer

Mr Charles Welwood   Kirknewton House, Kirknewton EH27 8DA

Gardens open on a specific date

61 Fountainhall Road, Edinburgh	Sunday 7 April	2:00pm	-	5:00pm
Dean Gardens , Edinburgh	Sunday 7 April	2:00pm	-	5:00pm
10 Pilton Drive North, Edinburgh	Saturday 13 April	11:00am	-	4:00pm
61 Fountainhall Road, Edinburgh	Sunday 14 April	2:00pm	-	5:00pm
61 Fountainhall Road, Edinburgh	Sunday 12 May	2:00pm	-	5:00pm
Rocheid Garden, Edinburgh	Saturday 18 May	2:00pm	-	6:00pm
61 Fountainhall Road, Edinburgh	Sunday 19 May	2:00pm	-	5:00pm
Moray Place & Bank Gardens, Edinburgh	Sunday 19 May	2:00pm	-	5:00pm
The Glasshouses at The Royal Botanic Gardens, Edinburgh	Sunday 2 June	10:00am	-	5:30pm
Dr Neil's Garden, Duddingston Village	Saturday 15 June	2:00pm	-	5:00pm
Rocheid Garden, Edinburgh	Saturday 15 June	2:00pm	-	6:00pm
Dr Neil's Garden, Duddingston Village	Sunday 16 June	2:00pm	-	5:00pm
101 Greenbank Crescent, Edinburgh	Sat & Sun 22-23 June	2:00pm	-	5:00pm
61 Fountainhall Road, Edinburgh	Sunday 23 June	2:00pm	-	5:00pm
15 Morningside Park, Edinburgh	Sunday 21 July	2:00pm	-	5:00pm
Hunter's Tryst, Edinburgh	Sunday 28 July	2:00pm	-	5:00pm
15 Morningside Park, Edinburgh	Sunday 4 August	2:00pm	-	5:00pm
45 Northfield Crescent, Bathgate	Saturday 10 August	2:00pm	-	5:00pm
45 Northfield Crescent, Bathgate	Sunday 11 August	2:00pm	-	5:00pm
Rocheid Garden, Edinburgh	Saturday 7 September	2:00pm	-	6:00pm
61 Fountainhall Road, Edinburgh	Sunday 8 September	2:00pm	-	5:00pm
The Archivists' Garden, Edinburgh	Saturday 14 September	2:00pm	-	5:00pm
61 Fountainhall Road, Edinburgh	Sunday 15 September	2:00pm	-	5:00pm
The Archivists' Garden, Edinburgh	Sunday 15 September	2:00pm	-	5:00pm

Gardens open regularly

Newliston, Kirkliston	1 May - 2 June except Mons & Tues	2:00pm	-	6:00pm

EDINBURGH & WEST LOTHIAN

Scotland's Gardens 2013 Guidebook is sponsored by **INVESTEC WEALTH & INVESTMENT**

Gardens open by arrangement

45 Northfield Crescent, Bathgate	On request	07885 701642
61 Fountainhall Road, Edinburgh	On request	0131 667 6146
Hunter's Tryst, Edinburgh	On request	0131 477 2919
Newliston, Kirkliston	On request	0131 333 3231
Rocheid Garden, Edinburgh	On request	0131 311 7000

Hunter's Tryst

Key to symbols

 New in 2013

 Teas

 Cream teas

 Homemade teas

 Dogs on a lead allowed

 Wheelchair access

 Accommodation

 Plant stall

 Scottish Snowdrop Festival

Garden locations

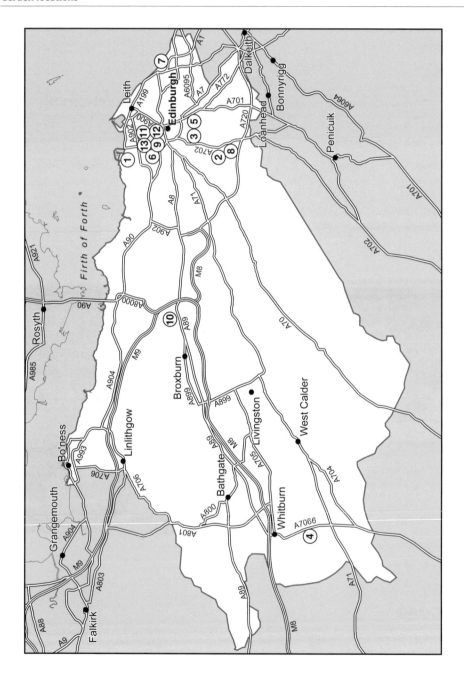

10 PILTON DRIVE NORTH
Edinburgh EH5 1NX
Fraser Drummond T: 0131 467 6811
E: fdrummond@hotmail.co.uk www.thegrantongarden.webs.com

Divided into three areas, the garden is 90 x 40 feet. In April, fritillarias, Erythronium 'Pagoda' and other plants, flower in the woodland area. In May the rockery and herbaceous bed are in flower. There are ponds, a greenhouse and numerous unusual species, e.g. Vestia, Actinidia, Kolomikta and Ribes Speciosum. The last area is evergreen with Polyanthus and Tulips.

Directions: From Crewe Road roundabout, pass the nearby Morrisons on Ferry Road and turn left into Pilton Drive, carry on straight down to Pilton Drive North. On numbers 9 and 18 Bus Routes.

Disabled Access:
None

Opening Times:
Saturday 13 April
11:00am - 4:00pm

Admission:
£3.00

Charities:
Maggie's Cancer Caring Centres receives 40%, the net remaining to SG Beneficiaries.

101 GREENBANK CRESCENT
Edinburgh EH10 5TA
Mr and Mrs Jerry and Christine Gregson T: 0131 447 6492
E: jerry_gregson@yahoo.co.uk

Interesting spacious terraced garden with water feature, variety of shrubs, and wandering paths and steps. Marvellous views over hills and neighbouring park. Opening later than usual this year to show some different aspects of the garden.

Directions: From Edinburgh centre, via Morningside Station. Turn right at Greenbank Church crossing. Nos 16 and 5 buses. Stop opposite Greenbank Row.

Disabled Access:
None

Opening Times:
Saturday 22 June
2:00pm - 5:00pm
Sunday 23 June
2:00pm - 5:00pm

Admission:
£3.00, children free

Charities:
Macmillan Cancer Support receives 40%, the net remaining to SG Beneficiaries.

15 MORNINGSIDE PARK
Edinburgh EH10 5HD
Miller/Williams Family

Tiny town garden (50 feet x 25 feet) crammed with a wonderful variety of plants and interesting features including a Mediterranean-style patio and water feature.

Other Details: Cold drinks and biscuits served.

Directions: Turn west off Morningside Road at M&S. On bus routes 11,15, 16, 5, 23.

Disabled Access:
None

Opening Times:
Sunday 21 July
2:00pm - 5:00pm
Sunday 4 August
2:00pm - 5:00pm

Admission:
£3.00

Charities:
The Citizen's Income Trust receives 40%, the net remaining to SG Beneficiaries.

45 NORTHFIELD CRESCENT
Longridge, Bathgate EH47 8AL
Mr Jamie Robertson T: 07885 701642
E: jamierobertson04@hotmail.co.uk

A delightful garden with a wide variety of shrubs and herbaceous plants. Large pond with a small waterfall and a colourful decked area with an attractive selection of bedding plants. Good vegetable patch and a 12 feet x 8 feet greenhouse. The owner has held the "West Lothian Gardener of the Year" award.

Directions: From A71: turn right after Breith at traffic lights, go about a mile and turn right into the Crescent. From Whitburn: take A706 Longridge Road to Longridge and last left into Crescent.

Disabled Access:
None

Opening Times:
Saturday 10 August
2:00pm - 5:00pm
Sunday 11 August
2:00pm - 5:00pm
Also by arrangement on request

Admission:
£4.00

Charities:
World Cancer Research Fund receives 40%, the net remaining to SG Beneficiaries.

61 FOUNTAINHALL ROAD
Edinburgh EH9 2LH
Dr J A and Mrs A Hammond T: 0131 667 6146
E: froglady@blueyonder.co.uk www.froglady.pwp.blueyonder.co.uk

Large walled town garden in which trees and shrubs form an architectural backdrop to a wide variety of flowering plants. The growing collection of hellebores and trilliums and a large variety of late blooming flowers provide interest from early March to late October. In addition there are now several alpine beds which include a large collection of Sempervivums. Three ponds, with and without fish, have attracted a lively population of frogs.

Directions: See "Contact Details" on Website.

Disabled Access:
Full

Opening Times:
Sundays: 7 and 14 April
12 and 19 May
23 June
8 and 15 September
2:00pm - 5:00pm
Also by arrangement on request

Admission:
£4.00

Charities:
Froglife receives 40%, the net remaining to SG Beneficiaries.

DEAN GARDENS
Edinburgh EH4
Dean Gardens Management Committee

Private 13.5 acre gardens on north bank of the Water of Leith. Spring bulbs, daffodils and shrubs with lovely views over the Dean Valley. The Victorian Pavilion has been reinstated and there is seating throughout.

Directions: Entrance at Ann Street or Eton Terrace.

Disabled Access:
Partial

Opening Times:
Sunday 7 April
2:00pm - 5:00pm

Admission:
£4.00

Charities:
All proceeds to SG Beneficiaries

DR NEIL'S GARDEN
Duddingston Village EH15 7DG
Dr Neil's Garden Trust
E: info@drneilsgarden.co.uk www.drneilsgarden.co.uk

Wonderful secluded landscaped garden on the lower slopes of Arthur's Seat including conifers, heathers, alpines, physic garden, herbaceous borders and ponds. Thompson's Tower with the Museum of Curling and beautiful views across Duddingston Loch.

Other Details: 2013 is the gardens Golden Anniversary. Please come and join us.

Directions: Kirk car park on Duddingston Road West. Then follow signposts through the Manse garden.

Disabled Access:
Partial

Opening Times:
Saturday 15 June
2:00pm - 5:00pm
Sunday 16 June
2:00pm - 5:00pm

Admission:
£3.00, children free

Charities:
Dr. Neil's Garden Trust
receives 40%, the
net remaining to SG
Beneficiaries.

HUNTER'S TRYST
95 Oxgangs Road, Edinburgh EH10 7BA
Jean Knox T: 0131 477 2919
E: jean.knox@blueyonder.co.uk

Well stocked, mature, medium-sized town garden comprising herbaceous/shrub beds, lawn, vegetables and fruit, water feature, seating areas and trees.

Directions: From Fairmilehead crossroads head down Oxgangs Road to Hunter's Tryst roundabout, last house on the left. Bus Nos. 4, 5, 18, 27. Bus Stop at Hunter's Tryst. Garden opposite Hunter's Tryst.

Disabled Access:
Partial

Opening Times:
Sunday 28 July
2:00pm - 5:00pm
Also by arrangement on
request

Admission:
£3.00

Charities:
Lothian Cat Rescue receives
40%, the net remaining to
SG Beneficiaries.

MORAY PLACE AND BANK GARDENS
Edinburgh EH3 6BX
The Gardeners of Moray Place and Bank Gardens

Moray Place: Private garden of 3½ acres in Georgian New Town recently benefited from five-year programme of replanting. Shrubs, trees and beds offering atmosphere of tranquillity in the city centre. Bank Gardens: Nearly six acres of secluded wild gardens with lawns, trees and shrubs with banks of bulbs down to the Water of Leith. Stunning vistas across Firth of Forth.

Directions: Moray Place: Enter by north gate in Moray Place. Bank Gardens: Enter by gate at top of Doune Terrace.

Disabled Access:
None

Opening Times:
Sunday 19 May
2:00pm - 5:00pm

Admission:
£3.00

Charities:
The Euan Macdonald Centre
for Motor Neurone Disease
Research receives 40%,
the net remaining to SG
Beneficiaries.

NEWLISTON

Kirkliston EH29 9EB
Mr and Mrs R C Maclachlan T: 0131 333 3231
E: mac@newliston.fsnet.co.uk

18th century designed landscape with good rhododendrons and azaleas. The house, designed by Robert Adam, is open.

Other Details: Please note there are no catering facilities.
On Sundays there is a ride-on steam model railway from 2:00pm - 5:00pm.

Directions: Four miles from Forth Road Bridge, entrance off B800.

Disabled Access:
Full

Opening Times:
1 May to 2 June except
Mondays and Tuesdays
2:00pm - 6:00pm
Also by arrangement on
request

Admission:
£3.00, children free

Charities:
Children's Hospice
Association receives 40%,
the net remaining to SG
Beneficiaries.

ROCHEID GARDEN

Rocheid House, 20 Inverleith Terrace, Edinburgh EH3 5NS
Mrs Anna Guest T: 0131 311 7000
E: anna@afguest.co.uk

A young but rapidly maturing garden with an impressive diversity of plants, shrubs, trees, including native, exotic and rare, providing a tranquil retreat in the midst of the city. The transition from Eastern leads one through ribbons of bamboo and ornamental grasses into the Mediterranean. The natural swimming pond forms a dramatic focus and is surrounded by rich planting and overlooked by olive trees. The planted tunnel leads to the woodland by the river. Mature trees above an exciting variety of planting, creating a mosaic of colour, diversity and interest. Award-winning compost shed with a roof creating waves of ornamental grasses.

Other Details: Teas will be dependent on weather.

Directions: The Garden is on the southern side of the Royal Botanic Garden, Edinburgh.

Disabled Access:
Partial

Opening Times:
Saturdays 18 May, 15 June
and 7 September
2:00pm - 6:00pm
Also by arrangement on
request

Admission:
£4.50

Charities:
The Safe Garden at Ferryfield
Nursing Home receives 40%,
the net remaining to SG
Beneficiaries.

THE ARCHIVISTS' GARDEN

HM General Register House, 2 Princes Street, Edinburgh EH1 3YY
T: 0131 535 1313
E: enquiries@nas.gov.uk www.scotlandspeoplehub.gov.uk

The Archivists' Garden is planted with about 60 species, including heather, iris, birch, hawthorn, violet, male fern, rosemary and Scotch thistle. The plants are all connected in some way to Scotland's collective memory, whether through myth and folklore, heraldry or by association with famous Scots. A visit to the garden shows the role that plants play in our national heritage.

Other Details: Cafe open in Scotland's People Centre.

Directions: The garden lies behind General Register House and next to New Register House, at the east end of Princes Street. Enter through the courtyard gates on West Register Street (next to the Guildford Arms). Close to Waverley Station and many bus routes.

Disabled Access:
Full

Opening Times:
Saturday 14 September
2:00pm - 5:00pm
Sunday 15 September
2:00pm - 5:00pm

Admission:
£3.00

Charities:
Maggie's Centre receives
40%, the net remaining to
SG Beneficiaries.

THE GLASSHOUSES AT THE ROYAL BOTANIC GARDEN EDINBURGH
20A Inverleith Row, Edinburgh EH3 5LR
Royal Botanic Gardens T: 0131 552 7171
www.rbge.org.uk

The Glasshouses with 10 climatic zones are a delight all year round. The Orchids and Cycads House brings together primitive Cycads which dominated the land flora some 65 million years ago, and a diverse range of orchids, the most sophisticated plants in the world. In summer, giant water lillies, Victoria amazonica, are the star attraction in the Tropical Aquatic House. Plants with vibrant flowers and fascinating foliage thrive in the Rainforest Riches House and the complex ecosystems of life in the world's deserts are explored in the Arid Lands House. A large collection of gingers, (Zingiberaceae), one of the largest collections of Vireya rhododendrons in the world and a case housing carnivorous plants are among other attractions.

Directions: Located off the A902, one mile north of city centre. Entrances at Inverleith Row and Arboretum Place. Lothian Buses 8, 23 and 27 stop close to the East Gate entrance on Inverleith Row. The Majestic Tour Bus stops at Arboretum Place.

Disabled Access:
Full

Opening Times:
Sunday 2 June
10:00am - 5:30pm

Admission:
£4.50, concessions £3.50, children £1.00, family £9.00

Charities:
Donation to SG Beneficiaries

Rocheid Garden

ETTRICK & LAUDERDALE

Scotland's Gardens 2013 Guidebook is sponsored by **INVESTEC WEALTH & INVESTMENT**

District Organiser

To be advised

Area Organiser

Mrs M Kostoris   Wester Housebyres, Melrose TD6 9BW

Treasurer

Mrs D Muir   Torquhan House, Stow TD1 2RX

Gardens open on a specific date

2 Whytbank Row, Clovenfords	Sunday 9 June	1:00pm	- 5:00pm
Fairnilee House, near Clovenfords	Sunday 23 June	2:00pm	- 5:00pm
Harmony Garden, Melrose	Sunday 23 June	1:00pm	- 4:00pm
Priorwood Gardens, Melrose	Sunday 23 June	1:00pm	- 4:00pm
Gattonside Village Gardens	Saturday 29 June	2:00pm	- 6:00pm
Lowood House, Melrose	Sunday 30 June	2:00pm	- 6:00pm
Carolside, Earlston	Saturday 13 July	2:00pm	- 6:00pm
Ravensheugh House, Selkirk	Sunday 14 July	2:00pm	- 5:00pm
2 Whytbank Row, Clovenfords	Sunday 4 August	1:00pm	- 5:00pm

Gardens open regularly

Carolside, Earlston	23 June - 4 August	11:00am	- 5:00pm
	Weds, Fris & Suns		

Gardens open by arrangement

Fairnilee House, Near Clovenfords	1 May - 31 August	01896 754393

Key to symbols

 New in 2013   Homemade teas   Accommodation

 Teas   Dogs on a lead allowed   Plant stall

 Cream teas   Wheelchair access   Scottish Snowdrop Festival

Garden locations

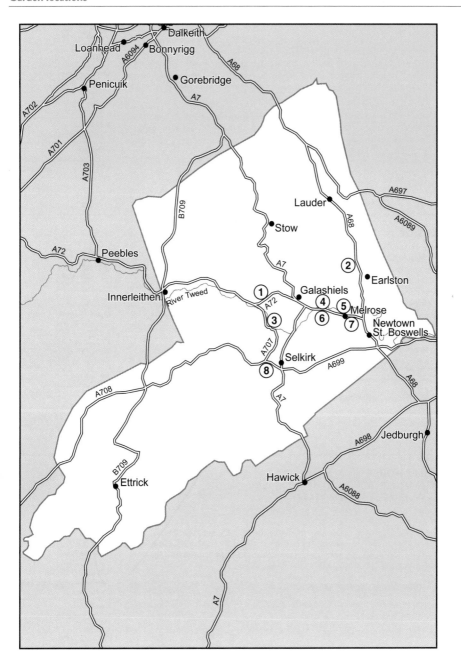

2 WHYTBANK ROW
Clovenfords, Galashiels TD1 3NE
Mr and Mrs A Martin

Large rural garden (1.4 acres) with fruit trees, raised vegetable beds, greenhouses, polytunnel, pond and an active beehive. Various types of layout with cottage garden borders, shrub beds, container planting. All of the features have been designed and created by the owners and are good examples of organic gardening and what can be done with a bit of imagination and some hard work.

Directions: A72 Galashiels to Peebles road, 3 miles from Galashiels. At the roundabout in the village centre turn up the hill behind the hotel and Whytbank Row is 2nd street on the left.

Disabled Access:
None

Opening Times:
Sunday 9 June
1:00pm - 5:00pm
Sunday 4 August
1:00pm - 5:00pm

Admission:
£3.00, children free

Charities:
Alzheimers Scotland receives 40%, the net remaining to SG Beneficiaries.

CAROLSIDE
Earlston TD4 6AL
Mr and Mrs Anthony Foyle T: 01896 849272
E: info@carolside.com www.carolsidegardens.com

A traditional and romantic garden set in a beautiful 18th century landscape, comprising lawns, shrubberies, mixed borders, a secret garden, a winter garden and an oval walled garden containing herbaceous borders, fruits, vegetables, parterres and an historically important collection of roses that has been carefully assembled over 23 years. Kenneth Cox in his book "Scotland for Gardeners" describes Carolside as "one of Scotland's finest private gardens".

Other Details: National Plant Collection ®: Pre 19th century Gallica Roses. Plant Stall on Saturday 13 July only.

Directions: One mile north of Earlston on A68. Entrance faces south.

Disabled Access:
Full

Opening Times:
Saturday 13 July
2:00pm - 6:00pm
23 June to 4 August
Weds, Fris & Suns
11:00am - 5:00pm

Admission:
£5.00, children free

Charities:
Marie Curie Cancer Care receives 40%, the net remaining to SG Beneficiaries.

FAIRNILEE HOUSE
Near Clovenfords TD1 3PR
Mr and Mrs D Mason T: 01896 754393

Mature extensive gardens which have been beautifully restored over the past 10 years having been totally neglected for 40 years previously surrounding impressive family house. Woodland, orchard, shrubs, herbaceous borders, parterre and stunning rose arbours, allees and terraces. Greenhouses.

Other Details: Guide dogs allowed.

Directions: On A708 between Caddonfoot and Yair. Turn off A7 to Yair between Galashiels and Selkirk.

Disabled Access:
Full

Opening Times:
Sunday 23 June
2:00pm - 5:00pm
Also by arrangement 1 May to 31 August

Admission:
£4.00, children free.

Charities:
Guide Dogs for the Blind receives 40%, the net remaining to SG Beneficiaries.

4

GATTONSIDE VILLAGE GARDENS
Gattonside TD6
Gardeners of Gattonside

Various interesting and colourful village gardens, some open for the first time. Tickets and maps from Village Hall on Main Street.

Other Details: Teas and plant stall in the village hall.

Directions: Two miles from Leaderfoot Bridge, on A68, North side of the River Tweed on B6360.

Disabled Access:
Partial

Opening Times:
Saturday 29 June
2:00pm - 6:00pm

Admission:
£5.00, children free

Charities:
Village Hall Funds receives 20%, The Helen Maude Garfit Fund Supporting research of Fragile X Syndrome & Fragile X Associated Tremor Ataxia Syndrome receives 20%, the net remaining to SG Beneficiaries.

5

HARMONY GARDEN (JOINT WITH PRIORWOOD GARDENS)
St. Mary's Road, Melrose TD6 9LJ
The National Trust for Scotland T: 01896 822493
E: ggregson@nts.org.uk www.nts.org.uk

Wander through this tranquil garden, wonderful herbaceous borders, lawns, fruit and vegetable plots, and enjoy fine views of the Abbey and Eildon Hills. Seasonal fruits and vegetable sales on trolly at entrance.

Other Details: Plant stall and dried flowers are available at Priorwood.

Directions: Road: Off A6091, in Melrose, opposite the Abbey. Bus: First from Edinburgh and Peebles.

Disabled Access:
Full

Opening Times:
Sunday 23 June 1:00pm - 4:00pm

Admission:
£6.00 for both gardens. N.B. Price correct at time of going to print

Charities:
Donation to SG Beneficiaries.

6

LOWOOD HOUSE
Melrose TD6 9BJ
Mr and Mrs Alexander Hamilton

Entry beside Lowood Bridge, past a tiny lodge, half mile drive through a small wood and park. Lowood House sits on the south bank of the Tweed and has been added to over the years in somewhat haphazard fashion. South of the house is a large garden with some nice shrubs, trees and a lot of roses, including climbing and rambling roses. Features are a sunken garden, woodland walk, a walk through the park by the lochan, a river walk, a secret garden and a walled garden mainly used as a kitchen garden.

Other Details: Cake stall.

Directions: Entrance from the B6374 at the south end of the single lane Lowood Bridge leading from Melrose to Gattonside.

Disabled Access:
Full

Opening Times:
Sunday 30 June
2:00pm - 6:00pm

Admission:
£4.00, OAPs £3.00, children free

Charities:
Scottish Motor Neurone receives 40%, the net remaining to SG Beneficiaries.

PRIORWOOD GARDENS (JOINT WITH HARMONY GARDEN)
Abbey Road, Melrose TD6 9PX
The National Trust for Scotland T: 01896 822493
E: ggregson@nts.org.uk www.nts.org.uk

In Melrose, overlooked by the Abbey ruins, this unique garden produces plants for a superb variety of dried flower arrangements made and sold here. The orchard contains many historic apple varieties.

Other Details: Dried flowers available.

Directions: Road: Off A6091, in Melrose opposite the Abbey. Bus: First from Edinburgh and Peebles.

Disabled Access:
Full

Opening Times:
Sunday 23 June
1:00pm - 4:00pm

Admission:
£6.00 for both gardens.
N.B. Price correct at time of going to print

Charities:
Donation to SG Beneficiaries.

RAVENSHEUGH HOUSE
Selkirk TD7 5LS
Mr and Mrs C A Anderson

Ravensheugh is a fine sheltered garden of some 3 acres of mature trees and shrubs, including wellingtonias, tulip tree and cut leaf beeches. With the Long Philip Burn running through it, and a water garden, it is a work in progress. There is a small walled garden, created after the flood of 2003 of traditional herbaceous plants and roses, and a kitchen garden of raised beds.

Other Details: The Waterwheel restaurant and tearoom, beside the Philiphaugh Salmon viewing centre is ½ mile on up A708 Moffat road.

Directions: On A708, 100 yds outside Selkirk 30 mile limit.

Disabled Access:
Partial

Opening Times:
Sunday 14 July
2:00pm - 5:00pm

Admission:
£4.00, children free

Charities:
ABF The Soldiers' Charity receives 40%, the net remaining to SG Beneficiaries.

Lowood House

FIFE

Scotland's Gardens 2013 Guidebook is sponsored by **INVESTEC WEALTH & INVESTMENT**

District Organiser

Lady Erskine	Cambo House, Kingsbarns KY16 8QD

Area Organisers

Mrs Jeni Auchinleck	2 Castle Street, Crail KY10 3SQ
Mrs Jayne Clarke	Marine House, Ordnance Road, Crombie KY12 8JZ
Mrs Evelyn Crombie	West Hall, Cupar KY15 4NA
Mrs Sue Eccles	Whinhill, Upper Largo KY8 5QS
Mrs Kate Elliott	Lucklaw House, Logie, Cupar KY15 4SJ
Mrs Lisa Hall	Old Inzievar House, Oakley, Dunfermline KY12 8HA
Mrs Lindsay Murray	Craigfoodie, Dairsie KY15 4RU
Ms Louise Roger	Chesterhill, Boarhills, St Andrews KY16 8PP
Mrs April Simpson	The Cottage, Boarhills, St Andrews KY16 8PP
Mrs Fay Smith	37 Ninian's Field, Pittenweem, Anstruther KY10 2QU
Mrs Lucy Wright	91 Main Street, Newmills KY12 8ST
Mrs Julia Young	South Flisk, Blebo Craigs, Cupar KY15 5UQ

Treasurer

Mrs Sally Lorimore	Willowhill, Forgan, Newport-on-Tay DD6 8RA

Gardens open on a specific date

Falkland Palace and Garden, Falkland	Sunday 5 May	1:00pm	-	5:00pm
Culross Palace, Culross	Sunday 12 May	10:00am	-	5:00pm
Tayfield, Forgan	Sunday 12 May	2:00pm	-	5:00pm
Willowhill, Forgan	Sunday 12 May	2:00pm	-	5:00pm
Tayport Gardens, Tayport	Saturday 25 May	12:00pm	-	5:00pm
Lindores House, by Newburgh	Sunday 26 May	1:00pm	-	5:00pm
Tayport Gardens, Tayport	Sunday 26 May	12:00pm	-	5:00pm
Earlshall Castle, Leuchars	Sunday 2 June	2:00pm	-	5:00pm
Freuchie Plant Sale and the Garden at Karbet	Sunday 9 June	12:00pm	-	4:00pm
Old Inzievar House	Sunday 16 June	2:00pm	-	5:00pm
Craigfoodie, Dairsie	Sunday 23 June	2:00pm	-	5:00pm
Pittenweem: Gardens in the Burgh	Sunday 30 June	11:00am	-	5:00pm
Strathmiglo Village Gardens	Sunday 30 June	1:00pm	-	5:00pm
Kemback House, Cupar	Saturday 6 July	12:00pm	-	5:00pm
Wormistoune House, Crail	Sunday 14 July	11:00am	-	5:00pm

FIFE

Crail: Small Gardens in the Burgh	Saturday 20 July	1:00pm	-	5:30pm
Crail: Small Gardens in the Burgh	Sunday 21 July	1:00pm	-	5:30pm
Balcaskie, Pittenweem	Sunday 28 July	12:00pm	-	5:00pm
Kellie Castle, Pittenweem	Sunday 28 July	12:00pm	-	5:00pm
Earlshall Castle, Leuchars	Sunday 4 August	2:00pm	-	5:00pm
Gilston House, by Largoward	Saturday 24 August	1:00pm	-	5:00pm
Tayfield, Forgan	Sunday 25 August	2:00pm	-	5:00pm
Willowhill, Forgan	Sunday 25 August	2:00pm	-	5:00pm
Hill of Tarvit Plant Sale and Autumn Fair, Cupar	Sunday 6 October	10:30am	-	4:00pm

Gardens open regularly

Cambo House, Kingsbarns	Daily	10:00am	-	5:00pm
The Tower, Wormit	18 April - 12 Sept, Thurs	2:00pm	-	7:00pm
Willowhill, Forgan	26 June - 28 August, Weds	2:00pm	-	5:00pm

Gardens open by arrangement

Barham, Bow of Fife	1 April - 30 September	01337 810227
Earlshall Castle, Leuchars	On request	01334 839205
Glassmount House, by Kirkcaldy	1 April - 30 September	01592 890214
Teasses Gardens, nr. Ceres	On request	01334 828048
Willowhill, Forgan, Newport-on-Tay	1 June - 30 August	07948 286031
Wormistoune House, Crail	On request	ktaylor.home@googlemail.com

Plant sales

Freuchie Plant Sale and the Garden at Karbet	Sunday 9 June	12:00pm	-	4:00pm
Hill of Tarvit Plant Sale and Autumn Fair, Cupar	Sunday 6 October	10:30am	-	4:00pm

Events

The Fife Garden Trail	Various days from 1 May - 30 June	Various times

Key to symbols

🌷	New in 2013	☕	Homemade teas	B&B	Accommodation
☕	Teas	🐕	Dogs on a lead allowed	🌷	Plant stall
☕	Cream teas	♿	Wheelchair access	🌾	Scottish Snowdrop Festival

Garden locations

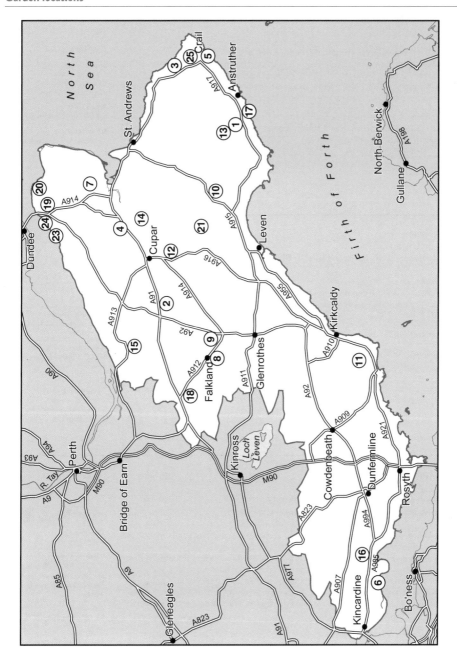

BALCASKIE (IN CONJUNCTION WITH KELLIE CASTLE)
Pittenweem KY10 2RD
The Anstruther Family

In 1905 George Elgood wrote that Balcaskie was 'one of the best and most satisfying gardens in the British Isles'. Over the centuries, the gardens have seen input from Gilpin, Bryce and Nesfield. Today the gardens are at the start of a period of restoration. As part of a collaboration with the National Trust for Scotland, the gardens are being restored by the gardening team from Kellie Castle.

Directions: Access is via Kellie Castle only, a free minibus will take visitors from Kellie Castle to Balcaskie. Road: B9171, 3 miles NNW of Pittenweem. Bus: Flexible from local villages by pre-booking.

Disabled Access:
Partial

Opening Times:
Sunday 28 July
12:00pm - 5:00pm

Admission:
£8.00 includes both gardens

Charities:
Donation to SG Beneficiaries

BARHAM
Bow of Fife KY15 5RG
Sir Robert and Lady Spencer-Nairn T: 01337 810227

A small woodland garden with snowdrops, spring bulbs, trilliums, rhododendrons and ferns. Also a summer garden with rambling roses, herbaceous borders and island beds.

Other Details: Small plant nursery selling unusual plants.

Directions: A914 miles west of Cupar.

Disabled Access:
None

Opening Times:
By arrangement 1 April to 30 September

Admission:
£3.00, OAPs £2.50, children free

Charities:
Pain Association Scotland receives 40%, the net remaining to SG Beneficiaries.

CAMBO HOUSE
Kingsbarns KY16 8QD
Sir Peter and Lady Erskine T: 01333 450313
E: cambo@camboestate.com www.camboestate.com

Best known for snowdrops (mail order in February), but exciting at all times of year, this Victorian walled garden with magnificent herbaceous displays is constantly evolving. Head Gardener, Elliott Forsyth, aided by students and volunteers, has created irresistible planting combinations with drifts of bold perennials and grasses in the style originally devised by Piet Oudolf and an outrageous annual potager garden. Outside the main garden, a Winter Garden and North American prairie are developing. Woodland walks to sea. Featured in 'The Garden' and 'Weekend Telegraph Magazine' August 2012.

Other Details: National Plant Collection ®: Snowdrops. Champion Trees: Bundle Beech. Tea room and plant stall all year. Tulip and Rose Festivals. Events throughout the year.

Directions: A917 between Crail and St Andrews.

Disabled Access:
Full

Opening Times:
Daily 10:00am - 5:00pm including the Snowdrop Festival 2 February - 17 March

Admission:
£5.00, children free

Charities:
Donation to SG Beneficiaries

CRAIGFOODIE
Dairsie KY15 4RU
Mr and Mrs James Murray

Restored formal walled garden adjoining 17th century house with extensive range of plants and enjoying fine aspect to the south. Parterre, clock lawn, mixed/herbaceous borders, shrub roses, terraces with exotic plantings, fruit and vegetable gardens.

Other Details: Tennis lawn, woodland garden and knoll walk.

Directions: On A91 from Cupar to St Andrews turn left at Dairsie School then follow signs.

Disabled Access:
Partial

Opening Times:
Sunday 23 June
2:00pm - 5:00pm

Admission:
£4.00

Charities:
AICR (The Association
for International Cancer
Research) receives 40%,
the net remaining to SG
Beneficiaries.

CRAIL: SMALL GARDENS IN THE BURGH
KY10 3SQ
The Gardeners of Crail

A number of small gardens in varied styles: cottage, historic, plantsman's, bedding as featured in "Scotland on Sunday" July 2012.

Other Details: Tickets and maps available from: Mrs Auchinleck, 2 Castle Street and David and Sue Jerdan, 44 Marketgate South KY10 3TL. Teas in British Legion Hall.

Directions: Approach Crail from either St Andrews or Anstruther by A917. Park in the Marketgate.

Disabled Access:
None

Opening Times:
Saturday 20 July
1:00pm - 5:30pm
Sunday 21 July
1:00pm - 5:30pm

Admission:
£5.00, children free

Charities:
Crail British Legion
Hall receives 10%, Crail
Preservation Society receives
30%, the net remaining to SG
Beneficiaries.

CULROSS PALACE
Culross KY12 8JH
The National Trust for Scotland T: 0844 4932189
E: mjeffery@nts.org.uk www.nts.org.uk

Relive the domestic life of the 16th and 17th centuries amid the old buildings and cobbled streets of this Royal Burgh on the River Forth. A model 17th century garden has been recreated behind Culross Palace to show the range of plants available and includes vegetables, culinary and medicinal herbs, soft fruits and ornamental shrubs. Don't miss the adorable Scots Dumpy chickens!

Other Details: Fruit and vegetable stalls.

Directions: Off A985, 12 miles east of Kincardine Bridge, 6 miles west of Dunfermline. Stagecoach, Stirling to Dunfermline or First, Edinburgh to Dunfermline. Falkirk station 12 miles, Dunfermline station 6 miles.

Disabled Access:
None

Opening Times:
Sunday 12 May
10:00am - 5:00pm

Admission:
£5.00 including NTS
members
Admission includes tea/coffee
and cakes
N.B. Prices correct at time of
going to print

Charities:
Donation to SG Beneficiaries.

EARLSHALL CASTLE
Leuchars KY16 0DP
Paul & Josine Veenhuijzen T: 01334 839205

Garden designed by Sir Robert Lorimer. Topiary lawn, for which Earlshall is renowned, rose terrace, croquet lawn with herbaceous borders, shrub border, box garden, orchard, kitchen and herb garden.

Other Details: Wheelchair access is difficult but possible.

Directions: On Earlshall road, ¾ of a mile east of Leuchars Village (off A919).

Disabled Access:
Partial

Opening Times:
Sun 2 Jun 2:00pm - 5:00pm
Sun 4 Aug 2:00pm - 5:00pm
Also by arrangement on request

Admission:
£5.00, children free

Charities:
RAF Benevolent Fund receives 40% June opening, St Athernase Church receives 40% August opening, the net remaining to SG Beneficiaries.

FALKLAND PALACE AND GARDEN
Falkland KY15 7BU
The National Trust for Scotland T: 0844 4932186
E: gardens@nts.org.uk www.nts.org.uk

Set in a medieval village, the Royal Palace of Falkland is a superb example of Renaissance architecture. Garden enthusiasts will appreciate the work of Percy Cane who designed and cultivated the gardens between 1947 and 1952. On the day Falkland Palace Garden will have a Blossom Day, dedicated to wildlife and families. The blossom in the Orchard and cherry blossom in the main garden will be spectacular and are not to be missed.

Directions: Road: A912, 10 miles from M90, junction 8, 11 miles north of Kirkcaldy. Bus: Stagecoach Fife stops in High Street (100 metres). OS Ref: NO253075.

Disabled Access:
Partial

Opening Times:
Sunday 5 May
1:00pm - 5:00pm

Admission:
£6.00 including NTS members. N.B. Prices correct at time of going to print.

Charities:
Donation to SG Beneficiaries

FREUCHIE PLANT SALE AND THE GARDEN AT KARBET
KY15 7EY
Major and Mrs A B Cran

A good plant sale with a wide selection for garden and container.

Directions: In the centre of Freuchie on the B936.

Disabled Access:
Partial

Opening Times:
Sunday 9 June
12:00pm - 4:00pm

Admission:
£1.00

Charities:
Charity to be confirmed, details of which will be shown on our website.

10 GILSTON HOUSE

By Largoward, Leven KY8 5QP
Mr and Mrs Edward Baxter T: 01333 360245
E: catherine@cathbrown.com   www.eastneukestates.co.uk

Large mature garden surrounding Gilston House (not open) including revamped terrace garden. Established shrubs mixed with gorgeous perennials. Specimen trees, wide lawns and extensive parkland. Children are free and are very welcome. Plenty of space to run around in. Pond walk and woodland walk. Dogs on leads please. Feel free to bring picnics. 40% of the day's proceeds go to RHET which promotes bringing farmers into classrooms and children onto farms.

Other Details: Homemade tea £2.50. Free car parking (at owner's risk).

Directions: Signposted on A915 between Largoward and Upper Largo.

Disabled Access:
Full

Opening Times:
Saturday 24 August
1:00pm - 5:00pm

Admission:
£5.00, children free

Charities:
RHET receives 40%,
the net remaining to SG
Beneficiaries.

11 GLASSMOUNT HOUSE

by Kirkcaldy KY2 5UT
James and Irene Thomson T: 01592 890214
E: peterlcmclaren@yahoo.co.uk

Intriguing densely planted walled garden with surrounding woodland. An A-listed sun dial, Mackenzie and Moncur greenhouse and historical doocot are complemented by newer structures including an atmospheric water feature/fish pond. Snowdrops and daffodils are followed by a mass of candelabra and cowslip primula, meconopsis and Cardiocrinum giganteum. Then hedges and topiary form backdrops for an abundance of bulbs, clematis, rambling roses and perennials, creating interest through the summer into September. Featured in 'Country Living'. Winner The Times/Fetzer Back Gardens of the Year 2008 Green garden category.

Directions: Take the road signposted 'Kinghorn' off the B9157 2 miles west of Kirkcaldy (from Kirkcaldy to Aberdour/Dalgety Bay), then take second road on right. Glassmount drive is fifty yards up this road on right. From Kinghorn (B923 to Kinghorn Loch) take first road on right and then third on left. Glassmount drive is fifty yards up road on right. Surrounded by trees, Glassmount House is on the highest point overlooking Kinghorn and Kirkcaldy.

Disabled Access:
None

Opening Times:
By arrangement
1 April to 30 September

Admission:
£3.00

Charities:
Parkinson's UK receives 40%,
the net remaining to SG
Beneficiaries.

12 HILL OF TARVIT PLANT SALE AND AUTUMN FAIR

Hill of Tarvit, Cupar KY15 5PB
The National Trust for Scotland

Hill of Tarvit is one of Scotland's finest Edwardian mansion houses with superb paintings by Sir Henry Raeburn, Allan Ramsay and eminent Dutch artists. Surrounding the mansion house are spectacular gardens designed by Robert Lorimer, woods, open heath and parkland to explore. For the energetic, a walk to the monument situated on the hill behind the house is rewarded with spectacular views over the Fife countryside. Monument at the top of the hill.

Other Details: Generous divisions of herbaceous plants plus a large selection of potted alpines, shrubs etc. A wide range of stalls displaying local foods and crafts. Cooking and handicraft demonstrations. Guided walks around the estate by fungi and wild food experts. Mansion House open (reduced entry fee) 1:00pm - 5:00pm. Hatters Edwardian Tearoom 11:00am - 5:00pm.

Directions: 2 miles south of Cupar off A916.

Disabled Access:
Partial

Opening Times:
Plant sale Sunday 6 October
10:30am - 4:00pm
garden also open.

Admission:
£2.00, children free.

Charities:
All proceeds to SG
Beneficiaries

KELLIE CASTLE (IN CONJUNCTION WITH BALCASKIE)
Pittenweem KY10 2RF
The National Trust for Scotland T: 0844 4932184
E: marmour@nts.org.uk www.nts.org.uk

This superb garden around 400 years old was sympathetically restored by the Lorimer family in the late 19th century. The Arts and Crafts style garden has a selection of old-fashioned roses and herbaceous plants cultivated organically and hosts an amazing 30 varieties of rhubarb and 75 different types of apple.

Other Details: Access to Balcaskie and Kellie Castle via Kellie Castle only, a free minibus will transport visitors between both gardens. Exciting mix of artist and craft stalls.

Directions: Road: B9171, 3 miles NNW of Pittenweem. Bus: Flexible from local villages by pre-booking.

Disabled Access:
Partial

Opening Times:
Sunday 28 July
12:00pm - 5:00pm

Admission:
£8.00 includes both gardens

Charities:
Donation to SG Beneficiaries

KEMBACK HOUSE
Kemback, by Cupar KY15 5TN
Christopher and Claire Thomson

The house and gardens of Kemback hark back to the 15th century when they were owned by the Archbishop of St Andrews and the University. The house was restored in the 17th century and in 2010 was completely renovated. It is one of the finest contemporary homes in Scotland.
Fruit trees, including apple, pear, plum, peach, red and white currant, line the walled garden. There are fine herbaceous borders and a working potager garden, beside which sits a series of small greenhouses and a rose garden. There is the sound of a lovely rill fed from a source in the Kemback woods.
The woodland walk takes visitors past two waterfalls that feed a series of interconnected ponds. The beautiful fifty acre policy parks have many extraordinary specimen trees, including ancient yews, beech, auricaria, sequoia and maple. Visitors are encouraged to walk the many pathways and discover the ponds and the Neolithic mound.

Directions: Off the minor road which runs through Dura Den from Pitscottie to Dairsie. Will be signposted from Dairsie and Pitscottie.

Disabled Access:
Partial

Opening Times:
Saturday 6 July
1:00pm - 5:00pm

Admission:
£5.00, children free, guided tour of the house £5.00

Charities:
All proceeds to SG Beneficiaries.

LINDORES HOUSE
by Newburgh KY14 6JD
Mr and Mrs R Turcan

Stunning lochside position, rhododendrons, trilliums and herbaceous borders. Woodland walks and amazing seventeenth century yew believed to be the largest in Fife.

Other Details: Lyn's Crafts.

Directions: Off A913 2 miles east of Newburgh.

Disabled Access:
Partial

Opening Times:
Sunday 26 May
1:00pm - 5:00pm

Admission:
£4.50, children free

Charities:
First Newburgh Guides receives 40%, the net remaining to SG Beneficiaries.

OLD INZIEVAR HOUSE
KY12 8HA
Mr and Mrs Tim Hall

A recently restored walled garden with lime walk, herbaceous borders, knot garden, rose gardens, fruit trees and a small amount of vegetables. Lovely views over the lower south facing wall.

Directions: A985 heading west for Kincardine Bridge turn right at sign to Oakley two miles after Cairneyhill roundabout. After ½ mile take a right turn to Linvid Pet Hotel. Follow SG signs.

Disabled Access:
Partial

Opening Times:
Sunday 16 June
2:00pm - 5:00pm

Admission:
£3.50

Charities:
Holy Name Church restoration fund receives 40%, the net remaining to SG Beneficiaries.

PITTENWEEM: GARDENS IN THE BURGH
KY10 2PQ
The Gardeners of Pittenweem   T: 01333 311988

A variety of garden designs: from well established traditional, to open aspect landscaped and from tiny walled secluded, to a recently established large herb garden.

Other Details: Tickets and maps available from 3 Seaview Row, Pittenweem (near West Braes car park), 'Craignish' 41 Viewforth Place, Pittenweem and some other gardens.
Refreshments available in village pubs and coffee shops.

Directions: On the A917 coast road enter Pittenweem and follow signs to the West Braes car park at the St Monans end of the village. Some off-street, short term parking available at 'Craignish' which is on the way into Pittenweem from St. Monans.

Disabled Access:
Partial

Opening Times:
Sunday 30 June
11:00am - 5:00pm

Admission:
£4.50

Charities:
Trellis (supporting therapeutic gardening in Scotland) receives 20%, Pittenweem in Bloom receives 20%, the net remaining to SG Beneficiaries.

STRATHMIGLO VILLAGE GARDENS
Fife   KY14 7PR
The Gardeners of Strathmiglo

Strathmiglo offers a selection of lovely village and walled gardens, nestling beneath the stunning Lomond Hills. Beautiful walks in and around the village; an historic tollbooth and a pictish standing stone provide further interest.

Directions: Off the A91, two miles west of Auchtermuchty, enter village from the west end, passing the primary school on the left. Follow signs in the High Street to parking and ticket sales.

Disabled Access:
Partial

Opening Times:
Sunday 30 June
1:00pm - 5:00pm

Admission:
£4.00

Charities:
CHAS (Rachel House, Kinross) receives 20%, Crossroads (Fife Central) receives 20%, the net remaining to SG Beneficiaries.

19 TAYFIELD (IN CONJUNCTION WITH WILLOWHILL)
Forgan, Newport-on-Tay DD6 8RA
William and Elizabeth Berry

A wide variety of shrubs and fine trees many to mark celebrations of the family who have lived here for over 200 years. Some trees are of a great age and Tayfield has the tallest beech tree recorded in Scotland at 39 metres. A picturesque approach to Tayfield House is enhanced by wonderful large tree rhododendrons in May and views across the Tay all year round. The grounds are wildlife rich and contain two large ponds. Look out for red squirrels which are often seen.

Other Details: Craft Stalls at Forgan Arts Centre on 12 May.

Directions: 1½ miles south of Tay Road Bridge. Take the B995 to Newport off the Forgan roundabout.

Disabled Access:
Partial

Opening Times:
Sunday 12 May
2:00pm - 5:00pm
Sunday 25 August
2:00pm - 5:00pm

Admission:
£4.00

Charities:
Forgan Arts Centre receives 40% 12 May opening, RIO Community Centre receives 40% 25 August opening, the net remaining to SG Beneficiaries.

---

20 TAYPORT GARDENS
Tayport DD6 9HX
The Gardeners of Tayport

Located at the mouth of the river Tay, Tayport is an historic harbour town with attractive views of the Broughty Ferry coastline and Tentsmuir Forest. Six gardens open of varied age and style.

Other Details: Tickets and maps available from Mr and Mrs McCormick, Craigmore, 9 Reform Street, Tayport DD6 9HX.

Directions: On the south of the Tay Road Bridge take the B946 to Tayport.

Disabled Access:
None

Opening Times:
Saturday 25 May
12:00pm - 5:00pm
Sunday 26 May
12:00pm - 5:00pm

Admission:
£4.00

Charities:
Tayport Community Trust receives 40%, the net remaining to SG Beneficiaries.

---

21 TEASSES GARDENS
Nr. Ceres KY8 5PG
Sir Fraser and Lady Morrison T: 01334 828048
E: Kate@teasses.com

Teasses Gardens have been developed by the present owners for twelve years and now extend to approximately 60 acres. In addition to the traditional oval walled garden with fruit, vegetables, cut flowers and large greenhouse, there are formal and informal areas of garden linked by numerous woodland walks with many woodland gardens. There are extensive areas of spring bulbs. Please allow two hours for a tour with a member of the gardening staff to enjoy these large and peaceful gardens.

Other Details: The garden is open for individuals or groups.

Directions: Between Ceres and Largo. Enter by farm entrance two miles west of New Gilston village. Follow tarmac road to Estate Office.

Disabled Access:
None

Opening Times:
By arrangement on request

Admission:
£5.00 (includes tour)

Charities:
All proceeds to SG Beneficiaries.

22 THE FIFE GARDEN TRAIL
See the events page on our website for details.
The Fife Gardeners

Barham, Bow of Fife KY15 5RG (Sir Robert & Lady Spencer-Nairn)
Wednesdays 15, 22, 29 May and 5, 12 June 2:00pm - 5:00pm.
Earlshall Castle, Leuchars KY16 0DP (Paul & Josine Veenhuijzen)
Mondays, Tuesdays & Wednesdays 1 May - 30 June 8:00am - 4:00pm.
Gilston House, by Largoward KY8 5QP (Mr & Mrs Edward Baxter)
Wednesdays 5, 12, 19, 26 June 1:00pm – 5:00pm.
Greenhead Farmhouse, Greenhead of Arnot KY6 3JQ (Mr & Mrs M Strang Steel)
Tuesdays 21, 28 May and 4, 11 June 1:00pm – 4:00pm.
Logie House, Crossford KY12 8QN (Mr & Mrs John Hunt)
Wednesdays 22, 29 May and 5, 12 June 11:00am – 4:00pm.
Rosewells, Pitscottie KY15 5LE (Birgitta & Gordon MacDonald)
15, 22, 29 May and 5, 12, 19 June Wednesdays 3:00pm – 8:00pm.
South Flisk, Blebo Craigs KY15 5UQ (George & Julia Young)
Thursdays 2, 9, 30 May and 6, 13 June 3:00pm – 7:00pm.
The Tower, Wormit DD6 8PP (Peter & Angela Davey)
Thursdays all May and June 2:00pm – 7:00pm.
Willowhill, Newport-on-Tay DD6 8RA (Eric Wright & Sally Lorimore)
Tuesdays & Thursdays 21 May - 30 June 2:00pm – 8:00pm.

Other Details: Plant sales at Barham, Willowhill and Gilston House. Barham has a small nursery of rare and unusual plants grown from seed collected or plants divided from the garden.
Soup and sandwiches at Greenhead Farmhouse and homemade teas at Gilston House.

Directions: Details will be shown in leaflet provided on purchase of ticket(s).

Disabled Access:
Partial

Opening Times:
1 May to 30 June
8:00am - 8:00pm times vary
see main body text.

Admission:
£15.00 for all gardens,
accompanied children under
16 free
Entry to all gardens by presold
ticket only.
A limited number of tickets
are available and can be
purchased from
www.scotlandsgardens.org
by credit card or by cheque
payable to Scotland's Gardens
from S. Lorimore, Willowhill,
Forgan, Newport on Tay, Fife
DD6 8RA

Charities:
AICR receives 40%,
the net remaining to SG
Beneficiaries.

See more
details of the
Fife Garden Trail
on pages 28 - 29

23 THE TOWER
1, Northview Terrace, Wormit DD6 8PP
Peter and Angela Davey T: 01382 541635 M: 07768406946

Situated four miles south of Dundee, this one acre Edwardian landscaped garden has panoramic views over the river Tay. Special features include rhododendron walk, rockeries, informal woodland planting schemes using native and exotic plants, offering year round interest. Original raised paths lead to a granite grotto with waterfall pool. A boardwalk leads to four further ponds joined by a stream. Of additional interest are raised vegetable beds made from granite sets.

Other Details: Garden set into a hill with steep paths, therefore not suitable for those with poor mobility.

Directions: From B946 park on Naughton Road outside Spar shop and walk up path left following signs.

Disabled Access:
None

Opening Times:
18 April to 12 September
Thursdays 2:00pm - 7:00pm

Admission:
£3.00

Charities:
Barnardos receives 40%,
the net remaining to SG
Beneficiaries.

24 **WILLOWHILL (IN CONJUNCTION WITH TAYFIELD)**
Forgan, Newport-on-Tay DD6 8RA
Eric Wright & Sally Lorimore T: 07948 286031

An evolving three acre garden featured in "Scotland for Gardeners" and "Scotland on Sunday". The house is surrounded by a vegetable plot and a series of mixed borders designed with different vibrant colour combinations for effect all season. Newly developed area containing borders of bulbs, roses and perennials. A stepped terrace of alpines leads to a wildlife pond in grassland planted with trees, bulbs and herbaceous perennials through which wide sweeping paths are mown.

Other Details: Plant stalls with many perennials from Willowhill and other gardens in Fife. Craft stalls at Forgan Arts Centre on 12 May.

Directions: 1½ miles south of Tay Road Bridge. Take the B995 to Newport off the Forgan roundabout. Willowhill is the first house on the left hand side next to the Forgan Arts Centre.

Disabled Access:
Partial

Opening Times:
Sunday 12 May
2:00pm - 5:00pm
Sunday 25 August
2:00pm - 5:00pm
26 June to 28 August,
Weds 2:00pm - 5:00pm
Also by arrangement
1 June to 30 August

Admission:
£4.00

Charities:
Forgan Arts Centre receives 40% 12 May opening, RIO Community Centre receives 40% 25 August opening, the net remaining to SG Beneficiaries.

SCOTTISH
SNOWDROP
FESTIVAL

Scotland's Gardens season starts with the popular Snowdrop Openings.

We are very keen to add more Snowdrop Gardens in 2014 so please let us know if you would like to share your snowdrops with us next year.

Snowdrop Gardens are listed on pages 26 - 27

25 WORMISTOUNE HOUSE
Crail KY10 3XH
Baron and Lady Wormiston
E: ktaylor.home@googlemail.com (Head Gardener)

A 17th century Scots Tower House and its gardens which have been painstakingly restored over the last 20 years. The charming 1.5 acre walled garden is divided into a series of 'rooms', each one with its own individual enchantment. These include a wildlife meadow, productive potager, intricate formal parterre, magical Grisselinia garden (with Scotland's largest listed Grisselinia) and a recently planted late-season perennial border. The backbone of the garden is the splendid double herbaceous border which peaks in midsummer - as featured on the cover of Kenneth Cox's "Scotland for Gardeners". The walled garden also contains two award-winning Georgian-style Garden Pavilions - one representing the male, the other the female in the Garden of Eden. Outside the walled garden enjoy woodland walks, pond and mosaic celtic cross.

Other Details: Soup and roll lunches from 11:30am -2:00pm.
Cream teas 2:00pm-5:00pm.
Dogs not allowed in the walled garden.

Directions: One mile north of Crail on the A917 Crail to St Andrews road. Signposted at end of lane on a sharp bend. Car park is a 5 minute walk from the garden but passengers may be dropped at main gate before parking.

Disabled Access:
None

Opening Times:
Sunday 14 July
11:00am - 5:00pm
Also by arrangement on request.

Admission:
£4.50, children free

Charities:
CHAS receives 40%, the net remaining to SG Beneficiaries.

Wormistoune House

GLASGOW & DISTRICT

Scotland's Gardens 2013 Guidebook is sponsored by **INVESTEC WEALTH & INVESTMENT**

District Organiser

Mrs J Millar   3 Cochrane Court, Milngavie G62 6QT

Area Organisers

Mrs S Elliot   46 Corrour Road, Newlands G42 2DX
Mrs A Murray   44 Gordon Road, Netherlee G44 3TW
Mrs Sandra Wilson   Robinsfield Gatehouse, Bardowie G62 6ER

Treasurer

Mr J Murray   44 Gordon Road, Netherlee G44 3TW

Gardens open on a specific date

Greenbank Garden, Clarkston	Saturday 9 March	9:30am	-	Dusk
5 Ellergreen Road, Bearsden	Saturday 18 May	2:00pm	-	5:00pm
Kilsyth Gardens, Kilsyth	Sunday 19 May	2:00pm	-	5:00pm
Kirklee Circus Pleasure Garden & Beyond	Saturday 8 June	1:30pm	-	6:00pm

Gardens open by arrangement

Kilsyth Gardens, Allanfauld Road, Kilsyth	1 April - 30 September	01236 821667

Key to symbols

 New in 2013

 Homemade teas

 Accommodation

 Teas

 Dogs on a lead allowed

 Plant stall

 Cream teas

 Wheelchair access

Scottish Snowdrop Festival

Garden locations

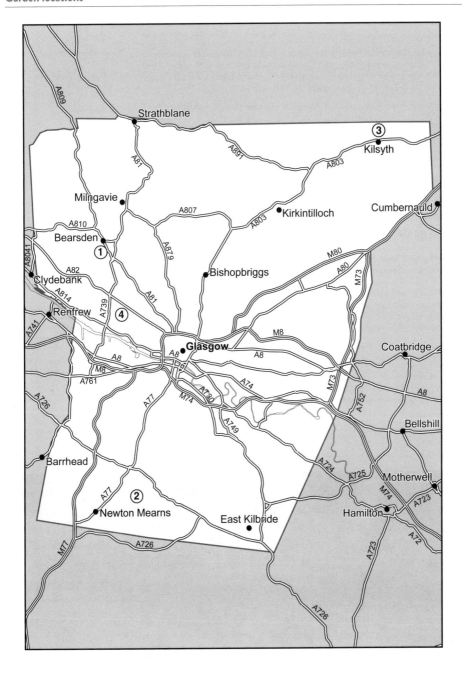

5 ELLERGREEN ROAD
Bearsden G61 2RJ
Mr and Mrs A MacSween

Nestled at the edge of St Germains Loch in Bearsden this garden is reached via a 400 foot drive bordered by lovely Spring planting and shrubs. Wonderful lochside setting with a large range of acers, azaleas and rhododendrons, a hidden gem, where it is hard to believe you are not miles from civilization.

Directions: From Canniesburn Toll roundabout take the Drymen Road (A809) towards the centre of Bearsden. After ½ mile Ellergreen Road is on the left just before, and parallel to, Station Road. Parking in station car park. No parking on Ellergreen Road. From the station it is a short walk to the house and garden at the very end of Ellergreen Road.

Disabled Access:
Partial

Opening Times:
Saturday 18 May
2:00pm - 5:00pm

Admission:
£5.00 includes teas,
children free

Charities:
Make a Wish Foundation
UK receives 40%, the
net remaining to SG
Beneficiaries.

GREENBANK GARDEN
Flenders Road, Clarkston G76 8RB
The National Trust for Scotland T: 0844 493 2201
E: dferguson@nts.org.uk www.nts.org.uk

A unique walled garden with plants and designs of particular interest to suburban gardeners. There are also fountains and a woodland walk. Gardens are perfect for wildlife. There will be a garden walk on 'Gardening with wildlife in mind'. Join the friendly Greenbank gardeners for tips on encouraging wildlife in your garden.

Other Details: National Plant Collection ®: Bergenia.   Gardening demonstrations throughout the year. Shop. Soups, sandwiches, teas and cake served.

Directions: Flenders Road, off Mearns Road, Clarkston. Off M77 and A727, follow signs for East Kilbride to Clarkston Toll. Bus: No. 44a, Glasgow to Newton Mearns. Rail: Clarkston station 1¼ miles.

Disabled Access:
Full

Opening Times:
Saturday 9 March 9:30am
- Dusk

Admission:
£6.00, Concessions £5.00,
Guided Tour £2.00. N.B.
Prices correct at time of going
to print.

Charities:
Donation to SG Beneficiaries

Kilsyth Gardens -Blackmill

KILSYTH GARDENS
Allanfauld Road, Kilsyth G65 9DE
Mr and Mrs George Murdoch and Mr and Mrs Alan Patrick T: 01236 821667

Aeolia (Mr and Mrs G Murdoch): A ⅓ acre garden developed since 1960 by the owners. Mature specimen trees and shrubs, a large variety of rhododendrons, primulas, hardy geraniums and herbaceous plants.
Blackmill (Mr and Mrs Alan Patrick): Across the road from Aeolia. An acre of mature and recent planting of specimen trees and shrubs on the site of an old mill. There is an ornamental pond and rock pool built into the remains of an old mill building. A further acre of natural woodland glen. Paths along the Garrel Burn with views to the cascading waterfalls.

Other Details: See green energy being made on site with small hydro scheme. Official test site for West of Scotland Drystone Walling Association. Come along and see a wall being built or better still try yourself. WC at Blackmill available but unsuitable for disabled.

Directions: A803 to Kilsyth, through main roundabout. Turn left into Parkburn Road up to the crossroads. Short walk up Allanfauld Road. Buses: No. 27 Glasgow-Falkirk, No. 24 Glasgow-Stirling, No. X86 Glasgow-Kilsyth (not Sunday).

Disabled Access:
Partial

Opening Times:
Sunday 19 May
2:00pm - 5:00pm
Also by arrangement
1 April to 30 September

Admission:
£6.00 includes both gardens
and homemade teas

Charities:
Strathcarron Hospice receives
40%, the net remaining to SG
Beneficiaries.

KIRKLEE CIRCUS PLEASURE GARDEN AND BEYOND
Kirklee Circus G12 OTW
Lisella Hutton (Kirklee Circus Gardens Convenor) T: 0141 334 2052
E: lisellahutton@kirkleelandscape.com

Kirklee Circus Garden is a delightful oasis of calm enclosed by a discreet enclave of Victorian houses west of the Botanic Gardens. Over the years a dense circle of 32 lime trees has been reduced to five and replaced in stages with a large variety of interesting plants, many defying the shady location. This process will be continued into the future which will encourage a return visit. To the rear of the villas and terraced houses are the residents walled gardens, many of which will be on show. These display an amazing variety reflecting the aspirations and character of generations of owners as well as present residents.

Other Details: Various stalls, photographic exhibition.

Directions: Enter from Kirklee Road, second on the right from the Great Western Road/Kirklee Road junction and traffic lights.
Parking on Kirklee Road.
There are frequent bus services along Great Western Road.
Nearest subway station is Hillhead Station on Byres Road.
Kirklee Circus is a 10 minute walk from the station, either along Great Western Road or through the Botanic Gardens to the Kirklee Gate.

Disabled Access:
Partial

Opening Times:
Saturday 8 June
1:30pm - 6:00pm

Admission:
£5.00

Charities:
Friends of the Beatson,
Teenage Cancer Trust and
Save the Children share
40%, the net remaining to
SG Beneficiaries.

ISLE OF ARRAN

Scotland's Gardens 2013 Guidebook is sponsored by **INVESTEC WEALTH & INVESTMENT**

District Organiser

Mrs S C Gibbs   Dougarie, Isle of Arran KA27 8EB

Treasurer

Mrs E Adam   Bayview, Pirnmill, Isle of Arran KA27 8HP

Gardens open on a specific date

Brodick Castle & Country Park, Brodick	Sunday 5 May	10:00am - 4:30pm
Strabane, Brodick	Sunday 19 May	2:00pm - 5:00pm
Strabane, Brodick	Sunday 26 May	2:00pm - 5:00pm
Dougarie	Sunday 30 June	2:00pm - 5:00pm
Brodick Castle & Country Park, Brodick	Sunday 7 July	10:00am - 4:30pm

Strabane

Key to symbols

	New in 2013		Homemade teas		Accommodation
	Teas		Dogs on a lead allowed		Plant stall
	Cream teas		Wheelchair access		Scottish Snowdrop Festival

BRODICK CASTLE & COUNTRY PARK
Brodick KA27 8HY
The National Trust for Scotland T: 0844 493 2152
E: brodickcastle@nts.org.uk www.nts.org.uk

At any time of year the gardens are well worth a visit, though especially in spring when the internationally acclaimed rhododendron collection bursts into full bloom. Venture out into the country park and discover wildflower meadows where Highland cows graze, woodland trails and tumbling waterfalls. Exotic plants and shrubs. Walled garden. Woodland garden.

Other Details: National Plant Collection ®: Three rhododendron collections.

Directions: Brodick 2 miles. Service buses from Brodick Pier to Castle. Regular sailings from Ardrossan and Claonaig (Argyll). Information from Caledonian MacBrayne, Gourock. (T: 01475 650100)

Disabled Access:
Partial

Opening Times:
Sunday 5 May
10:00am - 4:30pm
Sunday 7 July
10:00am - 4:30pm

Admission:
£5.50, concessions £4.50, family £15.00. including NTS members
N.B. Prices correct at time of going to print

Charities:
Donation to SG Beneficiaries

DOUGARIE
KA27 8EB
Mr and Mrs S C Gibbs
E: office@dougarie.com

Most interesting terraced garden in castellated folly. Tender shrubs, herbaceous border, traditional kitchen garden. Small woodland area.

Directions: Blackwaterfoot 5 miles. Regular ferry sailing from Ardrossan and Claonaig (Argyll). Information from Caledonian MacBrayne, Gourock. (Telephone 01475 650100).

Disabled Access:
None

Opening Times:
Sunday 30 June
2:00pm - 5:00pm

Admission:
£3.50, children free

Charities:
Pirnmill Village Association receives 40%, the net remaining to SG Beneficiaries.

STRABANE
Brodick KA27 8DP
Lady Jean Fforde

Woodland garden with fine rhododendrons and azaleas. Walled garden with good herbaceous borders.

Directions: On east side of Brodick - Corrie road 100 yards before Duchess's Shopping Centre. Parking in front of house.

Disabled Access:
Partial

Opening Times:
Sunday 19 May
2:00pm - 5:00pm
Sunday 26 May
2:00pm - 5:00pm

Admission:
£4.00, children free

Charities:
Royal Agricultural Benevolent Institution receives 40% 19 May opening Arran Youth Foundation receives 40% 26 May opening the net remaining to SG Beneficiaries.

KINCARDINE & DEESIDE

Scotland's Gardens 2013 Guidebook is sponsored by **INVESTEC WEALTH & INVESTMENT**

District Organisers

Tina Hammond	Bardfield, Inchmarlo, Banchory AB31 4AT
Julie Nicol	Bogiesheil, Ballogie, Aboyne AB34 5DU

Area Organisers

Mrs Andrea Bond	Rosebank, Crathes, Banchory AB31 5JE
Mrs Helen Jackson	
Ms. Frieda Morrison	
Mr and Mrs David Younie	Bealltainn, Ballogie, Aboyne AB34 5DL

Treasurer

Lesley Mitchell	13 Highgate Gardens, Ferryhill, Aberdeen AB11 7TZ

Gardens open on a specific date

Crathes Castle, Banchory	Saturday 26 January	10:00am	- 5:00pm
Ecclesgreig Castle, St Cyrus	Sunday 24 February	1:00pm	- 4:00pm
Woodend House, Banchory	Sunday 26 May	1:30pm	- 4:30pm
Inchmarlo House Garden, Inchmarlo	Saturday 8 June	1:30pm	- 4:30pm
Kincardine, Kincardine O'Neil	Sunday 9 June	1:00pm	- 5:00pm
Ecclesgreig Castle, St Cyrus	Sunday 16 June	1:00pm	- 5:00pm
Crathes Castle, Banchory	Saturday 22 June	9:00am	- 5:00pm
Finzean House, Finzean, Banchory	Sunday 23 June	2:00pm	- 5:00pm
Drum Castle, Drumoak, by Banchory	Thursday 4 July	2:00pm	
Findrack, Torphins	Sunday 7 July	2:00pm	- 5:00pm
Drum Castle, Drumoak, by Banchory	Thursday 11 July	2:00pm	
Drumlithie Village, Drumlithie	Saturday 13 July	2:00pm	- 5:00pm
Douneside House, Tarland	Sunday 14 July	2:00pm	- 5:00pm
Drum Castle, Drumoak, by Banchory	Thursday 18 July	2:00pm	
Mill of Benholm Project, Benholm by Johnshaven	Sunday 21 July	10:00am	- 5:00pm
Drum Castle, Drumoak, by Banchory	Thursday 25 July	2:00pm	
Mallamauch, Banchory	Sunday 28 July	1:00pm	- 5:00pm
Glenbervie House, Drumlithie, Stonehaven	Sunday 4 August	2:00pm	- 5:00pm
Drum Castle, Drumoak, by Banchory	Sunday 22 September	11:00am	- 5:00pm
Inchmarlo House Garden, Inchmarlo	Sunday 20 October	1:30pm	- 4:30pm

KINCARDINE & DEESIDE

Scotland's Gardens 2013 Guidebook is sponsored by **INVESTEC WEALTH & INVESTMENT**

Glenbervie House

Key to symbols

 New in 2013

 Teas

 Cream teas

 Homemade teas

 Dogs on a lead allowed

 Wheelchair access

 Accommodation

 Plant stall

 Scottish Snowdrop Festival

Garden locations

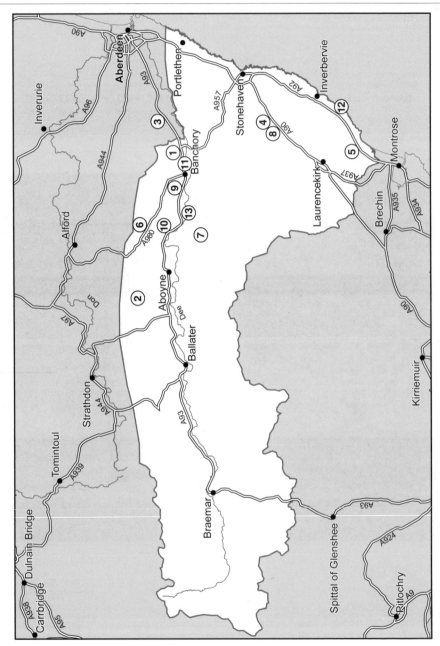

CRATHES CASTLE
Banchory AB31 5QJ
The National Trust for Scotland T: 0844 493 2166
E: crathes@nts.org.uk www.nts.org.uk

26 January: Join our expert Head Gardener for a day workshop about the principles and practicalities of pruning a garden. The programme will cover practical sessions on roses, renovations and removals as well as trees, shrubs and formative pruning.
22 June: Visit the beautiful Crathes gardens for its annual SG open day. The walled garden is divided into eight themed gardens, ranging from the formal to the modern! See the massive yew hedges and herbaceous borders. Seasonal highlight being the famous June border.

Other Details: Booking esential via NTS website for 26 January event, places are limited.

Directions: On A93, 15 miles west of Aberdeen and 3 miles east of Banchory.

Disabled Access:
Full

Opening Times:
Saturday 26 January
10:00am - 5:00pm
Saturday 22 June
9:00am - 5:00pm

Admission:
26 Jan: £50.00 (includes tea/coffee and light lunch)
22 June: £4.00 Admission also applicable to NTS members. N.B. Prices correct at time of going to print

Charities:
Donation to SG Beneficiaries

DOUNESIDE HOUSE
Tarland AB34 4UD
The MacRobert Trust

The former home of Lady MacRobert who designed and developed the gardens from farmland in the early to mid 1900s. The house and gardens are now in Trust and from March to October are used exclusively by retired and serving Officers of The Armed Forces, and as a conference centre in the winter months. Overlooking the Deeside Hills, ornamental terraced borders, woodland and water gardens surround a spectacular elevated lawn. The garden also boasts a large walled garden which supplies vegetables and cut flowers and also houses a large ornamental greenhouse. The Trust offers horticultural placements each year and the gardens have recently been accredited as a 'Royal Horticultural Society Approved Learning Centre'.

Other Details: Local pipe band.

Directions: B9119 towards Aberdeen. Tarland 1½ miles.

Disabled Access:
Partial

Opening Times:
Sunday 14 July
2:00pm - 5:00pm

Admission:
£4.00, OAPs £2.00, children free

Charities:
Perennial receives 40%, the net remaining to SG Beneficiaries.

DRUM CASTLE
Drumoak, by Banchory AB31 5EY
The National Trust for Scotland T: 0844 4932161
www.nts.org.uk

Each Thursday at 2:00pm join the Head Gardener for a walk through the historic rose garden: The main theme of walks is 'Romancing the Rose' (other themes are available). The Trust has established a collection of old-fashioned roses, at its peak for blossom and colour during July. See the Trust's website for details, booking is essential. 22 September walks at 11:30am, 1:30pm and 3:30pm looking at September borders. Please telephone for further information.

Other Details: Castle and castle tearoom open. Light lunches available.
See NTS website for castle admission prices.

Directions: On A93 3 miles west of Peterculter. 10 miles west of Aberdeen and 8 miles east of Banchory.

Disabled Access:
Partial

Opening Times:
Thursdays 4, 11, 18, & 25 July, 2:00pm
Sunday 22 September
11:00am - 5:00pm

Admission:
July walks: £7.50 incl. teas or £12.00 incl. lunch (booking essential).
22 Sept: £7.50 incl. teas
Admission also applicable to NTS members.

Charities:
Donation to SG Beneficiaries

DRUMLITHIE VILLAGE
Drumlithie AB39 3YF
The Gardeners of Drumlithie Village T: 01569 740378
E: jon.hayati@yahoo.co.uk

Walk round the delightful historical village of Drumlithie with Meg the local historian as your guide (2:00pm and 3:30pm) or visit a variety of attractive colourful village gardens or do both.

Other Details: Tickets on sale at the Village Hall, you will also be able to collect a plan showing where to find the gardens. An art exhibition by the local art group will be on display in the village hall.

Directions: Drumlithie, 6 miles south of Stonehaven, is 1 mile off the A90. It is well signed and on entering the village there are directions to the Village Hall for parking.

Disabled Access:
Partial

Opening Times:
Saturday 13 July
2:00pm - 5:00pm

Admission:
£4.00, children free

Charities:
Glenbervie and District Community Association receives 40%, the net remaining to SG Beneficiaries.

ECCLESGREIG CASTLE
St Cyrus DD10 0DP
Mr Gavin Farquhar T: 01674 850100
E: enquiries@ecclesgreig.com www.ecclesgreig.com

Ecclesgreig Castle, Victorian Gothic on a 16th century core, is internationally famous as an inspiration for Bram Stoker's Dracula. The snowdrop walk starts at the castle, meanders around the estate, along woodland paths and the pond, ending at the garden. The woodlands contain some very interesting trees and shrubs. Herbaceous borders 10 feet wide 140 feet long in Italian balustraded gardens. The garden has classical statues and stunning shaped topiary with views across St Cyrus to the sea. Started from a derelict site, development continues.

Directions: Ecclesgreig will be signposted from the A92 Coast Road and from the A937 Montrose / Laurencekirk Road.

Disabled Access:
Partial

Opening Times:
Sunday 24 February
1:00pm - 4:00pm for the Snowdrop Festival
Sunday 16 June
1:00pm - 5:00pm

Admission:
£4.00, accomp. children free

Charities:
Scottish Guide Assoc. (Montrose) receives 20%, Scottish Civic Trust receives 20%, the net remaining to SG Beneficiaries.

FINDRACK
Torphins AB31 4LJ
Mr and Mrs Andrew Salvesen

The gardens of Findrack are set in beautiful wooded countryside and are a haven of interesting plants and unusual design features. There is a walled garden with circular lawns and deep herbaceous borders, stream garden leading to a wildlife pond, vegetable garden and woodland walk.

Other Details: Excellent selection of plants for sale all grown in the garden.

Directions: Leave Torphins on A980 to Lumphanan after ½ mile turn off signposted Tornaveen. Stone gateway 1 mile up on left.

Disabled Access:
Partial

Opening Times:
Sunday 7 July
2:00pm - 5:00pm

Admission:
£4.50 children under 12
£1.00

Charities:
The Breadmaker receives 40%, the net remaining to SG Beneficiaries.

FINZEAN HOUSE
Finzean, Banchory AB31 6NZ
Mr and Mrs Donald Farquharson

Finzean House was the family home of Joseph Farquharson, the Victorian landscape painter, and the garden was the backdrop for several of his paintings. The garden has lovely views over the historic holly hedge to the front of Clachnaben. There is a spring woodland garden, extensive lawns with herbaceous and shrub borders and a working cut flower garden for late summer alongside a recently restored pond area.

Directions: On B976, South Deeside Road, between Banchory and Aboyne.

Disabled Access:
Full

Opening Times:
Sunday 23 June
2:00pm - 5:00pm

Admission:
£4.00, OAPs £3.00,
children free

Charities:
Forget-Me- Not receives
40%, the net remaining to
SG Beneficiaries.

GLENBERVIE HOUSE
Drumlithie, Stonehaven AB39 3YB
Mr and Mrs A Macphie

Nucleus of present day house dates from 15th century with additions in 18th and 19th centuries. A traditional Scottish walled garden on a slope with roses, herbaceous and annual borders along with fruit and vegetables. One wall is taken up with a fine Victorian style conservatory with many varieties of pot plants and climbers giving a dazzling display. There is also a woodland garden by a burn with primulas and ferns.

Other Details: Please note paths are quite steep in parts of the garden.

Directions: Drumlithie 1 mile. Garden 1½ miles off A90.

Disabled Access:
None

Opening Times:
Sunday 4 August
2:00pm - 5:00pm

Admission:
£4.00, children under 12 free

Charities:
Friends of Anchor
(Haematology and Oncology
Department ARI) receives
40%, the net remaining to SG
Beneficiaries.

INCHMARLO HOUSE GARDEN
Inchmarlo, Banchory AB31 4AL
Skene Enterprises (Aberdeen) Ltd T: 01330 826242
E: info@inchmarlo-retirement.co.uk www.inchmarlo-retirement.co.uk

An ever-changing 5 acre Woodland Garden, featuring ancient Scots Pines, Douglas Firs and Silver Firs, some over 42 metres tall, beeches and rare and unusual trees, including Pindrow Firs, Pere David's Maple, Erman's Birch and a mountain snowdrop tree. The Oriental Garden features a Kare Sansui, a dry slate stream designed by Peter Roger, an RHS Chelsea gold medal winner. The Rainbow Garden, within the keyhole-shaped purple Prunus Cerasifera hedge, has been designed by Billy Carruthers, an eight times gold medal winner at the RHS Scottish Garden Show.

Directions: From Aberdeen via North Deeside Road on A93, one mile west of Banchory turn right at the main gate to the Inchmarlo Estate.

Disabled Access:
Partial

Opening Times:
Sat 8 June 1:30pm - 4:30pm
Sun 20 Oct 1:30pm - 4:30pm

Admission:
£5.00, senior citizens £4.00,
children 14 and under free

Charities:
Alzheimer Scotland receives
40% June opening,
Deeside Forget-Me-Not
Dementia Support receives
40% October opening,
the net remaining to SG
Beneficiaries.

KINCARDINE
Kincardine O'Neil AB34 5AE
Mr and Mrs Andrew Bradford

A woodland or wilderness garden in development with some mature rhododendrons and azaleas and new planting amongst mature trees. A walled garden with a mixture of herbaceous and shrub borders, a sensational laburnum walk, vegetables and fruit trees. Extensive lawns and wild-flower meadows and a thought-provoking Planetary Garden. Also a free treasure trail for children. All with a background of stunning views across Royal Deeside.

Directions: Kincardine O'Neil on A93. Gates and lodge are opposite village school.

Disabled Access:
Partial

Opening Times:
Sunday 9 June
1:00pm - 5:00pm

Admission:
£5.00 children £2.00
including entry to treasure trail.

Charities:
Children 1st receives 20%, Kincardine O'Neil Village Hall receives 20%, the net remaining to SG Beneficiaries.

MALLAMAUCH
Banchory AB31 6HY
Mr and Mrs J Stripling

Situated in a challenging north facing quarry this is a relatively new garden which has been developed from scratch over the last 7 years. The garden boasts a huge array of herbaceous plants and shrubs to suit the different soil conditions in the quarry. There is a large pond and the beginnings of a collection of unusual trees. The garden is a true plantsmans garden. A small but interesting alpine garden adjoins Mallamauch garden alongside a vegetable plot with raised beds, fruit and a poly tunnel. The garden is still developing and has the potential to keep its owners busy over the coming years.

Directions: Situated on the B9077 travel 1 mile east of the Feugh Bridge on the right or approx 3 miles west from Crathes Bridge on the left. The road entrance is marked with a sign Maryfield Farm and Tilquhillie puddings and has a picture of a Christmas pudding and chicken on it.

Disabled Access:
Partial

Opening Times:
Sunday 28 July
1:00pm - 5:00pm

Admission:
£4.00, children free

Charities:
Stonehaven Renal Unit receives 40%, the net remaining to SG Beneficiaries.

MILL OF BENHOLM PROJECT
Benholm by Johnshaven DD10 0HT
Mill of Benholm Project T: 01561 362466
E: mill_of_benholm@btconnect.com

The Project provides training for SVQ gardening awards (with Aberdeen College). There are student gardens and a cottage garden. There is a delightful river and woodland walk through Millbrae Wood where there is an abundance of wildlife. There are mill wheel demonstrations and guided tours of the mill as well as plants for sale, raised by the students. This is a work in progress which warrants an annual visit to follow the efforts of students, staff, volunteers and members.

Directions: Turn off the A92 onto the Kirk of Benholm road. We are south of Inverbervie and north of Johnshaven.
Large visitors parking area with disabled parking for two cars directly by tearoom.

Disabled Access:
None

Opening Times:
Sunday 21 July
10:00am - 5:00pm

Admission:
£3.50

Charities:
Mill of Benholm receives 40%, the net remaining to SG Beneficiaries.

WOODEND HOUSE
Banchory AB31 4AY
Mr and Mrs J McHardy

Tucked away in a secluded woodland location. Mature rhododendrons and azaleas with extensive lawns create a stunning backdrop for Woodend House set on the banks of the River Dee. There is a small walled cottage garden and a glorious riverside walk amongst the cowslips and wildflowers giving way to ancient and majestic beech trees.

Directions: Four miles west of Banchory on the A93 (Banchory to Aboyne road).

Disabled Access:
Partial

Opening Times:
Sunday 26 May
1:30pm - 4:30pm

Admission:
£4.00, children free

Charities:
Sandpiper Trust receives 40%, the net remaining to SG Beneficiaries.

Kincardine

KIRKCUDBRIGHTSHIRE

District Organiser

Dr J Brennan	Barholm Castle, Gatehouse of Fleet DG7 2EZ

Area Organisers

Mrs P Addison	Killeron Farm, Gatehouse of Fleet DG7 2BS
Mrs Val Bradbury	Glenisle, Jubilee Path, Kippford DG5 4LW
Mrs W N Dickson	Chipperkyle, Kirkpatrick, Durham DG7 3EY
Mrs B Marshall	Cairnview, Carsphairn DG7 3TQ
Mrs M McIlvenna	Braeneuk, Balmaclellan, Castle Douglas DG7 3QS
Mrs C McIver	Loxley, Abercrombie Road, Castle Douglas DG7 1BA
Mrs K Ross	Slate Row, Auchencairn, Castle Douglas DG7 1QL
Mrs C V Scott	14 Castle Street, Kirkcudbright DG6 4JA

Treasurer

Mr P Phillips	The Old Manse, Crossmichael DG7 3AT

Gardens open on a specific date

Danevale Park, Crossmichael	Date to be advised			
Threave Garden, Castle Douglas	Sunday 12 May	10:00am	-	5:00pm
Corsock House, Castle Douglas	Sunday 26 May	2:00pm	-	5:00pm
Broughton House Garden, Kirkcudbright	Thursday 13 June	6:00pm	-	9:00pm
The Waterhouse Gardens at Stockarton, Kirkcudbright	Sunday 23 June	1:00pm	-	5:00pm
Cally Gardens, Gatehouse of Fleet	Sunday 30 June	10:00am	-	5:30pm
Crofts, Kirkpatrick Durham	Sunday 14 July	2:00pm	-	5:00pm
Glensone Walled Garden, Southwick	Sunday 21 July	2:00pm	-	5:00pm
Southwick House, Southwick	Sunday 28 July	2:00pm	-	5:00pm
Southwick House, Southwick	Monday 29 July	9:00am	-	5:00pm
Southwick House, Southwick	Tuesday 30 July	9:00am	-	5:00pm
Southwick House, Southwick	Wednesday 31 July	9:00am	-	5:00pm
Southwick House, Southwick	Thursday 1 August	9:00am	-	5:00pm
Southwick House, Southwick	Friday 2 August	9:00am	-	5:00pm
Seabank, Rockcliffe	Sunday 4 August	2:00pm	-	5:00pm
Threave Garden, Castle Douglas	Sunday 4 August	10:00am	-	5:00pm
Barholm Castle, Gatehouse of Fleet	Sunday 11 August	2:00pm	-	5:00pm
Cally Gardens, Gatehouse of Fleet	Sunday 18 August	10:00am	-	5:30pm

KIRKCUDBRIGHTSHIRE

Scotland's Gardens 2013 Guidebook is sponsored by **INVESTEC WEALTH & INVESTMENT**

Gardens open by arrangement

Corsock House, Castle Douglas	1 April - 30 June	01644 440250
Cosy Cottage, Borgue	On request	01557 870648
Danevale Park, Crossmichael	Until 1 June	01556 670223
		E: danevale@tiscali.co.uk
Margrie Cottage, Borgue	On request	01577 870313
Steadstone, Dalbeattie	On request	01556 611565
Stockarton, Kirkcudbright	1 April - 31 August	01557 330430

Corsock House

Key to symbols

New in 2013	Homemade teas	Accommodation
Teas	Dogs on a lead allowed	Plant stall
Cream teas	Wheelchair access	Scottish Snowdrop Festival

Garden locations

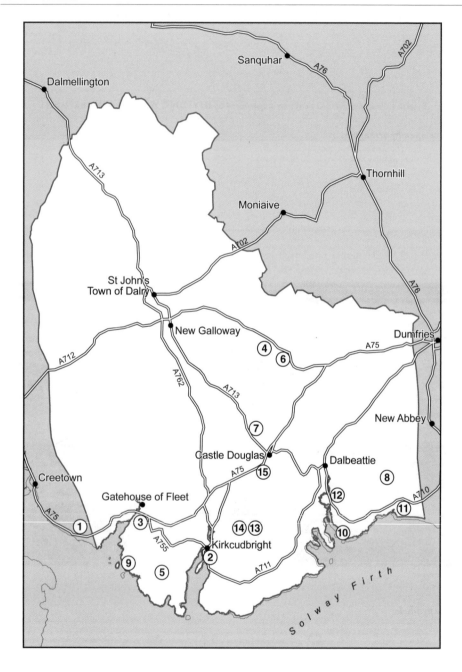

BARHOLM CASTLE

Gatehouse of Fleet DG7 2EZ

Mr and Dr Brennan

Barholm Castle, a 16th century tower, was restored from a ruin in 2006 and the owners moved in permanently in 2011. Since the restoration, the 3 acre gardens surrounding the tower have been slowly developing from scratch. There is a small walled garden, a wooded ravine, which is gradually being won over from 7 foot high nettles, a greenhouse and newly developing shrub borders, ponds, rockeries and herbaceous beds. The views over Wigtown Bay are magnificent.

Directions: Off the A75 at the Cairn Holy turn-off, fork right 3 times up a steep narrow road for ½ mile. Parking is limited, so those who are able to walk up should park just off the A75.

Disabled Access:
Partial

Opening Times:
Sunday 11 August
2:00pm - 5:00pm

Admission:
£4.00

Charities:
Lepra receives 40%, the net remaining to SG Beneficiaries.

BROUGHTON HOUSE GARDEN

12 High Street, Kirkcudbright DG6 4JX

The National Trust for Scotland T: 01557 330437

E: broughtonhouse@nts.org.uk www.nts.org.uk

This event will offer visitors an evening of live music, gardens walks and refreshments. It is a chance to see the garden by a different light! Broughton House Garden is a fascinating town house garden that belonged to E A Hornel - artist, collector and one of the 'Glasgow boys'. Full of colour, mostly herbaceous, old apple trees, greenhouse with old pelargonium varieties, fruit and vegetable garden and the newly named Dactylorhiza "Tizzy Hornell".

Other Details: Self-catering accommodation available. Refreshments included for evening.

Directions: In Kirkcudbright High Street.

Disabled Access:
Full

Opening Times:
Thursday 13 June
6:00pm - 9:00pm

Admission:
£4.00. Including NTS members. N.B. Prices correct at time of going to print

Charities:
Donation to SG Beneficiaries

CALLY GARDENS

Gatehouse of Fleet DG7 2DJ

Mr Michael Wickenden T: 01557 814703

E: info@callygardens.co.uk www.callygardens.co.uk

A specialist nursery in a fine 2.7 acre 18th century walled garden with old vinery and bothy, all surrounded by the Cally Oak Woods. Our collection of 3,500 varieties of plants can be seen and a selection will be available pot-grown. Excellent range of rare herbaceous perennials.

Other Details: Forestry nature trails nearby.

Directions: From Dumfries take the Gatehouse turning off A75 and turn left through the Cally Palace Hotel gateway from where the gardens are well signposted.

Disabled Access:
Full

Opening Times:
Sunday 30 June
10:00am - 5:30pm
Sunday 18 August
10:00am - 5:30pm

Admission:
£2.50

Charities:
ROKPA Tibetan Charity receives 40%, the net remaining to SG Beneficiaries.

CORSOCK HOUSE
Corsock, Castle Douglas DG7 3DJ
The Ingall Family T: 01644 440250

Rhododendrons, woodland walks with temples, water gardens and loch. One acre formal walled garden being re-made. David Bryce turretted "Scottish Baronial" house in background.

Directions: Off A75 Dumfries 14 miles, Castle Douglas 10 miles, Corsock village ½ mile on A712.

Disabled Access:
Partial

Opening Times:
Sunday 26 May
2:00pm - 5:00pm
Also by arrangement 1 April
to Sunday 30 June

Admission:
£4.00, concessions £3.00

Charities:
Kirkpatrick Durham
Church receives 40%,
the net remaining to SG
Beneficiaries.

COSY COTTAGE
Borgue DG6 4SH
Mr and Mrs A Broome T: 01557 870648

Village garden with herbaceous borders, rockeries, greenhouse and alpine troughs.

Directions: Borgue Village is on the B727 between Kirkcudbright and Gatehouse of Fleet 3m off the A75 route Carlisle to Stranraer.

Disabled Access:
Partial

Opening Times:
By arrangement on request

Admission:
£2.00

Charities:
Cancer Research UK receives
40%, the net remaining to
SG Beneficiaries.

CROFTS
Kirkpatrick Durham, Castle Douglas DG7 3HX
Mrs Andrew Dalton T: 01556 650235

Victorian garden with mature trees, a walled garden, hydrangea garden and a water garden.

Directions: A75 to Crocketford, then 3 miles on A712 to Corsock & New Galloway

Disabled Access:
Partial

Opening Times:
Sunday 14 July
2:00pm - 5:00pm

Admission:
£4.00

Charities:
Kirkpatrick Durham
Church receives 40%,
the net remaining to SG
Beneficiaries.

DANEVALE PARK
Crossmichael DG7 2LP
Mrs M R C Gillespie T: 01556 670223
E: danevale@tiscali.co.uk

Mature policies with woodland walk alongside the River Dee. One of the finest displays of snowdrops in Scotland. We also get great praise for our teas.

Directions: On the A713. Crossmichael 1 mile, Castle Douglas 2 miles.

Disabled Access:
Partial

Opening Times:
Date to be advised, see website for details
Also open by arrangement until 1 June

Admission:
£2.50

Charities:
Poppyscotland receives 40%, the net remaining to SG Beneficiaries.

GLENSONE WALLED GARDEN
Southwick DG2 8AW
William & Josephine Millar T: 01387 780215
E: josephine.millar@btconnect.com

A restored walled garden complete with central water feature. Borders of perennials; shrubs with beds interspersed through the lawn. Large kitchen garden with a variety of vegetables; fruit occupies a section of the garden. Bee Bowls, a unique feature, are positioned in two opposite corners of the wall. Set in an idyllic valley with views of the Solway Firth and the Cumbrian hills.

Directions: Off the A710 Dumfries to Dalbeattie coast road at Caulkerbush. Take the B793 to Dalbeattie for two miles then turn right and follow the arrows.

Disabled Access:
Full

Opening Times:
Sunday 21 July
2:00pm - 5:00pm

Admission:
£3.50

Charities:
Combat Stress receives 40%, the net remaining to SG Beneficiaries.

MARGRIE COTTAGE
Borgue DG6 4UE
Mr and Mrs George Hill T: 01577 870313

Garden of over an acre with mature shrubs and trees. Natural rock features and a pond.

Directions: From Borgue village on B727 between Kirkcudbright and Gatehouse of Fleet go uphill past the church. Follow the road along the coast for two miles passing Knockbrex, a large property on the left. At the junction bear right, Margrie Cottage is the first property on the right.

Disabled Access:
Partial

Opening Times:
By arrangement on request, except last two weeks in both May and July.

Admission:
£2.00

Charities:
Cancer Research UK receives 40%, the net remaining to SG Beneficiaries.

10 SEABANK
Seabank, Merse Road, Rockcliffe DG5 4QH
Mr and Mrs P J Stanning

The 1½ acre gardens extend to the high water mark with fine views across the Urr estuary, Rough Island and beyond. Herbaceous borders surround the house and there is a new walled garden for fruit and vegetables. A plantswoman's garden with a range of interesting and unusual plants.

Directions: Park in the public car park at Rockcliffe. Walk down the road about 50 metres towards the sea and turn left along The Merse, a private road. Seabank is the sixth house on the left.

Disabled Access:
Partial

Opening Times:
Sunday 4 August
2:00pm - 5:00pm

Admission:
£3.50

Charities:
Marie Curie (Solway Group) receives 40%, the net remaining to SG Beneficiaries.

11 SOUTHWICK HOUSE
Southwick DG2 8AH
Mr and Mrs R H L Thomas

Traditional formal walled garden with greenhouses and potager containing fruit, vegetables and cutting flowers. Roses now a prominent feature together with herbaceous borders, shrubs and a lily pond. A water garden with trees, shrubs, ponds and lawns running alongside the Southwick Burn.

Directions: On A710 near Caulkerbush. Dalbeattie 7 miles, Dumfries 17 miles.

Disabled Access:
Partial

Opening Times:
Sunday 28 July
2:00pm - 5:00pm
Mon - Fri 29 July - 2 August
9:00am - 5:00pm

Admission:
£4.00

Charities:
Loch Arthur Community receives 20%, Gardener's Royal Benevolent Fund receives 20%, the net remaining to SG Beneficiaries.

12 STEADSTONE
Colvend Road, Dalbeattie DG5 4QT
Mr and Mrs R Kinnaird T: 01556 611565
E: rg.kinnaird@live.co.uk

A garden in a quarry. Lovely in spring and autumn with a large variety of shrubs and seas of mecanopsis and primulas.

Directions: One and a half miles out of Dalbeattie on the A710 towards Kippford.

Disabled Access:
Partial

Opening Times:
By arrangement on request

Admission:
£3.00

Charities:
Colliston Youth Club receives 40%, the net remaining to SG Beneficiaries.

STOCKARTON
Kirkcudbright DG6 4XS
Lt. Col. and Mrs Richard Cliff T: 01557 330 430

A garden begun in 1994. Our aim has been to create informal and small gardens around a Galloway farmhouse, leading down to a lochan.

Other Details: Holiday cottage to rent within the garden, overlooking the lochan. Sleeps 4-6

Directions: On B727 Kirkcudbright to Gelston Road. Kirkcudbright 3 miles, Castle Douglas 7 miles.

Disabled Access:
Partial

Opening Times:
By arrangement Monday 1 April to Saturday 31 August

Admission:
£3.00

Charities:
Friends of Loch Arthur Community receives 40%, the net remaining to SG Beneficiaries.

THE WATERHOUSE GARDENS AT STOCKARTON
Kirkcudbright DG6 4XS
Martin Gould & Sharon O'Rourke T: 01557 331266
E: waterhousekbt@aol.com www.waterhousekbt.co.uk

One acre of densely planted terraced cottage style gardens attached to a Galloway cottage. Three ponds surround the oak framed eco-polehouse 'The Waterhouse' available to rent 52 weeks a year. Climbing roses, clematis and honeysuckles are a big feature as well as pond-side walk. Over 50 photos on our website. Featured on BBC Scotland's 'Beechgrove Garden' 2007.

Directions: On B727 Kirkcudbright to Gelston - Dalbeattie road.   Kirkcudbright 3 miles, Castle Douglas 7 miles.

Disabled Access:
None

Opening Times:
Sunday 23 June
1:00pm - 5:00pm

Admission:
£3.00

Charities:
Loch Arthur Community receives 40%, the net remaining to SG Beneficiaries.

THREAVE GARDEN
Castle Douglas DG7 1RX
The National Trust for Scotland T: 01556 502 575
E: sinnes@nts.org.uk www.nts.org.uk

Home of the Trust's School of Practical Gardening. Spectacular daffodils in spring, colourful herbaceous borders in summer, striking autumn trees and heather garden. There is also a working walled garden. For more information on the Scotland's Gardens event, please contact the property for more information or visit http://www.nts.org.uk/Events/.

Other Details: Self-catering accommodation available. Restaurant open for full dining.

Directions: Off A75, one mile west of Castle Douglas.

Disabled Access:
Full

Opening Times:
Sunday 12 May
10:00am - 5:00pm
Sunday 4 August
10:00am - 5:00pm

Admission:
£6.50, concessions £5.50, including NTS members. N.B. Prices correct at time of going to print

Charities:
Donation to SG Beneficiaries

LANARKSHIRE

Scotland's Gardens 2013 Guidebook is sponsored by **INVESTEC WEALTH & INVESTMENT**

District Organiser

Mrs M Maxwell Stuart   Baitlaws, Lamington ML12 6HR

Treasurers

Mr & Mrs D Onions   Allium Croft, 21 Main Street, Braehead ML11 8EZ

Gardens open on a specific date

Cleghorn , Stable House, Cleghorn Farm	Sunday 24 February	2:00pm	-	4:00pm
Nemphlar Village Garden Trail	Sunday 19 May	1:30pm	-	5:00pm
Allium Croft, Braehead	Sunday 16 June	1:00pm	-	5:00pm
Dippoolbank Cottage, Carnwath	Sunday 23 June	2:00pm	-	6:00pm
Thankerton/Covington Village Gardens	Sunday 30 June	1:00pm	-	5:00pm
Dippoolbank Cottage, Carnwath	Sunday 21 July	2:00pm	-	6:00pm
Wellbutts, Elsrickle	Sunday 11 August	1:00pm	-	5:00pm
Culter Allers, Coulter	Sunday 18 August	2:00pm	-	5:00pm
New Lanark Roof Garden	Sunday 18 August	1:00pm	-	5:00pm

Gardens open regularly

New Lanark Roof Garden	Daily	11:00am	-	5:00pm

Gardens open by arrangement

Baitlaws, Lamington	1 June - 31 August	01899 850240
Biggar Park, Biggar	1 May - 31 July	01899 220185
Carmichael Mill, Hyndford Bridge	On request	01555 665880
The Scots Mining Company House, Leadhills	On request	01659 74235

Key to symbols

	New in 2013		Homemade teas		Accommodation
	Teas		Dogs on a lead allowed		Plant stall
	Cream teas		Wheelchair access		Scottish Snowdrop Festival

Garden locations

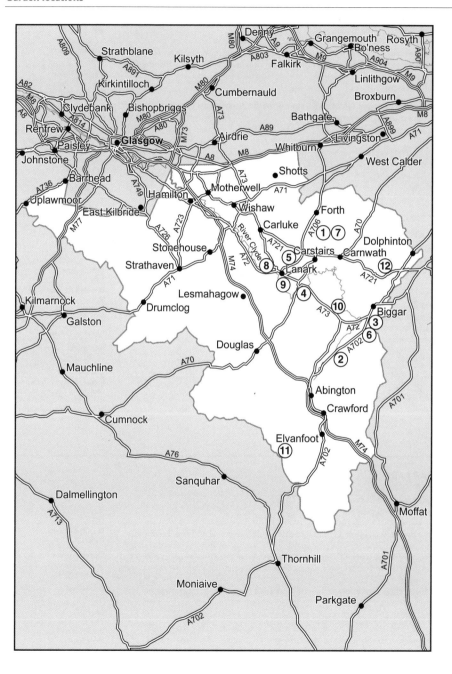

ALLIUM CROFT
21 Main Street, Braehead ML11 8EZ
David and Pat Onions T: 01555 812843
E: pat@alliumcroft.plus.com

This is a new garden established only three years ago, with new plants and over 700 brought in our own furniture van from our previous garden in Perthshire. This garden is an example of what can be achieved in a very windy and wet location and in only a short time.

Directions: The garden is in Main Street off the B7016 (Forth - Carnwarth), turn opposite Last Shaft Inn and Restaurant.

Disabled Access:
None

Opening Times:
Sunday 16 June
1:00pm - 5:00pm

Admission:
£3.00

Charities:
Braehead Village Fund receives 40%, the net remaining to SG Beneficiaries.

BAITLAWS
Lamington, Biggar ML12 6HR
Mr and Mrs M Maxwell Stuart T: 01899 850240
E: ms.kirsty@gmail.com

The garden is set at over 900 ft. above sea level and has been developed over the past 25 years with a particular emphasis on colour combinations of shrubs and herbaceous perennials which flourish at that height. A small pond is a recent addition. The surrounding hills make an imposing backdrop. Featured in "Good Gardens' Guide".

Other Details: Groups welcome.

Directions: Off A702 above Lamington Village. Biggar 5 miles, Abington 5 miles, Lanark 10 miles.

Disabled Access:
None

Opening Times:
By arrangement
1 June to 31 August

Admission:
£4.00

Charities:
Biggar Museum Trust, Lamington Chapel Restoration Fund receives 40%, the net remaining to SG Beneficiaries.

BIGGAR PARK
Biggar ML12 6JS
Mr and Mrs David Barnes T: 01899 220185
E: sue@smbarnes.com

Ten acre garden starred in "Good Gardens' Guide", featured on "The Beechgrove Garden" and in "Country Life", "Scottish Field" and many others. Incorporating traditional walled garden with long stretches of herbaceous borders, shrubberies, fruit, vegetables and a potager. Lawns, walks, pools, small Japanese garden and other interesting features. Glades of rhododendrons, azaleas and blue poppies in May and June. Good collection of old fashioned roses in June and July; interesting young trees.

Other Details: Groups welcome.

Directions: On A702, ¼ mile south of Biggar.

Disabled Access:
Partial

Opening Times:
By arrangement
1 May to 31 July

Admission:
£5.00

Charities:
ZANE receives 40%, the net remaining to SG Beneficiaries.

CARMICHAEL MILL
Hyndford Bridge, Lanark ML11 8SJ
Chris, Ken and Gemma Fawell T: 01555 665880
E: ken.fawell@btinternet.com

Riverside gardens surrounding the only remaining workable, water powered grain mill in Clydesdale. Admission includes entry to the mill which will be turning, river levels permitting. Diverse plant habitats from saturated to bone dry allow a vast range of trees and shrubs, both ornamental and fruit, with a vegetable garden. Herbaceous perennials, annuals and biennials with ornamental/wildlife pond complementing the landscape. Also, archaeological remains of medieval grain mills from c.1200 and foundry, lint mill and threshing mill activity within the curtilage of the Category B Listed Building.

Other Details: Teas and light refreshments by prior arrangement.

Directions: Just off A73 Lanark to Biggar road ½ mile east of the Hyndford Bridge.

Disabled Access:
Partial

Opening Times:
By arrangement on request

Admission:
£4.00, children over 12
£2.00

Charities:
Donation to SG Beneficiaries.

CLEGHORN
Stable House, Cleghorn Farm, Lanark ML11 7RN
Mr and Mrs R Elliott Lockhart T: 01555 663792
E: info@cleghornestategardens.com www.cleghornestategardens.com

18th century garden which is currently being renovated. Mature trees and shrubs, with masses of snowdrops spread around. Beautiful views to the south of Tinto Hill and the Cleghorn Glen.

Directions: Cleghorn Farm is situated two miles north of Lanark on the A706.

Disabled Access:
None

Opening Times:
Sunday 24 February
2:00pm - 4:00pm
for the Snowdrop Festival

Admission:
By Donation

Charities:
Marie Curie Cancer
Care receives 40%, the
net remaining to SG
Beneficiaries.

CULTER ALLERS
Coulter, Biggar ML12 6PZ
The McCosh Family

Culter Allers, a late-Victorian baronial house, has maintained its traditional one-acre walled kitchen garden, half with fruit and vegetables, the other half with mainly cut flowers and herbaceous. The policies of the house are open and include woodland walks and an avenue of 125 year old lime trees leading to the village church.

Directions: In the village of Coulter, 3 miles south of Biggar on A702.

Disabled Access:
Partial

Opening Times:
Sunday 18 August
2:00pm - 5:00pm

Admission:
£4.00, children free

Charities:
Coulter Library Trust receives
40%, the net remaining to SG
Beneficiaries.

DIPPOOLBANK COTTAGE
Carnwath ML11 8LP
Mr Allan Brash

Artist's intriguing cottage garden. Vegetables grown in small beds. Herbs, fruit, flowers, pond in woodland area with tree house and summer house. Fernery completed in 2007. This is an organic garden mainly constructed with recycled materials.

Directions: Off B7016 between Forth and Carnwath near the village of Braehead on the Auchengray road. Approximately 8 miles from Lanark. Well signed.

Disabled Access:
None

Opening Times:
Sunday 23 June
2:00pm - 6:00pm
Sunday 21 July
2:00pm - 6:00pm

Admission:
£4.00

Charities:
The Little Haven receives 40%, the net remaining to SG Beneficiaries.

NEMPHLAR VILLAGE GARDEN TRAIL
Nemphlar, Lanark ML11 9JG
The Gardeners of Nemphlar Village

A number of medium and small gardens in the village of Nemphlar. A pleasant stroll of one mile covers all the gardens. Extensive views over the Clyde Valley and Tinto Hill.

Other Details: Homemade teas served in village hall.

Directions: Leave A73 at Cartland Bridge (Lanark to Carluke Road) or A72 (Clyde Valley Road) at Crossford. Both routes well signposted.

Disabled Access:
None

Opening Times:
Sunday 19 May
1:30pm - 5:00pm

Admission:
£4.00, children under 12 free

Charities:
Clydesdale Branch of the Riding for Disabled Association receives 40%, the net remaining to SG Beneficiaries.

NEW LANARK ROOF GARDEN
New Lanark Mills, Lanark ML11 9DB
New Lanark Visitor Centre T: 01555 661345
E: visit@newlanark.org www.newlanarkroofgarden.co.uk

This amazing 9,000 square feet garden has been created on the roof of the historic A Listed Mill No. 2, in the heart of the New Lanark World Heritage Site. Designed by Douglas Coltart of Viridarium to meet these challenging conditions, the garden and viewing platform offer splendid and seasonally changing views. The Roof Garden is part of the New Lanark Visitor Centre, and is accessed by lift or stairs.

Other Details: Disabled access via ramps and lifts.

Directions: New Lanark is one mile south of Lanark and around an hour from Glasgow (M74/A72) and Edinburgh (A70). From the south, the village is 30 mins from M74 Junction 13/Abington - main trunk road to Edinburgh.

Disabled Access:
Full

Opening Times:
Sunday 18 August
1:00pm - 5:00pm for Scotland's Gardens
Daily 11:00am - 5:00pm as part of New Lanark Visitor Centre

Admission:
Price included in passport ticket for visitor centre - see New Lanark website for details

Charities:
Donation to SG Beneficiaries

THANKERTON/COVINGTON VILLAGE GARDENS
ML12 6PA
Thankerton/Covington Village Gardeners

Nestled at the foot of Tinto Hill in the upper Clyde Valley, the villages of Thankerton and Covington offer nine gardens to be explored. Each garden has its own character and style. With imaginative plantings and a broad range of plants, shrubs and trees, there is something to inspire everyone. Six of the gardens lie within the village of Thankerton, with a further three a short scenic drive away through the conservation area of Covington with its ancient tower and quaint thatched cottages.

Disabled Access:
Partial

Opening Times:
Sunday 30 June
1:00pm - 5:00pm

Admission:
£4.00

Charities:
Lanarkshire Cancer Care Trust receives 20%, Woodland Trust Scotland receives 20%, the net remaining to SG Beneficiaries.

Directions: Thankerton lies half a mile east of the A73 between Lanark and Biggar.

THE SCOTS MINING COMPANY HOUSE
Leadhills, Biggar ML12 6XP
Charlie and Greta Clark T: 01659 74235

The site is c.400m above sea level, which is high for a cultivated garden. The surrounding landscape is open moorland with sheep grazing. The garden is largely enclosed by dense planting, but the various walks allow views through the trees into the surrounding countryside. Historic Scotland in their register of "Gardens and designed landscapes" describe the garden as "An outstanding example of a virtually unaltered, small, 18th century garden layout connected with James Stirling, the developer of the profitable Leadhills mining enterprise, and possibly William Adam." Say goodbye to spring walking among what must be amongst the last daffodils of the year.

Disabled Access:
Partial

Opening Times:
By arrangement on request

Admission:
£3.50, children free

Charities:
Scots Mining Company Trust receives 40%, the net remaining to SG Beneficiaries.

Other Details: Homemade teas may be available by prior request.

Directions: On Main Street, Leadhills (B797) 6 miles from M74 Junction 13 (Abington).

WELLBUTTS
Elsrickle, by Biggar ML12 6QZ
Mr and Mrs N Slater

Started in 2000 from a bare brown site around a renovated croft cottage, with additional field ground obtained in 2005, the garden is now approximately 2 acres. Due to the exposed and elevated (960 ft.) position the ongoing priority is hedge and shrub planting to give some protection for the many and varied herbaceous borders leading to the duckhouse, two large ponds and 'boggery'.

Disabled Access:
None

Opening Times:
Sunday 11 August
1:00pm - 5:00pm

Admission:
£4.00

Charities:
CHAS receives 40%, the net remaining to SG Beneficiaries.

Directions: Parking on main road (A721) near to bus stop. Walk to garden (approximately 200 yards)

LOCHABER & BADENOCH

District Organiser

Mr and Mrs Norrie Maclaren	Ard-Daraich, Ardgour, Nr. Fort William PH33 7AB

Area Organisers

Mrs Philip MacKenzie	Glenkyllachy, Tomatin IV13 7YA
Mrs Anne Moore	Polgreggan, Newtonmore PH20 1BD

Treasurer

Mr Norrie Maclaren	Ard-Daraich, Ardgour, Nr. Fort William PH33 7AB

Gardens open on a specific date

Canna House Walled Garden, Isle of Canna	Saturday 4 May	10:30am - 4:00pm
Aberarder, Kinlochlaggan	Sunday 2 June	2:00pm - 5:30pm
Ardverikie, Kinlochlaggan	Sunday 2 June	2:00pm - 5:30pm
Craigmore Mill , Nethybridge	Sunday 7 July	1:00pm - 6:00pm
Canna House Walled Garden, Isle of Canna	Wednesday 14 August	10:30am - 4:00pm

Gardens open regularly

Ardtornish, by Lochaline	Daily	10:00am - Dusk

Gardens open by arrangement

Ard-Daraich, Ardgour	On request	01855 841348

Key to symbols

	New in 2013		Homemade teas		Accommodation
	Teas		Dogs on a lead allowed		Plant stall
	Cream teas		Wheelchair access		Scottish Snowdrop Festival

Garden locations

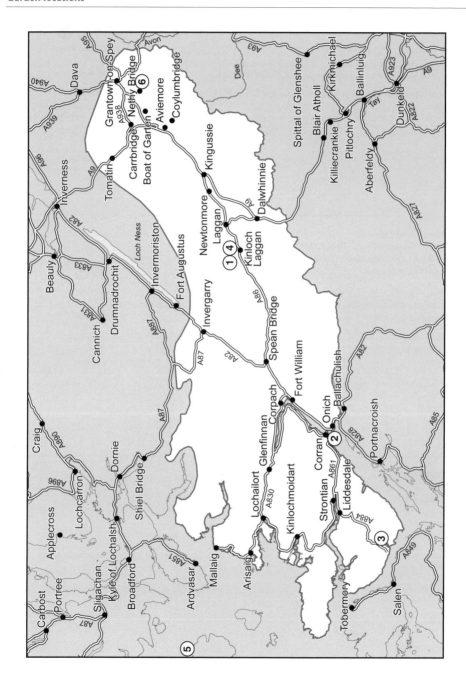

ABERARDER (JOINT OPENING WITH ARDVERIKIE)
Kinlochlaggan PH20 1BX
The Feilden Family T: 01528 544300

The garden has been laid out over the last twenty years to create a mixture of spring and autumn plants and trees, including rhododendrons, azaleas and acers. The elevated view down Loch Laggan from the garden is exceptional.

Directions: On A86 between Newtonmore and Spean Bridge at east end of Loch Laggan.

Disabled Access:
Partial

Opening Times:
Sunday 2 June
2:00pm - 5:30pm

Admission:
£5.00 includes entrance to Ardverikie

Charities:
Marie Curie receives 20%, Laggan Church receives 20%, the net remaining to SG Beneficiaries.

ARD-DARAICH
Ardgour, By Fort William PH33 7AB
Norrie and Anna Maclaren T: 01855 841348
www.arddaraich.co.uk

Seven acre hill garden, in a spectacular setting, with many fine and uncommon rhododendrons, an interesting selection of trees and shrubs and a large collection of camellias, acers and sorbus.

Directions: West from Fort William, across the Corran Ferry, turn left and a mile on the right further west.

Disabled Access:
None

Opening Times:
By arrangement on request

Admission:
£4.00

Charities:
Donation to SG Beneficiaries

ARDTORNISH
By Lochaline, Morvern PA80 5UZ
Mrs John Raven

Wonderful gardens of interesting mature conifers, rhododendrons, deciduous trees, shrubs and herbaceous set amid magnificent scenery.

Directions: A884 Lochaline 3 miles.

Disabled Access:
None

Opening Times:
Daily
10:00am - 6:00pm or Dusk

Admission:
£3.50

Charities:
Donation to SG Beneficiaries.

❹ ARDVERIKIE (JOINT OPENING WITH ABERARDER)
Kinlochlaggan PH20 1BX
Mrs P Laing and Mrs E T Smyth-Osbourne T: 01528 544300

Lovely setting on Loch Laggan with magnificent trees. Walled garden with large collection of acers, shrubs and herbaceous. Architecturally interesting house (not open). Site of the filming of the TV series "Monarch of the Glen".

Other Details: Teas at Aberarder.

Directions: On A86 between Newtonmore and Spean Bridge. Entrance at east end of Loch Laggan by gate lodge over bridge.

Disabled Access:
Partial

Opening Times:
Sunday 2 June
2:00pm - 5:30pm

Admission:
£5.00 includes entrance to Aberarder

Charities:
Marie Curie receives 20%, Laggan Church receives 20%, the net remaining to SG Beneficiaries.

❺ CANNA HOUSE WALLED GARDEN
Isle of Canna PH44 4RS
National Trust for Scotland T: 01687 462998
E: sconnor@nts.org.uk www.nts.org.uk

Formerly derelict 2 acre walled garden brought back to life following a 5 year restoration project started in 2007. Soft fruit, top fruit, vegetables, ornamental lawns and flower beds. 80ft Escallonia arch. Garden has been replanted to attract bees, butterflies and moths. Woodland walks outside walls. Spectacular views of neighbouring islands.

Directions: Access Isle of Canna via Calmac ferry from Mallaig pier. Gardener will meet you in the Garden.

Disabled Access:
Full

Opening Times:
Saturday 4 May
10:30am - 4:00pm
Wednesday 14 August
10:30am - 4:00pm

Admission:
£3.00 Including NTS members. N.B. Prices correct at time of going to print.

Charities:
Donation to SG Beneficiaries.

CRAIGMORE MILL
Dorback Road, Nethybridge PH25 3ED
Chris and Harry Jamieson

Half acre garden set outside Nethybridge village surrounded by Scots Pines, silver birches and fields mostly on a sloping terrain facing east. The Aultmore Burn borders the garden and feeds a natural pond containing bog plants. Mixed borders, rockeries and paths have evolved over the years since the Old Meal Mill was converted into a house by the present owners in 1976. Wide range of shrubs and herbaceous plants including meconopsis, incarvillea, primulas, celmisias, hostas etc. with the main focus on foliage.

Other Details: Teas available in workshop, garage or garden! Toilets available.

Directions: From A9: Take B970 to Boat of Garton then Nethybridge. Go over humpback bridge, turn right before Nethybridge Hotel. Continue uphill on Dorback/Tomintoul road, at next cross-roads go straight on. One minute later sign for parking on left at Woodside. Proceed by foot to garden which will be signposted.
From East: Near Grantown take B970 to Nethybridge and after Nethybridge Hotel turn left (before bridge). Then follow directions from Dorback/Tomintoul road as above.

Disabled Access:
None

Opening Times:
Sunday 7 July
1:00pm - 6:00pm

Admission:
£3.50

Charities:
Marie Curie Cancer Care receives 40%, the net remaining to SG Beneficiaries.

MIDLOTHIAN

Scotland's Gardens 2013 Guidebook is sponsored by **INVESTEC WEALTH & INVESTMENT**

District Organiser

Mrs Sarah Barron	Laureldene, Kevock Road, Lasswade EH18 1HT

Area Organisers

Mrs Margaret Drummond	Pomathorn House, Penicuik EH26 8PJ
Mrs R Hill	Law House, 27 Biggar Road, Silverburn EH26 9LJ
Mrs Elidh Liddle	21 Craigiebeild Crescent, Penicuik EH26 9EQ

Treasurer

Mrs Margaret Drummond	Pomathorn House, Penicuik EH26 8PJ

Gardens open on a specific date

Kevock Garden, Lasswade	Sunday 3 March	12:00pm - 3:00pm
Kevock Garden, Lasswade	Saturday 15 June	2:00pm - 5:00pm
Kevock Garden, Lasswade	Sunday 16 June	2:00pm - 5:00pm
Silverburn Village	Sunday 4 August	12:30pm - 5:00pm
Harvieston Walled Garden, Gorebridge	Sunday 18 August	2:00pm - 5:00pm

Gardens open by arrangement

The Old Sun Inn, Newbattle	1 June - 31 July	0131 663 2648

Plant sales

SG & Midlothian Council Plant Sale, Vogrie	Saturday 25 May	10:00am - 4:00pm

Key to symbols

	New in 2013		Homemade teas		Accommodation
	Teas		Dogs on a lead allowed		Plant stall
	Cream teas		Wheelchair access		Scottish Snowdrop Festival

Garden locations

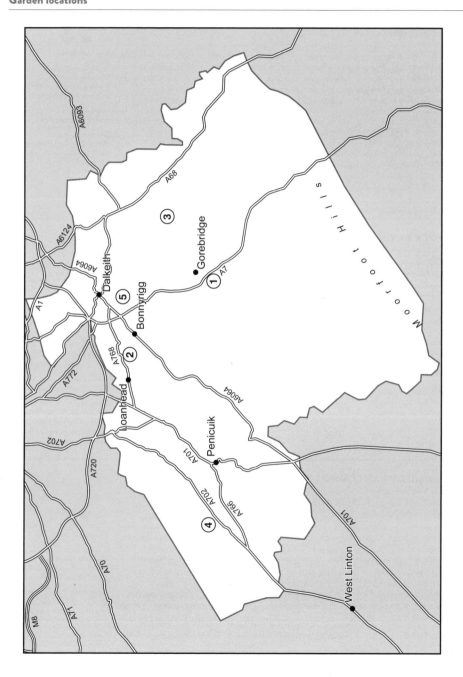

HARVIESTON WALLED GARDEN
Harvieston Cottage, Gorebridge, Midlothian EH23 4QA
Mr and Mrs Bill Crook
E: lornacrook@live.co.uk

Beautiful walled garden, originally early 19th century, part of the Harvieston Estate. It has been carefully redeveloped over the past 15 years by the current owners, who have created a wonderful contemporary garden, full of interesting and unusual trees and shrubs. There are informal borders and island beds of perennial planting and a pond with water lilies, iris and other damp loving plants. Lots to interest the keen gardener.

Directions: Take A7 south from Edinburgh to crossroads/junction with B6372 Gorebridge to Temple road. The entrance to Harvieston House and Walled Garden is at crossroads. There is very limited parking available at the Walled Garden, reserved for disabled visitors only. Parking on B6372, Powdermill Brae and surrounding roads. Ten minute walk along driveway to walled garden follow directional signs.Take Lothian Buses 3, 29 and 33 to Gorebridge, Bus stop/terminus, right outside gates to Walled Garden, X95 bus stops just before Gorebridge/Temple junction.

Disabled Access:
Partial

Opening Times:
Sunday 18 August
2:00pm - 5:00pm

Admission:
£4.00 Children free

Charities:
Roma Chooses Life receives 40%, the net remaining to SG Beneficiaries.

KEVOCK GARDEN
16 Kevock Road, Lasswade EH18 1HT
David and Stella Rankin T: 0131 454 0660
E: info@kevockgarden.co.uk www.kevockgarden.co.uk

A wonderful compact hillside garden overlooking the North Esk Valley with rockeries and a pond with damp loving plants. Several mature specimen trees, azaleas, rhododendrons and unusual shrubs are infilled with a range of rare woodland plants. Kevock Garden which has featured in many magazine articles and at the 2011 Chelsea Flower Show is open in March for Snowdrops and in the Summer for interesting perennials and shrubs.

Other Details: Soup and rolls in March, teas in June.

Directions: Kevock Road lies to the south of A678 Loanhead/Lasswade Road.

Disabled Access:
None

Opening Times:
Sunday 3 March
12:00pm - 3:00pm for the Snowdrop Festival
Saturday & Sunday 15/16 June 2:00pm - 5:00pm

Admission:
£3.00 Children free

Charities:
The Building for the Future of Nepal. receives 40%, the net remaining to SG Beneficiaries.

SG & MIDLOTHIAN COUNCIL PLANT SALE
Vogrie Walled Garden, Vogrie Country Park, Gorebridge EH23 4NU
Midlothian Council T: 01875 821986
E: ld9kevock@aol.com

Stock up your gardens with a wide variety of interesting plants from the Midlothian Council and SG Plant Sale, held within Vogrie Walled Garden in the beautiful grounds of Vogrie Country Park. A range of plants will include bedding, baskets, herbaceous, and shrubs from local gardens and Vogrie Nursery as well as unusual plants from a specialist grower. For beginners and connoisseurs alike. Fun for the family with woodland walks, adventure playground, picnic area, 9 hole golf course, pony rides, scavenger hunt with Countryside Ranger and miniature railway running 12:00-2:00pm.

Other Details: Garden accessories, composting demonstrations. Tea/coffee will be available in the walled garden.

Directions: From Edinburgh travel south along A68 through Dalkeith towards Jedburgh. Just before Pathhead, turn right onto B6372 signposted Vogrie Country Park continue for approx 2 km, main park entrance gates on left.

Disabled Access:
Full

Opening Times:
Plant sale Saturday 25 May
10:00am - 4:00pm

Admission:
Free entry, but £1.00 charge to park in the car park at Vogrie Country Park

Charities:
Maggie's Cancer Care Centres Scotland receives 20%, Cancer Research UK receives 20%, the net remaining to SG Beneficiaries.

SILVERBURN VILLAGE
Silverburn Village EH26 9LJ
The Gardeners of Silverburn

Nestling in the foothills of the Pentlands, Silverburn has a selection of village gardens of varying size and planting style growing at 800ft. Wonderful views and many ideas for growing plants in exposed locations. Come and have tea in Silverburn's Village Hall and enjoy the Beechgrove 2008 Community Garden.

Directions: A702, Edinburgh/Biggar Road, 13 miles south of Edinburgh and 1 mile before Ninemileburn.

Disabled Access:
Partial

Opening Times:
Sunday 4 August
12:30pm - 5:00pm

Admission:
£4.00

Charities:
Silverburn Community Ltd. receives 40%, the net remaining to SG Beneficiaries.

THE OLD SUN INN
Newbattle, Dalkeith EH22 3LH
Mr and Mrs James Lochhead T: 0131 663 2648
E: randjlochhead@uwclub.net

An interesting small, half acre garden of island and raised beds, containing a collection of species lilies, rock plants and some unusual bulbs. There are also two small interconnecting ponds and a conservatory.

Other Details: Teas possible.

Directions: B703 (Newtongrange) from Eskbank Toll. Garden is immediately opposite Newbattle Abbey College entrance. First bus 95 & 95X to Eskbank Toll only. Parking at Newbattle Abbey College.

Disabled Access:
Partial

Opening Times:
By arrangement 1 June to 31 July

Admission:
£3.00, children free

Charities:
All proceeds to SG Beneficiaries

MORAY & NAIRN

District Organiser

To be advised

Area Organisers

Mrs Lorraine Dingwall	Bents Green, 10 Pilmuir Road West, Forres IV36 2HL
Mrs Annie Stewart	33 Albert Street, Nairn IV12 4HF

Treasurer

Mr Michael Barnett	Drumdelnies, Nairn IV12 5NT

Gardens open on a specific date

Brodie Castle, Forres	Saturday 13 April	10:30am - 4:30pm
Brodie Castle, Forres	Sunday 14 April	10:30am - 4:30pm
Cuddy's Well, Clephanton	Saturday 29 June	12:30pm - 8:30pm
Cuddy's Well, Clephanton	Sunday 30 June	12:30pm - 8:30pm
Bents Green, Forres	Sunday 14 July	2:00pm - 8:00pm
Castleview, Auchindoun	Sunday 4 August	2:00pm - 5:00pm

Gardens open regularly

Boath House, Auldearn	1 June - 30 September	2:00pm - 4:00pm

Gardens open by arrangement

Bents Green, Forres	1 July - 1 September	01309 674634

Key to symbols

	New in 2013		Homemade teas		Accommodation
	Teas		Dogs on a lead allowed		Plant stall
	Cream teas		Wheelchair access		Scottish Snowdrop Festival

Garden locations

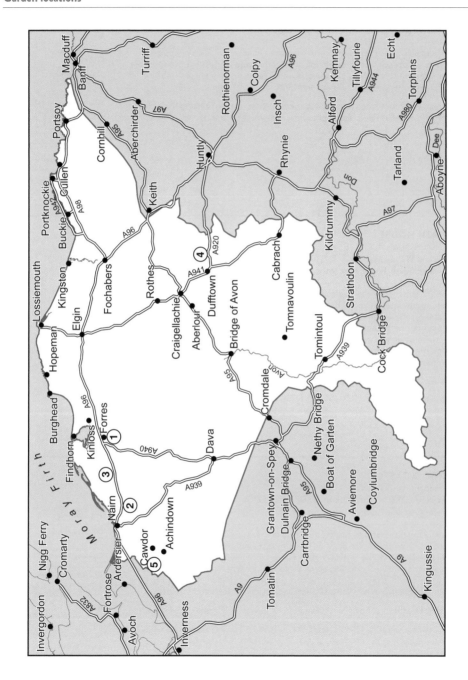

BENTS GREEN
10 Pilmuir Road West, Forres IV36 2HL
Mrs Lorraine Dingwall T: 01309 674634
E: fixandig@aol.com www.simplesite.com/hosta

Plantsman's small town garden with over three hundred cultivars of hostas, an extensive collection of hardy geraniums together with many other unusual plants. Managed entirely without the use of artificial fertilizers or chemicals, the owner encourages hedgehogs, toads and wild birds to control slugs.

Directions: From Tesco roundabout at Forres continue along Nairn Road. Take first left onto Ramflat Road, then right at the bottom, then first left onto Pilmuir Road West.

Disabled Access:
None

Opening Times:
Sunday 14 July
2:00pm - 8:00pm
Also by arrangement 1 July to
1 September

Admission:
£3.00

Charities:
Macmillan Nurses receives
40%, the net remaining to
SG Beneficiaries.

BOATH HOUSE
Auldearn, Nairn IV12 5TE
Don and Wendy Matheson T: 01667 454896
E: info@boath-house.com www.boath-house.com

The 20 acres of lawns, woodland and streams are home to swans, wild geese, ducks and various types of Scottish native birdlife. Bee hives and pet bantam hens can be seen in the walled garden along with an orchard, vegetable potager, greenhouse and various herbaceous borders. The two acre ornamental lake is stocked with brown and rainbow trout. A bog garden has been designed which has produced large amounts of pond life including newts, frogs, toads and dragonflies. A large wildflower meadow with mown pathways flanks the western boundary of the estate.

Other Details: Open for lunch, afternoon teas and dinner, pre-booking essential.

Directions: Located 1½ miles east of Nairn on the A96. Situated to the north of the A96 a short distance from a junction signposted for 'Boath'.

Disabled Access:
Partial

Opening Times:
1 June to 30 September
2:00pm - 4:00pm
Please note garden is
occasionally closed for
functions

Admission:
£4.00

Charities:
The Highland Hospice
receives 40%, the
net remaining to SG
Beneficiaries.

BRODIE CASTLE
Brodie, Forres IV36 2TE
The National Trust for Scotland T: 0844 4932156
E: sferguson@nts.org.uk www.nts.org.uk

Brodie Castle's Daffodil Tea Event: The garden team will lead guided walks in support of Scotland's Gardens. In springtime the grounds are carpeted with the daffodils for which the castle is rightly famous. Bred by Ian Brodie, these daffodils are internationally significant. Some are found nowhere else in the world but the castle grounds! There is also a shrubbery garden with rhododendrons and a good tree collection, plus wildflowers. Contact property for further information.

Other Details: National Plant Collection ®: Narcissus (Brodie cultivars).

Directions: Off A96 4½ miles west of Forres and 24 miles east of Inverness.

Disabled Access:
Full

Opening Times:
Saturday 13 April
10:30am - 4:30pm
Sunday 14 April
10:30am - 4:30pm

Admission:
Garden tour £3.00 (including
NTS Members)
N.B. Prices correct at time of
going to print

Charities:
Donation to SG Beneficiaries.

CASTLEVIEW
Auchindoun, Dufftown AB55 4DY
Mr and Mrs Ian Sharp T: 01340 820941
E: castleview10@hotmail.com

B&B

A small secluded riverside garden, created on three levels from scrub land by two enthusiastic beginners in 2005. The garden consists of two interconnected ponds, one formal, one natural and an abundance of herbaceous plants and shrubs. There are several sitting areas where you can admire the garden from many view points.

Directions: From Dufftown on the A920, travel approximately three miles towards Huntly. Drive until a small cluster of houses is reached, garden on the left approximately 20 yards off the main road.

Disabled Access:
None

Opening Times:
Sunday 4 August
2:00pm - 5:00pm

Admission:
£3.00

Charities:
Cat Protection League receives 40%, the net remaining to SG Beneficiaries.

CUDDY'S WELL
Clephanton, Inverness IV2 7QS
Jim and Jacque Smith T: 01667 493639
E: jimjacq1@btinternet.com

A relatively young family-friendly garden (started in 2005) designed to blend in with the surrounding rural woodland setting and to provide colour and interest throughout the year. There are colourful mixed herbaceous borders enclosing lawns, with ponds, rockeries and a herb garden to provide interest. A raised terrace contains productive rotational vegetable plots, a fruit garden and a well-stocked polytunnel.

Other Details: Families and children welcome.

Directions: From the A96 Inverness-Nairn road take the B9090 road south towards Cawdor. Clephanton is 1 mile up the hill. Cuddy's Well is the last house on the left going towards Cawdor.

Disabled Access:
Partial

Opening Times:
Saturday 29 June
12:30pm - 8:30pm
Sunday 30 June
12:30pm - 8:30pm

Admission:
£3.00, children free

Charities:
Save the Children receives 20%, Raigmore Renal Unit receives 20%, the net remaining to SG Beneficiaries.

Bents Green

PEEBLESSHIRE

Scotland's Gardens 2013 Guidebook is sponsored by INVESTEC WEALTH & INVESTMENT

District Organiser

Mrs Mary Carrel	14 Leeburn View, Cardrona, Peebles EH45 9LS

Area Organisers

Mr J Bracken	Gowan Lea, Croft Road, West Linton EH46 7DZ
Mr Graham Buchanan-Dunlop	The Potting Shed, Broughton Place, Broughton ML12 6HJ
Ms R Hume	Llolans, Broughton ML12 6HJ
Mrs R Parrott	An Sparr, Medwyn Road, West Linton EH46 7HA
Mr K St C Cunningham	Hallmanor, Peebles, Tweeddale EH45 9JN
Mr Brian Taylor	5 Fawnburn Crescent, Cardrona EH45 9LG

Treasurer

Mr J Birchall	The Old Manse, Drumelzier, Biggar ML12 6JD

Gardens open on a specific date

Traquair House, Innerleithen	Saturday 23 February	11:00am	-	3:00pm
Traquair House, Innerleithen	Sunday 24 February	11:00am	-	3:00pm
Kailzie Gardens, Peebles	Sunday 3 March	2:00pm	-	4:00pm
8 Halmyre Mains, West Linton	Sunday 21 July	2:00pm	-	5:00pm
Portmore, Eddleston	Sunday 28 July	1:30pm	-	5:00pm
West Linton Village Gardens	Sunday 11 August	2:00pm	-	5:00pm
Dawyck Botanic Garden, Stobo	Sunday 6 October	10:00am	-	5:00pm

Gardens open regularly

Dawyck Botanic Garden, Stobo	1 February - 30 November	10:00am	-	6:00pm
Kailzie Gardens, Peebles	1 January - 24 March	Dawn	-	Dusk
	25 March - 31 October	11:00am	-	5:00pm
	1 November - 31 December	Dawn	-	Dusk
Traquair House, Innerleithen	29 March - 30 November	11:00am	-	5:00pm
	Open weekends only in Nov.			

Gardens open by arrangement

Portmore, Eddleston	On request	01721 730383

PEEBLESSHIRE

Dawyck Botanic Garden

Key to symbols

	New in 2013		Homemade teas		Accommodation
	Teas		Dogs on a lead allowed		Plant stall
	Cream teas		Wheelchair access		Scottish Snowdrop Festival

Garden locations

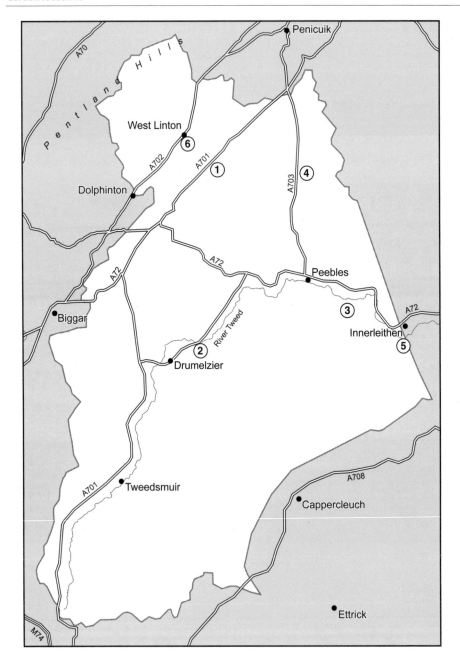

8 HALMYRE MAINS
West Linton, Borders   EH46 7BX
Joyce Andrews and Mike Madden   T: 07774 609 547
E: romanno@btinternet.com

Half-acre organic garden, formal beds, large pond, vegetable plot, greenhouse, keder house, gazebo and polytunnel, 25ft pergola to large composting area. Further developments since last year.

Other Details: Teas will be provided in The Hub at Lamancha.

Directions: Five miles South of Leadburn Junction on the A701 (Moffat). Signposted Newlands Hall .

Disabled Access:
Full

Opening Times:
Sunday 21 July
2:00pm - 5:00pm

Admission:
£4.00, children free

Charities:
Whitmuir Project receives 40%, the net remaining to SG Beneficiaries.

DAWYCK BOTANIC GARDEN
Stobo   EH45 9JU
Royal Botanic Gardens Edinburgh   T: 01721 760254
www.rbge.org.uk/dawyck

Stunning collection of rare trees and shrubs. With over 300 years of tree planting Dawyck is a world famous arboretum with mature specimens of Chinese conifers, Japanese maples, Brewer's spruce, the unique Dawyck beech and Sequoiadendrons from North America which are over 45 metres tall. Bold herbaceous plantings run along the burn. Range of trails and walks. Fabulous autumn colours.

Other Details: National Plant Collection ®: Larix and Tsuga.
Opening for the Snowdrop Festival 2 February to 17 March.
Autumn Magic Guided Walks at 11.30am and 2:00pm - £3.50 (Please book with Dawyck Botanics).

Directions: Eight miles south west of Peebles on B712.

Disabled Access:
Partial

Opening Times:
Sunday 6 October
10:00am - 5:00pm
for Scotland's Gardens.
1 February to 30 November
Apr - Sep 10:00am - 6:00pm
Feb & Nov 10:00am - 4:00pm
Mar & Oct 10:00am - 5:00pm

Admission:
£5.50, concessions £4.50, family £11.00, guided walks £3.50.

Charities:
Donation to SG Beneficiaries

West Linton Village Gardens

KAILZIE GARDENS
Peebles EH45 9HT
Lady Buchan-Hepburn T: 01721 720007
E: angela.buchanhepburn@btinternet.com www.infokailziegardens.com

Semi-formal walled garden with shrubs and herbaceous borders, rose garden, well stocked Victorian greenhouses, chicken village, including rare poultry breeds. Woodland and burnside walks amongst spring bulbs, rhododendrons and azaleas. The garden is set among fine old trees including an old larch planted in 1724. Osprey watch with live C.C.T.V. recordings of Ospreys nesting in the recently extended nature centre. Kailzie has been featured on Landward and the Beechgrove Garden.

Other Details: Champion Trees: 1725 European Larch.
Teas and lunches available.

Directions: On B7062 2½ miles east of Peebles.

Disabled Access:
Partial

Opening Times:
Sunday 3 March
2:00pm - 4:00pm
for Scotland's Gardens
1 January to 24 March
Dawn - Dusk
For wild garden and woodland walks and the Snowdrop Festival (2 Feb. to 17 March)
25 March to 31 October
11:00am - 5:00pm
For walled, wild gardens and woodland walks
1 November to 31 December
Dawn - Dusk
For wild garden and woodland walks

Admission:
1 January - 24 March (including SG opening) & 1 November - 31 December:
Adults £2.50, children 5-12 £1.00
25 March - 1 June:
Adults £3.50, concessions £3.00, children 5-12 £1.00 (under 5 free)
2 June - 31 October:
Adults £4.00, concessions £3.50, children £1.00 (under 5 free)
Apply for group rates

Charities:
Erskine Hospital receives 40%, the net remaining to SG Beneficiaries.

PORTMORE
Eddleston EH45 8QU
Mr and Mrs David Reid T: 01721 730383

Lovingly created by current owners over the past 20 years the gardens surrounding the David Bryce mansion house contain mature trees and offer fine views of the surrounding countryside. Large walled garden with box-edged herbaceous borders planted in stunning colour harmonies, potager, rose garden, pleached lime walk and ornamental fruit cages. The Victorian glasshouses contain fruit trees, roses, geraniums, pelargoniums and a wide variety of tender plants. Italianate grotto. Water garden with shrubs and meconopsis and woodland walks lined with rhododendrons, azaleas and shrub roses. Starred in "Good Gardens Guide".

Other Details: Homemade cream teas and plant stall on the 28 July opening.

Directions: Off A703 one mile north of Eddleston. Bus no.62.

Disabled Access:
Partial

Opening Times:
Sunday 28 July
1:30pm - 5:00pm
Also by arrangement on request

Admission:
£5.00

Charities:
The Margaret Kerr Unit receives 40%, the net remaining to SG Beneficiaries.

TRAQUAIR
Traquair House, Innerleithen, Peeblesshire EH44 6PW
Traquair Charitable Trust T: 01896 830323
E: catherine@traquair.co.uk www.traquair.co.uk

The woodlands and grounds of Traquair House have a spectacular showing of snowdrops. Traquair is Scotland's oldest inhabited house and the grounds and gardens are an eighteenth century designed landscape.

Directions: Traquair House is on the B708 1½ miles from Innerleithen and is well signposted.

Disabled Access:
Partial

Opening Times:
Saturday & Sunday 23/24 February 11:00am - 3:00pm
29 March to 30 November
Mar - Sep 11:00am - 5:00pm
Oct 11:00 am - 4:00pm Nov 11:00 am - 3:00pm.
Nov. open at weekends only

Admission:
£4.00, concessions £3.00

Charities:
Traquair Charitable Trust receives 40%, the net remaining to SG Beneficiaries.

WEST LINTON VILLAGE GARDENS
West Linton EH46 7EL
West Linton Village Gardeners

At least five gardens (two of which recently featured on the Beechgrove Garden) situated in the heart of the village and within close proximity to each other. All large/medium gardens with completely contrasting styles and some very interesting features, including large herbaceous borders, specimen trees and shrubs, garden ornaments and an eco-friendly garden using novel techniques.

Directions: A701 or A702 and follow signs.

Disabled Access:
Partial

Opening Times:
Sunday 11 August
2:00pm - 5:00pm

Admission:
£4.00

Charities:
The Ben Walton Trust receives 20%, Margaret Kerr Unit, Borders General Hospital receives 20%, the net remaining to SG Beneficiaries.

Portmore © Ray Cox

PERTH & KINROSS

District Organisers

Mrs Miranda Landale	Clathic House, By Crieff PH7 4JY
Mrs Judy Nichol	Rossie House, Forgandenny PH2 9EH

Area Organisers

Mrs Sonia Dunphie	Wester Cloquhat, Bridge of Cally, Perthshire PH10 7JP
Mrs Margaret Gimblett	Croftcat Lodge, Grandtully PH15 2QS
Miss Henrietta Harland	Easter Carmichael Cottage, Forgandenny Road, Bridge of Earn PH2 9EZ
Lady Lavinia Macdonald Lockhart	Thornton Hill, Fossoway, Kinross KY13 7PB
Mrs Elizabeth Montgomery	Burleigh House, Milnathort, Kinross KY13 7PB
Miss Judy Norwell	Dura Den, 20 Pitcullen Terrace, Perth PH2 7EG
Miss Bumble Ogilvy Wedderburn	Garden Cottage, Lude, Blair Atholl PH18 5TR

Treasurers

Mr Michael Tinson	Parkhead House, Parkhead Gardens, Burghmuir Road, PerthPH1 1JF

Gardens open on a specific date

Kilgraston, Bridge of Earn	Sunday 24 February	2:00pm	- 4:30pm
Megginch Castle, Errol	Sunday 14 April	2:00pm	- 5:00pm
Branklyn, Perth	Sunday 5 May	10:00am	- 4:00pm
Glendoick, by Perth	Sunday 5 May	2:00pm	- 5:00pm
Bonhard Garden, Perth	Sunday 12 May	10:00am	- 4:00pm
Glendoick, by Perth	Sunday 12 May	2:00pm	- 5:00pm
Rossie House, Forgandenny	Saturday 18 May	11:00am	- 5:00pm
Croftcat Lodge, Grandtully	Sunday 26 May	10:30am	- 4:00pm
Fingask Castle, Rait	Sunday 26 May	2:00pm	- 5:00pm
Explorers Garden, Pitlochry	Sunday 9 June	10:00am	- 5:00pm
Bradystone House, Murthly	Thursday 13 June	2:00pm	- 5:00pm
Bradystone House, Murthly	Thursday 20 June	2:00pm	- 5:00pm
Bradystone House, Murthly	Thursday 27 June	2:00pm	- 5:00pm
The Bield at Blackruthven, Tibbermore	Saturday 29 June	2:00pm	- 5:00pm
Bradystone House, Murthly	Thursday 4 July	2:00pm	- 5:00pm
Bradystone House, Murthly	Thursday 11 July	2:00pm	- 5:00pm

PERTH & KINROSS

Scotland's Gardens 2013 Guidebook is sponsored by **INVESTEC WEALTH & INVESTMENT**

Auchleeks House, Calvine	Sunday 21 July	2:00pm - 5:30pm
Boreland, Killin	Sunday 21 July	2:00pm - 5:30pm
Croftcat Lodge, Grandtully	Sunday 28 July	10:30am - 4:00pm
Drummond Castle Gardens, Crieff	Sunday 4 August	1:00pm - 5:00pm
Mount Tabor House, Perth	Sunday 4 August	12:00pm - 4:30pm

Gardens open regularly

Ardvorlich, Lochearnhead	1 May - 31 May	9:00am - Dusk
Blair Castle Gardens, Blair Atholl	12 January - 24 March	10:00am - 4:00pm
Blair Castle Gardens, Blair Atholl	25 March - 25 October	9:30am - 5:30pm
Bolfracks, Aberfeldy	1 April - 31 October	10:00am - 6:00pm
Braco Castle, Braco	1 March - 31 October	10:00am - 5:00pm
Cluny House, Aberfeldy	1 January - 31 December	10:00am - 4:00pm
Dowhill, Cleish	2 May - 27 June, Tues & Thurs	10:00am - 4:00pm
Drummond Castle Gardens, Crieff	1 May - 31 October	1:00pm - 6:00pm
Easter Meikle Fardle, Meikleour	12 April - 31 August, Fris	12:00pm - 5:30pm
Fingask Castle, Rait	10 February - 10 March, Suns	12:00pm - 5:00pm
Glenbeich, Lochearnhead	22 July - 4 August	11:00am - 5:00pm
Glendoick, by Perth	1 April - 31 May	10:00am - 4:00pm

Gardens open by arrangement

Bradystone House, Murthly	On request	01738 710308
Croftcat Lodge, Grandtully	On request	01887 840288
Easter Meikle Fardle, Meikleour	On request	01738 710330
Glendoick, by Perth	On request	01738 860205
Parkhead House, Perth	1 June - 31 August	01738 625983

Plant sales

Rossie House, Forgandenny	Saturday 18 May	11:00am - 5:00pm

Key to symbols

	New in 2013	Homemade teas		Accommodation	
 Teas		Dogs on a lead allowed		Plant stall	
Cream teas		Wheelchair access		Scottish Snowdrop Festival	

Garden locations

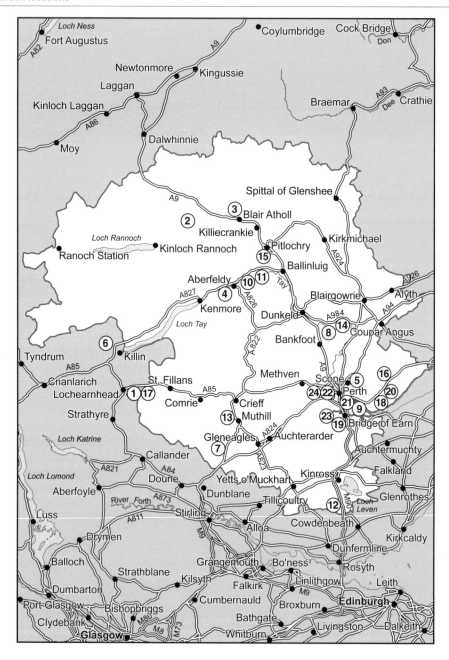

ARDVORLICH
Lochearnhead FK19 8QE
Mr and Mrs Sandy Stewart

Beautiful hill garden featuring over 300 different species and hybrid rhododendrons, grown in a glorious setting of oaks and birches on either side of the Ardvorlich Burn. Quite steep in places. Boots advisable.

Directions: On South Loch Earn Road 3 miles from Lochearnhead, 5 miles from St Fillans.

Disabled Access:
None

Opening Times:
1 May to 31 May
9:00am - Dusk

Admission:
£4.00

Charities:
The Gurkha Welfare Trust receives 40%, the net remaining to SG Beneficiaries.

AUCHLEEKS HOUSE
Calvine PH18 5UF
Mr and Mrs Angus MacDonald

Auchleeks is a classical Georgian house with a large herbaceous walled garden in a beautiful glen setting surrounded by hills and mature trees.

Directions: North of Blair Atholl turn off A9 at Calvine. B847 towards Kinloch Rannoch, 5 miles on right.

Disabled Access:
None

Opening Times:
Sunday 21 July
2:00pm - 5:30pm

Admission:
£4.00

Charities:
Sandpiper Trust receives 40%, the net remaining to SG Beneficiaries.

Boreland

BLAIR CASTLE GARDENS
Blair Atholl PH18 5TL
Blair Charitable Trust T: 01796 481207
E: office@blair-castle.co.uk www.blair-castle.co.uk

Blair Castle stands as the focal point in a designed landscape of some 2,500 acres within a large and traditional estate. Hercules Garden is a walled enclosure of about 9 acres recently restored to its original 18th century form with landscaped ponds, a Chinese bridge, plantings, vegetables and an orchard of more than one hundred fruit trees. The glory of this garden in summer are the herbaceous borders which run along the 275m south facing wall. A delightful sculpture trail incorporates contemporary and 18th century sculpture as well as 8 new works, letter-carving on stone from the Memorial Arts Charity's Art and Memory Collection. Diana's Grove is a magnificent stand of tall trees including Grand Fir, Douglas Fir, Larch and Wellingtonia in just two acres. In February, enjoy the seasonal delight of snowdrops in a walk around the grounds. A gentle meandering route passes through the Hercules Garden and weaves along to St Brides Kirk. The walk also includes access to two new paths (only open to the public at snowdrop time).

Disabled Access:
Partial

Opening Times:
12 January to 24 March
(Includes the Snowdrop Festival) weekends only
10:00am - 4:00pm
25 March to 25 October
9:30am - 5:30pm

Admission:
Adults, seniors, students
£5.25, children £2.40

Charities:
Donation to SG Beneficiaries

Other Details: An electric limited mobility scooter may be hired at a charge of £3.85 giving access to the garden, all proceeds are passed to Highland Perthshire Shop Mobility to help them extend the provision of such services.

Directions: Off A9, follow signs to Blair Castle, Blair Atholl.

BOLFRACKS
Aberfeldy PH15 2EX
The Douglas Hutchison Trust T: 01887 820344
E: athel@bolfracks.com www.bolfracks.com

Special 3 acre garden with wonderful views overlooking the Tay Valley. Burn garden with rhododendrons, azaleas, primulas, meconopsis in woodland garden setting. Walled garden with shrubs, herbaceous borders, rose rooms with old fashioned roses. Rose and clematis walk. Peony beds underplanted with tulips and Japanese anemone. Great selection of bulbs in spring and good autumn colour. Slippery paths in wet weather.

Disabled Access:
None

Opening Times:
1 April to 31 October
10:00am - 6:00pm

Admission:
£4.50, children under 16 free

Charities:
Donation to SG Beneficiaries

Other Details: Refreshments available for groups by prior arrangement.

Directions: 2 miles west of Aberfeldy on A827. White gates and Lodge on left. Brown tourist signs.

BONHARD GARDEN
Perth PH2 7PQ
Stephen and Charlotte Hay T: 01738552471

A traditional 19ᵗʰ century garden of 5 acres with mature trees, lawns, rhododendrons, azaleas, oak drive lined with primulas and daffodils. Kitchen garden, herbaceous borders, Pinetum, wooded area, ponds. Sensible footwear should be worn. Teas and coffee available at adjacent Bonhard nursery, leading to arboretum.

Other Details: Teas and coffee available at adjacent Bonhard nursery.

Directions: From Perth take A94 north to Scone. Turn right at sign to Murrayshall Hotel. Continue about 1 mile. House drive on right where road turns sharp left. From Balbeggie take A94. Turn left signed for Bonhard one mile north of Scone and in ½ mile turn right. House drive on left where road turns sharp right shortly after Bonhard Nursery.

Disabled Access:
Partial

Opening Times:
Sunday 12 May
10:00am - 4:00pm

Admission:
£3.50

Charities:
Freedom from Fistula Foundation receives 40%, the net remaining to SG Beneficiaries.

BORELAND
Killin FK21 8TT
Mrs Angus Stroyan

A varied garden with borders as the main feature. Very pretty walk along river leading to arboretum.

Other Details: Raffle

Directions: Off A827 through Killin, first turning left at Bridge of Lochay Hotel. House approx. 2 miles on left.

Disabled Access:
Full

Opening Times:
Sunday 21 July
2:00pm - 5:30pm

Admission:
£4.00

Charities:
Cancer Research UK, Killin Branch receives 40%, the net remaining to SG Beneficiaries.

BRACO CASTLE
Braco FK15 9LA
Mr & Mrs M van Ballegooijen T: 01786 880437

A 19ᵗʰ century landscaped garden comprising woodland and meadow walks with a fine show of spring flowering bulbs, many mature specimen trees and shrubs, with considerable new planting. The partly walled garden is approached on a rhododendron and tree-lined path and features an ornamental pond, extensive hedging and lawns with shrub and herbaceous borders. The planting is enhanced by spectacular views over the castle park to the Ochils. Good autumn colour.

Other Details: Catering facilities are not available.

Directions: 1 to 1½ mile drive from gates at north end of Braco Village, just west of bridge on A822.

Disabled Access:
Partial

Opening Times:
1 March to 31 October
10:00am - 5:00pm

Admission:
£3.50

Charities:
The Woodland Trust receives 40%, the net remaining to SG Beneficiaries.

BRADYSTONE HOUSE
Murthly PH1 4EW
Mrs James Lumsden T: 01738 710308

True cottage courtyard garden converted 16 years ago from derelict farm steadings beautifully planted to produce an ever changing picture. Unusual plants complimenting others in wonderful combinations. Ponds, free roaming ducks and hens and many interesting shrubs and ornamental trees.

Other Details: Food and refreshments available on request.

Directions: From south/north follow A9 to Bankfoot, then sign to Murthly. At crossroads in Murthly take private road to Bradystone.

Disabled Access:
Full

Opening Times:
Thursdays 13, 20 & 27 June and Thursdays 4 & 11 July
2:00pm - 5:00pm
Also by arrangement on request

Admission:
£4.00

Charities:
Canine Partners receives 40%, the net remaining to SG Beneficiaries.

BRANKLYN
116 Dundee Road, Perth PH2 7BB
The National Trust for Scotland T: 0844 493 2193
E: smcnamara@nts.org.uk www.nts.org.uk

This attractive garden in Perth was once described as "the finest two acres of private garden in the country". It contains an outstanding collection of plants particularly rhododendrons, alpine, herbaceous and peat-loving plants, which attract gardeners and botanists from all over the world.

Other Details: National Plant Collection ®: Cassiope, Lilium, Meconopsis (Himalayan poppy) and Rhododendron.   Weather permitting homemade scones will be served on the patio.

Directions: On A85 Perth/Dundee road.

Disabled Access:
Partial

Opening Times:
Sunday 5 May
10:00am - 4:00pm

Admission:
£6.00, family £16.00, concessions £5.00 (including NTS members). N.B. Prices correct at time of going to print

Charities:
Donation to SG Beneficiaries

CLUNY HOUSE
Aberfeldy PH15 2JT
Mr J and Mrs W Mattingley T: 01887 820795
E: wmattingley@btinternet.com www.clunyhousegardens.com

A wonderful, wild woodland garden overlooking the scenic Strathtay valley. Experience the grandeur of one of Britain's widest trees, the complex leaf variation of the Japanese maple, the beauty of the American trillium or the diversity of Asiatic primulas. A good display of snowdrops. Cluny's red squirrels are usually very easily seen. A treasure not to be missed.

Other Details: Plant seeds available for sale.

Directions: 3½ miles from Aberfeldy on Weem to Strathtay Road

Disabled Access:
Partial

Opening Times:
Daily 10:00am - 4:00pm but 16 March - 31 October open times are 10:00am - 6:00pm

Admission:
2 February - 15 March:
£4.00, children £1.00
16 March - 31 October:
£5.00 Children £1.00
Other Dates:
Free, but donations towards squirrel food are welcome

Charities:
Donation to SG Beneficiaries

CROFTCAT LODGE
Grandtully, Perthshire PH15 2QS
Margaret and Iain Gimblett T: 01887 840288
E: iain@gimblettsmill.plus.com

An odd shaped 1 acre set on a windy, stoney hill side with spectacular views. There is a small walled garden with climbing plants, herbaceous beds and at its centre a mirror pool. Surrounding the house are lawns, an autumn/spring garden, small alpine and rock gardens, rose terraces, heathers, azaleas, clipped beehive laurels, a growing clematis collection and a Japanese water garden with "tea house'". The garden has mainly gravel and grass paths. There are garden seats wherever you might like to rest or just sit and look. This is a garden for all seasons, created and cared for by its owners. It is welcoming, inspiring and well worth seeing especially if you would like to arrange a visit outwith the opening dates. Beautiful bluebell walk just a short walk from the garden

Other Details: Wheelchair access is possible to most of the garden with help. There is an outside toilet.
May opening: hot homemade soup, buttered rolls, tea/coffee will be available. Bring your own picnic or sausages to BBQ. Take a walk through the woods and enjoy the wonderful displays of bluebells.
July opening: teas, homebaking, strawberries and cream available. Plant stall.

Directions: From A9 take A827 signed Aberfeldy. Through Grandtully village and 1 mile from traffic lights on bridge turn left by cream house set back from road. Croftcat is on left 300 yards up lane.

Disabled Access:
Partial

Opening Times:
Sunday 26 May
10:30am - 4:00pm
Sunday 28 July
10:30am - 4:00pm
Also by arrangement

Admission:
May: £3.00
July: £4.00

Charities:
MND Scotland (Motor Neurone Disease) receives 40%, the net remaining to SG Beneficiaries.

DOWHILL
Cleish KY4 0HZ
Mr and Mrs Colin Maitland Dougall

A garden set off by the background of Benarty Hill and magnificent old trees. Lovely woodland walks to the ruins of Dowhill Castle. Nine linked ponds. Blue poppies and primulas together with temptingly placed seats make the garden a wonderful place for a picnic in fine weather.

Directions: ¾ mile off M90, exit 5, towards Crook of Devon on the B9097 in the trees.

Disabled Access:
None

Opening Times:
2 May to 27 June
10:00am - 4:00pm
Tuesdays & Thursdays

Admission:
£4.00

Charities:
Motor Neurone Disease receives 40%, the net remaining to SG Beneficiaries.

DRUMMOND CASTLE GARDENS
Crieff PH7 4HZ
Grimsthorpe & Drummond Castle Trust Ltd
www.drummondcastlegardens.co.uk

The Gardens of Drummond Castle were originally laid out in 1630 by John Drummond, 2nd Earl of Perth. In 1830 the Parterre was changed to an Italian style. One of the most interesting features is the multi-faceted sundial designed by John Mylne, Master Mason to Charles I. The formal garden is said to be one of the finest in Europe and is the largest of its type in Scotland.

Other Details: Teas, stalls, raffle and entertainment on Sunday 4 August.

Directions: Entrance 2 miles south of Crieff on Muthill road (A822).

Disabled Access:
Partial

Opening Times:
Sunday 4 August 1:00pm -
5:00pm opening for SG.
1 May to 31 October
1:00pm - 6:00pm

Admission:
£4.00, OAPs £3.00,
children £2.00

Charities:
British Limbless Ex-
Servicemen's Association
receives 40% on 4 August,
the net remaining to SG
Beneficiaries.

EASTER MEIKLE FARDLE
Meikleour PH2 6EF
Rear Admiral and Mrs John Mackenzie T: 01738 710330

A delightful old-fashioned 2 acre garden. Herbaceous borders backed by soft sandstone walls or beech hedges. Small enclosed garden with raised beds. There is also a maturing water garden and walks through maturing woodland.

Other Details: Homemade lunches and light refreshments available on request. Groups preferred on Monday to Friday; not weekends. Large groups welcome.

Directions: Take A984 Dunkeld to Coupar Angus 1½ miles, from Spittalfield towards Meikleour, third house on left after turning to Lethendy.

Disabled Access:
Partial

Opening Times:
12 April to 31 August
12:00pm - 5:30pm
Fridays only.
Also by arrangement

Admission:
£4.00

Charities:
Seafarers UK receives 40%,
the net remaining to SG
Beneficiaries.

EXPLORERS GARDEN
Pitlochry PH16 5DR
Pitlochry Festival Theatre
www.explorersgarden.com

This six acre woodland garden, now seven years old, is maturing nicely. More and more visitors are coming to see the wonders this four star VisitScotland attraction reveals art and architecture, wildlife and birds, exotic plants, peat and rock gardens, extraordinary landscaping and magnificent views. Try the guided tours that reveal the stories of the Scottish Plant Hunters who risked their lives travelling the globe in search of new plants and trees. In this garden, which is divided into different parts of the world, you will see the plants they collected for cultivation, commerce and conservation.

Directions: A9 to Pitlochry town, follow signs to Pitlochry Festival Theatre.

Disabled Access:
Partial

Opening Times:
Sunday 9 June
10:00am - 5:00pm

Admission:
£4.00, guided tour (inluding
entry) £5.00.

Charities:
Acting for Others receives
40%, the net remaining to SG
Beneficiaries.

16 FINGASK CASTLE
Rait PH2 7SA
Mr and Mrs Andrew Murray Threipland T: 01821 670777
E: andrew@fingaskcastle.com   www.fingaskcastle.com

The magical grounds of Fingask Castle are testament to both the present owner and his ancestors' eccentricity and architectural scavenging. Explore the grounds and discover statues, gargoyles, gravestones, bamboo forest, large collection of topiary and much, much more.

Other Details: Homemade teas available 26 May.

Directions: Halfway between Perth and Dundee. From A90 follow signs to Rait until small crossroad, turn right and follow signs to Fingask.

Disabled Access:
Full

Opening Times:
10 Feb to 10 Mar 12:00pm - 5:00pm Suns only.Open for the Snowdrop Festival. Sunday 26 May 2:00pm - 5:00pm

Admission:
Feb/Mar: £3.00, children free
26 May: £4.00, children free

Charities:
All Saints Church, Glencarse and Fingask Follies receives 40%, the net remaining to SG Beneficiaries.

17 GLENBEICH
Lochearnhead FK19 8PZ
Mrs Tim Holcroft

Two acre garden in spectacular setting overlooking Loch Earn. Formal planting near the house, with interesting selection of trees and perennials, giving way to more naturalistic planting along a burnside walk.

Other Details: Boots advisable.

Directions: On A85, 1¾ miles east of Lochearnhead, 5 miles west of St Fillans.

Disabled Access:
Partial

Opening Times:
22 July to 4 August
11:00am - 5:00pm

Admission:
£4.00

Charities:
The Falls of Dochart Retirement Home, Killin receives 40%, the net remaining to SG Beneficiaries.

Parkhead House

GLENDOICK
by Perth PH2 7NS
Peter, Patricia, Kenneth and Jane Cox T: 01738 860 205
E: orders@glendoick.com www.glendoick.com

Glendoick was included in The Independent on Sunday's exclusive survey of Europe's top 50 Gardens, boasts a unique collection of plants collected by three generations of Coxes from their plant-hunting expeditions in China and the Himalaya. You can see one of the finest collections of rhododendrons and azaleas, *Primula, Meconopsis, Kalmia and Sorbus* in our woodland garden, peat garden and nursery. Many of the Rhododendron and azalea species and hybrids have been introduced from the wild or bred by the Cox family and the gardens boast a huge range of plants from as far afield as Chile, Tasmania and Tibet. Three new waterfall viewing platforms have been built in the woodland gardens. You can also take a glimpse into the fascinating world of hybridising in the walled garden where you'll find new as yet unnamed hybrids from the Glendoick breeding programme trial beds. Peter and Kenneth Cox have written numerous books on rhododendrons and gardens. Kenneth Cox's book *Scotland for Gardeners* describes 500 of Scotland's finest gardens.

Other Details: National Plant Collection ®: collections of Rhododendron.
For group bookings contact Jane Cox by post at the above address or E: jane@glendoick.com.
Refreshments for groups should be pre-booked.
The woodland garden is not easily accessible to wheelchairs but some of the gardens by the house are.
Disabled toilets at the garden centre only.

Directions: Follow brown signs to Glendoick Garden Centre off A90 Perth - Dundee road. Gardens are ½ mile behind Garden Centre. After buying tickets at the garden centre please drive up and park at gardens (free parking).

Disabled Access:
None

Opening Times:
Sundays 5 & 12 May
2:00pm - 5:00pm
Glendoick 60th anniversary celebrations with guided tour at 2:30pm with Peter or Kenneth Cox
1 April to 31 May
10:00am - 4:00pm except weekends which are open 2:00pm - 5:00pm.
Also by arrangement

Admission:
Sundays 5 & 1 2 May: £5.00
bookings: by
E: gardencentre@glendoick.com
or T: 01738 860260
Other Dates: £4.00
per person. Tickets
from garden centre.
School age children free
A 32-page guidebook is available at £2.95

Charities:
Donation to SG Beneficiaries

KILGRASTON
Bridge of Earn PH2 9BQ
Kilgraston School T: 01738 815517
E: marketing@kilgraston.com www.kilgraston.com

Set within the grounds of Kilgraston School, this is a wonderful opportunity to see the snowdrops whilst exploring the woodlands and surroundings of this unique garden. Kilgraston has been a girls boarding school since 1930. The house dates from the first decade of the 19th century and was the home of the Grant family. Impressive art sculptures (including work by Hew Lorimer) intermingle with ancient trees, snowdrops and even the resident red squirrels. Spend a Sunday afternoon wandering along wild woodland pathways and through the extensive grounds whilst taking in the surrounding winter landscape. There is also an opportunity to explore the chapel, main hall and artistic works within the school itself.

Other Details: Homemade teas available in the main hall.

Directions: Bridge of Earn is 3 miles South of Perth on the A912. Kilgraston School is signposted from the main road.

Disabled Access:
Partial

Opening Times:
Sunday 24 February
2:00pm - 4:30pm
Open for the Snowdrop Festival

Admission:
£4.00

Charities:
Save the Children receives 40%, the net remaining to SG Beneficiaries.

20 MEGGINCH CASTLE
Errol PH2 7SW
Mr Giles Herdman & The Hon. Mrs Drummond-Herdman of Megginch

15th century turreted castle (not open) with Gothic stable yard and pagoda dovecote. 19th century formal front garden, topiary and ancient yews. Splendid array of daffodils and rhododendrons. Double walled kitchen garden and orchard.

Directions: Approach from Dundee only, directly off A90, on south side of carriageway ½ mile on left after Errol flyover, between lodge gatehouses. 7 miles from Perth, 8 from Dundee.

Disabled Access:
Full

Opening Times:
Sunday 14 April
2:00pm - 5:00pm

Admission:
£4.00, children free

Charities:
All Saints Church, Glencarse receives 40%, the net remaining to SG Beneficiaries.

---

21 MOUNT TABOR HOUSE
Mount Tabor Road, Perth PH2 7DE
Mr and Mrs John McEwan

Mature terraced town garden originally laid out in the late 19th century but constantly evolving. A sheltered and peaceful garden surrounded by mature trees and hedges with well filled herbaceous borders. Cascade of ponds filled with carp and other wildlife. Lots of places to sit in the sun and relax.

Other Details: Homemade soups and rolls from 12:00pm until 2:00pm - teas and traybakes from 2:00pm until 4.30pm.

Directions: From Dundee Road in Perth at Isle of Skye Hotel, turn right into Manse Road, over mini-roundabout and into Mount Tabor Road.

Disabled Access:
Partial

Opening Times:
Sunday 4 August
12:00pm - 4:30pm

Admission:
£3.50

Charities:
The Katie McKerracher Trust receives 40%, the net remaining to SG Beneficiaries.

---

22 PARKHEAD HOUSE
Parkhead Gardens, Burghmuir Road, Perth PH1 1JF
Mr & Mrs M.S. Tinson T: 01738 625983
E: maddy.tinson@gmail.com

Parkhead is an old farmhouse sited within an acre of beautiful gardens. Mature trees include an outstanding 300 year old Spanish chestnut. This hidden gem is a garden for all seasons. Gentle terracing and meandering paths lead you past a large variety of unusual and interesting plants and shrubs. Holder of the National Collection of "Mylnefield Lilies" originally developed by Dr Christopher North at the Scottish Horticultural Research Institute, Dundee.

Other Details: National Plant Collection ®: Mylnefield Lilies in flower July/August. Homemade teas by request only. Plant stall when available.

Directions: Parkhead Gardens is a small lane off the west end of Burghmuir Road in Perth. More detailed directions on request.

Disabled Access:
Partial

Opening Times:
By arrangement
1 June to 31 August

Admission:
£3.50

Charities:
All proceeds to SG Beneficiaries

ROSSIE HOUSE
Forgandenny PH2 9EH
Mr & Mrs David B. Nichol T: 01738
E: judynichol@rossiehouse.co.uk

Rossie dates from 1657. Many of the trees in the garden and surrounding park date back to this time. The undulating terrain is full of magnificent trees, shrubs and many beautiful rhododendrons which are all set off by a carpet of bluebells, trillium and other woodland plants. Paths take you down by the stream, over bridges and eventually into the walled garden. Sculptures by Nigel Ross and David Annand grace the garden whilst Castlemilk sheep graze the paddocks.

Other Details: Mega plant sale, BBQ lunch, homemade teas, stalls and trade stands.

Directions: Forgandenny is on the B935 between Bridge of Earn and Dunning.

Disabled Access:
Partial

Opening Times:
Plant sale Saturday 18
May 11:00am - 5:00pm
garden also open.

Admission:
£4.00, OAPs £3.00, children free

Charities:
Camphill Village Trust receives 40%, the net remaining to SG Beneficiaries.

Rossie House Open Day

• MEGA PLANT SALE •
• GARDEN OPENING •
CARPET OF BLUEBELLS
AND OTHER WOODLAND PLANTS

Saturday 18 May 2013 : 11am to 5pm
Rossie House, Forgandenny
On the B935 between Bridge of Earn and Dunning.

Many Stalls • Children's Entertainment • Homemade Teas
• BBQ: Heather & Glen Venison • Pipe Band

For further details see www.scotlandsgardens.org.
Camphill Village Trust receives 40% of proceeds, the net remaining to SG Beneficiaries.

THE BIELD AT BLACKRUTHVEN
Blackruthven House, Tibbermore, Perth PH1 1PY
The Bield Christian Co. Ltd. T: 01738 583238
E: info@bieldatblackruthven.org.uk www.bieldatblackruthven.org.uk

The Bield is set in extensive grounds comprising well maintained lawns and clipped hedges, a flower meadow and a large collection of specimen trees. Visitors are encouraged to stroll around the grounds and explore the Labyrinth cut into the grass of the old orchard. The main garden is a traditional walled garden containing extensive herbaceous borders, manicured lawns and an organic vegetable plot. The walled garden also contains a wide variety of trained fruit trees, a fruit cage, glasshouse and a healing garden.

Other Details: Refreshments will be available.

Directions: From Dundee or Edinburgh, follow signs for Glasgow, Stirling Crianlarich which lead onto the Perth bypass. Head west on the A85 signed to Crieff/Crianlarich to West Huntingtower. Turn left at the crossroads to Madderty/Tibbermore. The entrance is on your left after ½ a mile and is marked by stone pillars and iron gates. Take a left up the tarmac road passing the gate lodge. Turn right to park at the Steading.

Disabled Access:
Full

Opening Times:
Saturday 29 June
2:00pm - 5:00pm

Admission:
£5.00 including refreshments

Charities:
Southton Smallholding receives 40%, the net remaining to SG Beneficiaries.

RENFREWSHIRE

Scotland's Gardens 2013 Guidebook is sponsored by **INVESTEC WEALTH & INVESTMENT**

District Organisers

Mrs Rosemary Leslie	High Mathernock Farm, Auchentiber Road, Kilmacolm PA13 4SP T: 01505874032
Mrs Alexandra MacMillan	Langside Farm, Kilmacolm PA13 4SA T: 01475 540423

Area Organisers

Mrs Helen Hunter	2 Bay Street, Fairlie KA29 0AL
Mrs B McLean	49 Middlepenny Road, Langbank PA14 6XE
Mr J A Wardrop OBE DL	St Kevins, Victoria Road, Paisley PA2 9PT

Treasurer

Mrs Jean Gillan	Bogriggs Cottage, Carlung, West Kilbride KA23 9PS

Gardens open on a specific date

Ardgowan, Inverkip	Sunday 17 February	2:00pm	-	5:00pm
Carruth, Bridge of Weir	Sunday 26 May	2:00pm	-	5:00pm
Sma' Shot Cottages , Paisley	Sunday 23 June	12:00pm	-	4:00pm
Duchal, Kilmacolm	Sunday 30 June	2:00pm	-	5:00pm

Plant sales

SG Plant Sale at Kilmacolm, Kilmacolm	Saturday 20 April	10:00am	-	12:00pm
SG Plant Sale at St Fillan's Episcopal Church, Kilmacolm	Saturday 14 September	10:00am	-	12:00pm

Key to symbols

	New in 2013		Homemade teas	**B&B**	Accommodation
	Teas	🐕	Dogs on a lead allowed		Plant stall
	Cream teas	♿	Wheelchair access		Scottish Snowdrop Festival

Garden locations

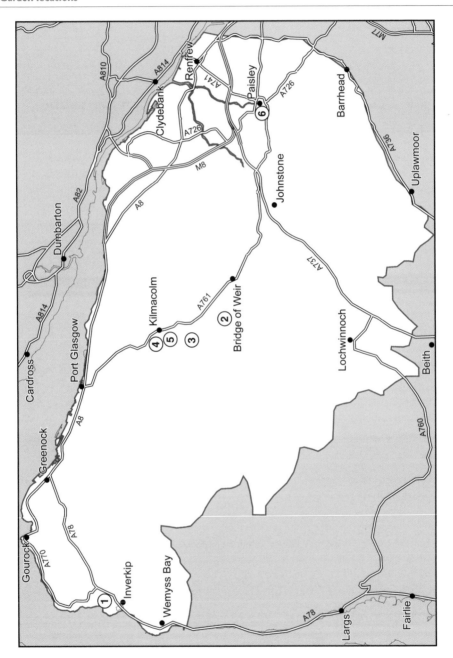

ARDGOWAN
Inverkip PA16 0DW
Lady Shaw Stewart T: 01475 521656/226
E: info@ardgowan.co.uk

Woodland walks carpeted with snowdrops. Strong waterproof footwear/boots advised as some paths may be wet/muddy depending on the weather.

Other Details: Snowdrop plant stall. Wheelchair access not advisable in wet weather.

Directions: Inverkip 1½ miles. Glasgow/Largs buses to and from Inverkip Village. Entrance at roundabout or via Marina.

Disabled Access:
Partial

Opening Times:
Sunday 17 February
2:00pm - 5:00pm for the
Snowdrop Festival

Admission:
£2.00

Charities:
Ardgowan Hospice receives
40%, the net remaining to
SG Beneficiaries.

CARRUTH
Bridge of Weir PA11 3SG
Mr and Mrs Charles Maclean

Over 20 acres of long established rhododendrons, woodland with good bluebells and lawn gardens in lovely landscaped setting. Young arboretum.

Directions: Access from B786 Kilmacolm/Lochwinnoch road or from Bridge of Weir via Torr Road.

Disabled Access:
Partial

Opening Times:
Sunday 26 May
2:00pm - 5:00pm

Admission:
£3.50, children under 16 free

Charities:
Marie Curie Cancer
Care receives 40%, the
net remaining to SG
Beneficiaries.

DUCHAL
Kilmacolm PA13 4RS
Lord Maclay

18th century walled garden particularly well planted and maintained, entered by footbridge over the Greenwater. Specie trees, hollies, old fashioned roses, shrubs and herbaceous borders with fruit orchards and vegetable garden. Lily pond.

Other Details: Large plant sale with wide selection of plants.

Directions: On B788 1 mile from Kilmacolm (this road links B786 Lochwinnoch Road and A761 Bridge of Weir Road) Greenock/Glasgow bus via Bridge of Weir. Knapps Loch stop is ¼ mile from garden.

Disabled Access:
Partial

Opening Times:
Sunday 30 June
2:00pm - 5:00pm

Admission:
£4.00, children under 16 free

Charities:
Ardgowan Hospice receives
40%, the net remaining to SG
Beneficiaries.

SG PLANT SALE AT KILMACOLM
Outside Kilmacolm Library, Lochwinnoch Road, Kilmacolm PA13 4EL
Scotland's Gardens

Spring plant sale in the centre of Kilmacolm.

Directions: To be held at the cross outside the Library and Cargill Centre.

Disabled Access:
Full

Opening Times:
Plant sale Saturday 20 April
10:00am - 12:00pm

Admission:
Free - donations welcome

Charities:
Kilmacolm Local Association
of Guiding receives 40%,
the net remaining to SG
Beneficiaries.

SG PLANT SALE AT ST FILLAN'S EPISCOPAL CHURCH
Moss Road, Kilmacolm PA13 4LX
SG Renfrewshire and St Fillan's Episcopal Church

A wide variety of interesting and good locally grown plants and shrubs.

Other Details: Small charge for coffee/teas.

Directions: Turn off A761 Port Glasgow-Bridge of Weir Road in centre of Kilmacolm into Moss Road.

Disabled Access:
Full

Opening Times:
Plant sale Saturday 14
September
10:00am - 12:00pm

Admission:
Free but donations welcome.

Charities:
St Fillans Episcopal
Church receives 40%,
the net remaining to SG
Beneficiaries.

SMA' SHOT COTTAGES
2 Sma' Shot Lane, Paisley PA1 2HG
Old Paisley Society T: 0141 889 1708
www.smashot.co.uk

Sma' Shot Cottages is a heritage museum comprising a weaver's cottage from the 1750's and a small row of three cottages from the early 19th century. They are linked by a small courtyard with a 19th century garden containing only plants from that era with the exception of the Dianthus "Paisley Gem" and the Viola "Sma' Shot Cottage".

Other Details: Guided tours available. Tearoom providing light lunches and home baking. Small gift shop.

Directions: Off New Street in Paisley town centre. Walking distance from Paisley Gilmour Street train station.

Disabled Access:
Full

Opening Times:
Sunday 23 June
12:00pm - 4:00pm

Admission:
£2.00

Charities:
Accord Hospice receives
40%, the net remaining to
SG Beneficiaries.

ROSS, CROMARTY, SKYE & INVERNESS

Scotland's Gardens 2013 Guidebook is sponsored by **INVESTEC WEALTH & INVESTMENT**

District Organiser

Lady Lister-Kaye	House of Aigas, Beauly IV4 7AD

Treasurer

Mrs Sheila Kerr	Lilac Cottage, Struy, By Beauly IV4 7JU

Gardens open on a specific date

Brackla Wood, Culbokie	Monday 15 April	2:00pm	-	4:00pm
Brackla Wood, Culbokie	Tuesday 16 April	2:00pm	-	4:00pm
Brackla Wood, Culbokie	Wednesday 17 April	2:00pm	-	4:00pm
Brackla Wood, Culbokie	Thursday 18 April	2:00pm	-	4:00pm
Dundonnell House, Little Loch Broom	Thursday 18 April	2:00pm	-	5:00pm
Brackla Wood, Culbokie	Friday 19 April	2:00pm	-	4:00pm
Inverewe, Poolewe	Wednesday 22 May	10:00am	-	4:00pm
Aultgowrie Mill, Aultgowrie	Sunday 26 May	1:00pm	-	5:00pm
House of Gruinard, Laide,	Wednesday 29 May	2:00pm	-	5:00pm
Dundonnell House, Little Loch Broom	Thursday 30 May	2:00pm	-	5:00pm
Novar, Evanton	Sunday 2 June	2:30pm	-	5:00pm
Brackla Wood, Culbokie	Wednesday 5 June	2:00pm	-	5:00pm
Inverewe, Poolewe	Wednesday 5 June	10:00am	-	4:00pm
Field House, Belladrum	Sunday 9 June	2:00pm	-	5:00pm
House of Aigas and Field Centre, by Beauly	Sunday 30 June	2:00pm	-	5:00pm
House of Gruinard, Laide	Wednesday 10 July	2:00pm	-	5:00pm
Hugh Miller's Birthplace Cottage & Museum, Cromarty	Saturday 13 July	12:00pm	-	5:00pm
House of Aigas and Field Centre, by Beauly	Sunday 28 July	2:00pm	-	5:00pm
Aultgowrie Mill, Aultgowrie	Sunday 4 August	1:00pm	-	5:00pm
Dundonnell House, Little Loch Broom	Thursday 15 August	2:00pm	-	5:00pm
Dundonnell House, Little Loch Broom	Thursday 19 September	2:00pm	-	5:00pm

Gardens open regularly

Abriachan Garden Nursery, Loch Ness Side	1 February - 30 November	9:00am	-	7:00pm
Applecross Walled Garden, Strathcarron	15 March - 31 October	11:00am	-	9:00pm
Attadale, Strathcarron	28 March - 31 October Except Sundays	10:00am	-	5:30pm
Balmeanach House, Struan	6 May - 30 October Mondays & Wednesdays	10:30am	-	3:30pm

ROSS, CROMARTY, SKYE & INVERNESS

Scotland's Gardens 2013 Guidebook is sponsored by INVESTEC WEALTH & INVESTMENT

Clan Donald Skye, Armadale	Daily	9:30am	-	5:30pm
Dunvegan Castle and Gardens	1 April - 15 October	10:00am	-	5:30pm
Leathad Ard, Upper Carloway	1 June - 31 August	1:45pm	-	6:00pm
	Except Fridays & Sundays			
	Also closed Wed 7 August			
Leckmelm Shrubbery & Arboretum, Ullapool	1 April - 31 October	10:00am	-	6:00pm
Oldtown of Leys Garden, Inverness	Daily	Dawn	-	Dusk
The Lookout, Kilmuir	2 April - 26 September	11:00pm	-	4:00pm

Gardens open by arrangement

Brackla Wood, Culbokie	20 April - 21 April	01349 877765
	& 8 - 14 September	01349 877765
Coiltie Garden, Divach	On request	01456 450219
Dundonnell House, Little Loch Broom	On request	07789 390028
Dunvegan Castle and Gardens	3 January - 31 March	01470 521206
	& 16 October - 31 December	01470 521206
House of Aigas and Field Centre, by Beauly	On request	01463 782443
Leathad Ard, Upper Carloway, Isle of Lewis	1 April - 30 September	01851 643204
The Lookout, Kilmuir, North Kessock	1 April - 31 October	01463 731489

Key to symbols

	New in 2013	Homemade teas			Accommodation
	Teas	 Dogs on a lead allowed			Plant stall
	Cream teas	Wheelchair access			Scottish Snowdrop Festival

Garden locations

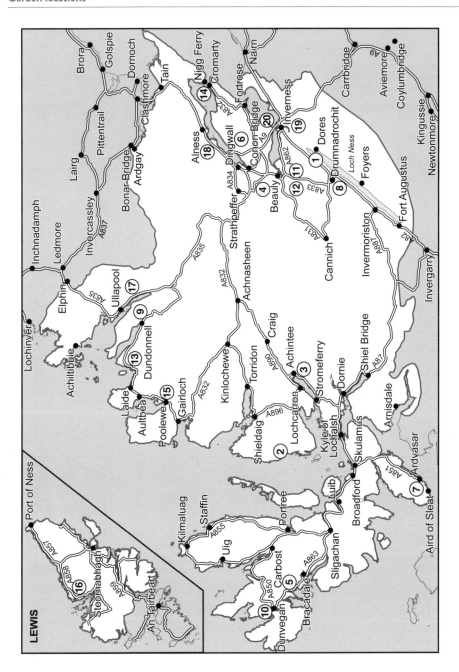

ABRIACHAN GARDEN NURSERY
Loch Ness Side IV3 8LA
Mr and Mrs Davidson T: 01463 861232
E: info@lochnessgarden.com www.lochnessgarden.com

An outstanding garden. Over 4 acres of exciting plantings with winding paths through native woodlands. Seasonal highlights - snowdrops, hellebores, primulas, meconopsis, hardy geraniums and colour-themed summer beds. Views over Loch Ness. New path to pond through the Bluebell Wood.

Other Details: Working retail nursery. Drinks machine in nursery.

Directions: On A82 Inverness/Drumnadrochit road, approximately 8 miles south of Inverness.

Disabled Access:
Partial

Opening Times:
1 February to 30 November
9:00am - 7:00pm
which includes opening for
the Snowdrop Festival 2
February - 17 March

Admission:
£3.00

Charities:
Highland Hospice receives
40%, the net remaining to
SG Beneficiaries.

APPLECROSS WALLED GARDEN
Strathcarron IV54 8ND
Applecross Organics T: 01520 744440

Walled garden of 1.25 acres in spectacular surroundings. Derelict for 50 years but lovingly restored since 2001. Lots of herbaceous borders, fruit trees and raised vegetable beds. We try to have an interesting plant table in this wonderful peaceful setting.

Award winning cafe/restaurant within the garden.

Other Details: Restaurant open from 11:00am till late, last orders 8:30pm.

Directions: Take the spectacular Bealach na Ba hill road after Kishorn. At the T-junction in Applecross, turn right for half a mile. Entrance to Applecross House is immediately in front of you.

Disabled Access:
Full

Opening Times:
15 March to 31 October
11:00am - 9:00pm

Admission:
Admission by donation

Charities:
Smile Train receives 40%,
the net remaining to SG
Beneficiaries.

ATTADALE
Strathcarron IV54 8YX
Mr and Mrs Ewen Macpherson T: 01520 722603
E: info@attadalegardens.com www.attadalegardens.com

The Gulf Stream and surrounding hills and rocky cliffs create a microclimate for 20 acres of outstanding water gardens, old rhododendrons, unusual trees and fern collection in a geodesic dome, there is also a sunken fern garden developed on site of early 19th century drain, new pool with dwarf rhododendrons, sunken garden, kitchen garden. Conservatory, Japanese garden, sculpture collection and giant sundial.

Other Details: Major collections of meconopsis and ferns. Some plants for sale.

Directions: On A890 between Strathcarron and South Strome. Car parking for disabled by the house.

Disabled Access:
Partial

Opening Times:
28 March to 31 October
10:00am - 5:30pm except
Sundays

Admission:
£6.00, senior citizens £4.00,
children £1.00, wheelchair
users free

Charities:
Howard Doris Centre
Lochcarron/Highland
Hospice receives 40%,
the net remaining to SG
Beneficiaries.

AULTGOWRIE MILL
Aultgowrie, Urray, Muir of Ord IV6 7XA
Mr and Mrs John Clegg T: 01997 433699
E: john@johnclegg.com

Aultgowrie Mill is an eighteenth century converted water mill set in gardens and woodland river walks of 13 acres. Features include a wooded island, a half-acre wildflower meadow and a wildlife pond, all with outstanding views of the surrounding hills. The gardens are being developed with much new landscaping and planting, including terraces, lawns, an orchard and raised vegetable beds.

Other Details: Homemade teas on the balcony or millpond lawn. Plant Stall. Plans of the river and island walks will also be supplied on arrival and there is ample field parking.

Directions: from the south, turn left at Muir of Ord Distillery, Aultgowrie Mill is 3.2 miles. From the North & West, after Marybank Primary School, Aultgowrie Mill is 1.7 miles up the hill.

Disabled Access:
Partial

Opening Times:
Sunday 26 May
1:00pm - 5:00pm
Sunday 4 August
1:00pm - 5:00pm

Admission:
£4.00

Charities:
R.N.L.I. receives 40%,
the net remaining to SG
Beneficiaries.

BALMEANACH HOUSE
Struan, Isle of Skye IV56 8FH
Mrs Arlene Macphie T: 01470 572320
E: info@skye-holiday.com www.skye-holiday.com

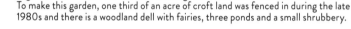

A garden with herbaceous border, bedding and a small azalea/rhododendron walk. To make this garden, one third of an acre of croft land was fenced in during the late 1980s and there is a woodland dell with fairies, three ponds and a small shrubbery.

Other Details: Plant stall at Plants n Stuff, Atholl Service Station. Teas at Waterside Cafe, Atholl Service Station.

Directions: A87 to Sligachan, turn left, Balmeanach is 5 miles north of Struan and 5 miles south of Dunvegan.

Disabled Access:
None

Opening Times:
6 May to 30 October
10:30am - 3:30pm
Mondays & Wednesdays

Admission:
£3.00

Charities:
SSPCA receives 40%,
the net remaining to SG
Beneficiaries.

BRACKLA WOOD
Culbokie, Dingwall IV7 8GY
Susan and Ian Dudgeon T: 01349 877765
E: smdbrackla@aol.com

Mature 1 acre plot consisting of woodland, wildlife features, ponds, mixed borders, a kitchen garden, a rockery and a mini-orchard. Spring bulbs and hellebores, rhododendron, wisteria and roses followed by crocosmia, clematis and deciduous trees provide continuous colour and interest throughout the season. Chance of seeing red squirrels. New beds for 2013.

Other Details: 5 June: Raffle

Directions: From the north: Take the A9 and turn off to Culbokie. At the far end of the village, turn right after the playing fields signposted "Munlochy". A mile up the road, turn right into "No Through Road" signposted "Upper Braefindon"
From the south: Take the A9 and turn off to Munlochy. At the far end of the village, turn right and then sharp left up road signposted "Culbokie" and "Killen". After about 4½ miles turn left onto road signposted "Upper Braefindon". Brackla Wood is first house on left.

Disabled Access:
Partial

Opening Times:
15 April to 19 April
2:00pm - 4:00pm
Wednesday 5 June
2:00pm - 5:00pm
By arrangement 20 to 21
April and 8 to 14 September

Admission:
£3.00, homemade teas £2.50

Charities:
MacMillan Nurses (Black
Isle branch) receives 40%,
the net remaining to SG
Beneficiaries.

CLAN DONALD SKYE
Armadale, Isle of Skye IV45 8RS
Clan Donald Lands Trust T: 01471 844305
E: office@clandonald.com   www.clandonald.com

Exotic trees, shrubs and flowers, expansive lawns and stunning scenery combine to make this a real treat for garden lovers. The warming influence of the Gulf Stream allows the sheltered gardens to flourish. When the Clan Donald Lands Trust took over, the gardens were overgrown and neglected. Years of hard pruning, rebuilding and planting around the centrepiece of historic Armadale Castle has resulted in 40 acres of stunning woodland gardens and lawns that provide a tranquil place to sit or walk. Specimen trees, some planted in the early 1800s, tower above the gardens. Beyond the formal gardens visitors can enjoy woodland walks and nature trails, with beautiful views to the Sound of Sleat, the mountains of Knoydart forming a spectacular backdrop. A new children's adventure playground was added to the gardens in 2011 and new garden interpretation is planned for 2013.

Other Details: Two retail and one gardening outlet.
Coffee, tea and homebaking. Lunches, evening meals, alcoholic beverages at The Stables Restaurant. 4* self catering accommodation.

Directions: From Skye Bridge: Head north on A87 and turn left just before Broadford onto A851 signposted Armadale 15 miles. From Armadale Pier: ¼ mile north on A851 to car park.

Disabled Access:
Full

Opening Times:
1 April to 31 October
9:30am - 5:30pm
1 January to 31 March and
1 November to 31 December
dawn - dusk

Admission:
£6.95, concessions/children
£4.95, under 5 free, families
£20.00
Free admission
January - March and
November - December

Charities:
Donation to SG Beneficiaries

COILTIE GARDEN
Divach, Drumnadrochit IV63 6XW
Gillian and David Nelson T: 01456 450219

A garden made over the past 35 years from a long neglected Victorian garden, now being somewhat reorganised to suit ageing gardeners. Many unusual trees, shrubs, herbaceous borders, roses, all set in beautiful hill scenery with a fine view of 100ft Divach Falls. Trees planted 30 years ago are showing well now.

Other Details: Other dates outwith those opening by arrangement will be confirmed on the SG website.

Directions: Take turning to Divach off A82 in Drumnadrochit village. Proceed two miles uphill, passing Falls. 150 metres beyond Divach Lodge.

Disabled Access:
Full

Opening Times:
By arrangement on request

Admission:
£3.00, children free

Charities:
Amnesty International
receives 40%, the
net remaining to SG
Beneficiaries.

DUNDONNELL HOUSE
Dundonnell, Little Loch Broom, Wester Ross IV23 2QW
Dundonnell Estates T: 07789 390028

Camellias, magnolias and bulbs in spring, rhododendrons and laburnum walk in this ancient walled garden. Exciting planting in new borders gives all year colour centred around one of the oldest yew trees in Scotland. Midsummer roses, restored Edwardian glasshouse, riverside walk, arboretum - in the valley below the peaks of An Teallach.

Other Details: On 30 May home teas available in the house. On 18 April, 15 August and 19 September teas are available at Maggie's Tearoom 3 miles towards Little Loch Broom.

Directions: Off A835 at Braemore on to A832. After 11 miles, take Badralloch turn for half a mile.

Disabled Access:
Partial

Opening Times:
Thursdays 18 April, 30 May, 15 August, 19 September 2:00pm - 5:00pm
Also by arrangement on request

Admission:
£3.50, children free.

Charities:
Atlantic Salmon Trust receives 40% on 2 days, The Stroke Assoc. receives 40% on 2 days, the net remaining to SG Beneficiaries.

DUNVEGAN CASTLE AND GARDENS
Isle of Skye IV55 8WF
Hugh Macleod of Macleod T: 01470 521206
E: info@dunvegancastle.com www.dunvegancastle.com

Dunvegan Castle's five acres of formal gardens began life in the 18th century. In stark contrast to the barren moorland that dominate Skye's landscape, the gardens are a hidden oasis featuring an eclectic mix of plants, woodland glades, shimmering pools fed by waterfalls and streams flowing down to the sea.
After experiencing the Water Garden with its ornate bridges and islands replete with a rich and colourful plant variety, wander through the elegant surroundings of the formal Round Garden featuring a Box-wood Parterre as its centrepiece. The Walled Garden is well worth a visit. In what was formerly the castle's vegetable garden, there is a garden museum and a diverse range of plants and flowers which complement the attractive features including a waterlily pond, a neoclassical urn and a Larch Pergola.
A considerable amount of replanting and landscaping has taken place over the last thirty years to restore and develop the gardens at Dunvegan.

Directions: 1 mile from Dunvegan Village, 23 miles west of Portree.

Disabled Access:
Partial

Opening Times:
1 April to 15 October 10:00am - 5:30pm
Also by arrangement 3 Jan. to 31 Mar. and 16 Oct. to 31 Dec. except weekends and Christmas & New Year

Admission:
Garden: £7.50, conc. £6.00, child 5-15 £4.00.
Castle and Garden: £9.50, conc. £7.00, child 5-15 £5.00

Charities:
Donation to SG Beneficiaries

FIELD HOUSE
Belladrum, Beauly IV4 7BA
Mr & Mrs D Paterson
www.dougthegarden.co.uk

Informal country garden in one acre site. Mixed borders with some unusual plants - a plantsman's garden.

Directions: 4 miles from Beauly on A833 Beauly to Drumnadrochit road, then follow signs to Belladrum.

Disabled Access:
None

Opening Times:
Sunday 9 June 2:00pm - 5:00pm

Admission:
£4.00

Charities:
Highland Hospice receives 40%, the net remaining to SG Beneficiaries.

HOUSE OF AIGAS AND FIELD CENTRE
by Beauly IV4 7AD
Sir John and Lady Lister-Kaye T: 01463 782443
E: sheila@aigas.co.uk www.aigas.co.uk

Aigas has a woodland walk overlooking the Beauly River with a collection of named Victorian specimen trees now being restored and extended with a garden of rockeries, herbaceous borders and shrubberies. Guided walks on nature trails.

Other Details: Homemade teas in house on both open days. For the "by arrangement" openings, lunches/teas available on request. Check out Aigas website for details of other events.

Directions: 4½ miles from Beauly on A831 Cannich/Glen Affric road.

Disabled Access:
Partial

Opening Times:
Sunday 30 June
2:00pm - 5:00pm
Sunday 28 July
2:00pm - 5:00pm
Also by arrangement on request

Admission:
£3.00, children free

Charities:
Highland Hospice (Aird Branch) receives 40%, the net remaining to SG Beneficiaries.

HOUSE OF GRUINARD
Laide, by Achnasheen IV22 2NQ
The Hon Mrs A G Maclay T: 01445 731235
E: office@houseofgruinard.com

Superb hidden and unexpected garden developed in sympathy with stunning west coast estuary location. Wide variety of interesting herbaceous and shrub borders with water garden and extended wild planting.

Other Details: Homemade teas on 29 May, no teas on 10 July.

Directions: On A832 12 miles north of Inverewe and 9 miles south of Dundonnell.

Disabled Access:
None

Opening Times:
Wednesday 29 May
2:00pm - 5:00pm
Wednesday 10 July
2:00pm - 5:00pm

Admission:
£3.50, children under 16 free

Charities:
Macmillan Nurses receives 40%, the net remaining to SG Beneficiaries.

HUGH MILLER'S BIRTHPLACE COTTAGE & MUSEUM
Church Street, Cromarty IV11 8XA
The National Trust for Scotland T: 0844 493 2158
E: apowersjones@nts.org.uk www.nts.org.uk

Garden of Wonders, created in 2008, with its theme of natural history, features fossils, exotic ferns, ornamental letter-cutting and a 'mystery' stone. Lydia Garden, a new garden completed in 2010. Walk around the crescent shaped sandstone path of fragrant climbing roses, herbs and wild plant areas.

Directions: By road via Kessock Bridge and A832 to Cromarty. 22 miles north east of Inverness.

Disabled Access:
None

Opening Times:
Saturday 13 July
12:00pm - 5:00pm

Admission:
£6.00 Concession £5.00, Family £16.00. N.B. Prices correct at time of going to print

Charities:
Donation to SG Beneficiaries.

INVEREWE

Poolewe, Achnasheen, Ross-shire IV22 2LG
The National Trust for Scotland T: 0844 493 2225
E: inverewe@nts.org.uk www.nts.org.uk

Magnificent 54 acre Highland garden, surrounded by mountains, moorland and sea-loch. Created by Osgood Mackenzie in the late 19th century, it now includes a wealth of exotic plants from Australian tree ferns to Chinese rhododendrons to South African bulbs.

Other Details: National Plant Collection ®. The Head Gardener's Walk on 22 May will focus on Woodland Gardening. Meet at Visitor Centre 2:00pm. The walk led by the First Gardener on 5 June will view some of the National Collection planting. Meet at Visitor Centre 2:00pm.

Directions: Signposted on A832 by Poolewe, 6 miles north east of Gairloch.

Disabled Access:
Full

Opening Times:
Wednesday 22 May
10:00am - 4:00pm
Wednesday 5 June
10:00am - 4:00pm

Admission:
£9.50 (including NTS members) N.B. Prices are correct at time of going to print

Charities:
Donation to SG Beneficiaries.

LEATHAD ARD

Upper Carloway, Isle of Lewis HS2 9AQ
Rowena and Stuart Oakley T: 01851 643204
E: oakley1a@clara.co.uk www.whereveriam.org/leathadard

¾ acre sloping garden with stunning views over East Loch Roag. It has evolved along with the shelter hedges that divide the garden into a number of areas. With shelter and raised beds the different conditions created permit a wide variety of plants to be grown. Beds include herbaceous borders, cutting borders, bog gardens, grass garden, exposed beds, patio, a new pond and vegetable and fruit patches, some of which are grown to show. A full tour by Stuart takes about 2 hours.

Directions: A858 Shawbost - Carloway. First right after Carloway football pitch. First house on right. The Westside circular bus ex Stornoway to road end - ask for the Carloway football pitch.

Disabled Access:
None

Opening Times:
1 June to 31 August 1:45pm
- 6:00pm except Fridays and Sundays. Closed Wednesday 7 August
Also by arrangement 1 April to 30 September except Suns

Admission:
By donation: recommended min. donation£4.00 per person

Charities:
Red Cross receives 40%, the net remaining to SG Beneficiaries.

LECKMELM SHRUBBERY & ARBORETUM

Ullapool IV23 2RH

The restored 12 acre arboretum, planted in the 1880s, is full of splendid and rare trees including 2 "Champions", specie rhododendrons, azaleas and shrubs. Warmed by the Gulf Stream, this tranquil woodland garden has alpines, palms and bamboos along winding paths which lead down to the sea.

Other Details: Champion Trees.

Directions: Situated by the shore of Loch Broom 3 miles south of Ullapool on the A835 Inverness/Ullapool road. Parking in walled garden.

Disabled Access:
None

Opening Times:
1 April to 31 October
10:00am - 6:00pm

Admission:
£3.00, children under 16 free

Charities:
Donation to SG Beneficiaries and Local Charities.

NOVAR
Evanton IV16 9XL
Mr and Mrs Ronald Munro Ferguson T: 01349 831062

Water gardens with recent restoration and new planting, especially rhododendrons and azaleas. Large, five acre walled garden with formal 18th century oval pond (restored). Newly planted apple orchard.

Other Details: Disabled access to most areas.

Directions: Off B817 between Evanton and junction with A836: turn west up Novar Drive.

Disabled Access:
Partial

Opening Times:
Sunday 2 June
2:30pm - 5:00pm

Admission:
£5.00, children free

Charities:
Diabetes Charities receives 40%, the net remaining to SG Beneficiaries.

OLDTOWN OF LEYS GARDEN
Inverness IV2 6AE
David and Anne Sutherland T: 01463 238238
E: ams@oldtownofleys.com

Large garden established 10 years ago, on the outskirts of Inverness and overlooking the town. Herbaceous beds with lovely rhododendron and azalea displays in spring. Specimen trees. Three ponds surrounded by waterside planting. Small woodland area.

Other Details: See SG website for special open days which will include teas/coffees, plant stalls.

Directions: Turn off Southern distributor road (B8082) at Leys roundabout towards Inverarnie (B861). At T-junction turn right. After 50 metres turn right into Oldtown of Leys.

Disabled Access:
Partial

Opening Times:
Daily Dawn - Dusk

Admission:
By donation.

Charities:
ARCHIE receives 20%, Highland Hospice receives 20%, the net remaining to SG Beneficiaries.

THE LOOKOUT
Kilmuir, North Kessock IV1 3ZG
Mr & Mrs David and Penny Veitch T: 01463 731489
E: david@veitch.biz

A ¾ acre elevated coastal garden with incredible views over the Moray Firth which is only for the sure-footed. This award winning garden is created out of a rock base with shallow pockets of ground, planted to its advantage to encourage all aspects of wildlife. There is a small sheltered courtyard, raised bed vegetable area, pretty cottage garden, scree and rock garden, rose arbour, rhododendrons, flowering shrubs, bamboos, trees and lily pond with waterside plants.

Other Details: Teas and baking only if outside weather permits. Studio with exhibition of landscape pictures for sale.

Directions: From Inverness: take North Kessock left turn from A9, and third left at roundabout to go on underpass then sharp left onto Kilmuir road.
From Tore: take slip road for North Kessock and immediately right for Kilmuir. Follow signs for Kilmuir (3 miles) until you reach the shore. The Lookout is near far end of village with a large palm tree on the grass in front.

Disabled Access:
None

Opening Times:
2 April to 26 September
11:00am - 4:00pm
Also by arrangement 1 April to 31 October

Admission:
£3.00

Charities:
Alzheimer Scotland receives 40%, the net remaining to SG Beneficiaries.

ROXBURGHSHIRE

Scotland's Gardens 2013 Guidebook is sponsored by INVESTEC WEALTH & INVESTMENT

District Organiser

Mrs Sally Yonge   Newtonlees, Kelso TD5 7SZ

Area Organiser

Mrs Clare Leeming   Loanend, Earlston, Berwickshire TD4 6BD

Treasurer

Mr Peter Jeary   Kalemouth House, Eckford, Kelso TD5 8LE

Gardens open on a specific date

Yetholm Village Gardens, Town Yetholm	Sunday 14 July	2:00pm	- 5:30pm
West Leas, Bonchester Bridge	Sunday 18 August	2:00pm	- 5:00pm

Gardens open regularly

Floors Castle, Kelso	1 May - 31 October	10:30am	- 5:00pm
Monteviot, Jedburgh	1 April - 31 October	12:00pm	- 4:00pm

Gardens open by arrangement

Lanton Tower, Jedburgh	On request	01835 863443
West Leas, Bonchester Bridge	On request	01450 860711

Key to symbols

	New in 2013		Homemade teas		Accommodation
	Teas		Dogs on a lead allowed		Plant stall
	Cream teas		Wheelchair access		Scottish Snowdrop Festival

Garden locations

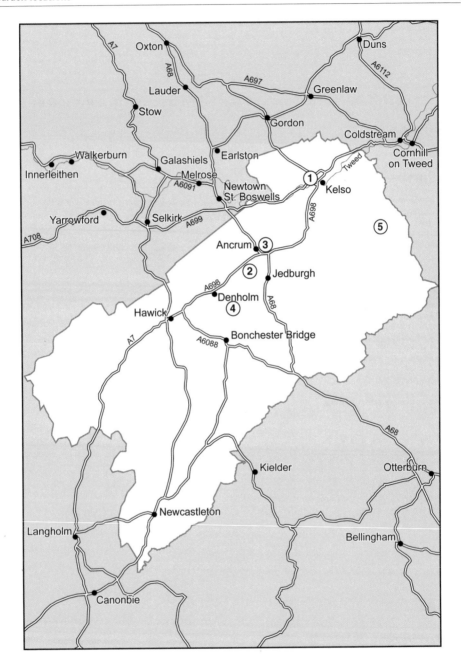

FLOORS CASTLE
Kelso TD5 7SF
The Duke of Roxburghe T: 01573 223333
www.floorscastle.com

The largest inhabited house in Scotland enjoys glorious views across parkland, the River Tweed and the Cheviot Hills. Woodland garden, riverside and woodland walks, formal French style Millennium Parterre and the traditional walled garden. The walled garden contains colourful herbaceous borders, vinery and peach house, and in keeping with the tradition the kitchen garden still supplies vegetables and soft fruit for the castle.

Other Details: Onsite plant centre and Floors Castle nursery , Terrace cafe and Courtyard restaurant, gift shop, woodland and riverside walks, adventure playground.

Directions: Floors Castle can be reached by following the A6089 from Edinburgh; the B6397 from Earlston or the A698 from Coldstream. Go through Kelso, up Roxburgh Street to the Golden Gates.

Disabled Access:
Partial

Opening Times:
1 May to 31 October
10:30am - 5:00pm
except special event days

Admission:
£4.50, senior £4.00, children £2.00

Charities:
Donation to SG Beneficiaries.

LANTON TOWER
Jedburgh TD8 6SU
Lady Reid T: 01835 863443

The garden, divided into 'rooms' by beech, holly and yew hedges and stone walls is architectural rather than botanical, with an emphasis on shrubs, bulbs and fruit trees. A parterre near the tower, with steps leading to a croquet lawn, is surrounded by shrub borders, with orchards on each side of a beech hedge and wall. An azalea and mixed shrub border is next to a pond surrounded by bog garden. Nearby, lies a border of low-growing herbaceous plants with a york stone path leading to a large curved bench, the space contained by hedges of Charles de Mills roses. There is a vegetable garden, and a herb garden near the house. A walk between a holly and rosa spinosissima hedge towards a large mirror framed in ivy leads to a paddock well-furnished with trees and a fine view towards the Eildon Hills.

Directions: 2½ miles west of Jedburgh.

Disabled Access:
Full

Opening Times:
By arrangement on request

Admission:
£4.00

Charities:
Maggie's Cancer Caring Centres receives 40%, the net remaining to SG Beneficiaries.

MONTEVIOT
Jedburgh TD8 6UQ
Marquis & Marchioness of Lothian T: 01835 830380
www.monteviot.com

Series of differing gardens including herb garden, rose garden, water garden linked by bridges, and river garden with herbaceous shrub borders. Dene garden featuring ponds and bridges and planted with a variety of foliage plants.

Directions: Turn off A68, 3 miles north of Jedburgh B6400.

Disabled Access:
Partial

Opening Times:
1 April to 31 October
12:00pm - 4:00pm

Admission:
£5.00

Charities:
Donation to SG Beneficiaries.

WEST LEAS
Bonchester Bridge TD9 8TD
Mr and Mrs Robert Laidlaw T: 01450 860711
E: ann.laidlaw@btconnect.com

The visitor to West Leas can share in the exciting and dramatic project on a grand scale still in the making. At its core is a passion for plants allied to a love and understanding of the land in which they are set. Collections of perennials and shrubs, many in temporary holding quarters, lighten up the landscape to magical effect. New landscaped water features, bog garden and extensive new shrub and herbaceous planting.

Directions: Signposted off the Jedburgh/Bonchester Bridge Road.

Disabled Access:
Partial

Opening Times:
Sunday 18 August
2:00pm - 5:00pm
Also by arrangement on request

Admission:
£4.00

Charities:
Macmillan Cancer Relief, Borders Appeal receives 40%, the net remaining to SG Beneficiaries.

YETHOLM VILLAGE GARDENS
Town Yetholm TD5 8RL
The Gardeners of Yetholm Village

The village of Town Yetholm is situated at the north end of the Pennine Way and lies close to the Bowmont Water in the dramatic setting of the foothills of the Cheviots. A variety of gardens with their own unique features have joined the Yetholm Village Gardens Open Day this year.
Gardens open will include: Copsewood, Almond Cottage, 5 Yew Tree Lane, Rosebank, The Old Manse, The Hall House, Thirlestane, Hillview, 3 Morebattle Road, 2 Grafton Court and Grafton House. In addition "The Yew Tree Allotments" running along the High Street will open again this year in turn providing an ever popular feature.
Yetholm Village Gardens open day offers visitors the chance to walk through several delightful gardens planted in a variety of styles and reflecting many distinctive horticultural interests. From newly established, developing and secret gardens to old and established gardens there is something here to interest everyone. The short walking distance between the majority of the gardens provides the added advantage of being able to enjoy the magnificence of the surrounding landscape to include "Staerough" and "The Curr" which straddle both the Bowmont and Halterburn Valleys where evidence of ancient settlements remains.

Other Details: Tickets will be sold in the Wauchope Hall.
Plant stall and garden produce, home baking, bric-a-brac, wood craft and book stall.
Cream teas in the Youth Hall.
Music in one of the gardens plus poetry readings at the "Old Manse".

Directions: Equidistant between Edinburgh and Newcastle. South of Kelso in the Borders take the B6352 to Yetholm Village. Ample parking available along the High Street.

Disabled Access:
Partial

Opening Times:
Sunday 14 July
2:00pm - 5:30pm

Admission:
£4.00 (includes all gardens), children under 10 years free

Charities:
Riding for the Disabled Association, Borders Group receives 40%, the net remaining to SG Beneficiaries.

STIRLINGSHIRE

Scotland's Gardens 2013 Guidebook is sponsored by INVESTEC WEALTH & INVESTMENT

District Organiser

Carola Campbell	Kilbryde Castle, Dunblane FK15 9NF

Area Organisers

Gillie Drapper	Kilewnan Cottage, Fintry, By Glasgow G63 0YH
Maurie Jessett	The Walled Garden, Doune FK16 6HJ
Pippa Maclean	Quarter, Denny FK6 6QZ
Iain Morrison	Clifford House, Balkerach Street, Doune FK16 6DE
Rachel Nunn	1 Laurelhill Place, Stirling FK8 2JH
Philip Penfold	Craigend House, Auchenbowie FK7 9QW
Douglas Ramsay	The Tors, 2 Slamannan Road, Falkirk FK1 5LG
Mandy Readman	Hutchison Farm, Auchinlay Road, Dunblane FK15 9JS
Gillie Welstead	Ballingrew, Thornhill FK8 3QD

Treasurer

John McIntyre	18 Scott Brae, Kippen FK8 3DL

Gardens open on a specific date

West Plean House, by Stirling	Sunday 24 February	1:00pm	-	4:00pm
Kilbryde Castle, Dunblane	Sunday 3 March	1:00pm	-	4:00pm
The Linns, Sheriffmuir	Sunday 10 March	10:00am	-	4:00pm
The Pass House, Kilmahog	Sunday 21 April	2:00pm	-	5:00pm
Kilbryde Castle, Dunblane	Sunday 12 May	2:00pm	-	5:00pm
Drymen Gardens	Sunday 19 May	2:00pm	-	5:00pm
Gargunnock House, Gargunnock	Sunday 26 May	2:00pm	-	5:00pm
Kilbryde Castle, Dunblane	Sunday 9 June	2:00pm	-	5:00pm
Stirling Gardens	Sunday 16 June	2:00pm	-	5:00pm
Blair Drummond Gardens	Sunday 30 June	2:00pm	-	5:00pm
Row House, Dunblane	Wednesday 3 July	1:00pm	-	4:00pm
Row House, Dunblane	Wednesday 10 July	1:00pm	-	4:00pm
Row House, Dunblane	Wednesday 17 July	1:00pm	-	4:00pm
The Walled Garden, Kincardine	Sunday 21 July	10:00am	-	4:00pm
Gean House , Alloa	Tuesday 23 July	2:00pm	-	5:00pm
Row House, Dunblane	Wednesday 24 July	1:00pm	-	4:00pm
The Tors, Falkirk	Sunday 28 July	2:00pm	-	5:00pm
Row House, Dunblane	Wednesday 31 July	1:00pm	-	4:00pm
Thorntree, Arnprior	Sunday 11 August	2:00pm	-	5:00pm

Gardens open regularly

Gargunnock House, Gargunnock	2 February - 17 March Daily	11:00am - 3:30pm
	& 14 April - 16 June	11:00am - 3:30pm
	Saturdays & Sundays	
The Walled Garden, Righead Farm, Kincardine	23 January - 29 December	10:00am - 4:00pm
	Except Mondays & Tuesdays	

Gardens open by arrangement

Arndean, by Dollar	15 May - 15 June	01259 743525
Camallt, Fintry	1 April - 15 May	01360 860034
Duntreath Castle, Blanefield	On request	01360 770215
Gargunnock House, Gargunnock	15 September - 31 October	01786 860392
Kilbryde Castle, Dunblane	On request	01786 824897
Milseybank, Bridge of Allan	On request	01786 833866
Rowberrow, Dollar	On request	01259 742584
The Tors, Falkirk	On request	01324 620877
Thorntree, Arnprior	On request	01786 870710

Events

Scotland's Gardens Autumn Seminar, Stirling	1 October	10:30am - 4:00pm

The Pass House

Key to symbols

 New in 2013   Homemade teas   Accommodation

 Teas   Dogs on a lead allowed   Plant stall

 Cream teas   Wheelchair access   Scottish Snowdrop Festival

Garden locations

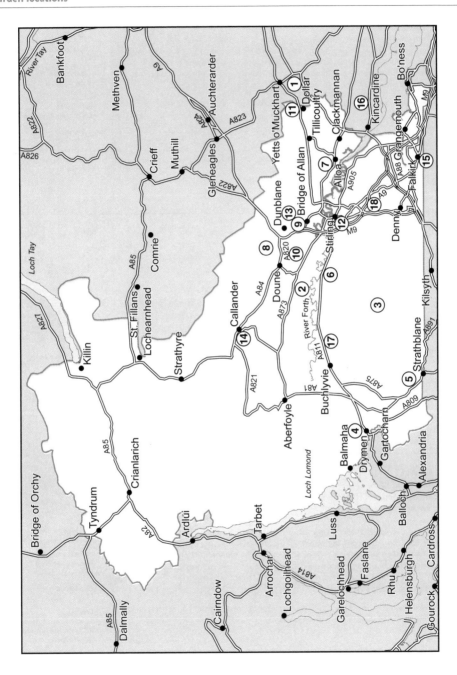

ARNDEAN
By Dollar FK14 7NH
Johnny and Katie Stewart T: 01259 743525
E: johnny@arndean.co.uk

This is a beautiful mature garden extending to 15 acres including the woodland walk. There is a formal herbaceous part, a small vegetable garden and orchard. In addition there are flowering shrubs, abundant and striking rhododendrons and azaleas and many fine specimen trees. Tree house for children.

Directions: Arndean is well sign posted off A977.

Disabled Access:
Full

Opening Times:
By arrangement 15 May to
15 June

Admission:
£5.00, children free

Charities:
Scots Guards Colonel's
Fund receives 40%, the
net remaining to SG
Beneficiaries.

BLAIR DRUMMOND GARDENS

T: 01786 850671
E: gillie.welstead@gmail.com

Country gardens and farmhouse gardens with interesting shrubs, trees, herbaceous borders and some vegetable gardens; including Coldoch and Struan House.

Other Details: Maps and tickets at all gardens.
Teas at Camphill, Blair Drummond.

Directions: Follow yellow signs from A84.

Disabled Access:
Partial

Opening Times:
Sunday 30 June
2:00pm - 5:00pm

Admission:
£5.00, children free

Charities:
Camphill Village Trust
receives 40%, the
net remaining to SG
Beneficiaries.

CAMALLT
Fintry G63 0XH
William Acton and Rebecca East T: 01360 860034
E: enquiries@camallt.com

8 acre garden previously open for its old and interesting daffodil cultivars dating from 1600 which carpet the woodland beside waterfalls and burn, at their best during April and early May. These are followed by bluebells, rhododendrons and azaleas. Herbaceous terraced gardens under continued progression of change meet lawns which run down to the Endrick Water. Other features include ponds and bog garden still under development.

Directions: From Fintry village B822 to Lennoxtown, approx 1 mile then turn left to Denny on B818, Camallt entrance on right.

Disabled Access:
None

Opening Times:
By arrangement 1 April to
15 May

Admission:
£3.50, children free

Charities:
Strathcarron Hospice receives
40%, the net remaining to SG
Beneficiaries.

DRYMEN GARDENS
G63
Drymen Gardeners T: 01786 841007 or 07981 920156
E: Mor990@aol.com

A selection of delightful village and country house gardens with rhododendrons, azaleas, specimen trees and bulbs.

Other Details: Maps and tickets available at all gardens.

Directions: Follow the yellow signs to Drymen village from A811.

Disabled Access:
Partial

Opening Times:
Sunday 19 May
2:00pm - 5:00pm

Admission:
£5.00, children free

Charities:
Preshal Trust receives 40%, the net remaining to SG Beneficiaries.

DUNTREATH CASTLE
Blanefield G63 9AJ
Sir Archibald & Lady Edmonstone T: 01360 770215
E: juliet@edmonstone.com   www.duntreathcastle.co.uk

Extensive gardens with mature and new plantings. Ornamental landscaped lake and bog garden. Sweeping lawns below formal fountain and rose parterre with herbaceous border leading up to an attractive waterfall garden with shrubs and spring plantings. Woodland walk. 15th century keep and chapel.

Directions: A81 north of Glasgow between Blanefield and Killearn.

Disabled Access:
Full

Opening Times:
By arrangement on request

Admission:
£4.00, children free

Charities:
All proceeds to SG Beneficiaries.

Gean House

GARGUNNOCK HOUSE
Gargunnock FK8 3AZ
By kind permission of the Gargunnock Trustees T: 01786 860392
E: william.campbellwj@btinternet.com

Five acres of mature gardens, woodland walks, walled garden and 18th century Doocot. Snowdrops in February/March, daffodils in April/May. Glorious display of azaleas and rhododendrons in May/June. Wonderful trees and shrubs, glorious autumn colour. Garden featured in articles in "The Scotsman" and "Scottish Field". Guided tours can be arranged for parties.

Other Details: Plant stall always available at rear of Gargunnock House. February/March: Snowdrops for sale.
26th May: **Major** plant sale with a wonderful selection of azaleas and rhododendrons for sale.
Homemade teas in Gargunnock House on 26th May only.
For Guided Walks contact Head Gardener.

Directions: On A811 5 miles west of Stirling.

Disabled Access:
Full

Opening Times:
Sunday 26 May
2:00pm - 5:00pm
2 February to 17 March
11:00am - 3:30pm
open daily for the Snowdrop Festival
Sunday 14 April to Sunday 16 June 11:00am - 3:30pm
except weekdays
Also by arrangement
15 September to 31 October

Admission:
26th May: £4.00, children free
Other dates: £3.00, children free

Charities:
Children's Hospice Assciation receives 20%, Gargunnock Community Centre receives 20%, the net remaining to SG Beneficiaries.

GEAN HOUSE
Tullibody Road, Alloa FK10 2EL
Ceteris (Scotland)
E: ebowie@geanhouse.co.uk www.geanhouse.co.uk

Gean House is an early 20th century Arts & Crafts style mansion. On arrival the sweeping driveway from the main road takes you through beautiful parkland lined with trees to the mansion set on top of the hill facing north east. The gardens surrounding the house were originally 40 acres and included a Japanese garden in the woods. All that remains now are seven acres on the southern and eastern aspects of the house.

Other Details: Cream teas in Gean House.

Directions: Gean House is located on the Tullibody Road, Alloa.

Disabled Access:
None

Opening Times:
Tuesday 23 July
2:00pm - 5:00pm

Admission:
£4.00, children free

Charities:
Scottish Society for Autism receives 40%, the net remaining to SG Beneficiaries.

KILBRYDE CASTLE
Dunblane FK15 9NF
Sir James & Lady Campbell & Jack Fletcher T: 01786 824897
E: kilbryde1@aol.com www.kilbrydecastle.com

The Kilbryde Castle gardens cover some 12 acres and are situated above the Ardoch Burn and below the castle. The gardens are split into 3 parts: formal, woodland and wild. Huge drifts of snowdrops are in the wild garden during March. Natural planting (azaleas, rhododendrons, camellias and magnolias) in the woodland garden. There are glorious spring bulbs and autumn colour.

Other Details: Plant stall by Carol Seymour on 12 May and 9 June. Cream teas on 12 May only.

Directions: Three miles from Dunblane and Doune, off the A820 between Dunblane and Doune. On Scotland's Gardens days signposted from A820.

Disabled Access:
Partial

Opening Times:
Sunday 3 March
1:00pm - 4:00pm
for the Snowdrop Festival
Sunday 12 May and 9 June
2:00pm - 5:00pm
Also by arrangement on request

Admission:
£4.00, children free

Charities:
Leighton Library receives 40%, the net remaining to SG Beneficiaries.

MILSEYBANK
Bridge of Allan FK9 4NB
Murray and Sheila Airth T: 01786 833866
E: smairth@hotmail.com

Wonderful and interesting sloping garden with outstanding views, terraced for ease of access. Woodland with bluebells, rhododendrons, magnolias and camellias, and many other unusual plants, a true plantsman's garden.

Directions: Situated on A9, 1 mile from junction 11, M9 and ¼ mile from Bridge of Allan. Milseybank is at top of lane at Lecropt Nursery 250 yards from Bridge of Allan train station.

Disabled Access:
Full

Opening Times:
By arrangement on request

Admission:
£4.00, children free

Charities:
Strathcarron Hospice receives 40%, the net remaining to SG Beneficiaries.

ROW HOUSE
Dunblane, Perthshire FK15 9NZ
Mr & Mrs P Wordie
E: a.wordie@madasafish.com

Mature garden with wonderful views to the River Teith and Ben Lomond. Many unusual trees and shrubs and stunning herbaceous borders.

Directions: From Keir Roundabout take the B824 to Doune, Row House will be sign posted off the B824.

Disabled Access:
Partial

Opening Times:
Wednesdays 3, 10, 17, 24 & 31 July
1:00pm - 4:00pm

Admission:
£4.00, children free

Charities:
Crossroads Caring Scotland West (Stirling Branch) receives 40%, the net remaining to SG Beneficiaries.

ROWBERROW
18 Castle Road, Dollar FK14 7BE
Bill and Rosemary Jarvis T: 01259 742584
E: rjarvis1000@hotmail.com

On the way up to Castle Campbell overlooking Dollar Glen, this colourful garden has several mixed shrub and herbaceous borders, a wildlife pond, two rockeries, alpine troughs, fruit and vegetable gardens, and a mini-orchard. The owner is a plantaholic and likes to collect unusual specimens. Rowberrow was featured on Beechgrove Garden in summer 2011.

Directions: Pass along the burn side in Dollar, turn right at T junction follow signs for Castle Campbell & Dollar Glen. Park at bottom of Castle Road or in Quarry car park just up from house.

Disabled Access:
Partial

Opening Times:
By arrangement on request

Admission:
£4.00, children free.

Charities:
Hillfoot Harmony Barbershop Singers receives 40%, the net remaining to SG Beneficiaries.

STIRLING GARDENS
FK8 2JH
Stirling Gardeners T: 07758 784732
E: rachellnunn@yahoo.co.uk

A selection of town house gardens with unusual trees, shrubs and herbaceous borders. Some vegetable gardens.

Other Details: Tickets and maps available at each house. Teas at 1 Laurelhill Place.

Directions: Follow the garden open signs.

Disabled Access:
Partial

Opening Times:
Sunday 16 June 2:00pm - 5:00pm

Admission:
£5.00, children free.

Charities:
Forth Environment Link Ltd receives 40%, the net remaining to SG Beneficiaries.

THE LINNS
Sheriffmuir, Dunblane FK15 0LP
Drs Evelyn and Lewis Stevens T: 01786 822295
E: evelyn@thelinns.org.uk

A specialist collection of snowdrops. Open by arrangement on a first come first served basis as parking is limited.

Directions: Sheriffmuir by Dunblane, telephone for additional directions.

Disabled Access:
None

Opening Times:
Sunday 10 March 10:00am - 4:00pm for theSnowdrop Festival

Admission:
£4.00, children free.

Charities:
Sophie North Charitable Trust receives 40%, the net remaining to SG Beneficiaries.

THE PASS HOUSE
Kilmahog, Callander FK17 8HD
Dr and Mrs D Carfrae

Well planted medium sized garden with steep banks down to swift river. Garden paths not steep. Camellias, rhododendrons, azaleas, alpines and shrubs. The Scotland's Gardens plaque awarded for 25 years of opening is on display.

Directions: 2 miles from Callander on A84 to Lochearnhead.

Disabled Access:
None

Opening Times:
Sunday 21 April
2:00pm - 5:00pm

Admission:
£4.00, children free

Charities:
Crossroads receives 40%, the net remaining to SG Beneficiaries.

THE TORS
2 Slamannan Road, Falkirk FK1 5LG
Dr and Mrs D M Ramsay T: 01324 620877

The Tors is an award winning Victorian garden of just over one acre with a secret woodland garden to the side and a small orchard and wild area to the rear. Many unusual maple trees and rhododendrons are the main interest of this garden and there are several wildlife ponds and water features. The Tors was featured on the 'Beechgrove Garden' for autumn colour in September 2010, but the best time to see this garden is at the end of July or the beginning of August.

Directions: The B803 to the South of Falkirk leads to Glenbrae Road. Turn right at traffic lights into Slamannan Road and The Tors is a Victorian building immediately on the left.

Disabled Access:
Partial

Opening Times:
Sunday 28 July
2:00pm - 5:00pm
Also by arrangement on request

Admission:
£3.50

Charities:
Strathcarron Hospice receives 40%, the net remaining to SG Beneficiaries.

THE WALLED GARDEN
Righead Farm, Kincardine, By Alloa FK10 4AT
Anna Crawford T: 07951 530571
E: acrawford67@hotmail.co.uk

Newly built walled garden laid out in a symmetrical design based on a central gravel path that runs under a pergola smothered in roses and clematis. Wide perimeter beds planted with a combination of shrubs and herbaceous plants. The large vegetable patch produces many varieties of seasonal vegetables also a recently added orchard outside the garden.

Other Details: Inside the walled garden, The Summer House will be open for teas, coffees, home baking and light lunches. The Potting Shed sells plants, produce, homemade jams, chutneys and other goods.

Directions: Righead Farm is signposted off the A985.

Disabled Access:
Partial

Opening Times:
Sunday 21 July
10:00am - 4:00pm
23 January to 29 December
10:00am - 4:00pm except
Mondays and Tuesdays

Admission:
£3.50

Charities:
Macmillan Cancer Support receives 40% on 21 July opening, the net remaining to SG Beneficiaries.

THORNTREE
Arnprior FK8 3EY
Mark and Carol Seymour T: 01786 870710
E: info@thorntreebarn.co.uk www.thorntreebarn.co.uk

Charming country garden with flower beds around courtyard. Apple walk, fern garden and Saltire garden. Lovely views from Ben Lomond to Ben Ledi. A good display of primroses at end of April beginning of May.

Other Details: John Coyle, Beekeeping Scotland, will be available to answer your questions on bee keeping on 11 August and will have an inspection hive on display.

Directions: A811. In Arnprior take Fintry Road, Thorntree is second on right.

Disabled Access:
Full

Opening Times:
Sunday 11 August
2:00pm - 5:00pm
Also by arrangement on request

Admission:
£4.00, children free

Charities:
Riding for the Disabled receives 40%, the net remaining to SG Beneficiaries.

 WEST PLEAN HOUSE
Denny Road, By Stirling FK7 8HA
Tony and Moira Stewart T: 01786 812208
E: moira@westpleanhouse.com www.westpleanhouse.com

Woodland walks with snowdrops in February. Well established garden including site of iron age homestead and panoramic views over seven counties. Woodlands with mature rhododendrons, specimen trees, extensive lawns, shrubs and walled garden with variety of vegetables. Includes woodland walk with planting of azaleas and rhododendrons.

Directions: Leave all routes at Junction 9 roundabout where M9/M80 converge. Take A872 for Denny, go less than mile, turn left at house sign and immediately after lodge cottage. Carry on up drive.

Disabled Access:
Full

Opening Times:
Sunday 24 February
1:00pm - 4:00pm for the Snowdrop Festival

Admission:
£3.50, children free

Charities:
Scottish Motor Neurone Disease Association receives 40%, the net remaining to SG Beneficiaries.

SCOTLAND'S GARDENS AUTUMN SEMINAR
The Albert Halls, Dumbarton Road, Stirling FK8 2QL

Speakers at the Autumn Seminar will be:
   Richard Baines, Curator, Logan Botanical Gardens
   Elizabeth Banks, Chairman, Royal Horticultural Society
   Chris Marchant, Orchard Dene Nurseries

Other Details: Entrance includes morning coffee, sandwich lunch, wine and stalls

For Tickets: Please contact Lady Edmonstone, Duntreath Castle, Blanefield, Glasgow G63 9AF. T: 01360 770215 E: juliet@edmonstone.com. or go to: www.scotlandsgardens.org

Disabled Access:
Full

Opening Times:
Tuesday 1 October
10:30am to 4:00pm

Admission:
£45.00, children free

Charities:
All proceeds to SG Beneficiaries.

WIGTOWNSHIRE

Scotland's Gardens 2013 Guidebook is sponsored by INVESTEC WEALTH & INVESTMENT

District Organiser

Mrs Ann Watson	Doonholm, Cairnryan Road, Stranaer DG9 8AT

Area Organisers

Mrs Francis Brewis	Ardwell House, Stranraer DG9 9LY
Mr Giles Davies	Elmlea Plants, Minnigaff, Newton Stewart DG8 6PX
Mrs Andrew Gladstone	Craichlaw, Kirkcowan, Newton Stewart DG8 0DQ
Mrs David Hannay	Cuddyfield, Carsluith DG8 7DS
Mrs T Roberts	Logan House Gardens, Port Logan, by Stranraer DG9 9ND

Treasurer

Mr George Fleming	Ardgour, Stoneykirk, Stranraer DG9 9DL

Gardens open on a specific date

Kirkdale, Carsluith	Sunday 10 February	1:00pm	-	4:00pm
Dunskey Gardens and Maze, Portpatrick	Saturday 16 February	10:00am	-	4:00pm
Dunskey Gardens and Maze, Portpatrick	Sunday 17 February	10:00am	-	4:00pm
Dunskey Gardens and Maze, Portpatrick	Saturday 23 February	10:00am	-	4:00pm
Dunskey Gardens and Maze, Portpatrick	Sunday 24 February	10:00am	-	4:00pm
Logan House Gardens, Port Logan	Sunday 5 May	9:00am	-	6:00pm
Claymoddie Garden, Whithorn	Sunday 12 May	2:00pm	-	5:00pm
Logan Botanic Garden, Port Logan	Sunday 26 May	10:00am	-	5:00pm
Woodfall Gardens, Glasserton	Sunday 2 June	2:00pm	-	5:00pm
Glenwhan Gardens, Dunragit	Sunday 9 June	10:00am	-	5:00pm
Castle Kennedy & Gardens, Stranraer	Sunday 16 June	10:00am	-	5:00pm
Woodfall Gardens, Glasserton	Saturday 6 July	10:00am	-	5:00pm
Woodfall Gardens, Glasserton	Saturday 3 August	10:00am	-	5:00pm
Woodfall Gardens, Glasserton	Saturday 7 September	10:00am	-	5:00pm
Woodfall Gardens, Glasserton	Saturday 5 October	10:00am	-	5:00pm

Gardens open regularly

Ardwell House Gardens, Ardwell	1 April - 30 September	10:00am	-	5:00pm
Castle Kennedy & Gardens, Stranraer	4 February - 30 October	10:00am	-	5:00pm
Claymoddie Garden, Whithorn	31 March - 29 September Fridays, Saturdays & Sundays	2:00pm	-	5:00pm

WIGTOWNSHIRE

Dunskey Gardens and Maze, Portpatrick	29 March - 31 October	10:00am - 4:00pm
Glenwhan Gardens, Dunragit	1 April - 31 October	10:00am - 5:00pm
Logan Botanic Garden, Port Logan	1 March - 31 October	10:00am - 5:00pm

Gardens open by arrangement

Castle Kennedy & Gardens, Stranraer	1 November - 31 December	01581 400225
Claymoddie Garden, Whithorn	On request	01988 500422
Craichlaw, Kirkcowan	On request	01671 830208
Dunskey Gardens and Maze, Portpatrick	On request	01776 810211
Woodfall Gardens, Glasserton	On request	REKKSLmuir@aol.com

CANCELLATIONS

On the rare occassions that garden openings are cancelled, details will be posted on the Cancellation page of our website www.scotlandsgardens.org

Key to symbols

 New in 2013

 Homemade teas

 Accommodation

Teas

 Dogs on a lead allowed

 Plant stall

Cream teas

 Wheelchair access

 Scottish Snowdrop Festival

Garden locations

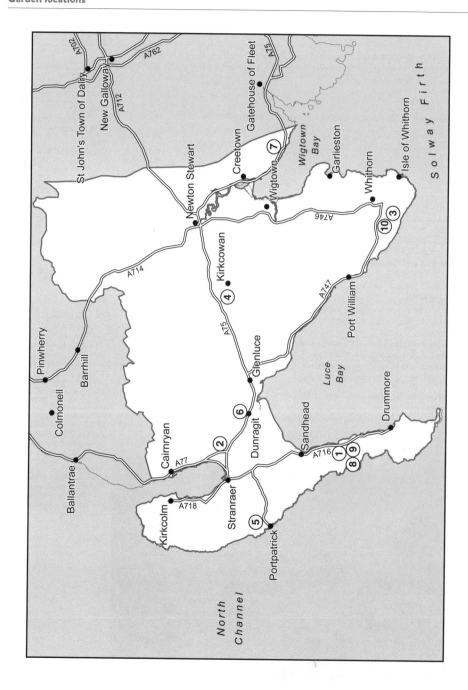

ARDWELL HOUSE GARDENS
Ardwell, Stranraer DG9 9LY
Mr and Mrs Francis Brewis

Daffodils, spring flowers, rhododendrons, flowering shrubs, coloured foliage and rock plants. Moist garden at smaller pond and a walk around larger ponds with views over Luce Bay. Collection Box.

Other Details: Self-pick fruit in season. Picnic site on shore. House not open.

Directions: A716 towards Mull of Galloway. Stranraer 10 miles.

Disabled Access:
None

Opening Times:
1 April to 30 September
10:00am - 5:00pm

Admission:
£3.00, concessions £2.00, children under 14 free

Charities:
Donation to SG Beneficiaries.

CASTLE KENNEDY & GARDENS
Stranraer DG9 8RT
The Earl and Countess of Stair T: 01581 400225

These famous 75 acre gardens of landscaped terraces and avenues are located on an isthmus surrounded by 2 large natural lochs. At one end the ruined Castle Kennedy overlooks a stunning herbaceous walled garden with Lochinch Castle at the other. Over 300 years of planting has created an impressive collection of rare trees, rhododendrons and exotic shrubs featuring many spectacular Champion Trees (tallest or largest of their type). Snowdrop walks, daffodils, spring flowers, rhododendrons and magnolia displays, tree trails and herbaceous borders make this a 'must visit' garden throughout the year.

Other Details: Champion Trees: 6 British, 11 Scottish and 25 for Dumfries and Galloway.
Charming tearoom serving homemade teas and light lunches.

Directions: On A75 5 miles east of Stranraer.

Disabled Access:
Partial

Opening Times:
Sunday 16 June
10:00am - 5:00pm
4 February to 31 March
10:00am - 5:00pm
for the Snowdrop Festival
1 April to 30 October
10:00am - 5:00pm
Also by arrangement
1 November to 31 December

Admission:
£5.00, concessions £3.00, children £1.50, disabled free, families £11.00 (two adults & three children).

Charities:
Scots Guards Colonels Fund for Injured Soldiers and their Families receives 40%, the net remaining to SG Beneficiaries.

CLAYMODDIE GARDEN
Whithorn, Newton Stewart DG8 8LX
Mr and Mrs Robin Nicholson T: 01988 500422

This romantic garden, developed over the last 40 years, with its backdrop of mature trees was designed by the owner, an enthusiastic plantsman. Imaginative hard and soft landscaping provides a wide range of settings, both shady and sunny, for a mass of meticulously placed plants, both old favourites and exotic species, all helped by the proximity of the Gulf Stream. Running through the lower part of the garden is the burn which feeds the pond, all newly planted. There are changes in levels, but most of the garden is accessible to wheelchairs.

Other Details: All plants in the nursery shop are propagated from the garden. Teas available on Sunday 12 May only.

Directions: Claymoddie is off the A746, 2 miles south of Whithorn.

Disabled Access:
Partial

Opening Times:
Sunday 12 May
2:00pm - 5:00pm
31 Mar. to 29 Sept. Fris - Suns
2:00pm - 5:00pm
Also by arrangement on request

Admission:
£3.00, children under 14 free

Charities:
Macmillan Cancer
Support receives 40%,
the net remaining to SG
Beneficiaries.

CRAICHLAW
Kirkcowan, Newton Stewart DG8 0DQ
Mr and Mrs A Gladstone T: 01671 830208

Formal garden with herbaceous borders around the house. Set in extensive grounds with lawns, lochs and woodland. A path around the main loch leads to a water garden returning past an orchard of old Scottish apple varieties.

Directions: Signposted off A75, 8 miles west of Newton Stewart, and B733 one mile west of Kirkcowan.

Disabled Access:
Partial

Opening Times:
By arrangement on request

Admission:
£4.00, concessions £3.00,
children under 14 free

Charities:
Donation to SG Beneficiaries

Claymoddie Garden

DUNSKEY GARDENS AND MAZE
Portpatrick, Stranraer DG9 8TJ
Mr and Mrs Edward Orr Ewing T: 01776 810211
E: garden@dunskey.com www.dunskey.com

Come and enjoy welcoming walled garden and woodland snowdrop walks. There are 43 named varieties including: Galanthus 'Dunskey Talia', Galanthus 'Fred's Giant', Galanthus 'Robin Hood', Galanthus 'Sickle'.
Gardener led strolls at 2:00pm each Sunday.

Other Details: National Plant Collection ®: Clianthus and Sutherlandia
Dogs are allowed on the walks but not allowed in walled garden, shaded dog parking.
Disabled loos and mobility scooter.
Plants for sale have all been raised at Dunskey.
Tearoom with warming soups and teas.

Directions: 1 mile from Portpatrick on B738 off A77.

Disabled Access:
Partial

Opening Times:
Saturday 16 February
10:00am - 4:00pm
Sunday 17 February
10:00am - 4:00pm
Saturday 23 February
10:00am - 4:00pm
Sunday 24 February
10:00am - 4:00pm
February dates are for the
Snowdrop Festival
29 March to 31 October
10:00am - 4:00pm
Garden open for the season
Also by arrangement on
request

Admission:
Snowdrop openings: £3.60,
children under 14 £0.50,
family £10.00 (includes
maze).
Season dates: £5.00,
concessions £4.20, children
£2.00, family £12.00, season
ticket £15.00.

Charities:
Donation to SG Beneficiaries.

GLENWHAN GARDENS
Dunragit, By Stranraer DG9 8PH
Mr and Mrs W Knott

Glenwhan Garden has been described as one of the best newly created gardens in recent times. 25 years ago there was nothing but bracken, gorse and willows but careful planting has created a 12 acre garden filled with glorious collections of plants from around the world. There is colour in all seasons and the winding paths, well placed seats, sculptures and water all add to the tranquil atmosphere. There is a 17 acre moorland wildflower walk, the chance to see red squirrels and magnificent views over Luce Bay, the Mull of Galloway and the Isle of Man.

Other Details: No dogs allowed in the garden but dog walk available.
Shop and tea room.

Directions: 7 miles east of Stranraer, 1 mile off A75 at Dunragit (follow signs).

Disabled Access:
None

Opening Times:
Sunday 9 June
10:00am - 5:00pm
1 April to 31 October
10:00am - 5:00pm

Admission:
£4.50, children £1.50, family
£10.00, concessions £3.50,
season ticket £15.00

Charities:
World Wildlife Fund receives
40%, the net remaining to SG
Beneficiaries.

KIRKDALE
Carsluith, Newton Stewart DG8 7EA
Mr and Mrs Neil Hannay

Fabulous woodland snowdrop walks around historic 18th century property. A chance to view the only working water driven sawmill in south of Scotland and nature trail.

Directions: On A75 six miles west of Gatehouse of Fleet. Signposted Cairnholy Chambered Cairn.

Disabled Access:
Partial

Opening Times:
Sunday 10 February
1:00pm - 4:00pm for the
Snowdrop Festival

Admission:
£3.00, children free

Charities:
Homestart, Wigtownshire
receives 40%, the
net remaining to SG
Beneficiaries.

LOGAN BOTANIC GARDEN
Port Logan, By Stranraer DG9 9ND
The Royal Botanic Gardens Edinburgh
www.rbge.org.uk

At the south western tip of Scotland lies Logan which is unrivalled as the country's most exotic garden. With a mild climate washed by the Gulf Stream, a remarkable collection of bizarre and beautiful plants, especially from the southern hemisphere, flourish out of doors. Enjoy the colourful walled garden with its magnificent tree ferns, palms and borders along with the contrasting woodland garden with its unworldly gunnera bog. Explore the Discovery Centre or take an audio tour.

Other Details: Home baking, botanic shop, Discovery Centre, guided tours.

Directions: 10 miles south of Stranraer on A716 then 2½ miles from Ardwell village.

Disabled Access:
Partial

Opening Times:
Sunday 26 May
10:00am - 5:00pm for
Scotland's Gardens.
1 March to 31 October
10:00am - 5:00pm

Admission:
£4.00, concessions £3.50,
children £1,00, family £9.00

Charities:
Royal Botanic Garden,
Edinburgh receives 40%,
the net remaining to SG
Beneficiaries.

LOGAN HOUSE GARDENS
Port Logan, By Stranraer DG9 9ND
Mr and Mrs T Roberts

1701 Queen Anne House. Spectacular woodland gardens with rare and exotic tropical plants, shrubs and champion trees. Very fine species and hybrid rhododendrons.

Other Details: Exhibition of work by local artists.

Directions: On A716 14 miles south of Stranraer. 2½ miles from Ardwell village.

Disabled Access:
Partial

Opening Times:
Sunday 5 May
9:00am - 6:00pm

Admission:
£3.00, children under 16 free

Charities:
Port Logan Hall Fund receives
40%, the net remaining to SG
Beneficiaries.

WOODFALL GARDENS
Glasserton DG8 8LY
Ross and Liz Muir
E: REKKSLmuir@aol.com

This lovely 3 acre eighteenth-century triple walled garden has been thoughtfully restored to provide year round interest. Many mature trees and shrubs including some less common species; herbaceous borders and shrub roses surround the foundations of original greenhouses; grass borders; a knot garden; extensive beds of fruit and vegetables; a herb garden: woodland walk. This unusual garden is well worth a visit.

Directions: 2 miles south-west of Whithorn at junction of A746 and A747 (behind Glasserton Church).

Disabled Access:
Partial

Opening Times:
Sunday 2 June
2:00pm - 5:00pm for
Scotland's Gardens
Saturday 6 July
10:00am - 5:00pm
Saturday 3 August
10:00am - 5:00pm
Saturday 7 September
10:00am - 5:00pm
Saturday 5 October
10:00am - 5:00pm
Alos by arrangement on
request

Admission:
£4.00, children free but
must be accompanied by a
responsible adult.

Charities:
Glasserton Parish Church
receives 20%, Macmillan
Cancer Support receives
20%, the net remaining to
SG Beneficiaries.

Logan Botanic Gardens - Cordyline Walk

GARDENS INDEX

INDEX OF ADVERTISERS

OUR GUIDEBOOK FOR 2014

ORDER NOW
and your copy will be posted to you on publication in December 2013.

Send order to:

Scotland's Gardens, 42a North Castle Street, Edinburgh EH2 3BN

Please send me ____ copy / copies of **Our Guide for 2014**,

price £7.50, to include postage and packing, as soon as it is available.

I enclose a cheque / postal order made payable to Scotland's Gardens.

Name _____

Address _____

_____

Postcode _____

Copies of Our Guide for 2014 may also be purchased on our website:
www.scotlandsgardens.org

WOULD YOU LIKE TO OPEN YOUR GARDEN FOR CHARITY?

If you would like information on how to open your garden for charity please write to us at the address below, call 0131 226 3714 or email info@scotlandsgardens.org

We welcome gardens large and small and also groups of gardens.

To: Scotland's Gardens, 42a North Castle Street, Edinburgh EH2 3BN

Please send me more information about opening my garden for charity.

Name _____

Address _____

_____

Postcode _____ Tel _____

Email _____

NOTES